F R A M E W O R K S

Each book in the Frameworks series is a
comprehensive and concise introduction to
the subject. The books are well structured
and provide a step-by-step guide to essential
principles. They develop a basic framework
of understanding to underpin further study
of core business, financial and legal subjects
in the higher education curriculum.

FRAMEWORKS

Business Law

Richard Lawson

Consultant
Formerly Senior Lecturer in Law
University of Southampton

FINANCIAL TIMES
PITMAN PUBLISHING

FINANCIAL TIMES

MANAGEMENT

LONDON · SAN FRANCISCO
KUALA LUMPUR · JOHANNESBURG

*Financial Times Management delivers the knowledge,
skills and understanding that enable students,
managers and organisations to achieve their ambitions,
whatever their needs, wherever they are.*

London Office:
128 Long Acre, London WC2E 9AN
Tel: +44 (0)171 447 2000
Fax: +44 (0)171 240 5771
Website: www.ftmanagement.com

A Division of Financial Times Professional Limited

First published in Great Britain in 1998

© Financial Times Professional Limited 1998

The right of Richard Lawson to be identified as author of
this work has been asserted by him in accordance with the
Copyright, Designs and Patents Act 1988.

ISBN 0 273 63403 8

British Library Cataloguing in Publication Data
A CIP catalogue record for this book can be obtained from the British Library

10 9 8 7 6 5 4 3 2

Typeset by Land & Unwin (Data Sciences) Ltd, Northampton
Printed and bound in Great Britain by Bell and Bain Ltd, Glasgow

The Publishers' policy is to use paper manufactured from sustainable forests.

Contents

Table of Cases

Table of Statutes

Table of Regulations and Orders

Addendum

The following makes reference to recent cases which it was not possible to incorporate into the body of the text but which are significant enough to include in the book.

Page 33: If an employee in a firm is held out as a partner he is not liable for loss caused by negligent advice given by the firm if there is a lack of evidence to show either that he played any part in that advice or that the client relied on the holding out: *Nationwide Building Society* v *Lewis* (1998).

Page 81: France was also held to be in breach of Articles 5 and 30 by failing to take proper measures against farmers who held up or attacked imports: *European Commission* v *France* (1997). Article 5 requires member states to take appropriate action to fulfil their Treaty obligations.

Page 82: A member state cannot rely on Article 36 to justify restrictions on the export of live calves so long as the calves were exported under conditions laid down in the relevant Directive (EC Council Directive 91/629). A state could not in such a case rely on that Article and in particular on the grounds of public morality, public policy or the protection of health or life of animals laid down in that Article in order to justify restrictions on the export of live calves to prevent them being reared in the veal crate systems used by other member states: *R* v *MAFF, ex parte Compassion in World Farming Ltd* (1988).

Page 212: Eighteen days between delivery and rejection was not too long, bearing in mind that the seller attempted to rectify matters, and given the complexity of the goods: *Peakman* v *Express Circuits* (1998).

1

The structure of the business unit

In this chapter, we look at how various 'business units' are formed, notably companies and partnerships, and examine the legal incidents attaching to each such unit.

COMPANIES

The law relating to companies is almost entirely statutory. The law is presently consolidated in the Companies Act 1985, as subsequently amended. All section references are to this Act except where otherwise stated.

1. The legal status of companies

It is important to understand that a company enjoys a separate legal status of its own, quite separate from its shareholders, members and employees.

Case law In *Lee* v *Lee's Air Farming Ltd* (1961), Lee was the founder, principal shareholder, managing director and chief pilot of the company. He was killed while on company business. It was held that he and the company were distinct legal entities, so that he had been able to enter into a contract of employment with the company, thus enabling his widow to claim compensation under a scheme limited to widows of employees.

It is because the company is separate from its shareholders and directors that the latter are not normally responsible for the debts of the company.

The Companies Act does, however, provide for some *exceptions* to the rule that the company has its own separate legal status. These exceptions are sometimes referred to under the heading of 'lifting the veil'.

These are some of the occasions when the veil is lifted:

(a) Where the number of shareholders falls to just the one, that shareholder becomes personally liable for debts accruing more than six months after he became the sole shareholder: Companies Act s. 24.

(b) If, when the company is wound up, it appears that the company transacted business with a view to defrauding its customers, shareholders who connived in the fraud assume personal liability: Companies Act s. 630.

(c) It may be that the company was nothing more than a sham which was formed to promote some fraudulent scheme on the part of the shareholders. In such a case, the court may treat the shareholders and the company as one and the same.

> *Case law* In *Jones* v *Lipman* (1962), the seller of property attempted to avoid performance of a binding contract of sale by conveying it to a company formed by himself. The court gave an order for the specific performance of the contract against both the vendor and the company.

(d) A director who knows, or who should have known, that the company has no reasonable prospect of avoiding liquidation, and who fails to take reasonable steps to minimise the company's losses, is guilty of wrongful trading and may be required to contribute to the assets of the company: Insolvency Act 1986 s. 213.

(e) A director signing a company cheque is personally liable on it if the company name does not appear in full: Companies Act s. 349(4).

> *Case law* Directors have been held personally liable when the cheque omitted the word 'limited' (*Penrose* v *Martyn* (1858)); and when the company was described by the wrong name (*Nassau Steam Press* v *Tyler* (1894)).

> *Case law* Between 1987 and 1990, a holding company, PPI, set up a special-purpose, wholly owned subsidiary, PPIF, in order to raise finance to develop the group's business activities by means of a number of bond issues. PPIF issued the bonds to a group of banks which managed the issues and which also acted as principal paying agents. PPIF's repayment obligations were guaranteed by PPI and all funds received by PPIF were on-loaned to PPI. Each bond issue included a provision for PPI to be substituted for PPIF as the principal obligor and was formally documented by a public bond issue agreement, and a prospectus. In practice, once PPIF had formally joined in a bond issue, its subsequent involvement was minimal; in particular, it had no current account at a bank and all payments of interest, fees and costs in connection with the bonds were made by PPI. The court said that it was not open to the court to disregard the principle of separate corporate personality and to treat a closely-integrated group of companies as a single economic unit on the

basis merely of perceived injustice, particularly where the separate legal existence of those companies assumed greater importance once they became insolvent. Having regard to the legal documents entered into on the occasion of each bond issue, it was impossible to conclude that a relationship of agency or nomineeship could be inferred between the companies with the result that the on-loan could not be eliminated as a significant part of the composite transaction. Further, since PPIF was clearly more than an economic facade and there was no legal basis on which the PPIF group could be regarded as a single economic unit it followed that the claims were not, in substance, claims in respect of the same debt, and were not precluded by the rule against double proof (*Re Polly Peck plc* (1996)).

FORMATION AND DUTIES OF COMPANIES

It is possible for a company to be created by Royal Charter or by private Act of Parliament. The most important form of creation is by registration, and it is this that is dealt with below.

2. Public or private

A *public company* is defined by the Companies Act as a company limited by shares or guarantee but having a share capital: s. 1. The memorandum of the company (see **6** below) must state that it is a public limited company (plc) and it must comply with the special provisions for the registration of a plc. There is a minimum capital base required, whereas private companies are not required to have such a base: ss. 11 and 118. *Private companies* cannot offer their shares to the public. The overwhelming majority of companies (close to 98%) are private companies. A company is a public company only if its memorandum (see below) states that this is what it is.

As a safeguard, a plc is not entitled to do business or exercise any borrowing powers until it has satisfied the conditions required by the legislation and the Registrar of Companies has issued a certificate certifying such compliance and entitling it to do business: s. 117(1).

3. Liability

Companies can also be classified by reference to their members' liability. Companies registered under the Act may be limited by shares, limited by guarantee or be unlimited: s. 1.

The first is by far the most common, and it means that each member's liability is limited to the amount that remains unpaid in respect of his shareholding. In the case of a company *limited by guarantee*, the members' liability is limited to the amount which they have agreed to contribute to the company's assets in the event of an insolvent winding-up.

Unlimited companies are those where members' liability is unlimited in the event of the company becoming insolvent.

4. The promoters

The 'promoters' are the parties who seek to establish the company. They decide what the company will do, what purchases it will make, and who shall be its first directors. The term is 'a term not of law but of business, usefully summing up in a single word a number of business operations, familiar to the commercial world, by which a company is generally brought into existence' (*Twycross* v *Grant* (1877) per Bowen LJ).

Under the rule in *Foss* v *Harbottle* (1843), they are regarded as being in a fiduciary position and so cannot make an undisclosed profit from their role.

Any disclosure must be made either to an independent board of directors, which is one not containing any of the promoters, or to all the company's shareholders (*Lagunas Nitrate Co* v *Lagunas Syndicate* (1899)).

Remedies against promoter

If a promoter fails to make full disclosure of any profit or benefit obtained by him, the company has available to it the remedies of *rescission* of the contract (the property is returned to the promoter and the company recovers the purchase price); it may recover any secret profit; and it may obtain damages for breach of fiduciary duty.

> *Case law* In *Re Leeds and Hanley Theatre of Varieties Ltd* (1902), a company purchased two music halls which were to be sold to a new company when it was formed. In the meantime, it conveyed the properties to a nominee. It then promoted the new company and instructed the nominee to sell the properties to this company for a considerable profit. The prospectus was issued which gave the nominee as the vendor of the property and did not disclose the interest of the first company. The board of directors of the second company was not an independent board. It was held that the prospectus should have disclosed the interest of the first company, and that the promoters were liable in damages for the profit which they had made.

5. Pre-incorporation contracts

A contract made before a company is formally incorporated lacks binding effect: s. 361(4). Such contracts cannot be ratified by the company once formed. The same section provides that a person who purports to enter into a transaction on behalf of, or as agent for, an unformed company is, subject to any agreement to the contrary, personally liable on it.

Case law In *Phonogram Ltd* v *Lane* (1982), the Court of Appeal held that an agreement to the contrary could not be inferred from the fact that the agents had signed 'for and on behalf of' the unformed company.

6. The memorandum

Sections 1 and 2 provide for the deposit with the Registrar of Companies of a memorandum of association. This must show:

(*i*) The company name
(*ii*) Whether the registered office of the company is in England, Scotland or Wales
(*iii*) Whether the company is limited or unlimited (see **3** above) and the amount of the company's share capital if the company is to be limited by shares; and
(*iv*) The objects of the company.

The memorandum must be signed by at least two persons in the presence of at least one witness who must attest the signature. The Act provides a draft form of memorandum: s. 3.

The clauses in a registered memorandum can be altered by the shareholders if acting in accordance with procedures laid down in the Act: ss. 4–6, 28 and 121.

7. Articles of Association

A company's articles of association contain regulations for the internal management of its affairs. A company which is limited by shares need not submit articles. In such a case, the articles given in Table A contained in the Act will apply. A company may submit its own articles and adopt a part of Table A. A company may expressly exclude Table A. If this is not done, it will apply to matters not dealt with in the articles.

The articles of a guarantee company (see **3** above) must always register articles which must correspond with Tables C or D. An unlimited company (see **3** above) must submit articles which correspond with Table E.

Contents of articles

The articles usually contain provisions dealing with:

- Share capital and variation of rights

5

- Lien and calls on shares
- Transfer and transmission of shares
- Forfeiture of shares
- Conversion of shares into stock
- Alteration of capital
- General meetings
- Notice of general meetings
- Procedures at general meetings
- Votes of members
- Borrowing powers
- Appointment, power and duties of directors and managing director
- Disqualification of directors
- Secretary
- Dividends and reserves
- Accounts and audit
- Capitalisation of profits
- Special provisions relating to winding up.

A company may change its articles by special resolution. It is also possible to alter a company's articles without such a resolution if the consent of all the members is obtained.

> *Case law* In *Cane* v *Jones* (1981), all the members agreed to change an article which gave the chairman a casting vote. They did not meet formally to sanction the change nor sign a document to that effect. Even so, it was held that the article had been changed so that the chairman had a casting vote.

A company is entitled to alter its articles even though minority shareholders consider that the change will prejudice their interests. The courts will not interfere unless the change is not bona fide for the benefit of the company.

> *Case law* In *Greenhalgh* v *Ardene Cinemas* (1951), the majority shareholders wished to sell their shares to an outsider. The articles provided that any shareholder who wished to sell his shares must first offer them to other members of the company at a fair price. The articles were altered to allow sale to an outsider if approved by ordinary resolution. The majority could therefore sell to an outsider on the passing of such resolution, while the minority would have to sell to other members if the majority exercised their right. It was nevertheless held that the alteration was to the benefit of the company as a whole as all the members would be able to sell to an outsider.

> *Case law* In *Dafen Tinplate Co* v *Llanelly Steel Co* (1920), a company was controlled by its directors who were appointed by a number of steel

firms who were among the shareholders. The company sought to alter its articles to enable the shares of existing shareholders to be bought out at a fair price, this to be determined by the board. The proposed alteration was held to be invalid as it conferred an unrestricted power on the majority to expropriate the shares of the minority. The change was wider than necessary to protect the interests of the company.

8. Effect of memorandum and articles

The memorandum and articles create a contract between the company and each shareholder, and also between shareholder and shareholder: s. 14.

Case law In *Hickman* v *Kent or Romney Marsh Sheep-Breeders Association* (1915), the articles provided that any dispute between a member and the company should go to arbitration. Hickman, a member, was in dispute with the company which threatened to expel him. He then, in breach of the articles, brought court proceedings to prevent his expulsion. It was held that this action should be stayed as the articles constituted a contract between the company and the members in respect of their rights as members. The matter should, therefore, be referred to arbitration.

Case law In *Eley* v *Positove Government Security Life Assurance Co Ltd* (1876), the articles named as company solicitor for life a party who was a shareholder. The company employed another solicitor. The court refused to find a contract between the shareholder and the company in the articles, since the right to be the company solicitor could not be regarded as a right granted to all shareholders.

9. 'Limited'

The final words of a limited company's name must be either 'public limited company', which may be abbreviated to 'plc'; or 'limited', which may be abbreviated to 'Ltd', if it is a private limited company: s. 25. Companies registered in Wales may use the Welsh equivalents.

10. Contractual capacity

On registration, a company becomes a legal person with capacity to enter into contracts. It was originally the position that, if a contract was made by a company outside its authorised powers, any such contract was *ultra vires* and was hence void and incapable of enforcement. However, amendments introduced by the Companies Act 1989 effectively do away with the *ultra vires* rule. Third parties dealing with the company are no longer under any obligation to check the company's capacity and there is no question of a contract made by a company being invalid because it was outside the powers of the company as defined in its memorandum. However, a shareholder could still obtain an injunction to restrain any actions outside the company's powers and the company would itself have an action against directors who act outside their powers.

11. Members

The members of a company become members by one of the following means:

(a) The subscribers of the memorandum. These are deemed to have agreed to become members and, on the registration of the company, they are entered as members in its register of members.

(b) By application and allotment followed by entry on the register of members.

(c) By transfer from another member followed by registration.

(d) By transmission on death or bankruptcy followed by registration: s. 22.

Every company must keep a register of members: s. 110.

12. Directors

Every public company must have at least two directors: Companies Act s. 282. The articles (see **6** above) usually name the first directors, or they are appointed by the subscribers to the memorandum (see **5** above) or by the company at a general meeting. Matters such as the co-option of a maximum number of directors, the filling of casual vacancies, and the retirement of directors by rotation are normally dealt with in the company's articles. The length of any service contract entered into by an executive director (that is to say, one who is engaged in the running of a company) with the company needs shareholder approval if it is to last for more than five years: s. 319.

Notwithstanding anything in the articles, a director can be dismissed by the shareholders in a general meeting by ordinary resolution: s. 303. In addition, the court is empowered under the Company Directors Disqualification Act 1986 to disqualify a person from acting as a director where this is considered appropriate.

> *Case law* In *R* v *Goodman* (1993), a director was convicted of illegal insider dealing contrary to the Company Securities (Insider Dealing) Act 1985, and was disqualified from acting as a director under the provisions of the 1986 Act. This Act refers to offences 'in connection with the ...

management ... of a company'. The court ruled that the correct test to be applied in interpreting these words was whether the offence had some relevant factual connection with the management of the company and not whether the offence related to the management of the company, such as keeping accounts or filing returns, or had been committed in the course of managing a company. Since the director's conduct in this case had been the disposition of his shares before he resigned, and the results announced, that clearly had a relevant factual connection with the management of the company, and was an offence in connection with the management of the company for the purposes of the 1986 Act.

Case law It was held in *Secretary of State for Trade and Industry* v *Bannister* (1996) that the courts have an inherent power to stay or suspend a disqualification order, but that this was a power only to be used in exceptional circumstances.

Case law In *Re Continental Assurance Company of London plc* (1996), it was held that a failure to read and understand statutory accounts did amount to such incompetence or neglect as to make a finding of unfitness appropriate. The failure of this director to know the purpose of certain loans showed a lack of competence which would not be expected from a director of his level with a background in corporate finance.

13. A director's duties

(a) *To act bona fide in the best interests of the company.* A director's actions must not only be honest, but must also be in the best interests of the company.

Case law In *Re Roith Ltd* (1967), the memorandum and articles were changed so that pensions could be paid to dependants of employees. A director was appointed general manager for life under a service agreement. Under the terms of the agreement, his widow was to be paid a pension. It was held that this agreement was not binding, since it was not reasonably incidental to carrying on the company's business and was not *bona fide* for its benefit.

(b) *To avoid a conflict of interests.*

Case law In *Aberdeen Rly. Co* v *Blaikie Bros* (1854), a company made a contract with a firm for the supply of certain manufactured articles. The chairman was, when the contract was made, managing partner of that firm. The company was held not to be bound by the contract.

As for contracts made with the company, the general rule is that a director may only enter into a contract with the company if this is permitted by the articles or if this is approved at a general meeting. Furthermore, s. 317 provides that a director who is in any way interested in a contract or proposed contract must disclose the nature of his interest at a board meeting.

Case law In *Neptune (Vehicle Washing Equipment) Ltd* v *Fitzgerald* (1995), the defendant was the sole director of the plaintiff company. The articles allowed him to vote on any contract or arrangement in which he was interested, but he was required under the articles to declare the nature of any contract or proposed contract in which he was interested at a meeting of directors in accordance with s. 317. At a meeting attended by himself and the secretary, the defendant passed resolutions purporting to terminate his contract of employment with the plaintiff and authorising a large payment to himself. The minutes made no reference to the defendant having made the declaration of his interest in the arrangement. The payment was made and the defendant retired. The plaintiff company subsequently asserted a proprietary claim in the money.

The deputy master upheld the claim on a summons for summary judgment and granted a declaration that the defendant's conduct in passing the resolutions constituted both an unlawful self-dealing and a breach of fiduciary duty.

The High Court allowed the appeal. It ruled that a sole director cold not evade s. 317 by considering or committing the company to a contract in which he was interested otherwise than at a director's meeting or by delegating the decision making to others. For the purposes of the section, there could be a valid directors' meeting in the case of a company with a sole directorship when holding the meeting on his own; the director would have to make the declaration to himself and, though this need not be out loud, it still had to be recorded in the minutes. If the meeting was attended by someone else, usually the company secretary, the declaration had to be made out loud and in the hearing of those attending, again being recorded in the minutes. In the present case, it was clear that the arrangement which was the subject of self-dealing involved self-dealing and that, for the defendant to justify self-dealing and invoke the articles, he would need to show that he had complied with the articles and s. 317. In the absence of any conclusive evidence, the issue of whether the statutory declaration had been made and, if not, whether that failure was fatal to a defence, would be decided at trial. It was said that the court would be slow to make a finding on an application for summary judgment that the defendant had acted in bad faith when he denied it and provided some justification for his conduct. Having regard to the defendant's affidavit evidence that he had acted honestly and reasonably, and the fact that the money in dispute was secure pending resolution of the claim, the defendant had a sufficient case to justify the grant of leave to defend on the issue of breach of fiduciary duty.

(c) *To act for the benefit of the company.* Directors must exercise their duties in good faith and for the benefit of the whole company, and not just certain members.

> *Case law* In *Percival* v *Wright* (1902), P, a shareholder in an unquoted company, the shares of which were transferable only with the consent of the board, wrote to the company offering to sell his shares. The shares were purchased by three directors at a valuation fixed by P. He later discovered that the directors were negotiating the sale of the company shares to a third party. If the negotiations had succeeded, the price realised for the shares would have been greater than the sum paid to P. The negotiations failed but P brought an action to set aside his sale to the directors. It was held that they were not under a duty to inform him as to the negotiations as they owed no duty to any one shareholder.

(d) *To have regard to the interests of employees.* Section 309 provides that the directors of a company are to have regard to the interests of the company's employees as well as the interests of its members.

(e) *To act with attention and diligence to the business of the company.* Although a director owes a duty to be diligent and to pay attention to the affairs of the company, the amount of time and attention given will vary from business to business. Three basic propositions were laid down in *Re City Equitable Fire Insurance Co* (1925):

> (*i*) A director must show that degree of care and skill which might be reasonably expected from a person with his knowledge and experience.
> (*ii*) A director is not bound to give continuous attention to the affairs of the company. He is not bound to attend board meetings, but should do so.
> (*iii*) A director may, in the absence of grounds for suspicion, trust company officials to perform duties which may properly be designated.

> *Case law* In *Re Cardiff Savings Bank* (1892) a director, appointed to the board of a company when just six months old, was held not liable for the negligent acts of the board even though he had only attended one board meeting in 38 years.

> *Case law* In *Dorchester Finance Co Ltd* v *Stebbing* (1989) two accountant-directors entrusted the running of the company to a co-director, and counter-signed blank cheques for the co-director's use. They were held liable for the actions of that co-director.

(f) *To exercise powers for a proper purpose.* Directors must exercise their powers for the purposes for which they were bestowed.

> *Case law* In *Hogg* v *Cramphorn Ltd* (1967), the articles gave the directors power to issue shares. The directors allotted shares to employees to forestall a take-over bid which they honestly believed was not in the best interests of the company. It was held that, while the directors had acted *bona fide* and in what they believed to be the best interests of the company, the allotment was not with a view to raising capital which had to be the main purpose of an allotment, and so it had to be set aside.

Breach of a duty to act for a proper purpose can, however, be ratified by the shareholders, and this was subsequently done in the *Hogg* case.

(g) *To account for profit.* A director must account to the company for any profit that he has made by reason of the opportunities that have arisen by virtue of his position as director.

> *Case law* In *Boardman* v *Phipps* (1967) the parties were trustees of an estate whose assets included shares in a private company. They concluded that the position of the company was unsatisfactory. With the knowledge of the other trustees, they sought to obtain control of that company by purchasing shares in their own name, as the trustees were not empowered to invest trust money in the company's shares. Boardman obtained information from the company as to the price at which shares had changed hands by purporting to act for the trustees. Both parties made a considerable profit. It was held that they were each constructive trustees and had to account for the profit to the beneficiaries of the trust. The information had come to them as a result of their position as trustees. See too *Regal (Hastings) Ltd* v *Gulliver* (1942).

There are exceptions to the rule. The articles may permit a director to enter into a contract or have an interest in a contract. The company in a general meeting may approve such a contract.

14. Directors' report

A company must attach a report by the directors to every balance sheet which must give a fair view of the developments of the business of the company and its subsidiaries during the financial year ending with the balance sheet date, and of their position at the end of it, and stating the amount, if any, which they propose to carry to reserves (s. 235).

15. The company secretary

Section 283 provides that every company must have a secretary, but a sole director may not also be the secretary. The Act does not define the general duties of a secretary but certain specific duties are imposed on the secretary. Thus:

(a) In a winding-up by the court, the secretary must verify the statement of the company's affairs submitted to the Official Receiver (s. 528).
(b) On the appointment of a receiver by the debenture holders, to verify the statement of the company's affairs submitted to the receiver (s. 496).
(c) To sign the annual return (s. 363).
(d) To sign the form on a limited company's application to re-register as unlimited or on the application of an unlimited company's application to re-register as limited (ss. 49, 51).

A company secretary's power and authority within a company is a matter of internal management and will vary with the nature and size of the company's business. The secretary is generally authorised by the board of the company to enter into contracts of an administrative nature on behalf of the company, such as taking on staff, ordering office machinery and stationery. The company secretary 'is an officer of the company with extensive duties and responsibilities. This appears not only in the modern Companies Act, but also by the role he plays in the day-to-day business of companies ... He regularly makes representations on behalf of the company and enters into contracts on its behalf which come within the day-to-day running of the company's business. So much so that he may be regarded as held out as having authority to do such things on behalf of the company. He is certainly entitled to do such things on behalf of the company. He is certainly entitled to sign contracts connected with the administrative side of a company's affairs, such as employing staff and ordering cars, and so forth. All such matters now come within the ostensible authority of a company secretary' (*Panorama Developments (Guildford) Ltd* v *Fidelis Furnishing Fabrics Ltd* (1971) per Lord Denning MR).

AUDIT AND FINANCE

16. Auditors

Qualifications

A person may only act as an auditor if he is a member of a body of chartered or certified accountants. None of the following may act as auditor:

(*i*) an officer or servant of the company

(*ii*) a person who is a partner or in the employment of an officer or servant of the company

(*iii*) a body corporate

(*iv*) a person who for any of the above reasons is disqualified from acting as auditor of the company's holding company, subsidiary or co-subsidiary.

A person may not act as an auditor of a company at a time when he knows that he is disqualified for appointment. If, to his knowledge, he becomes disqualified, he must vacate his office and give written notice to the company that he has done so because of his disqualification: s. 389.

Appointment of auditors

Every general meeting at which accounts are presented has to appoint an auditor to serve until the next such meeting: s. 384(1). Although an auditor can be removed during the term of his office by an ordinary resolution (s. 385(1)), any proposal to do so or to appoint as auditor someone other than the retiring auditor requires special notice: s. 388(1). The auditor who is to be removed or not re-appointed must be advised of the proposal and is entitled to have written representations circulated to the members and to speak at the general meeting: ss. 388(2)–(5), 387(2). If an auditor wishes to resign, he must do so in writing stating either that there are no circumstances connected with his resignation which he considers should be brought to the notice of the members of creditors of the company, or setting out what the circumstances are: s. 390(1), (2).

Duties of auditors

The principal duty of an auditor is to report on the company's accounts: s. 236(1). The report is read out at the general meeting and may be inspected by the members: s. 241(2). A copy of the report must be attached to the balance sheet (s. 238(2)) and it is one of the documents comprised in the accounts which must be sent to every member and debenture holder and which must be filed at the Companies Registry: ss. 240 and 241(3).

Every auditor's report must state whether the accounts of the particular company are prepared in accordance with the Companies Acts and whether they give a true and fair picture view of the state of the company's affairs as at the end of its financial year and of the profit and loss for that year: s. 236(2). If the auditors qualify their report on either of these two aspects, and the accounts are used as the basis for a distribution, the auditors must state, either in their report or in a separate statement, whether in their opinion the qualification is material in determining if the distribution is lawful: s. 271(3), (4). In preparing their report, the auditors must consider if proper accounting records have been kept, proper returns adequate for their audit have been received from branches not visited by them, and whether the balance sheet and profit and loss account are in agreement with the accounting records and returns: s. 237(1). If the auditors find that any of these is not the case, this must be stated in the report: s. 237(2).

To enable them to prepare their report, auditors are given a right of access at all times to the books and accounts of the company: s. 237(3). They may also require any necessary information or explanations from officers of the company itself but also from subsidiary companies incorporated in Great Britain and their auditors: s. 392.

Although the Directors' Report (see **14** above) is not audited, the auditors must consider whether information given in it is consistent with the audited accounts and, if not, this must be stated in the auditors' report: s. 237(6).

Auditors are also obliged to prepare their reports in accordance with Statements of Standard Accounting Practice prepared by their relevant association.

Case law In *Re Thomas Gerard and Son Ltd* (1968), the company's managing director falsified the account. The auditors noticed that certain invoices had been altered but negligently failed to investigate the matter further. The auditors gave a favourable view of the company's profits, and this resulted in the payment of dividends and tax on the payment of dividends. It was held that the auditors must repay the dividends, the cost of recovering the tax and any tax which was not recoverable. The judge said that: 'If the directors do not allow auditors time to conduct such investigations as are necessary in order to make these statements, the auditors must either refuse to make a report at all or make an appropriately qualified report. They cannot be justified in making a report containing a statement the truth of which they have not had an opportunity of ascertaining'.

Case law In *Re Kingston Cotton Mill Co (No 2)* (1896), the auditors accepted the certificate of the company's manager as to the value of the stock in trade. If they had compared the amount of stock at the start of the year with sales and purchases over the year, they would have been put on enquiry. It was held that the auditors were not liable: 'an auditor is not bound to be a detective ... or to approach his work with suspicion, or with a foregone conclusion that something is wrong. He is a watchdog, not a bloodhound. He is justified in believing tried servants of the company in whom confidence is placed by the company'.

Liability of auditors

Auditors can be liable if they prepare the accounts negligently.

Case law In *Twomax Ltd* v *Dickson, Mcfarlane and Robinson* (1982), T Ltd acquired a majority shareholding in a private company. It asserted that, in taking the shares, it had relied on accounts prepared by auditors, and alleged that these had been negligently prepared. It was held that the audit had been 'perfunctory and negligent'. The auditors should have foreseen that the accounts might have been relied on by a potential investors for the purpose of deciding whether or not to invest in the company.

Case law In *Caparo Industries plc* v *Dickman* (1990), the House of Lords ruled that the auditor of a public company's accounts owed no duty of care to a member of the public at large who relied on the accounts to buy shares in a company because the court would not deduce a relationship of proximity between the auditor and a member of the public when to do so would give rise to unlimited liability on the part of the auditor. Furthermore, an auditor owed no duty of care to an individual share-holder in the company who wished to buy more shares in the company, since an individual shareholder was in no better position than a member of the public at large and the auditor's statutory duty to prepare accounts was owed to the body of shareholders as a whole, the purpose for which accounts were prepared and audited being to enable the share-holders as a body to exercise informed control of the company and not to enable individual shareholders to buy shares with a view to profit.

Case law In *Galoo Ltd* v *Bright Grahame Murray* (1995), the court ruled that the fact that it was foreseeable that a potential bidder for shares in a company, or a potential lender might rely on the audited accounts, was not of itself enough to impose on an auditor a duty of care owed to the bidder or lender. However, if the auditor had been made aware that a particular identified bidder or lender would rely on the audited accounts or other statements approved by him and the auditor intended that that party should so rely, he owed a duty of care to the identified party and could be liable in damages for any breach thereof.

Case law In *Anthony* v *Wright* (1995), the plaintiffs were investors who had invested in GAA. GAA held these investments on trust for the investors and had paid them into a separate designated client account at GAA's bank. Thereafter, the investments were improperly used by the directors of GAA to meet their own and the company's liabilities. GAA collapsed. The plaintiffs sued the directors of GAA and its auditors. They contended that the auditors owed them a duty of care in auditing GAA's accounts and that, if they had exercised reasonable care and skill, the directors' actions would not have gone unnoticed. The court struck out the claim since the investors did not fall within the class of persons to whom the auditors owed a duty of care. It could not be said that such a duty arose from the fact that the auditors knew that the plaintiff's investments were held by GAA on trust. There was no apparent assumption by the auditors of any responsibility to the plaintiffs nor any reliance by the plaintiffs on the auditing of the accounts.

17. Shares

'A share is the interest of a shareholder in the company measured by a sum of money for the purpose of liability in the first place, and of interest in the second, but also consisting of a series of mutual covenants entered into by all the shareholders *inter se*' (*Borland's Trustee* v *Steel Brothers & Co* (1901) per Farwell J).

Each company having a share capital must state in its memorandum 'the division of the share capital into shares of a fixed amount': s. 2(5). A company cannot, therefore, issue shares having no par value.

A company must, within two months of allotment or lodging a valid transfer (so long as this is not a transfer which the company is entitled to refuse), complete and have ready for delivery share certificates in respect of these shares, unless the conditions of issue are to the contrary: s. 185. Every shareholder has the right to transfer his shares in the manner provided for in the articles. Such transfer must be in writing and the company cannot register a transfer unless a proper instrument of transfer has been delivered, notwithstanding any provision to the contrary in the articles: s. 183. The Stock Transfer Act 1963 provides a form of transfer which is adopted by the majority of companies.

Restrictions in relation to shares

There are a number of rules laid down by the Companies Act in relation to shares, of which the most important are the following:

(a) Shares must not be issued or allotted by the company to the initial shareholders for a price less than their nominal value: s. 100.

(b) There are restrictions on the acceptability of non-cash consideration for the purchase of shares. Further, if shares in public companies are to be paid for otherwise than in cash, the consideration must be valued by a qualified person: ss. 99, 103 and 108.

(c) Although it is a general rule that a company cannot buy its own shares, nor provide assistance to another so that he can buy them, there are many exceptions to this rule: ss. 137, 143, 151, 153–155, 159–164. These exceptions will generally apply only when shareholders approve the purchase or assistance. Shares may only be purchased when fully paid shares may be purchased from distributable profits or out of the proceeds of a fresh issue of shares made for the purpose of the purchase; a company may not purchase its shares if, as a result of the purchase, there would no longer be any member holding shares other than redeemable shares; and a public company must, after any such purchase, satisfy the capital requirements of the Act.

> *Case law* In *British and Commonwealth Holdings plc* v *Barclays Bank plc* (1996), it was said that, for a company to be liable for providing unlawful financial assistance for the purchase of its shares by way of indemnity, that indemnity had to give assistance of a financial nature for the purpose of the acquisition of the shares. The fact that there was a contract under which a party might recover the same amount by way of damages as he would have recovered under an indemnity was not enough to convert that contract into an indemnity. In the circumstances of the particular case, covenants in an option agreement were *bona fide* covenants, the purpose of which was to reassure the relevant party and the performance of which did not involve the giving of any financial assistance. The fact that breach of the covenants might render the company liable in damages did not mean that the company gave financial assistance thereby. It followed that the option agreement did not amount to financial assistance for the purpose of acquisition of the shares.

In addition to allotting shares, the directors may seek to sub-divide shares, increase share capital or re-arrange share capital. Such will require the agreement by ordinary resolution of the shareholders: s. 121. The directors may also seek to reduce the share capital. This too is permissible provided it is approved by the shareholders by special resolution and by the court: ss. 137–140.

Types of share

(a) *Ordinary shares*. The holders of such shares are entitled to the surplus profits after prior interests have been met. They will be entitled to a fixed rate of dividend and are entitled in a winding-up (see **20** below) to the surplus profits remaining after the payment of liabilities and the return of capital unless preference shareholders (see below) are given the right to participate in the distribution of any surplus assets.

(b) *Preference shares.* This term, which is not legally defined, is generally used to denote those shares which confer certain preferential rights. The principal such rights are to a dividend at a fixed rate before payment to other classes of shareholder and the right to receive a proportionate part of the capital or to participate in the distribution of the company's assets.

(c) *Deferred shares.* These shares are sometimes also called 'founders' or 'management' shares, and are seldom issued. A prospectus issued by a company must state the number of founders shares, their voting rights, their interest in company property and profits: sch. 3.

(d) *Redeemable shares.* A company limited by shares, or by guarantee and having a share capital, may issue shares which may be redeemed at the option of the shareholder: s. 159. A number of conditions are to be satisfied as set out in the Act: ss. 159, 160, 170, 173.

(e) *Employee shares.* The main feature of such shares is normally that they are to be issued only to employees and that they are to be transferred to trustees when the holder leaves the company. Normally, they have no voting rights.

(f) *Share warrants.* A company limited by shares may, if the shares are fully paid up and it is given authority by its articles, issue a share warrant stating that the bearer is entitled to the shares specified therein: s. 188. On the issue of a warrant, the member's name is struck off the register, and the following entered: the fact that a warrant has been issued; a statement of the shares included in the warrant; and the date of issue of the warrant.

Variation of class rights

A company may seek to amend or vary the rights attaching to one or more of its classes of shares. These rights are usually concerned with dividends, voting or the distribution of assets in a winding-up (see **20** below). The class rights are usually found in the articles of the company, but may also be found in the memorandum or the terms of the issue of the shares or, occasionally, in the terms of a special resolution.

18. Debentures

A debenture is a 'document which creates or acknowledges a debt'. The Act further provides that 'debenture' 'includes' debenture stocks, bonds and other securities of a company whether constituting a charge on the assets of the company or not: s. 744.

There are two main types of debenture.

The *fixed* charge is a mortgage over defined assets of a company, such as a warehouse, and the company cannot dispose of the property free from the charge without the consent of the debenture holders.

The *floating* charge is a charge over the assets of the company. It 'floats' over property which changes, such as the stock in trade. At all times, the company is free to deal with property subject to such a charge. The charge will 'crystallise' when: the company ceases trading; a receiver is appointed; the company goes into liquidation; conditions in the debenture deed giving rise to crystallisation arise.

Registration of charges

Charges are to be registered in the company's register of charges and certain charges must be registered with the Registrar of Companies: ss. 395, 407. In this latter case, registration is required within 21 days of the creation of the charge. If this is not done, the charge is void against the liquidator and other creditors of the company. The charge is not void, however, while the company is a going concern. It is also the case that, in the event of non-registration, the moneys secured by the charge becomes immediately repayable. The court, however, does have the power to extend time for registration and to rectify the register in respect of errors in the registration of the charge: s. 404.

Remedies of debenture holders

If the debenture is not secured by a charge, the remedies open to a holder are:

(*i*) to sue the company on its promise to repay the principal and/or interest and to obtain judgment from the court
(*ii*) to levy execution against the company if judgment has been obtained
(*iii*) to petition as a creditor, for the winding-up of the company, on the grounds that the company is unable to pay its debts
(*iv*) to provide in a winding-up for the debt owed.

If the debenture holder is secured, the deed creating the charge usually contains remedies (such as sale, appointment of a receiver) for enforcing the security without the need to seek the aid of the court. The power of sale is usually contained in the debenture or trust deed and may be exercised without the consent of the court. The secured party may also apply to the court for an order of foreclosure. The effect of such an order is to extinguish the interest of the company in the assets charged and to vest the title in the debenture holder.

The debenture or trust deed usually gives the debenture holder the power to appoint a receiver.

Case law In *Sheppard & Cooper Ltd* v *TSB Bank plc* (1996), the plaintiff company executed a debenture in favour of a bank granting a fixed and floating charge (see above) over its assets and undertakings. It was agreed that the debt would be discharged on demand. The court held that, where money was payable on demand, and the debtor failed to make payment, he would not be in default until he had had a reasonable opportunity of implementing whatever reasonable mechanics of payment he might need to employ to discharge the debt. The requirement that sufficient time be permitted to elapse to enable the debtor to make the necessary arrangements for payment assumed that that was the period needed if the debtor had the funds available. If, however, the debtor had made it clear that the required funds were not available, that admission established the necessary default and there was thus no need for the creditor to allow any time to elapse before treating the debtor as in default.

19. Dividends

The mechanics of paying a dividend will generally be governed by the articles. These give the power to pay an interim dividend if it appears that this is justified by the profits available for distribution.

A private or public company may only make distributions out of its profits available for distribution. These are its accumulated, realised profits so far as not previously distributed or capitalised, less its accumulated, realised losses so far as not previously written off in a reduction or reorganisation of capital: s. 263.

A public company may only make a distribution so long as the company's net assets do not fall below the aggregate of its called-up share capital and 'undistributable reserves'. Thus, for public companies, any excess of unrealised losses over unrealised profits must be covered by realised profits: s. 264. These tests are applied by reference to the relevant accounts complying with specified requirements, these usually being the last audited accounts: s. 270.

The following are expressly excluded from the above restrictions:

(*i*) An issue of shares as fully or partly paid bonus shares
(*ii*) The redemption or purchase of any of the company's own shares otherwise than out of distributable profits
(*iii*) Certain reductions of share capitals
(*iv*) Distributions in a winding up: s. 263.

20. Winding up

There are two methods of winding up: winding up by the court and voluntary winding up.

21

Winding up by the court

A company may be wound up by the court if:

(a) It has passed a special resolution to that effect.

(b) It has not been issued with a s. 177 certificate. This is a certificate issued by the Registrar of Companies that he is satisfied that the minimum share capital has been subscribed.

(c) The company does not commence business within a year from incorporation or suspends its business for a whole year.

(d) The number of members is reduced to less than two.

(e) The company is unable to pay its debts.

(f) The court considers it 'just and equitable' that the company be wound up: s. 122 Insolvency Act 1986.

> *Case law* In *Re Yenidje Tobacco* (1916) a company's two directors were the sole shareholders, and held an equal number of shares. They were not on speaking terms and communicated by passing notes and through the secretary. One of the directors petitioned for winding up and it was held that the company should be wound up.

> *Case law* In *Loch* v *John Blackwood Ltd* (1924), a company was formed to carry on John Blackwood's business. The directors failed to hold general meetings, submit accounts or recommend a dividend in order to keep shareholders in ignorance of the company's affairs. The directors' object was to acquire shares at an undervaluation. It was held just and equitable that the company be wound up.

Winding-up petitions may be presented by the following: the company itself; a creditor; the directors; a contributory (that is, a person liable to contribute to the assets of the company in a winding up); the Department of Trade and Industry; the Official Receiver; the Attorney General; s. 124 Insolvency Act 1986. It has been held that it is an abuse of the process of the courts to present a winding-up position against a solvent company as a means of putting pressure on it to pay money which is *bona fide* disputed, instead of applying for summary judgment for the relevant amount, and the court will in such circumstances issue an injunction to restrain presentation of the petition and may penalise the petitioner in costs (*Re A Company* (no. 0012209 of 1991) (1992)).

If a winding-up order is made, the Official Receiver 'becomes the provisional liquidator and continues in that capacity until he or another person is appointed liquidator': s. 130 Insolvency Act 1986. Within 21 days of the appointment of the provisional liquidator or the making of a winding-up order, a statement of affairs must be submitted to the Official Receiver. This must show: particulars of the company's assets, debts and liabilities; the names, addresses and occupations of its creditors; the securities held by them and the dates on which they were given and such further information as may be prescribed or the Official Receiver may require: s. 131 of the 1986 Act. When a company is being wound up, every invoice, order or business letter on which the name of the company appears must contain a statement that the company is being wound up: s. 188 Insolvency Act. During the 12 weeks from the day when the winding-up order was made, the Official Receiver must decide whether to summon separate meetings of creditors and contributories for the purpose of choosing a liquidator. If a meeting is summoned, the meetings may establish a liquidation committee: s. 141 Insolvency Act 1986.

The liquidator can continue the company's business, but only insofar as this is of benefit to the creditors: sch. 4 Insolvency Act 1986.

When the Registrar of Companies receives a notice of the final meeting of creditors and of vacation of office by the liquidator, or a notice from the Official Receiver that the winding-up of the company by the court is complete, the Registrar must forthwith register it, and, at the end of three months beginning with the date of registration, the company is dissolved: s. 205 Insolvency Act 1986.

Voluntary winding up

There are two types of voluntary winding up: a members' voluntary winding up where the company is insolvent; and a creditors' voluntary winding up.

Members' winding up

The directors, or if there are more than two, the majority of the directors, must make a statutory declaration: that they have made a full inquiry into the company's affairs; and, that having done so, they have formed the opinion that the company will be able to pay its debts in full within twelve months. This declaration of solvency must be: made within five weeks preceding the resolution to wind up; filed with the Registrar of Companies before the resolution is passed; and contain a statement of assets and liabilities: s. 89 Insolvency Act. The company may then appoint a liquidator: s. 91 Insolvency Act.

As soon as the company's affairs are wound up, the liquidator must call a general meeting of the company. He must then present an account of the winding up, showing how it has been conducted and how company property has been disposed of. Within a week of the meeting, the liquidator must send to the Registrar a copy of the accounts and a return of the holding of the meeting. If a quorum was not present at the meeting, the liquidator will make a return to that effect. The Registrar registers the accounts and returns and, on the expiry of three months from the registration of the return, the company is deemed to be dissolved: ss. 94, 201 Insolvency Act.

For the details of members' winding up, see generally Part IV Chapter III of the 1986 Act.

Creditors' winding up

If the directors are unable to make a declaration of solvency, the winding up proceeds as a creditors' voluntary winding up: s. 90 Insolvency Act. A meeting must be summoned and a statement of affairs must be laid by the directors before the creditors: ss. 98, 99 Insolvency Act. A liquidator is appointed and, if it is thought fit, a liquidation committee: s. 101 Insolvency Act. The Registrar registers the accounts and returns and, on the expiry of three months from the registration of the return, the company is deemed to be dissolved: ss. 106, 201 Insolvency Act

For the details of creditors' winding up, see generally Part IV Chapter IV of the 1986 Act.

Distribution of assets

When the liquidator is in a position to satisfy the claims of creditors, he makes the relevant payments in accordance with a strict order of priority. Secured creditors with fixed charges (see **18** above) are entitled to the benefit of their security ahead of all other claims. Thereafter, the classes and their order of priority are:

(a) The costs, charges and expenses of the winding up

(b) The preferential debts (such as money owed to the Inland Revenue; VAT; social security and pension scheme contributions; remuneration of employees; s. 386 and Sch. 6 Insolvency Act)

(c) The claims of holders of floating charges (see above)

(d) Ordinary unsecured creditors

(e) Certain deferred debts.

Should there still be funds available, the shareholders are entitled to the return of their capital and to a share in any surplus.

21. Administration order

The objective of administration is to secure, if possible, the return of the company to corporate health, or for a more advantageous realisation of the company's assets than would occur in the context of a winding up.

Before it makes an administration order, the court must be satisfied that the company is, or is likely to be, unable to pay its debts, and it must consider that the making of the order would be likely to achieve one or more of the following:

(a) The survival of the company, and the whole or part of its undertaking, as a going concern.

(b) The approval at a meeting of the company and its creditors of a composition in satisfaction of the company's debts or a scheme of its affairs.

(c) The sanctioning under the Companies Act of a compromise or arrangement.

(d) A more advantageous realisation of the assets than would otherwise be effected in a winding up.

The general effect of an administration order is that no steps can be taken to enforce any security over the company property, or to repossess goods under a hire purchase, leasing or retention of title agreement, without the consent of the administrator or the leave of the court. Such consent or leave is also required before other proceedings or legal processes are taken against the company. See generally ss. 8–27 Insolvency Act 1986.

PARTNERSHIPS

The law relating to partnerships has generally been codified in the Partnership Act 1890. In the discussion below, all section references are to this Act except where otherwise stated.

22. Definition of partnership

A partnership is 'a relationship which subsists between persons carrying on a business in common with a view to profit': s. 1(1). A partnership is within the definition even if the parties sought to exclude this result (*Weiner* v *Harris* (1910)).

Case law In *Stekel* v *Ellice* (1973), E took S into salaried partnership for 7 months on the basis that E would provide all the capital, would take all profits and bear all losses, and that during this period a full partnership agreement would be concluded. At the end of the period, no partnership had been arranged and the temporary arrangement continued for a further 14 months. It was held that S was a partner, the court being influenced by the fact that S had been so held out as by the printing of his name on the firm's letterhead.

23. Number of partners

Section 716 of the Companies Act 1985 provides that a partnership must consist of no more than 20 persons. Exemptions exist in relation to solicitors, accountants and members of a recognised stock exchange. These exemptions can be extended by Regulations. Such Regulations presently cover: patent agents, surveyors, auctioneers, valuers, estate agents, land agents and those engaged in land management, actuaries, consulting engineers, building designers and loss adjusters, insurance brokers, town planners, member firms of the London Stock Exchange, multi-national firms of lawyers and others. Reference should be made to the various Partnerships (Unlimited Size) Regulations 1968 No. 1222; 1970 No. 1319; 1982 No. 530; 1990 No. 1581; 1990 No. 1969; 1991 No. 2729; 1992 No. 1028; 1992 No. 1439; 1994 No. 644; 1996 No. 262; 1997 No. 1937

24. The name of the partnership

The Business Names Act 1985 stipulates that all orders, invoices, business letters and the like must disclose the true names of all the owners of the business and the addresses in Great Britain. In addition, such information must be displayed on a notice in a prominent position at the business premises. A customer is entitled to ask for a written list of the required information which is to be supplied immediately. If the partnership consists of more than 20 persons, these conditions are relaxed provided the document does not contain the names of any partners except as signatories, and provided that the document indicates that a full list of partners can be inspected.

Actions in contract by a person in breach of the 1985 Act can be dismissed if the defendant can show that he has a claim against the plaintiff because of the breach or if he has suffered loss because of such breach. The court can allow an action to proceed if it considers this just and equitable.

Breach of the Act is a criminal offence.

25. The partnership agreement

There are no legal requirements as to the form of a partnership agreement, and it may therefore be made orally, in writing, by deed or by a combination. The rights and duties of the partners as expressed in the agreement can be varied with the consent of the partners, which can be express or inferred from the course of dealing: s. 19. For example, the agreement may specify that no partner can draw or accept bills of exchange in his own name without the approval of all the other partners, but if the partners 'slide into' the practice of allowing this to be done as a matter of course, this will count as a variation (*Const* v *Harris* (1824)).

26. Partnership property

Partnership property, whether originally brought in or later acquired (see below), must be held and applied solely for partnership purposes and in accordance with the agreement: s. 20(1).

The persons in whom partnership land is vested hold the land in trust for those beneficiaries interested under the partnership agreement, such as the partners themselves or retired partners entitled to annuities: s. 20(2). The interests of those beneficially interested in partnership land are interests in personalty not realty: s. 22. This means that if, for example, a partner leaves his realty to R and his personalty to S, S will take the interest in the land.

A partner has a beneficial interest in the entirety of the partnership assets and can enforce that interest against the other partners to the extent of ensuring that the assets are used for the benefit of the partnership, but he cannot assign that interest to a third party (*Hadlee and Sydney Bridge Nominees* v *IRC* (1993)).

Property brought in

In most cases, the partnership agreement will give details of the property brought in by the partner and this will be credited to that partner in the capital accounts. A partner may bring an asset into the firm:

(i) by transferring that asset to the partnership
(ii) transferring the asset to trustees to be held by them on behalf of the partnership
(iii) by retaining title but holding it on trust for the partnership.

The mere use of property in the partnership does not make it partnership property.

Case law In *Singh* v *Nahar* (1965), A took B and C into partnership. A conducted the business from premises leased from D. D sought to repossess the premises on the ground that they had become partnership property and hence an assignment of A's interest to the partnership.

27

Under the lease, this was grounds for forfeiture. The partnership agreement did not refer to the lease specifically and it was held that it had not become partnership property. There had, accordingly, been no forfeiture. (See too *Miles* v *Clark* (1953) and *Eardley* v *Broad* (1970).)

Property later acquired

Property bought with funds belonging to the partnership is deemed to have been bought on account of the partnership unless a contrary intention appears: s. 21.

If land is used which is not partnership land, but the profits are used for the purchase of further land, or the enhancement of the existing land, then the extra land or enhancements belong to the partnership (*Davis* v *Davis* (1894)).

27. Capital

Unless the partnership agreement specifies otherwise, partners are entitled to capital in equal shares regardless of the value of the assets brought in: s. 24(1). Interest on capital is only payable if the partnership agreement expressly so provides and sufficient profits are generated by the partnership: s. 24(4).

28. Loans

A partner may loan the partnership money over and above his capital. Such payments are not deemed to have increased his capital unless the partners have otherwise agreed, but he is entitled to interest on the loan at 5%, payable whether or not profits are made: s. 24(3).

29. Profits and losses

In the absence of anything to the contrary in the agreement, partners share equally in the profits and contribute equally to the losses: s. 24(1).

30. Indemnity

The partnership must indemnify each partner in respect of payments made and personal liabilities incurred by him in the ordinary and proper conduct of its business, or in doing anything necessary to preserve the business or property of the partnership: s. 24(2). Thus, if a partner pays the firm's debts or a premium to insure the firm's professional liability, he can look to the partnership for reimbursement.

31. Remuneration

No partner is entitled to remuneration for simply acting in the partnership business: s. 24(6). Where a partnership consists of active and non-active partners, the agreement will often provide that the former are entitled to a salary in addition to their share of profits. Furthermore, if one partner wilfully refuses to attend to partnership business, it is probable that an allowance is due to the remaining active partners. This was held to be the case in a dissolution (*Airey* v *Borham* (1861)), and it is likely that the principle of this case applies also during the existence of the partnership.

32. Management

The partnership agreement will usually set out the powers of the partners in the matter of management. If not, every partner may take part in the management of the business: s. 24(5). It is also the case that a partner may also inspect and copy the firm's books which must be kept at the principal place of business: s. 24(9).

33. Change in partnership business

The consent of all partners is needed before there can be a change in the nature of the partnership business, but disputes as to matters connected with the ordinary business of the partnership can be settled by majority vote, regardless of the capital introduced by each partner: s. 24(7), (8).

34. Change in partners

New partners

The introduction of a new partner requires a unanimous vote.

Expulsion of partners

A partner cannot be expelled by majority vote, unless this is provided for in the agreement: s. 25. If this is provided for, the power of expulsion must still be exercised in good faith.

> *Case law* In *Carmichael* v *Evans* (1904), it was held that the expulsion of a partner who had been convicted of travelling on a train without a valid ticket was a proper exercise of a term in the agreement allowing expulsion for 'scandalous conduct detrimental to the partnership business' or for 'flagrant breach of the duties of a partner'.

A term in a partnership agreement requiring the signature of a particular partner to an expulsion does not apply where he is the partner to be expelled (*Hitchman* v *CBS Services* (1983)).

35. Duties of partners

The partners have the following duties:

(a) To render accounts and disclose information. The partners are bound to render a true account and full information to any partner or his legal representative in relation to all things which affect the partnership: s. 28. Disclosure must be made whether it is asked for or not (*Law* v *Law* (1905)).

(b) Duty to account for private profits. Each partner must account to the firm for any benefit earned by him from any transaction relating to the partnership or from any use by him of the partnership property, name or business transaction: s. 29(1). No account is due if the transaction could not have affected the partnership business (*Aas* v *Benham* (1891)).

This duty to account also applies to transactions undertaken after the partnership has been dissolved by death (see below) and before the affairs of the partnership have been completely wound up: s. 29(2).

A potential partner is accountable to the partnership when it comes into existence in relation to profits made during the negotiations leading to its formation, if the transaction from which the profits were made would have affected the partnership had it then existed (*Fawcett* v *Whitehouse* (1829)).

(c) Duty not to compete with the partnership. If a partner, without the consent of the others, carries on a business in competition with the partnership, he must account for the profits made and pay them over to the partnership: s. 30. This provision merely provides for an account of profits and does not actually prohibit participation in a competing business. If, however, the partnership agreement imposes such a prohibition, then an injunction could be sought.

36. Assignment of partnership share

The fact that a partner assigns his share of the partnership does not make the assignee a partner and gives him no rights as such. He is entitled only to receive the share of profits to which the assignor would be entitled and he must accept the account of profits agreed to by the partners: s. 31(1). Creditors of the partnership can sue the assignor but the assignee, unless there has been an agreement to the contrary, must indemnify the assignor (*Dodson* v *Downey* (1901)).

If the partnership is dissolved (see **40** below), the assignee is entitled to receive the share of the assets to which the assigning partner was entitled, and in order of dissolution: s. 31(2).

Transmission of share

When a partner dies or becomes bankrupt, his property vests by operation of law in his personal representative or trustee in bankruptcy.

37. Remedies for breach of partnership agreement

By virtue of the partnership agreement itself, the partners have a contractual relationship with each other, and hence can sue other partners for breach of the agreement as on a breach of contract. Furthermore, injunctions can also be obtained to restrain breaches of the agreement. Since a partnership is essentially a contract for personal services, the courts will not generally grant a degree of specific performance requiring adherence to the agreement.

38. Relation of partners to persons dealing with them

Every partner is an implied agent of the partnership and, as such, can make the partnership liable for debts which he incurs on its behalf: s. 5.

> *Case law* In *Mann* v *D'Arcy* (1968), the defendants carried on a partnership dealing with produce. One of the partners agreed with the plaintiff on the purchase and sale of a cargo of potatoes. This arrangement was to be managed by the defendants and they were to share the profits and losses with the plaintiff. It was held that this venture was by way of the usual business carried on by the defendants so that the partner had the authority to bind the partnership which had, therefore, to share the profits with the plaintiff. See too *Mercantile Credit Co Ltd* v *Garrod* (1962).

Where an act or instrument relating to the business of the partnership is done or executed in its name, or in any way showing an intention to bind the partnership, by an authorised agent, whether a partner or not, it is binding on the partnership and the partners: s. 6.

Where a partner pledges the credit of the partnership for a purpose which is apparently not connected with its ordinary business, the partnership is not bound unless the action was specially authorised by the partners: s. 7.

39. Partner's liabilities

Debts and obligations

Every partner is liable jointly with the other partners for all the debts and obligations of the firm incurred while he is a partner; and, after his death, his estate is also severally liable for such debts and obligations so far as they remain unsatisfied, subject to prior payment of his separate debts: s. 9.

It used to be the position that if judgment were obtained for the whole debt against one partner, the creditor could not later bring proceedings against the others even if the judgment were unsatisfied (the rule in *Kendall* v *Hamilton* (1879)). This, however, was altered by s. 3 of the Civil Liability (Contribution) Act 1996 which expressly allows for an action against another partner should the first judgment go unsatisfied.

The rule of joint liability does not apply as between the partners. Thus, if a partner has paid a firm's debt, he can seek a contribution from the other partners: s. 24(2).

Torts

The partnership is liable for the torts of the partners which are committed in the ordinary course of the partnership's business: s. 10.

> *Case law* The plaintiff in *Hamlyn* v *Houston & Co* (1903) carried on business in London buying grain. The defendant ran a similar business, also in London. One of the partners in the defendant bribed the plaintiff's clerk to obtain information. It was held that both partners were liable in damages to the plaintiff on the grounds that the tortious act of the partner actually offering the bribe was within the general scope of his authority as a partner. Every partner is liable jointly and severally for the wrongful acts or omission of the partnership (note that in the case of debts and other obligations liability is joint only): s. 12. Thus, a judgment against one partner is no bar to an action against the other partners.

If one partner is sued and pays damages in respect of the tort for which the firm is liable, he may seek a contribution under the terms of the Law Reform (Married Women and Joint Tortfeasors) Act 1935.

Misapplication of money or property

The partnership is liable to make good the loss incurred if a partner has tortiously misapplied the money or property of a third person where: the partner was acting within the scope of his apparent authority (*Plumer* v *Gregory* (1874)); or where the partnership in the course of its business received the money or property and it was misapplied by one or more partners while in partnership custody (*Cleather* v *Twisden* (1884)): s. 11. Here too, each partner is jointly and severally liable: s. 12.

Partnership by estoppel

Any person who 'by words spoken or written' or who 'by conduct' represents himself, or who knowingly allows himself to be held out or represented to be a partner, is liable as a partner to anyone who, on the basis of any such representation, has given credit to the partnership: s. 14(1).

Case law In *Tower Cabinet Co Ltd* v *Ingram* (1949), I and C had been in partnership. The partnership was dissolved by agreement and I arranged with C for the notification of those dealing with the firm that I was no longer a partner. Notice was given to the partnership's bankers, but no advertisement was placed in the *London Gazette*. C had new notepaper printed, but, in one case, placed an order on the old paper and which bore I's name. I had no knowledge of this and it was contrary to his arrangement with C. It was held that judgment could not be entered against I since he had not knowingly allowed himself to be held out still to be a partner.

Where, after a partner's death, the business is continued in the old firm name, the continued use of that name, or of the deceased's partner's name as part of it, shall not of itself render his personal representatives or his estate liable for partnership debts contracted after his death. (See *Addendum*.)

Liability of new and old partners

A new partner is not liable for debts incurred before he joined the partnership unless it has been otherwise agreed: s. 17(1).

A retiring partner is not liable for debts incurred after he retired, but he is liable for those pre-dating his retirement: s. 17(2). He will, however, remain liable for post-retirement debts if he has allowed creditors to believe that he remains with the partnership. To avoid any such liability, he must: *(i)* give express notice of retirement to persons who dealt with the firm before retirement; *(ii)* notify persons who trade with the partnership in the future by advertising his retirement in the *London Gazette*: s. 36.

The estate of a deceased or bankrupt partner is not liable for partnership debts incurred after death or bankruptcy, whether any notice is given or not: s. 36(3).

A retiring partner may be discharged from any existing liabilities by an agreement to that effect between himself, the other partners, and the creditors: s. 17(3).

It is always possible for a partnership to be a party to a continuing guarantee, either as guarantor, creditor or principal creditor. If the partnership which is the creditor or principal debtor then changes its composition, the guarantee is, in the absence of any agreement otherwise, revoked. If, however, there is a change in the composition of the guarantor, such a change has no effect and a retiring partner remains liable while a new partner does not become liable in the absence of a novation of the agreement or an indemnity from the remaining partners: s. 18.

A retiring partner will be entitled to his share of the partnership assets, but he is not entitled as of right to appoint a receiver since this would amount to an unwarranted interference in the business of the partnership: *Floydd* v *Cheney* (1970); *Sobell* v *Boston* (1975).

40. Dissolution of partnership

1. Without a court order

The partnership agreement will end on the expiry of any fixed term contained in the agreement: s. 32. A partnership will also automatically come to an end if it was formed to carry out a particular venture, and that venture has been completed.

Where the partnership is a partnership at will, it expires on any one party giving notice. A partnership is presumed to be a partnership at will unless the agreement specifies a fixed term: s. 26. A partnership is also presumed to be at will where an agreed fixed term partnership has expired and the partnership continues to operate with no new agreement being expressly made: s. 27.

The partners can of course agree on a dissolution

Case law In *Sobell* v *Boston* (1975), one partner in a firm of solicitors was under police investigation. He agreed with the other partners to withdraw from the partnership. A notice was inserted by agreement in the Law Society's Gazette to the effect that the partnership had been 'dissolved', but which also stated that the remaining partners were continuing in practice at the same address and under the same name. The court held that this was not a dissolution. The true inference was that the relevant partner had retired, and that his retirement had not worked a dissolution.

If the partnership agreement provides that it is to be terminated only by 'mutual agreement', this displaces the assumption that it is a partnership at will and hence precludes termination by a single partner

Case law In *Moss* v *Elphick* (1910), the partnership agreement provided for dissolution by mutual agreement only. This was held to mean that the partnership was to last for the joint lives of the partners, neither of whom could terminate the partnership unilaterally.

Any notice of termination must be clear and communicated to all the partners: s. 26. Once given, it cannot be withdrawn unless all partners agree (*Jones* v *Lloyd* (1874)), but a notice expressed to take effect only if the partners do agree only takes effect on such agreement (*Hall* v *Hall* (1855)). A partnership at will is also dissolved if the conduct of the parties makes such intention plain even if no formal notice is given (*Pearce* v *Lindsay* (1860)).

Illegal purpose

If the objects and activities of the partnership become illegal, though they were not so when the partnership was first entered into, it is automatically dissolved: s. 34

> *Case law* In *Stevenson & Sons* v *Aktiengesellschaft für Cartonnange-Industrie* (1917), a partnership agreement had been made between parties who reside in the United Kingdom and Germany. Since the continuance of the partnership during war would have meant trading with the enemy, the partnership was held to be dissolved.

Death

The death of a partner dissolves the firm unless there is an agreement to the contrary: s. 33. An agreement that the partnership is to last for a specific number of years is not an agreement to the contrary (*Gillespie* v *Hamilton* (1818)).

> *Case law* In *McLeod* v *Dowling* (1927), it was held that a partnership had been ended by death, and not by notice, where a partner who had sent a notice of dissolution died before the notice was received by his co-partner.

Bankruptcy

The bankruptcy of a partner dissolves the partnership unless there is an agreement to the contrary: s. 33.

Charging order

A partner who allows his partnership share to be charged gives the other partners the option of winding up the partnership: s. 33.

2. Dissolution by court order

Section 35 of the Act lists a number of grounds entitling the court to order the dissolution of a partnership.

(a) Where a partner becomes permanently incapable of performing his part of the partnership agreement. If a partner becomes of unsound mind, the partnership does not dissolve automatically, but it is grounds for asking the court for a decree of dissolution: *Jones* v *Noy* (1833); Mental Health Act 1983, s. 96(1)(g).

The jurisdiction of the court under s. 35 of the Partnership Act extends to other forms of incapacity than mental, covering any form of incapacity rendering a partner incapable of performing his partnership duties.

(b) The court can dissolve a partnership when a partner has been guilty of conduct prejudicial to the business of the partnership. The conduct in question need not actually relate directly to the partnership's business.

> *Case law* In *Carmichael* v *Evans* (1904), a partner in a firm of drapers was convicted more than once of not paying his train fare. The partnership was held to be dissolved since convictions for dishonesty were prejudicial to the interests of the partnership.

> *Case law* In *Snow* v *Milford* (1868), a banker's adultery with several parties, resulting in divorce, was held not to give grounds for dissolution in the absence of evidence of injury or likely injury to the partnership.

(c) The court may order the dissolution of a partnership when a partner wilfully or persistently breaks the partnership agreement, or so conducts himself, so that it ceases to be reasonably practicable for other partners to continue. The keeping of erroneous accounts and the failure to enter receipts into the partnership books justifies dissolution (*Cheesman* v *Price* (1865)).

Misconduct which is not directly related to the business of the firm may give rise to dissolution if it destroys the trust of the other partners in that individual. For instance, the fraud of a partner in respect of an earlier partnership can be enough to destroy the confidence of his current partners in a solicitors' practice (*Harrison* v *Tennant* (1856)).

(d) The partnership can be dissolved when its business can only be carried on at a loss.

(e) The court may finally order the dissolution of a partnership where the circumstances render this 'just and equitable'.

> *Case law* In *Re Yenidje Tobacco Co Ltd* (1916), the court accepted that it would be grounds for dissolution if there were: 'Refusal to meet on matters of business, continued quarrelling, and such a state of animosity as precludes all reasonable hope of reconciliation and friendly co-operation ... It is not necessary in order to induce the court to interfere, to show personal rudeness on the part of one partner to another or even gross misconduct as a partner. All that is necessary is to satisfy the court that it is impossible for the partners to place that confidence in each other which each has a right to expect, and that such impossibility has not been caused by the person seeking to take advantage of it ...'.

A partnership consisting of not less than eight members may be wound up as an unregistered company. A 'company' may be wound up under these provisions if *(a)* it is dissolved, or has ceased to carry on business, or is carrying on business solely to wind up its affairs; *(b)* is unable to pay its debts; or *(c)* the court is of the option that it is just and equitable that it be wound up: Companies Act 1985 s. 666.

41. After dissolution

Notification

On the dissolution of a partnership, any partner may issue a public notice of dissolution, and may require the other partner(s) to concur in all necessary and proper acts to achieve that purpose: s. 37.

Authority of partners

After dissolution, the authority of each partner to bind the partnership continues to the extent necessary to wind up its affairs and complete transactions begun but not finished prior to dissolution: s. 38. However, the partnership will not be bound by the acts of a partner who has become bankrupt unless they represented themselves as still his partners: s. 38.

Effect of dissolution

The effects of dissolution may be covered by the partnership agreement. If this is not the case, the provisions of the 1890 Act will apply.

(a) Every partner is entitled to have partnership property applied in payment of the debts and liabilities of the firm. He is entitled to have surplus assets after such payment applied in payment of what may be due to the partners after deducting what may be due from them: and, for that purpose, he may apply to the court to wind up the business and affairs of the firm: s. 39.

(b) Where a partner has paid a premium to another on entering a partnership for a fixed term, and the partnership is dissolved before the expiry of such term otherwise than by death, the court can order repayment, or part, of the premium, as it thinks just. Repayment is not ordered, however, where the cause of dissolution was wholly or mainly due to the misconduct of the partner who paid the premium: s. 40. No order for the repayment of a premium will be made where the partnership is dissolved by an agreement containing no provision for its repayment: *Lee* v *Page* (1851). Any order usually apportions the premium by reference to the unexpired part of the partnership: *Attwood* v *Maude* (1868).

(c) If the partnership was rescinded because of fraud or misrepresentation, the innocent partner is entitled, without prejudice to any other right, to:

(i) a lien over the surplus of any partnership assets, after liabilities of the partnership have been satisfied, for any sum of money paid by him for

the purchase of a share in the partnership and for any capital contributed by him

(ii) stand in the place of any creditor for any payments made by him in respect of partnership liabilities; and

(iii) be indemnified by the partner guilty of the fraud or making the representation against all debts and liabilities of the firm: s. 41.

Since these rights are without prejudice to other rights, the innocent partner may also claim damages under the Misrepresentation Act 1967.

(d) When a partner has died, or otherwise ceased to be a partner, and the business is carried on with no final settlement of accounts, the outgoing partner, or estate, is entitled to such share of the post-dissolution profits as is attributable to the use of his share of the partnership assets, or to interest at the rate of 5% p.a. on the amount of his share of the assets. These provisions do not apply if an option to buy the former partner's share, as specified in the partnership agreement, has been taken up: s. 42.

(e) Subject to any agreement between the partners, the amount due from the other partners in respect of the former partner's share is a debt accruing at the date of dissolution: s. 43.

(f) In settling accounts between partners after a dissolution of partnership, the following rules apply:

(i) Losses are paid first from profits, then from capital, and finally by the partners individually in the proportion in which they were entitled to share profits.

(ii) The partnership assets, including any sums contributed by the partners to make up losses or deficiencies in capital, are to be applied in the following manner and order:

- in paying debts and liabilities to persons who are not partners
- in paying to each partner pro rata what is due from the partnership to him in respect of capital
- in paying the residue to each partner in the proportion in which profits were payable: s. 44.

42. Goodwill

This is a partnership asset and means the good reputation and business connections which the partnership has developed: *Trego* v *Hunt* (1896). Unless agreed to the contrary in the partnership agreement, the goodwill must be sold on dissolution and the proceeds distributed as capital. If dissolution was caused by death, the estate is entitled to a share in the proceeds: *Re David & Mathews* (1899).

If the goodwill is not sold, and there is no agreement as to its disposal, any partner can carry on the business, even using the firm's name, provided that, in so doing, he does not expose former partners to liability: *Burchell* v *Wilde* (1900). If, though, the goodwill is assigned to any person, he can restrain partners from soliciting old customers of the partnership, or from using the partnership's name, but he cannot prevent it from competing: *Boorne* v *Wicker* (1927).

43. Limited partnerships

These are governed by the Limited Partnerships Act 1907, and references are to that Act unless there is an indication to the contrary.

Nature of limitation

The Act provides for a partnership to claim limited liability for partnership debts in relation to one or more of the partners. Limited partnerships are not common because, in most cases, the objectives can be better achieved by incorporation as a company.

A limited partnership must consist of one or more general partners, who are liable for all the debts and obligations of the firm, and of one or more limited partners, who contribute capital or property, and who are not liable for debts and obligations beyond that contribution: s. 4(2)

> *Case law* In *Rayner & Co* v *Rhodes* (1926), it was held that, despite a deed of partnership, which stated that a person was to be a limited partner, he was subject to unlimited liability because he had not contributed capital or property, but merely a running bank guarantee of the partnership debts, terminable with three months' notice.

During the continuance of the partnership, a limited partner cannot withdraw his contribution, and, if he does so, he is liable for partnership debts and obligations up to such amount: s. 4(3)

Number of partners

A limited partnership must not have more than 20 members. This number may be exceeded in the cases specified in relation to partnerships generally under s. 716 of the Companies Act 1985 (see **23** above) and see too the Limited Partnership (Unrestricted Size) Regulations 1971 No. 782, 1990 No. 1580 and 1992 No. 1027.

Registration

The limited partnership must be registered with the Registrar of Companies. Registration must be in a form signed by the partners and containing:

(i) Name

(ii) General nature of partnership business

(iii) Principal place of business

(iv) Full name of each partner

(v) The term, if any, of the partnership and the date of commencement (if no term is fixed, details of the condition of existence of the partnership are required)

(vi) A statement that the partnership is limited and the description of every limited partner as such

(vii) The sum contributed by each limited partner, and whether paid in cash or how otherwise: s. 8.

Any change in these particulars, or the fact that a general partner becomes a limited partner, must be notified within seven days. Failure to register means that a limited partner is fully liable as a general partner.

Limited partners and third persons

The law applicable to ordinary partnerships is applied to limited partnerships by s. 7 subject to such modifications as are effected by the 1907 Act. Thus s. 5 of the 1890 Act applies to a general partner and he has the same authority to bind the firm as a partner in an ordinary partnership. He will therefore be liable for the contracts entered into and torts committed by the partnership.

A limited partner, however, cannot take part in the management of the partnership business and cannot bind the partnership. If he does take part in the management, then he will be liable for debts and obligations as though he were a general partner: s. 6(1). The sub-section also provides that, if the partnership is not registered (see above), a limited partner will be deemed to be a general partner. A limited partner can, however, without losing his status, give general advice and can demand to inspect the books.

The relationship of the partners to each other

As already noted, the 1907 Act makes it clear that limited partners enjoy the privilege of limited liability only if they refrain from participation in the management of the business.

Section 5 provides that any differences as to ordinary matters connected with partnership business may be decided by a majority of the general partners, subject to any contrary agreement between them.

In contrast to the 1890 Act (see **34** above), which forbids the introduction of a partner without the consent of the others, s. 6(5)(b) of the 1907 Act permits a limited partner, subject to any contrary agreement between the partners, to assign his share in the partnership, but only with the consent of the general partners, and, on assignment, the assignee becomes a limited partner with all the rights of the assignor. Notice of the assignment must be advertised in the *Gazette*.

Dissolution

By virtue of s. 7 of the Act, extending to limited partnerships the provisions of the 1890 Act, a limited partnership may be dissolved, whether by order of the court or otherwise, as in the case of an ordinary partnership (see **40** above). On the dissolution of a limited partnership, its affairs are wound up by the general partners unless the court orders otherwise: s. 6(3).

Death, bankruptcy and mental disorder of limited partner

The death or bankruptcy of a limited partner does not of itself dissolve the partnership, while mental disorder need not necessitate dissolution by the court unless it is impossible to ascertain his share by other means: s. 6(2). Subject to any agreement to the contrary, the other partners shall not be entitled to dissolve the partnership by reason of any limited partner having his share charged for his debts (contrast the position above in relation to ordinary partnerships).

The winding up provisions for 'unregistered companies' (see above) do not apply to limited partnerships registered in England, Wales or Northern Ireland: Companies Act 1988 s. 665(d).

Notice

Subject to an agreement to the contrary, a limited partner is not entitled to dissolve the partnership by notice: s. 6(5)(c). In the absence of any such agreement, the partnership, whether formed for a fixed term, for a single adventure or even for an indefinite period, will continue notwithstanding notice of dissolution from a limited partner.

Special provisions apply in relation to death, bankruptcy and charging orders.

2

Employment law

In this chapter, we consider the duties imposed on an employer in relation to the formation of a contract of employment, and its contents. We also consider his liabilities with regard to providing a safe working environment. Much of the law is contained in the Employment Rights Act 1996, which is referred to below as 'the Act'. The Act served to consolidate previous measures on employment law, notably the Employment Protection (Consolidation) Act 1978.

CONTRACT OF EMPLOYMENT

1. Written statement of employment contract

The Act gives every employee the right to receive, within 13 weeks of the commencement of employment, a written statement of the main terms and conditions of employment. This right to a contract, however, applies only to those working for 16 hours a week or more; or who have worked for 8 hours a week or more for five years or more for the same employer.

The main requirements of the written statement
The 1996 Act lays down that the written statement should indicate:

(*i*) The identity of employer and employee
(*ii*) The date of commencement of employment
(*iii*) The scale and methods of remuneration
(*iv*) Any terms and conditions relating to hours of work
(*v*) Any entitlement to holidays, including public holidays, and holiday pay
(*vi*) Terms relating to sickness, notification of sickness and pay for sickness
(*vii*) Pension arrangements, including a statement as to whether or not a contracting-out certificate is in force

(viii) The length of notice which an employee is entitled to receive and give in the event of a proposed termination of employment

(ix) The title of the job which the person is employed to do

(x) Disciplinary rules, or an indication of where the person can go to find out about such rules

(xi) The name of the person to whom a grievance should be taken, and the steps or stages of an appeal procedure.

The Employment Act 1989 allows employers of less than 20 persons not to provide a written disciplinary procedure, though details of the grievance procedure must be given. The employee is required to sign and return a copy statement or a tear-off slip.

Once the terms and conditions have been agreed, they may not be changed unilaterally. Changes must be agreed by the employee. The most frequent change is in salary.

2. Pay

Under the 1996 Act, an employee is entitled to itemised pay statements stating the gross amount of the pay; the amounts of any variable and fixed deductions and the reasons for them; and the net amount payable. The fixed deductions can be aggregated so long as the employee is issued with a statement of fixed deductions which is re-issued every 12 months, and he is notified of any alterations when they are made.

There is no presumption in a contract of employment that sick pay will be paid.

> *Case law* In *Mears* v *Safecar Security Ltd* (1982), an employee was absent through illness for 6 months out of 14 months employment. During the period of sickness, no claim for payment was made and the written statement was silent on the matter. The Employment Appeal Tribunal (see below) held that there was no implied term relating to sick pay. All the facts had to be considered, and here there was no implied term. Statutory sick pay is, however, payable under the terms of the Social Security and Housing Benefits Act 1982, the Social Security and Benefits Act 1985 and implementing regulations.

Even if there is a contractual right to lay off an employee without pay, the employee is nonetheless guaranteed a level of payment under the provisions of the 1996 Act.

Under the Employment Rights Act 1996, an employer may not make any deduction from wages unless:

(a) It is required or authorised by legislation.

(b) It is required or authorised by a provision in the employment contract

- which is in writing and of which a copy has previously been given to the employee; *or*
- whose existence and effect has been notified previously to the employee in writing.

(c) The employee has previously indicated in writing his agreement or consent to the making of the deduction.

Case law In *Delaney* v *Staples* (1992), the employee was summarily dismissed and given a cheque in lieu of notice. The cheque was stopped, the employer arguing that her misconduct entitled him to dismiss the employee summarily and not to pay any sum in lieu. The employee claimed that stopping the cheque was an unauthorised deduction from wages contrary to the Wages Act 1986, which was to a large part replaced by the 1996 Act. It was held that a payment made in lieu of proper notice on summary dismissal without proper notice was a payment on account of damages and not a payment of wages. The 1986 Act, therefore, did not apply.

THE TERMS OF THE CONTRACT OF EMPLOYMENT

The terms of contract will not be fully expressed in the written statement. A number of terms will also be implied, in relation to both the employer and the employee.

3. Implied duties of the employer

(a) An employer is under an implied obligation to take reasonable care of the safety of employees. This duty of care is personal to the employer and cannot be avoided by proof that performance of the duty was delegated, for example, to a safety officer: *Wilsons and Clyde Coal Co Ltd* v *English* (1938); *McDermaid* v *Nash Dredging and Reclamation Co Ltd* (1987). These common law duties are now supplemented by health and safety legislation (see below).

Case law In *Pape* v *Cumbria County Council* (1992), the plaintiff was a cleaner required to use various detergents and chemical cleaning products. The defendant provided gloves for the work, which were worn on occasion, but not for the protection of hands from contact with the cleaning products. The defendants did not warn of the danger of dermatitis from sustained exposure of the skin to the cleaning products or instruct cleaners to wear the gloves provided.

It was held that, although the danger of dermatitis was sufficiently well known to put a reasonable employer under a duty to appreciate the risks, it was not so well known as to make the danger obvious to the staff without any necessity for warning or instructions. Accordingly, the employer's duty to provide a safe system of work for employees required to use detergent and chemical cleaning products in the course of their work was not met by the mere provision of rubber gloves, but the employer was instead obliged to warn staff of the danger of dermatitis from the sustained exposure of skin to the cleaning products and to instruct them to wear the gloves at all times.

Case law In *Walker v Northumberland County Council* (1995), the plaintiff, a social worker, suffered a nervous breakdown because of stress and pressure. Before he returned to work, he was promised assistance to lessen his load, but this was not provided in any material degree. He suffered a further breakdown and was forced to stop work permanently. It was held that, where it was reasonably foreseeable that an employee might suffer a nervous breakdown because of the stress and pressures of work, the employer, as part of his duty to provide a safe system of work, was obliged not to cause the employee psychiatric damage by reason of the volume or character of the work he was required to do. On the facts, the defendants were liable for the second breakdown, but not the first since it was not then reasonably foreseeable that the plaintiff's workload would give rise to a material risk of mental illness.

(b) An employer is under a duty not to act towards employees in a way which is unpleasant or insulting. Thus, the employer may be in breach of such a duty if he deliberately insults or abuses an employee: *Palmanor Ltd v Cedron* (1978); *Wetherall (Bond St W1) v Lynn* (1978). The employer is also likely to be in breach if he wrongly accuses the employee of misconduct, incompetence or dishonesty: *Robinson v Crompton Parkinson Ltd* (1978). There is similarly likely to be a breach if the employer behaves in a way which is contrary to good industrial practice to such a degree that the employee cannot be expected to put up with such behaviour: *British Aircraft Corpn v Austin* (1978). Generally, employers must treat employees with consideration and respect; or, at least, not to act in a way which is calculated or likely to damage or destroy the relationship of trust and confidence between them: *Woods v WM Car Services (Peterborough) Ltd* (1982); *Bliss v South East Thames Regional Health Authority* (1987). It is also the case that the implied term is broken not only by conduct directed at a particular employee but also by conduct which, viewed objectively, is likely seriously to damage the relationship of employer and employee, as when the employer is engaged in fraudulent activities: *Malik* v *Bank of Credit and Commerce International SA* (1995).

The breach of the terms of an employment contract by the employer does not give rise to a claim in damages for loss of reputation (see the *Malik* case).

(c) An employer can in some circumstances be under an implied duty to the effect that any references are compiled with reasonable care. This is likely to be the case where the current employment is one where it is the normal practice to require a reference and where an employee cannot be expected to enter into that class of employment except on the basis that the employer will provide a full and frank reference as to the employee: *Spring* v *Guardian Assurance plc* (1994).

4. Provision of work

There is no general duty on an employer to provide work, so long as he is prepared to pay the due wages: 'Provided I pay my cook her wages regularly she cannot complain if I choose to take all my meals out': *Collier* v *Sunday Referee Publishing Co* (1940).

There will, however, be special classes where this general rule will not apply and where there is a duty to provide work, such as piece-workers (*Devonold* v *Rosser & Sons* (1906)); apprentices and skilled employees (*Breach* v *Epsylon Industries Ltd* (1976)); and actors (*Herbert Clayton and Jack Walker Ltd* v *Oliver* (1930)).

5. Implied duties of the employee

(a) The employee is under an obligation of faithful service on the part of the employee. A refusal to work will amount to a breach of contract, and a strike accordingly is a breach of contract on the part of those striking.

(b) The employee is under a duty to obey lawful and reasonable orders. Whether an order is reasonable or not is a matter to be judged on the facts of the individual case.

> *Case law* In *Walmsley* v *Udec Refrigeration* (1972), an employee was dismissed for refusing to work in a part of the Irish Republic which he claimed was a centre of IRA activity. He could not prove these allegations and was held to have disobeyed a reasonable order.

An employee need not obey an order which would expose him to the risk of danger to life: *Ottoman Bank* v *Chakarian* (1930).

(c) An employee undertakes to perform his work competently using reasonable skill and care. Breach of this requirement entitles the employer to claim damages in respect of the negligent performance of the contract: *Janata Bank* v *Ahmed* (1981).

(d) The employee is under an obligation not to accept any secret bribes, commissions or gifts in respect of his work other than from his employer. A managing director placed orders with other companies for which he received commission. It was held that he was properly dismissed: *Boston Deep-Sea Fishing & Ice Co* v *Ansell* (1888). It is also in breach of an employee's duties for him to have an interest in a firm which is transacting business with his employer if that interest is not disclosed: *Horcal Ltd* v *Gatland* (1983).

The giving and taking of incentives and commissions to and by an employee can amount to an offence under the provisions of the Public Bodies Corrupt Practices Act 1889 and the Prevention of Corruption Acts 1901–1916.

(e) An employee must not, during his employment, enter into any activity which is in competition with his employer. It was held to be a breach of this duty for an employee to work in his spare time for a rival and even though no confidential information was revealed: *Hivac Ltd* v *Royal Scientific Instruments Ltd* (1946).

An employee is also in breach of his duty if he prepares to set up a competing business and canvasses his employer's customers or prepares a list of customers to take with him: *Sanders* v *Parry* (1967); *Wessex Dairies Ltd* v *Smith* (1935); *Robb* v *Green* (1895).

In terms of the employer's duty after leaving the employment, only information properly classed as a trade secret, or information of an equally confidential nature, can be protected by the implied term against disclosure: *Faccenda Chicken Ltd* v *Fowler* (1986).

Case law In *Johnson & Bloy (Holdings) Ltd* v *Wolstenholme Rink plc* (1989), an ex-employee was restrained from disclosing the formula used by his former employers to make gold ink. This was a trade secret and so could not be disclosed or used even though the employee would inevitably have carried that knowledge with him on leaving the employment.

6. Termination of contract of employment

A contract of employment is just like any other contract, and can therefore be terminated by mutual consent. A contract of employment can also be terminated by frustration, as where the employee is sick for long periods and hence unable to perform his job. Frustration in such a case would depend on the circumstances of the individual case, such as the nature of the employment, the nature of the employee's job and the length of absence: *Marshall* v *Harland and Woolf Ltd* (1972); *Eggs Stores (Stamford Hill) Ltd* v *Leibovici* (1977). Frustration is also likely if the employee is imprisoned: *Hare* v *Murphy Bros Ltd* (1974); *FC Sheppard & Co Ltd* v *Jerrom* (1986).

A contract may also be brought to an end by performance, as when it is for a fixed term. A similar result would follow if an employee was taken on for a particular task: due performance of that task would automatically bring the contract to an end. Employment also ceases on the winding-up of a company or on the cessation of business. If the business is transferred to another, this was termination at common law, but the position is now affected by the Transfer of Undertakings (Protection of Employment) Regulations 1981 No. 1974. These now provide that, in such a case, the contract of employment is transferred automatically to the new employer.

7. Resignation

Resignation by an employee will not be a breach of the contract of employment if it is resignation in accordance with the terms of the contract or is a justified response to a breach by the employer. If an employee is demoted without reason, that would be a breach of contract by the employer which would justify the employee's resignation. Whether or not a resignation, other than in response to a breach by the employer, is a breach of contract depends on the terms of that contract. If the employee is engaged for a fixed term, then premature resignation would be a breach. If the contract is for an indeterminate length, and no period of notice is specified for resignation, the employee will be able to resign on the giving of reasonable notice, this having to be determined on the basis of all the circumstances. The 1996 Act provides that an employee must give a minimum period of one week's notice, though the contract can specify a longer period.

8. Maternity rights

Under the provisions of the Employment Rights Act 1996, it is unfair to dismiss a woman because she is pregnant unless: she is incapable of continuing to do her work properly; she is prevented from continuing to do her work for statutory reasons (such as regulations dealing with ionising radiation). Such dismissal may, however, still be unfair if the employer fails to offer a suitable available vacancy.

Ante-natal care

Pregnant women are entitled to time off during working hours, with pay, in order to receive ante-natal care.

Maternity leave

An employer is required to re-instate or re-engage an employee who, having been absent or dismissed on account of pregnancy, returns to work within 29 weeks from the date of confinement. An employee refused a job in these circumstances may take her case to an industrial tribunal which may regard this as unfair dismissal.

Provision is also made for statutory maternity pay.

DISMISSAL AND REDUNDANCY

9. Dismissal

Period of notice

The 1996 Act guarantees a minimum period of notice as follows:

- One week's notice if the period of employment is less than 2 years
- One week's notice for each year of employment of 2 years or more, but less than 12
- 12 week's notice if the period of employment was 12 years or more.

These provisions override any shorter period which might be contained in the contract, though the contract can specify a longer period.

The Act allows the employee to waive his right to notice or to accept payment in lieu of notice.

The notice given must specify the date on which it is to take effect, or contain facts which allow that date to be determined: *Morton Sundour Fabrics Ltd* v *Shaw* (1966). Once notice is given, it can be withdrawn only by agreement: *Harris & Russell Ltd* v *Slingsby* (1973).

Right to explanation of dismissal

The 1996 Act gives an employee of at least two years' standing the right to request from his employer a written statement, within 14 days, of the reasons for dismissal. If the employer refuses, or gives untruthful or inadequate reasons for the dismissal, the employee may go to an industrial tribunal (see **24** below). If the complaint is upheld, it must order payment to the employee of a sum equal to two weeks' pay.

9A. Summary dismissal

An employer is entitled to disregard the period of notice, and summarily to dismiss an employee, where the latter has committed a particularly serious breach of the contract of employment. It is justified, however, only in the most exceptional of cases: *Jupiter General Insurance Co* v *Shroff* (1937). Such cases include: gross misconduct; wilful refusal to obey a lawful and reasonable order; gross neglect and dishonesty.

Case law In *Sinclair* v *Neighbour* (1967), a manager took £15 from a till replacing it with an IOU. He intended to replace the money a few days later. The court held that summary dismissal was justified.

Case law In *Ross* v *Aquascutum* (1973), the employee was a nightwatchman. He was seen to be absent from the building he was supposed to guard for 2 hours each night. This was held to justify summary dismissal.

Case law In *Wilson* v *Racher* (1974), a gardener swore at his employer. Although this could have been gross misconduct, the court held that there were special circumstances in that it was the employer who had provoked the outburst by his own conduct.

It has also been said that, if an employee deliberately used an unauthorised password to enter or to attempt to gain access to an employer's computer which he knew contained information to which he was not entitled, that of itself amounted to gross misconduct which prima facie justified instant dismissal, since what the employee was doing was a very serious industrial offence: *Denco Ltd* v *Joinson* (1992).

9B. Wrongful dismissal

Where an employee is dismissed in circumstances which give rise to a breach of contract, he is entitled to damages. These are calculated on the basis of what the employee would have earned had he received the proper notice: *British Transport Commission* v *Gourley* (1956); *Laverack* v *Woods of Colchester Ltd* (1967); *Hill* v *CA Parsons Co Ltd* (1972). The employee is, however, under a duty to mitigate, so his damages may be reduced by the amount he could have earned had he obtained other employment in mitigation: *Brace* v *Calder* (1895). Deductions will also be made for any social security benefits received, but not for pension benefits received as a result of the dismissal: *Parsons* v *BNM Laboratories* (1964); *Westwood* v *Secretary of State for Employment* (1985); *Hopkins* v *Norcoss plc* (1993). Damages will not, however, be awarded for any distress or humiliation which may have been suffered by the employee: *Addis* v *Gramophone Co* (1909); *Bliss* v *South East Thames Regional Health Authority* (1987).

Because of the personal nature of a contract of employment, the courts will not generally make an order for the specific performance of a contract of employment. The courts have 'never dreamed of enforcing agreements strictly personal in their nature, whether they are agreements of hiring and service, being contracts, being the common relation of master and servant ...': *Rigby* v *Connol* (1880). If, however, the employment contract lays down a procedure which must be gone through prior to dismissal, the courts can grant an order restraining an employer treating an employee as dismissed when in breach of that procedure: *Irani* v *Southampton and South West Hampshire Health Authority* (1985); *Powell* v *London Borough of Brent* (1988).

If an employer is required by statute to contract on specified terms and fails to do so, the employee will have public law rights, by way of judicial review or on the principles of natural justice, if the employer failed or refused to contract on those terms: *R* v *East Berkshire Health Authority* (1985).

9C. Unfair dismissal

Provided an employer does not break the contract of employment, the employee will have no grounds for an action for wrongful dismissal (see **9B** above). He might, however, have grounds for a complaint of unfair dismissal under rights contained in the Act.

Such rights do not extend to those who:

- have not been employed for two years
- have reached the normal retiring age for their category of employment or, if there is no normal age, the age of 65
- are employed under a contract for a fixed term of one year or more who have agreed in writing to exclude any claim for unfair dismissal in respect of the expiry of the term
- those who, under the contract, ordinarily work outside the country.

Where an employer announces a policy of setting a normal retiring age of 60 and this is properly announced to the employees, that is the 'normal retiring age', even though some employees could reasonably expect to retire at different ages for special reasons, unless it could be shown that the normal retiring age was a sham, never implemented or abandoned, and in that case the statutory pensionable age of 65 would apply: *O'Brien and others* v *Barclays Bank plc* (1995).

Some groups of employees are also outside the provisions as to unfair dismissal, such as policemen and domestic servants.

Under the Act, an employee is treated as dismissed if:

- The contract of employment is terminated by the employer with or without notice
- A fixed-term contract expires without being renewed under the same contract
- It is a case of constructive dismissal.

The test for constructive dismissal is whether the employer's conduct amounted to a breach of the employment contract which entitled the employee to resign: *Western Engineering Excavating Ltd v Sharp* (1978). Thus, if the employer changes the terms of employment, such as a change of job, lowering the employee's earnings, changing the job location or demoting the employee, and there is no contractual right to do such thing, such conduct will be constructive dismissal which entitles the employee to resign: *Hill Ltd v Mooney* (1981); *Courtaulds Northern Spinning Ltd v Sibson* (1987).

If a woman is entitled to return to work after giving birth, and has sought to exercise such right under the Act, but is not permitted to return, she will be treated as dismissed.

9D. Justifiable dismissal

The burden is on the employer to show that a dismissed employee was not dismissed unfairly. The Act lays down the following grounds which can give rise to a fair dismissal.

(a) Capability or qualifications.

Case law In *Alidair v Taylor* (1978), a pilot made a faulty landing, damaging the aircraft. The manner of landing was found to be due to a lack of flying knowledge on the part of the pilot who was then dismissed. It was held that this was not unfair since, in this case, one failure to reach a high degree of skill could have serious consequences.

(b) Conduct of the employee. Types of conduct which have been held to warrant dismissal include: a refusal to wear the appropriate clothing required for the job; wearing provocative badges contrary to instructions and warnings; carrying on sexual relationships during working hours; passing on information to a former employer now working for a competitor; refusing to cut particularly long hair after being warned of the safety hazard; breach of works rules; suspected dishonesty; breach of safety instructions; fighting; being a drug addict; refusal to go on a training course: *Atkin v Enfield Group Hospital Management Committee* (1975); *Boychuk v Symons Holdings Ltd* (1977); *Newman v Alarmco* (1976); *Smith v Du Pont (UK) Ltd* (1976); *Marsh v Judge International* (undated); *Palmer v Vauxhall*

Motors Ltd (1977); *Parkers Bakeries Ltd* v *Palmer* (1977); *Wilcox* v *Humphreys & Glasgow* (1976); *Parsons* v *McLaughlin* (1978); *Walton* v *TAC Construction Materials Ltd* (1981); *Minter* v *Wellingborough Foundries Ltd* (1981).

Case law In *Thomson* v *Alloa Motor Co Ltd* (1983), a petrol pump attendant finished work and drove off, damaging the pump. She was summarily dismissed because of the serious nature of the damage and because the employers would have to sue her for compensation. The dismissal was held to be unfair. The accident had no bearing on her ability to do her work, the incident was unlikely to recur, and her employers would undoubtedly be covered by insurance.

(c) Redundancy (for redundancy payments, see **10** below). Although redundancy may be grounds for dismissal, it does not follow that dismissal for redundancy will be fair in all cases. In particular, an employee can complain that he was unfairly selected for redundancy. In *Williams* v *Compair Maxam* (1982), an overall standard of fairness was laid down, referring to: the giving of as much notice as possible: consultations with unions, if any; taking the views of more than one person as to who should be dismissed; a requirement to follow any laid-down procedures; and an effort at finding employees other work within the organisation. However, these guidelines are more flexibly interpreted in relation to smaller businesses: *Meikle* v *McPhail (Charleston Arms)* (1983). It has been held that, unless the employer has reasonable grounds for supposing that a fair procedure would be useless, the lack of such a procedure will inevitably lead to a finding of unfair dismissal: *Polkey* v *A E Dayton Services Ltd* (1987).

Case law In *Allwood* v *William Hill Ltd* (1974), employers closed down 12 betting shops, making the managers redundant. No warning was given or alternative employment offered. It was held that, merely because there were circumstances involving redundancy, this did not of itself mean that the managers had to be made redundant. There was a high turnover in the industry, and more effort should have been made to transfer the managers to other outlets, even if on a temporary basis. The employers should also have considered retaining the managers until vacancies arose.

Case law In *Clyde Pipeworks* v *Foster* (1978), selection for redundancy was based on a points system, which took into account bad time-keeping, workmanship, absenteeism and conduct. This procedure had been agreed with the unions, but they were not consulted about its implementation. It was held that there was no need to involve the unions in the detailed arrangements for selection for redundancy, provided the method was fair in general terms.

In the absence of any other agreed procedure, the normal rule when selecting for redundancy is last-in-first-out. This is, however, subject to any reasonable and proper modification.

> *Case law* In *International Paint Co* v *Cameron* (1979), it was held that the customary arrangement of last-in-first-out, without further specification, had to be based on continuous service, and not cumulative service, so that an employer with longer continuous service ought to be retained as against one with longer overall, but less continuous, service.

(d) Legal restrictions imposed on continued employment of employee. If a person is employed as a driver, it would not necessarily be unfair to dismiss him if his licence were taken away. The employer must, however, consider all the relevant circumstances, such as whether the job can be done without driving, whether alternative arrangements can be made and whether the employee can be given other work to do until his licence is restored.

> *Case law* In *Mathieson* v *Noble & Son Ltd* (1972), a salesman was disqualified from driving but employed a driver at his own expense. He was dismissed, but it was held that the employers had acted unreasonably in not giving him a chance to see how the new arrangements worked out.

> *Case law* In *Appleyard* v *Smith (Hull) Ltd* (1972), it was an essential requirement that mechanics held licences so they could test drive the vehicles they had repaired. When the particular employee lost his licence, the company gave thought to placing him elsewhere, but this was not practicable for a small firm, and his dismissal was held to be fair.

> *Case law* In *Gill* v *Walls Meat Co Ltd* (undated), the employee was a Sikh. When he took on the job, he was clean shaven, but later decided to grow a beard as part of his religious practice. To have continued to employ him dealing with open meat would have meant a breach of hygiene law, and it was held that he had been rightly dismissed.

(e) 'Some other substantial reason'. This has been given a wide interpretation and has been held to cover such cases as an employee's refusal to accept a change to his terms of employment as a result of a business re-organisation or rationalisation; the dismissal of incompatible employees; and dismissal in order to make room for a relative in a family business: *Hollister* v *National Farmers' Union* (1979); *Treganowan* v *Robert Knee & Co Ltd* (1975); *Priddle* v *Dibble* (1978).

9E. Dismissals automatically unfair

The Act provides that it is automatically unfair to dismiss an employee on the grounds of membership of a trade union, or for taking part in the duties of a trade union. It will also be unfair to dismiss an employee because he is not a member of a trade union.

It is also automatically unfair to dismiss a woman because of pregnancy unless her pregnancy makes her incapable of doing her normal work and no other suitable work is available.

9F. Remedies for unfair dismissal

Where an industrial tribunal (see 24 below) finds a case of unfair dismissal, it must explain to the employee the remedies open to him which are, in essence, reinstatement or re-engagement. Reinstatement means getting the old job back on identical terms; re-engagement means being taken back, but on different terms. Such orders are made in very few cases.

As an alternative to such orders, the tribunal may order compensation. The Act provides that this will consist of two elements: the basic award and the compensation award. The basic element depends on age, length of service and wages. The compensatory award makes good loss of wages and other benefits lost because of the dismissal. Both elements can be reduced on the ground that the employee contributed to his own dismissal. In certain circumstances, extra compensation may be payable, as where dismissal relates to union membership.

10. Redundancy

The Act gives an employee the right to a redundancy payment if he is dismissed because of redundancy. The employer must make a redundancy payment where the employee is dismissed by reason of redundancy, or is eligible for such a payment by reason of being laid off or kept on short-time: s. 135. The employee must, however, have had at least two years' continuous service: s. 155.

What amounts to dismissal

A dismissal takes place if:

(a) The employer terminates the contract, with or without notice.

(b) A fixed-term contract expires without being renewed.

(c) The employee terminates the contract with or without notice in circumstances which are such that he is entitled to do so by the employee's conduct.

(d) The employment is terminated by death, dissolution or the appointment of a receiver: s. 136.

Dismissal for reasons of redundancy

An employee's dismissal is by reason of redundancy if it is attributable wholly or mainly to:

(a) The fact the employer has ceased, or intends to cease, to carry on the business for the purposes for which the employee was taken on, or has ceased, or intends to cease, to carry on that business in the place where the employee was employed; *or*

(b) The fact that the requirement of that business for employees to carry out work of a particular kind, or for employees to carry out work of a particular kind in the place where employed, have ceased or diminished, or are expected to do so: s. 139. An employee whose contract included a term that he was prepared and willing to work at any place in the United Kingdom was not dismissed for redundancy when there was insufficient work for him in Norfolk and he refused to comply with instructions to move to Scotland: *Sutcliffe* v *Hawker Siddley Aviation Ltd* (1973). An employee was who was dismissed because there was no longer a requirement for employees to work in the Caribbean Service of the BBC, in which he had always worked, was not redundant because there was still a requirement for employees to work as 'producers' which is what his contract required him to do: *Nelson* v *BBC* (1977).

> *Case law* In *North Riding Garages* v *Butterwick* (1967), the employee was the manager of a repair workshop. New employers took over the business and introduced working methods which the employee could not adapt to. He was dismissed for incompetence and inefficiency. It was held that if the new methods so altered the nature of the work that there was a lessening of the work of a kind he was formerly employed to do, this would amount to redundancy. On the facts, however, the overall requirements of the firm had not changed. It was the inability of the employee to change and adapt to new methods which brought about his dismissal. It is presumed, unless the contrary is proven, that dismissal is by reason of redundancy: s. 163.

Renewal or re-engagement

If the employer renews the contract of employment or, before the ending of the previous employment, makes an offer of renewal or of re-engagement in suitable alternative employment, which the employee unreasonably refuses, the employee will lose his right to a redundancy payment: s. 141.

Domestic difficulties, inadequate or inconvenient travel facilities, lack of suitable educational facilities for children, loss of friends, have all been matters which have been held to constitute reasonable grounds for the refusal of an offer: *Paton Calvert & Co Ltd* v *Westerside* (1979).

> *Case law* In *Fuller* v *Stephanie Bowman Ltd* (1977), the employee worked as a secretary in Mayfair. The employers moved to Soho. The employee refused to move to the new premises since these were above a sex shop which she found distasteful. Her attitude was a personal fad and it was held that she had unreasonably refused alternative employment.

Lay-off and short-time working

A lay-off occurs where there is no work for the employee and no pay is provided. Short-time working occurs when less than half a normal week's pay is earned: s. 147. If either has lasted for more than 4 consecutive weeks, or more than 6 weeks in any thirteen, the employee may give written notice, not more than 4 weeks after the lay-off or short-time has finished, that he intends to claim a redundancy payment. He must then give the requisite notice to terminate his contract and will be entitled to be considered redundant.

The amount of redundancy pay

Any special arrangements made by the employer for payment in the event of redundancy take priority. In their absence, however, the provisions of the Act apply: s. 162. Service under the age of 18 is not taken account of, nor is that over normal retiring age. In other cases, redundancy is calculated as follows: half a week's pay for years of service between the ages of 18 and 22; one week's pay for service between the ages of 22 and 41; one and a half week's pay for service between 41 and 64. For the purposes of calculating redundancy pay, there is a statutory limit on the amount of a week's pay, and this is reviewed annually. The maximum service which can be taken into account is 20 years, and the greatest amount of redundancy pay which is payable is 30 weeks.

On making a redundancy payment, except in pursuance of a tribunal award, the employer is to give the employee a written statement indicating how the amount has been arrived at. If a lump sum is given without so indicating, an offence is committed and the lump sum may be regarded as a gratuity not intended to be by way of a redundancy payment: *Galloway* v *Export Packing Services Ltd* (1975).

Procedure for handling redundancies

An employer wishing to make employees redundant must consult with representatives of a recognised trade union, if one is recognised, at the earliest opportunity. Any failure to do so can lead to the trade union presenting a complaint to an industrial tribunal. If the complaint is upheld, it may make a declaration to that effect and may also make a 'protective award', that is an award that, for a specified period, the employer shall pay remuneration to employees who are the subject of redundancy.

HEALTH AND SAFETY AT WORK

11. Common law duties

At common law, an employer is required to take reasonable care to avoid those dangers to employees which are reasonably foreseeable. This issue has been dealt with above in relation to the implied terms of employment (see 3 above).

12. Statutory duties

(a) The Factories Act 1961 contains general provisions dealing with health, safety and welfare in factories. It also contains specific provisions dealing with working conditions, accidents and diseases. Thus, s. 14 of the Act requires every dangerous part of any machinery to be securely fenced.

(b) The Offices, Shops and Railway Premises Act 1963 lays down detailed requirements relating to such matters as cleanliness, overcrowding, temperature, ventilation, floors and stairs, and the fencing of dangerous machinery.

(c) The Health and Safety at Work Act 1974 imposes a duty on every employer, so far as is practicable, to ensure the health, safety and welfare at work of his employees. In particular, this involves:

(i) Providing and maintaining, so far as is reasonably practicable, safe plant, safe premises and a safe system of work
(ii) Ensuring that 'articles and substances' are, again so far as is reasonably practicable, safe and free from health risks
(iii) Providing such information, training, instruction and supervision as is necessary to ensure the health and safety of employees; and
(iv) Ensuring that the working environment is, as far as is reasonably practicable, free from risks to health and adequate as regards facilities and arrangements for welfare.

Case law In *Page* v *Freight Hire (Tank Haulage) Ltd* (1981), a woman, aged 23, was employed as a lorry driver for a firm engaged in carrying chemicals between various chemical plants. The employers refused to allow her to transport a particular chemical since the manufacturers advised that it could adversely affect women of child-bearing age. It was held that the duty to provide for the health, safety and welfare of employees overrode any duty not to discriminate against her on grounds of sex.

An employer is also under a duty to conduct his business so as to ensure, as far as is reasonably practicable, that persons not in his employment who may be affected are not exposed to risks to their health or safety.

Case law In *R* v *Board of Trustees of the Science Museum* (1993), an inspection by health and safety inspectors showed that a bacteria was present in the water of the air cooling system which caused legionnaires disease. The Board was fined for failing to ensure that, as far as was reasonably practicable, members of the public were not exposed to risks to health and safety. The Court of Appeal upheld the conviction since it was enough for the prosecution to prove a risk that the bacteria might escape. There was no requirement to go further and show that the bacteria had emerged into the atmosphere and could be inhaled. The Board had been properly convicted since there was ample evidence of a risk of the disease escaping from their cooling towers, this being increased by the Board's failure to maintain an efficient water treatment regime.

13. Official bodies

The Health and Safety at Work Act 1974 created the Health and Safety Commission and the Health and Safety Executive (HSE). It is the duty of the Commission to:

- further the purposes of the Act
- carry out appropriate research
- advise on health and safety matters
- make proposals for health and safety regulations; and
- draft and approve codes of practice on health and safety.

The Executive, which is responsible to the Commission, carries out enforcement duties (see below) in conjunction with its inspectorate for the enforcement of the legislation.

14. Enforcement

The Act is enforced by inspectors appointed by the HSE. They may enter and inspect premises, collect information and data, and bring prosecutions for unsafe practices. They can also issue prohibition notices, which have the immediate effect of stopping machinery or processes, and improvement notices, which require an employer to remedy specific problems within a given time. They also have rights to seize, render harmless or destroy any article or substance that might be the cause of imminent danger or serious personal injury. Appeals against notices are to an industrial tribunal which can confirm, modify or cancel the notice.

> *Case law* In *Associated Dairies* v *Hartley* (1979), an improvement notice required the employer to issue free safety shoes. The year before, one employee had been hurt when the wheel of a truck ran over his foot. The company employed 1000 people, and had a high turnover. Free footwear would have cost £20,000 in the first year. The tribunal held that the expense was disproportionate to the risk and cancelled the notice.

> *Case law* In *South Surbiton* v *Co-operative Society* v *Wilcox* (1975), an improvement notice was issued in relation to a cracked washbasin. The Society argued that the breach was trivial, there was little risk to health, and that there were many others in breach who did not receive such notices. The tribunal still upheld the notice.

15. Written safety policy

Except where there are fewer than five employees and where there is no duty to consult with safety representatives or a safety committee (see **16** below), an employer must prepare a written statement of his general policy as to health and safety at work, and of the organisation and arrangements currently in force for carrying out that statement. This statement must be brought to the attention of all employees.

16. Safety representatives and safety committees

A trade union recognised by an employer may appoint safety representatives from among the employees, though the appointed person need not be a union member. The employer must consult with the representatives and, if at least two such representatives so request, a safety committee must be set up.

17. Codes of Practice

As mentioned above, it is the duty of the Health and Safety Commission to approve and issues Codes of Practice. Breach of a Code does not give rise to an offence of itself, but breach of or compliance with a Code can be taken into account when determining whether an offence has been committed.

SEX DISCRIMINATION AND RACE RELATIONS

18. The Sex Discrimination Act 1975 and the Race Relations Act 1976

Both Acts make it unlawful for an employer to discriminate against an employee in the way he affords access to opportunities for promotion, transfer or training, or other benefits, facilities or services or by dismissing or subjecting the employee to any detriment on the grounds of race, colour, nationality or ethnic origin, or sex or marital status. In *Batisha* v *Sky* (1977), a woman was turned down for a job as a cave guide because it was 'man's work'; and in *Munro* v *Allied Suppliers* (1977), a man was not taken on as a cook because female employees would not work with him. In each case, it was held that unlawful sex discrimination had occurred. The latter case illustrates the point that unlawful sex discrimination can be directed against men as well as women.

Where a woman finds herself incapable of work because of pregnancy, termination of her contract for an indefinite period on the ground of pregnancy could not be justified by the fact that the woman was prevented, on a temporary basis, from performing the work for which she had been engaged (*Webb* v *EMO Air Cargo* (No 2) (1995)).

The legislation prohibits both direct and indirect discrimination which latter occurs when an employer imposes a requirement, which is not necessary for the job, which can be fulfilled by, for example, a much smaller proportion of women than men.

> *Case law* In *Clarke* v *Eley (IMI) Kynoch Ltd* (1983), a redundancy scheme provided that part-timers would be selected for redundancy in preference to full-time workers. The proportion of women able to comply with this condition was much smaller than for men. The scheme was therefore held to be indirectly discriminatory.

Genuine occupational qualification

The Sex Discrimination and Race Relations Acts each provide that no offence arises where discrimination is based on genuine occupational qualifications. Male actors or white actors could apply, for example, where the role in a play called for a male or for a white person; persons of one particular sex might be stipulated for particular jobs on grounds of decency and privacy (such as lavatory attendants).

19. Equal pay

The Equal Pay Act 1970 provides that where a woman is employed in like work or on work rated as equivalent or on work of equal value with a man in the same employment, there is an equality clause implied in her contract of employment. This clause operates to modify terms in it which are less favourable than terms of a similar kind in the man's contract so as not to be less favourable. Such a clause also operates as to include in a woman's contract beneficial terms in the man's contract not included in hers. As with the Sex Discrimination Act, the Equal Pay Act applies equally to men.

Case law In *Capper Pass* v *Lawton* (1977), a woman worked as cook in a directors' dining room providing lunches for between 10 and 30 persons. She sought equal pay with two assistant chefs who worked in the factory canteen and who prepared 350 meals each day. She worked a 40 hour week, and had no one supervising her, while the men worked 45 hours and were under a head chef. She was held entitled to equal pay.

Case law In *Noble* v *David Gold & Son (Holdings) Ltd* (1980) men worked in a warehouse loading and unloading, whereas women did lighter work, such as sorting, packing and labelling. It was held that the women were not doing like work.

Case law In *Eaton Ltd* v *Nuttall* (1977), a man and woman worked on like work, but the man received a higher rate because his responsibilities were greater. He handled more expensive products, and, as a result, a mistake by him would have been costlier. It was held proper to take into account these additional responsibilities.

The Equal Pay Act was amended by the Equal Pay (Amendment) Regulations 1983, SI 1983 No. 1194 to provide that a claim for equal pay may be made on the basis that the particular person's work is of equal value in terms of the demands made on that person (under headings such as effort, skill and decision) to that done by a person of different sex in the same employment.

OFFICIAL BODIES

20. Commissions

The Sex Discrimination Act established the *Equal Opportunities Commission* to work towards the elimination of discrimination on grounds of sex, generally promote equality of opportunity, keep the Equal Pay and Sex Discrimination Acts under review and, where necessary, draw up and submit proposals for amendments and review of the relevant statutory provisions relating to health and safety at work insofar as they require different treatment for men and women. It can also draw up Codes of Practice offering practical guidance on the elimination of discrimination and the promotion of equality of opportunity between the sexes. The Commission may carry out formal enquiries and it can give financial or other support to actual or potential claims. It may also issue non-discrimination notices and seek injunctions.

The *Commission for Racial Equality*, established by the Race Relations Act, has the same broad functions and rights of enforcement in relation to the treatment of different races. The other important aspect of the Race Relations Act 1976 is that it gives complainants of race discrimination in employment access to the industrial tribunals to resolve their problems. Both the Equal Opportunities Commission and Commission for Racial Equality have published Codes of Practice which employers are expected to follow.

The *Health and Safety Commission* and Health and Safety Executive were set up under the Health and Safety at Work Act 1974. It is the responsibility of the Commission to:

(*i*) further the purposes of the Act
(*ii*) carry out appropriate research
(*iii*) advise on health and safety matters
(*iv*) make regulations under the proposals.

The Executive carries out functions and directions of the Commission.

21. Advisory, Conciliation and Arbitration Service (ACAS)

This independent service was established as a statutory body on 1 January 1976 under the Employment Protection Act 1975. It promotes the improvement of industrial relations, and encourages the extension of collective bargaining machinery. ACAS is governed by a council consisting of a full-time chairman and nine other members all appointed by the Secretary of State for Employment. Three members are appointed after consultation with the Confederation of British Industry and three after consultation with the Trade Union Congress. Additional members may also be appointed by the Secretary of State.

The service undertakes a range of activities:

(*i*) inquiring into any industrial relations matters
(*ii*) providing advice on industrial relations and the development of effective personnel practices
(*iii*) issuing codes of practice containing practical guidance on the improvement of industrial relations

(iv) helping to resolve industrial disputes through conciliation, or through providing facilities for arbitration, mediation or committees of investigation

(v) offering conciliation in disputes over statutory employment rights between individual employees and their employers

(vi) carrying out inquiries into wages councils if required to do so by the Secretary of State for Employment.

Advice on industrial relations and personnel practices is given in a number of ways:

(i) by answering queries on the operation of employment legislation

(ii) by short advisory visits

(iii) by in-depth assistance either to advise on a particular project or programme of work or to diagnose the causes of more deep-seated problems and make recommendations for action or to work with managements and unions jointly; and

(iv) by helping to organise seminars and courses.

22. Certification Office

The Certification Office was established in February 1976 and is responsible for:

(i) maintaining lists of trade unions and employers' associations

(ii) determining the independence of trade unions

(iii) seeing that trade unions and employers' associations keep accounting records, have their accounts properly audited and submit annual returns

(iv) ensuring periodical examination of members' superannuation schemes

(v) ensuring observance of the statutory procedures for transfer of engagements, amalgamations and changes of name

(vi) supervising the statutory requirements as to the setting up and operation of political funds and dealing with complaints by members about breaches of political fund rules.

Under the Employment Act 1980 the certification officer is responsible for administering payments towards expenditure incurred by trade unions in conducting secret ballots.

23. Central Arbitration Committee

The Central Arbitration Committee (CAC) was brought into operation in February 1976. The constitution and proceedings of the CAC are set out in Sch. 1 of the Employment Protection Act 1975. It provides for the Secretary of State for Employment to appoint a chairman, deputy chairman and members, the last named having experience as representatives of employers or works. The Committee has wide discretion to determine its own procedures but, except at informal hearings, a chairman and a member from each side of industry will normally hear a case. There is power to appoint assessors in addition to the normal committee. The Chairman has powers of umpire. Decisions of the Committee are published in the form of an award which includes the considerations taken into account in reaching that decision. The CAC provides both voluntary and unilateral arbitration. The power to provide voluntary arbitration derives from the Employment Protection Act 1975 which enables references to be made to the CAC by ACAS. The CAC is also specified as the final stage in the industrial disputes procedure of a number of organisations. The Committee provides statutory, unilateral arbitration under the Employment Protection Act 1975 on disclosure of information, and also determines references made under the Equal Pay Act 1970.

24. Industrial tribunals

Industrial tribunals are independent judicial bodies, each having a legally qualified chairman appointed by the Lord Chancellor in England and Wales, and in Scotland by the Lord President. Each tribunal has two other members drawn from two panels of members appointed by the Secretary of State for Employment after consultation with employees' and employers' organisations. Tribunals were originally established to hear appeals by employers against assessments of training levies under the Industrial Training Act 1964. They are now regulated by the Industrial Tribunals Act 1996. They now have jurisdiction in a number of areas concerned with individual rights under the following legislation:

Equal Pay Act 1970
Sex Discrimination Acts 1975 and 1986
Employment Protection Act 1975
Race Relations Act 1976
Employment Protection (Consolidation) Act 1978
Employment Acts 1980 and 1982
Transfer of Undertakings Regulations 1982
Equal Pay (Amendment) Regulations 1983
Wages Act 1986
Employment Rights Act 1996

In most types of cases coming before the tribunal, copies of relevant documents are sent to an ACAS conciliation officer who is required to try to assist the parties to reach a settlement. Since October 1980 pre-hearing assessments have been introduced to provide for a preliminary airing of the case. A tribunal may advise an appellant not to proceed. If a conciliated settlement by conciliation is not achieved, a hearing ensues at which employers and employees may present their own cases or be represented by persons of their choice. A tribunal decision may involve a monetary award which is payable by one party to the other or an order for reinstatement or re-engagement in unfair dismissal cases. There is a right of appeal to the Employment Appeal Tribunal on points of law. Under the Industrial Tribunals Act 1996, if an Industrial Tribunal or the chairman sitting alone, at a pre-hearing assessment, considers that the case of the appellant has no reasonable prospect of success or that pursuit of it would be frivolous, vexatious or otherwise unreasonable, it may require a deposit of up to £150 as a condition of proceeding further.

As from 1 April 1990 an award made by an industrial tribunal will attract interest if not paid within 42 days after the tribunal decision is notified to the parties. This applies whether or not an appeal is likely to be made against the decision or the tribunal is asked to review its decision.

Where an award is varied on appeal or review, interest will be payable on the revised sum backdated to 42 days after the original decision. Where a recoupment order has been made and complied with, interest will only be payable on the amount remaining.

25. Employment Appeal Tribunal

The Employment Appeal Tribunal is a superior court of record, an appellate body on questions of law from industrial tribunals. The Tribunal also hears appeals on questions of law or fact arising from certain proceedings before, or arising from certain decisions of, the certification officer, and, under the Employment Act 1980, on complaints of unreasonable exclusion from trade union membership. It consists of judges and other members. The judges are nominated both by the Lord Chancellor from among the judges of the High Court and the Lord President of the Court of Session from among the judges of that Court. The other members have experience of industrial relations, either as representatives of employers or of workers, and are appointed on the joint recommendation of the Lord Chancellor and the Secretary of State for Employment.

3

Competition law

In this chapter, we consider how the law, both domestic and EU, seeks to ensure that businesses do not indulge in activities which could be considered anti-competitive. One point that can be usefully made in advance is that there is no common law, in the sense of judge-made law, relating to anti-competitive activities. The law is wholly statutory.

MONOPOLIES AND MERGERS COMMISSION

1. The functions of the Commission

Under the provisions of the Fair Trading Act 1973 a Monopolies and Mergers Commission is appointed by the Secretary of State for Trade and Industry, having between 10 and 27 members. Its principal functions are to investigate and report on such questions as are referred to it relating to:

(a) The existence or possible existence of a monopoly (see below)

(b) A transfer of a newspaper or the assets of a newspaper under certain provisions of the Fair Trading Act designed to prevent undue concentration, by reason of mergers, in one newspaper proprietor

(c) The creation or possible creation of a merger situation which qualifies for investigation under provisions of that Act

(d) The efficiency and costs of the service provided by, or the possible abuse of a monopoly by, public bodies. This last is a function designated by the Competition Act 1980.

2. Monopolies

The Fair Trading Act sets out when a monopoly situation exists. In the case of both goods and services, this will be when at least one quarter of the supply of the goods or services is supplied by one person or one group, or where there is an agreement in operation which prevents the supply of the particular goods or services at all. Similar criteria are applied in relation to the export of goods. Monopolies may be either 'scale' monopolies, where the activity is in the hands of a particular company or connected group; or a 'complex' monopoly, where there are few producers in the field and economic behaviour can be co-ordinated without explicit agreement.

3. Monopoly references

The Monopolies and Mergers Commission cannot act on its own initiative: it must wait for a reference to be made to it. A reference can be made by the Director General of Fair Trading; or by the Secretary of State for Trade and Industry or by the Secretary of State and any other Minister acting jointly.

The Office of Fair Trading assesses the information it has gathered on the structure of the particular industry, its conduct and its economic performance. The Act gives the Director General powers to obtain information and an offence arises if a party wilfully neglects to furnish information required by notice in writing or supplies false information. The maximum penalty for the former is a fine not exceeding £5000; for the latter, a fine and a sentence not exceeding two years. In complex monopolies, the Director General is given additional powers under the Act to determine whether there are any overt or covert arrangements under which the parties are so conducting their affairs as to prevent, restrict or distort competition.

4. The operation of the Commission

Under the terms of the Fair Trading Act, a reference can be so framed that the Commission is required only to investigate the facts. More usually, however, it will also be asked to investigate and report on whether the monopoly 'operates, or may be expected to operate, against the public interest'. Such a reference requires the Commission to consider, amongst other matters, the desirability:

(a) of maintaining and promoting effective competition between suppliers

(b) of promoting the interests of consumers, purchasers and other users of goods and services in the United Kingdom as regards price, quality and variety

(c) of promoting, through competition, the reduction of costs and the development of new techniques and products, and of facilitating the entry of new competition into existing markets

(d) of maintaining and promoting the balanced distribution of industry and employment in the United Kingdom

(e) of maintaining and promoting competitive activity in the export markets of the United Kingdom.

The Commission must report within a time specified in the reference: should it fail to do so, the reference lapses.

If the Commission decides that there is a monopoly, it sends to the relevant parties setting out what appears to be the public interest, and receives submissions and holds a public hearing. The Commission then formulates its conclusions and recommendations and sends the report to the Secretary of State for Trade and Industry and, if the reference was a joint one (see above), also to the particular Minister. The report is then laid before Parliament and published. If the report concludes that the monopoly is contrary to the public interest, an order may be made by Statutory Instrument in exercise of the powers given by the Act.

The powers so granted include orders to prohibit carrying out an agreement to make a restrictive agreement, or to withhold or threaten to withhold supplies, or to charge prices other than those in a published list. The powers also include the transfer or vesting of property in other bodies and the creation, allotment, surrender or cancellation of any shares. In this latter case, a draft of the order must be approved by both Houses of Parliament; in the other cases, the Minister must publish his intention to make the order, such order being subject to annulment following a resolution by either House. If an order is infringed, no criminal sanctions apply, but 'any person' may bring civil proceedings, and the Crown may apply for an injunction or other appropriate form of relief.

As an alternative to the exercise of these powers (and this is generally how things turn out), the Act empowers the Director General of Fair Trading to seek an undertaking from the parties concerned for action to remedy the adverse effects identified in the Commission report. Such undertakings are enforceable.

5. Avoiding references

It is always open to a business to avoid a monopoly reference by changing its practices. For example, Milk Marque, the dairy farmers' co-operative which replaced the statutory Milk Marketing Board, agreed to change its system of selling milk to avoid concerns expressed by the Office of Fair Trading, and thus avoided a reference to the Commission (1996).

Under amendments to the Fair Trading Act introduced by the Deregulation and Contracting Out Act 1994, the Secretary of State for Trade and Industry can accept undertakings from companies as an alternative to a monopoly reference by the Office of Fair Trading, or by the Directors General of Telecommunications, Electricity Supply and Water Services or the Rail Regulator.

Examples The OFT expressed concerns about competition in the UK brick supply market after Ibstock Building Products, a subsidiary of Ibstock plc, announced plans to acquire the brick manufacturing business of Redland plc. Draft undertakings were amended after consultation indicated a belief that two plants which were agreed to be divested had a short life expectancy. Ibstock thus agreed to divest two more modern plants. All of the plants will, under the final undertakings, be run as viable businesses before disposal and sold as going concerns. These undertakings were accepted in place of a reference to the Commission.

In contrast, an order was made following a 1994 Commission report on the supply of films for exhibition in cinemas in the United Kingdom. This came after negotiations failed to produce undertakings from the five leading film distributors, four independent film distributors and six exhibitors named in the report as parties to a 'complex monopoly' (see **2** above). The undertakings sought related mainly to one particular practice concerning the insistence by distributors on lengthy minimum exhibition periods as a condition of supplying exhibitors with films. An order was made following advice by the OFT that undertakings could not be secured (1996).

6. Mergers

The duty to keep situations under review where there might be a merger situation calling for investigation is placed on the Director General of Fair Trading. Unlike the position with monopolies, however, the Director General cannot make a merger reference direct to the Commission. He can only advise the Secretary of State for Trade and Industry, who will then make a decision on a reference. In the annual report for 1995, the OFT reported that it had considered 473 mergers and merger proposals, a 24% increase on the year before. The Director General recommended reference in 11 cases and the Secretary of State accepted this advice in 9 of them.

Examples The Secretary of State decided not to permit the acquisition by Bass plc of Carlsberg-Tetley plc. She accepted the unanimous findings of the Monopolies and Mergers Commission that this merger may be expected to operate against the public interest.

However, she did not agree with the majority Commission view that the adverse effects of the merger could be adequately addressed by the divestment of around 1900 Bass pubs. In accordance with both the advice of the Director General of Fair Trading and the conclusion on remedies reached by one of the members of the MMC inquiry team the Secretary of State decided that the only means of adequately dealing with the competition concerns arising from the significant shift in market power caused by this merger was to prohibit it (June 1997).

Newspaper mergers require the consent of the Secretary of State if the resulting combined circulation is at least 500,000 copies. In other cases, a reference may be made where it appears to the Secretary of State that two or more businesses have ceased to be distinct and if either a monopoly would be thus created or the value of the assets taken over exceeds £15m. For example, plans for a merger between Scottish milk suppliers were investigated by the Commission following advice from the OFT. The proposed acquisition of Scottish Pride Holdings plc by Robert Wiseman Dairies plc was felt to raise concerns over the processing and wholesale supply of milk in Scotland.

If the merger has already occurred, no reference can be made if 6 months has elapsed. If a reference is made, the Commission must report within 6 months, with a possible further extension of 3 months. In its report, the Commission must indicate if a merger qualifying for investigation exists and whether it operates, or may operate, contrary to the public interest. If it finds the latter, it must specify the particular adverse effect in question. The criteria against which the public interest is determined are as for monopolies (see 3 above). The powers of the Secretary of State to make orders are also the same as in relation to monopolies.

As an alternative to making a merger reference, the Secretary of State may also accept undertakings to dispose of parts of the business or to accept non-divestment undertakings.

Under the EU Merger Regulation 4064/89 the Commission has the power to control certain large cross-border mergers or concentrations. The OFT receives details of all mergers notified to the Commission. It examines each case, consults with the Department of Trade and Industry and other interested Government departments and submits the United Kingdom's view to the Commission. Cases are referred to the European Commission only if the combined global turnover of the companies involved is more than ECU 5bn and at least two of the merging companies have a combined turnover of more than ECU 250m outside the EU.

RESTRICTIVE PRACTICES

7. The Restrictive Trade Practices Act 1976

The Act provides for the registration with the Office of Fair Trading of restrictive trade agreements. An agreement becomes subject to registration if the parties carry on business in the United Kingdom and the agreement is one under which restrictions are accepted by two or more parties in respect of such matters as the prices to be charged, the quantities or descriptions of goods to be produced, supplied or acquired, the manufacturing processes to be used, or the levels or amounts of goods to be manufactured, the terms and conditions of supply, or the persons to or for whom, or the areas or places in which, the goods or services are to be supplied. Similarly, recommendations made by a trade association or a service supply association to its members which specify action to be taken in respect of any matters which would be registrable, if the subject of a restrictive agreement between the parties, are themselves subject to registration.

The Act also applies to 'information agreements', being agreements under which obligations are accepted by parties to exchange information about their selling prices or the terms and conditions of supply.

8. Application to services

The Act also applies to such services as are designated by the Secretary of State, a power exercised in the Restrictive Trade Practices (Services) Order 1976, SI 1976 No. 98. The Order brings all services within the Act, except for professional services, such as: legal services of barristers, advocates and solicitors; medical, dental and ophthalmic services; veterinary services; nursing and midwifery services; architects' services; accounting and auditing services; patent agents' services; surveyors' services; the services of ministers of religion; the services of professional engineers or technologists (including civil, mechanical and mining engineers); and certain financing terms, such as the making of a loan. There are also exempted services relating to: international sea transport; carriage by air; road passenger transport; the activities of building societies; financial control by the Treasury or Bank of England; banking services in Northern Ireland; insurance services; unit trust schemes; and the implementation of decisions of the City Panel on Takeovers and Mergers.

9. Notifying the OFT

If an agreement is registrable as above defined, then particulars must be furnished to the Office of Fair Trading. This must be done before the agreement is to take effect, or, if the operation of the agreement is postponed for more than three months after it was made, then within three months from such date. If these requirements are not complied with, the agreement is void in respect of the particular restrictions and it is unlawful for any party to give effect to, or enforce, those restrictions. No criminal offence arises from giving effect to void restrictions, but the Director General of Fair Trading may apply to the Restrictive Practices Court (see **12** below) for an injunction. In addition, any person suffering loss as a result of the unlawful operation of a void restriction may bring civil proceedings for the recovery of damages for breach of a statutory duty.

10. Non-notifiable agreements

The Deregulation and Contracting Out Act 1994 introduced the 'non-notifiable' agreement. The Secretary of State for Trade and Industry may exempt certain categories of agreement (but not price-fixing agreements) from mandatory notification to the Office of Fair Trading. These agreements remain registrable, but are exempt from the requirement to notify particulars to the OFT unless it requests them.

11. Effect of registration

An agreement continues to have effect if registered within the required period. If the Director General considers it appropriate, he must refer the agreement to the Restrictive Practices Court (see **12** below). However, he may recommend to the Secretary of State that he be discharged from making such a reference if of the opinion that the restrictions are not of such significance to call for investigation by the Court.

12. Reference to the Restrictive Practices Court

The Restrictive Practices Court consists of five judges, one of whom is nominated as President, and has not more than ten other members with knowledge of industry or commerce. It is the function of the Court to consider whether agreements referred to it are or are not in the public interest, the presumption being that they are not.

For an agreement to be in the public interest, it must satisfy the Court that one or more of a number of specified circumstances apply, often called 'gateways'. These may be summarised as follows:

(a) that the restrictions are reasonably necessary, having regard to the character of the goods or services, to protect the public from injury

(b) that the removal of the restrictions would deny the public, as purchasers, consumers or users other specific and substantial benefits or advantages

(c) that the restrictions are reasonably necessary to counteract measures taken by a person not party to the agreement with a view to preventing or restricting competition

(d) that the restrictions are reasonably necessary to enable the parties to the agreement to negotiate fair terms of supply from persons who are not party to the agreement who control a preponderant part of the trade or business of supplying such goods or services

(e) that the removal of the restrictions would be likely to have a serious and persistent effect on the general level of unemployment in the conditions actually obtaining or reasonably foreseeable

(f) that in similar circumstances to **(e)** the removal of the restrictions would be likely to cause a reduction in the volume or earnings of substantial export business

(g) that the restrictions are reasonably required for the maintenance of the other restrictions not found by the court to be contrary to the public interest

(h) that the restrictions do not directly or indirectly restrict or discourage competition to any material degree and are not likely to do so.

In addition, the Court must be further satisfied (this is often called the 'tailpiece') that the restrictions are 'not unreasonable having regard to the balance between those circumstances and any detriment to the public or persons not parties to the agreement' resulting from operation of the restriction.

> *Case law* In *Re Yarn Spinners' Association's Agreement* (1959) it was accepted that the closing of mills on the removal of certain restrictions would result in unemployment, but it was held that this was outweighed by the benefits of free competition.

> *Case law* In *Re National Sulphuric Acid Association's Agreement* (1963), the Association successfully showed that it was only possible to keep prices down by presenting a common front against an American combine which monopolised the export of sulphur.

13. Resale price maintenance

The Resale Prices Act 1976 prohibits collective and individual resale price maintenance in relation to the charging of minimum prices. It is also unlawful for a supplier to withhold supplies in order to maintain resale prices. Breach of these provisions does not mean that a criminal offence has been committed, but civil proceedings may be taken either on behalf of the Crown for an injunction or other appropriate relief, or by 'any person' affected by a contravention who may sue for breach of statutory duty and obtain damages. There is, however, nothing to prevent the use of recommended prices, which is indeed expressly authorised by the Act, but a recommendation by a trade association on behalf of individual suppliers may be registrable under the provisions of the Restrictive Trade Practices Act (see above). As a frequent alternative to taking court action, the OFT will obtain an assurance. For instance, Golden Wonder agreed with the OFT not to attempt to maintain minimum resale prices on its goods. The OFT had requested this assurance after a complaint from a distributor of crisps and snack foods about its contract with the company. This stipulated that payment of bonuses to dealers was dependent on their not selling goods below specified prices (1996).

14. Lawful price maintenance

Provision is made in the Resale Prices Act for the Restrictive Practices Court to exempt goods from the ban on resale price maintenance. An applicant for exemption must show that the scope of at least one of five 'gateways' applies. These are that, in the absence of resale price maintenance, any of the following would occur to the detriment of the public as consumers or users:

(a) The quality or variety of those goods would be substantially reduced.

(b) The number of retail establishments selling the goods would be substantially reduced.

(c) The retail prices at which the goods are sold would in general and in the long run be increased.

(d) The goods would be sold by retail to the public under conditions likely to cause danger to health in consequence of mis-use by the public.

(e) Any necessary services actually provided in connection with or after the sale of goods by retail would cease or be substantially reduced. 'Necessary services' here means services which, having regard to the character of the goods, are required to guard against the risk of injury, whether to persons or premises, or in connection with the consumption, installation or use of the goods, or are otherwise reasonably necessary for the benefit of consumers or users.

The Court must also be satisfied that the resultant detriment to the public outweighs any detriment which would result from the maintenance of resale prices.

If the Court does grant an exemption, a condition as to resale price maintenance then becomes enforceable against any person:

(a) who is not a party to the sale, and

(b) who subsequently acquires the goods with notice of the condition, provided that the chain is not broken by a sale to a person who acquires the goods otherwise than for resale in the course of business.

> *Case law* In *Re Chocolate and Sugar Confectionery Resale Price Reference* (1967), no exemption was granted because there was insufficient evidence that larger outlets would squeeze out small sweet shops.

> *Case law* In *Re Medicaments Reference (No 2)* (1971), the Court found that medicaments and drugs should be granted exemption because, in the absence of resale price maintenance, the availability of the goods for sale and the necessary services accompanying sales would be substantially reduced because some distributors would tend to stock fast-moving items only and cut prices on popular items, thus making the more comprehensive service offered by chemists uneconomic. Readers are advised to check if this exemption is still in place since, at the time of going to press, the OFT had applied to the Court for its removal.

> *Case law* In *Re Net Book Agreement* (1962), the publishers of books agreed that the majority of their titles were not to be sold to the public at less than their net price and were to be subject to standard conditions of sale. The Court found that, while there was no valid argument for saying that there would be a loss of export earnings, there was a case for saying that the removal of the restrictions would deny to the public certain benefits, such as a large number of booksellers maintaining a good stock of books. Exemption was therefore granted.
>
> Since then, the Net Book Agreement was first suspended by the publishers and then, in a later court ruling, its exemption was removed: *Re Net Book Agreement 1957* (1997).

15. Loss leaders

Suppliers are permitted by the Act to take protective action to prevent the use of their goods as 'loss leaders'. Goods are 'loss leaders' if sold by a dealer, not for the purpose of making a profit, but for attracting customers likely to purchase other goods, or otherwise for the purpose of advertising the dealer's business. Supplies can be withheld from such a dealer if the supplier has reasonable cause to believe that, within the previous 12 months, the dealer used the same or similar goods as loss leaders.

ANTI-COMPETITIVE ACTIVITIES

The matters dealt with above are all aspects of the legal regulation of competitive activities. However, more broadly-based legislation exists in the Competition Act 1980. Furthermore, this is also an area where EU law is of particular significance.

16. The Competition Act 1980

The Competition Act gives the Director General of Fair Trading the power to carry out an investigation with a view to establishing whether a person has been pursuing a course of conduct which amounts to 'an anti-competitive practice'. Such a practice arises where, in the course of a business, that person pursues a course of conduct which, of itself or when taken together with a course of conduct by persons associated with him, has or is intended to have or is likely to have the effect of restricting, distorting or preventing competition in connection with the production, supply or acquisition of goods in the United Kingdom, or part of it, or for the supply or securing of services in the United Kingdom or any part of it. Such practices would include:

(a) Price discrimination between distinct and separate groups of customers according to their degree of sensitivity to price levels.

(b) Predatory pricing – the practice of temporarily selling at prices below cost, with the intention of driving a competitor from the market so that in future prices may be raised and profits enhanced.

(c) Vertical price squeezing – where a vertically integrated firm controls the total supply of an input which is essential to the production requirements of its subsidiary and also its competitors, and where it is possible to manipulate the position so that the profits of competitors are squeezed.

A number of anti-competitive practices can also exist in relation to distribution policy. One such example is a *tie-in sale*, where a supplier insists that the buyer takes all or part of his requirements of a second product from the supplier of the first product. Another example is *full-line forcing*, where a buyer is required to purchase quantities in the full range if he wishes to buy any of them. There are also:

- Rental-only contracts, where a supplier offers rental or lease terms only
- Exclusive supply contracts, where a supplier supplies only one buyer in a certain geographical area thus limiting competition between that buyer and his competitors
- Selective distribution and exclusive purchase, involving respectively the choosing as sales outlets only those which satisfy specific qualitative or quantitative criteria, and the agreement by a distributor to stock only the products of one manufacturer, possibly in return for an exclusive supply arrangement.

Those who are the subject of a report are free to give undertakings to the Director General of Fair Trading which are binding if accepted. If no undertakings are given and accepted, the Director General may make a 'competition reference' to the Monopolies and Mergers Commission.

The Act was amended by the Deregulation and Contracting Out Act 1994, so that it is now no longer essential for there to be a formal investigation and report before undertakings can be accepted or a competition reference made. It suffices that the Director General has reasonable grounds for supposing there to exist an anti-competitive practice. The 1994 Act similarly relieves the Directors General of Telecommunications, Electricity Supply, Water Services and the Rail Regulator from the need to undertake a formal investigation and to issue a report before they can ask the Commission to investigate anti-competitive practices or accept undertakings.

17. Commission reports

If a reference is made to the Commission, it investigates matters to determine if the alleged conduct took place within the last 12 months and, if so, whether it amounted to an anti-competitive practice which is contrary to the public interest. In the event of an adverse report, reports being made to the Secretary of State for Trade and Industry, he may by notice in writing ask the Director General to seek an undertaking. If no undertaking is accepted, or is not fulfilled, the Secretary of State has the power, by statutory instrument, to make an appropriate Order.

Example Attempts by local newspapers to prevent estate agents from advertising in other papers were held in a report by the Office of Fair Trading to be anti-competitive (1986). As a result, the local newspapers gave undertakings to the OFT that they would cease this practice.

Example The OFT reported (1984) that the Ford Motor Company Ltd was pursuing a course of conduct which constituted an anti-competitive practice in that it refused to grant licences for the supply of body parts on the ground that the parts were protected by copyright. No undertakings were provided and the matter was referred to the Commission. The Commission reported that, although the company did have the legal right to protect its copyright, the practice of preventing other suppliers from providing parts, as they had done since 1960, would lead to a monopoly and would therefore be anti-competitive.

The company was later released from these undertakings which it gave to the Commission. These had required the company to license, after a seven-year period, independent firms to manufacture or supply Ford Motor vehicle body replacement parts, subject to a 2% royalty. The OFT decided that the undertakings were no longer needed following a ruling of the House of Lords that Ford did not have design rights to the various body parts. This was the decision in *British Leyland* v *Armstrong Patents* (1986) which was in turn modified by s. 51 of the Copyright, Designs and Patents Act 1988.

Example A report concluded that United Automobile Services, operating buses in the Darlington area, had pursued a course of conduct which constituted an anti-competitive practice (1995). However, because there had been major changes in the competitive situation since the start of the investigation, the OFT proposed no remedies, nor did it refer the case to the Commission.

18. Exemptions

Certain sectors of trade and industry are excluded from the above regime by the Anti-Competitive Practices (Exclusion) Order 1980, SI 1980/979. The exemption includes international shipping and aviation, small firms having a turnover of less than £5m and having less than 25% of the relevant market and not being a member of a group whose turnover or share figures exceed these volumes. Likewise within the scope of the exemption are practices registrable under the Restrictive Trade Practices Act (see **12** above), precisely because they would be subject to scrutiny under that Act.

19. Efficiency references

The Competition Act also allows the Secretary of State for Trade and Industry to ask the Monopolies and Mergers Commission to investigate the efficiency and costs of the service provided by, or the possible abuse of a monopoly by, public bodies. These are usually referred to as 'efficiency references'. In its report, the Commission may make recommendations for remedying such adverse effects as it discovers. The Secretary of State is empowered to take action to implement the Commission's findings. There have been 27 such references.

There are also powers given in the Act for the Secretary of State to ask the Office of Fair Trading to investigate prices of 'major public concern'. No follow-up powers are provided for.

Certain bus operations are excluded from the operation of these provisions by the Competition (Exclusion of Bus Operators) Order 1989, SI 1980/981.

EU COMPETITION LAW

For present purposes, EU competition law may be regarded as relating to actions by the member states in relation to the free movement of goods and services; and actions by businesses in relation to their own conduct.

20. Free movement

Article 30 of the Treaty of Rome forbids the member states to set up barriers to trade between themselves, a prohibition which is stated also to apply to all measures which have 'equivalent effect'. A similar prohibition is imposed by Article 34 on barriers to exports.

Direct barriers to trade are rarely put in place, but examples held to be in breach of Article 30 are: the suspension by Italy of the import of pork products (*EEC Commission* v *Italy* (1961)); UK restrictions on the import of Dutch potatoes (*EC Commission* v *United Kingdom* (1979)); and the French refusal to accept sheepmeat from the United Kingdom (*EC Commission* v *French Republic* (1979)). More usually, the alleged infringement of Article 30 relates to measures said to have an 'equivalent effect' to barriers to trade.

> *Case law* In *Procureur du Roi* v *Dassonville* (1974), the Scotch Whisky case, the European Court of Justice offered a broad description of measures having equivalent effect to barriers to trade, saying that these included 'all trading rules enacted by Member States which are capable of hindering, directly or indirectly, actually or potentially, intra-Community trade'.
>
> This was taken a significant step further in the *Cassis de Dijon* case (1979). The then West Germany had refused to accept the import of a liqueur lawfully made and marketed in France because it was not described as required by West German law. The European Court ruled

that the effect of Article 30 was that, once a product had been lawfully marketed in any one Member State, it must be accorded access to all other Member States regardless of the domestic law of the Member State of import.

Sanitary inspection procedures for frozen meat and live cattle at the Italian frontier were held to be equivalent to quantitative restrictions. Similarly, a national marketing system incompatible with the Community common organisation of a market; or excessive checking or inspection of imported goods; or advertising rules designed to champion or protect domestic products at the expense of imported ones; or a pricing system discriminating against imported goods are measures equivalent to quantitative restrictions on trade. (See *Addendum*.)

21. Permitted barriers to trade

Article 36 of the Treaty allows Member States to act in what would otherwise be a breach of Article 30. These grounds include public morality, public policy, public security, the protection of health and life of humans, animals or plants, the protection of national treasures possessing artistic, historic or archaeological value, or the protection of industrial and commercial property.

Case law On 2 and 3 January 1995 the respondent company, ITF, which had been formed for the purpose of transporting livestock across the English Channel, attempted to commence operations out of a port in Sussex. The local police force mounted an operation to police the lorries through the port, but on both occasions the number of animal rights protesters prevented them doing so. Over the following ten-day period the number of police involved in escort duties was increased to 1,125 at considerable cost to the force so that ITF was able to ship its livestock cargo. The number of protesters subsequently dropped and the police were able to maintain control with about 315 officers.

Throughout the operation the chief constable did not ask the police authority to request special financial assistance from the Home Office. Indeed the Home Office indicated that any such application would be required to show that the expenditure was unforeseen, exceptional and threatened the efficiency of the force and that there was no reason to believe that that was the case with the Sussex port operation. On 10 April the chief constable wrote to ITP stating that he intended to restrict police services at the port to one movement of between seven and ten lorries per day on either two consecutive days per week or four consecutive days per fortnight on the basis that the resources being utilised at the port were significantly affecting his ability to deliver policing services efficiently and effectively in other areas of the community. The chief constable subsequently advised ITF that if export operations could not be safely accomplished with the reduced police presence, lorries would be turned back from the port on police instructions and confirmed his decision in a letter dated 24 April. ITF thereafter applied to quash the two decisions on the grounds *(i)* that they were unreasonable and *(ii)* that they contravened Article 34 of the EC Treaty, being 'measures having an equivalent effect' to quantitative restrictions on exports between member states.

The Divisional Court held that it would not intervene as a matter of domestic law, but that the decisions contravened Article 34 of the Treaty, being equivalent to a quantitative restrictions on exports, which could not be justified under Article 36 on public policy grounds since the chief constable had made no effort to increase the financial resources available to him and was therefore unable to prove that he had inadequate resources to police the port on a regular basis. The chief constable appealed in relation to Articles 34 and 36 of the Treaty and ITF challenged the court's decision in relation to domestic law. It was held, on the matter of European law, that the chief constable's decisions not to provide ITF with full-time protection against animal rights protesters and to limit that protection to two days a week could be justified on the grounds of public policy under Article 36 of the Treaty and did not therefore constitute an unlawful restriction on exports.

It was clear that the chief constable had acted under an obligation to use his available resources to police as well as he could the area for which he was responsible and that, in the absence of those decisions, the burden on the Sussex force would clearly have exceeded what would reasonably be required. In striking a balance between ITF's right to lawful protection for its lawful economic activity, the right of the residents of Sussex to protection from crime and the right of the animal rights protesters to protest peacefully which was not unreasonable, and in making the best use of available resources, the chief constable had acted within the principle of proportionality. He was therefore entitled to rely on Article 36 and his appeal succeeded (*R* v *Chief Constable of Sussex, ex parte International Trader's Ferry Ltd* (1997)). (See *Addendum.*)

22. Free movement of services

Freedom to supply services across state boundaries is guaranteed by Articles 59 and 60 of the Treaty. The freedom to supply services applies to companies and firms formed in accordance with the law of a Member State and having their registered office, central administration or principal place of business within the EU. The right to provide services is also connected to the right of establishment. In this context, a number of EU Directives have been adopted providing for the mutual recognition of certain professional qualifications (such as nurses, dental and veterinary professions).

23. Article 85 and prohibited agreements

Article 85 of the Treaty of Rome prohibits agreements between undertakings, decisions by associations of undertakings and concerted practices which have as their object or effect 'the prevention, restriction or distortion of competition within the common market'. Article 85 specifies certain practices in particular which it covers. These are those which:

(a) directly or indirectly fix purchase or selling prices or any other trading conditions

(b) limit or control production, markets, technical development, or investment

(c) share markets or sources of supply

(d) apply dissimilar conditions to equivalent transactions with other trading parties, thereby placing them at a competitive disadvantage

(e) make the conclusion of contracts subject to the acceptance by other parties of supplementary obligations which, by their nature or according to commercial usage, have no connection with the subject of such contracts.

It is provided that any agreements or decisions which are prohibited pursuant to this Article shall be automatically void.

Case law In *Belgian Roofing Felt* (1986), the European Commission took action against 7 members of a trade association who had been fixing prices and protecting their domestic market. Two non-members of the association were also held to be in breach, although they had argued that there was no agreement between them and the 7 members. To the extent that they had given the impression that they would fall in line, they said that this was so only because of a fear of retaliation. The Commission rejected this argument, saying that the mental state of the two firms and the reservations they may have felt did not mean the absence of an agreement for the purposes of Article 85.

Case law In the *Sugar Cartel* Case (1975), the European Commission had held that various sugar producers had taken part in concerted practices to protect the position of two Dutch producers in their domestic market.

The producers argued that they had not worked out a plan to this effect, so that there could not be said to be a concerted practice. The European Court of Justice held that there was no need to prove an actual plan. It said that Article 85 prohibited 'any direct or indirect contact between such operators, the object or effect whereof is either to influence the conduct on the market of an actual or potential competitor or to disclose to such a competitor the course of conduct which they themselves have decided to adopt or contemplate adopting on the market'.

Case law In *AEG Telefunken* v *Commission* (1983), the European Court rejected the claim that refusals to supply retail outlets were unilateral acts falling outside the Article. Instead, it held that such refusals arose from the contractual relationship between the supplier and its established distributors and their mutual acceptance, tacit or express, of AEG's intention to exclude from the network distributors who, though qualified technically, were not prepared to adhere to its policy of maintaining a high level of prices and excluding modern channels of distribution.

24. Negative clearance

An undertaking engaged in a practice of a restrictive nature may apply to the European Commission for 'negative clearance' under the provisions of Regulation 17/62, this being legislation adopted by the EU. The Commission will provide a statement that, 'on the basis of the facts in its possession', it sees no ground for action to be taken under Article 85. Such clearance is not an absolute guarantee against a finding that Article 85 has been infringed, but it could be pleaded in mitigation. The Regulation gives the Commission the power to impose fines for incorrect or misleading information.

25. Exemptions to Article 85

The foregoing provisions may, however, be declared inapplicable in the case of:

- Any agreement or category of agreements between undertakings
- Any decision or category of decisions by associations of undertakings
- Any concerted practice or category of concerted practices which contributes to improving the production or distribution of goods or promoting technical or economic progress, whilst allowing consumers a fair share of the resulting benefit, and which does not:

(*i*) impose on the undertakings concerned restrictions which are not indispensable to the attainment of these objectives

(*ii*) afford such undertakings the possibility of eliminating competition in respect of a substantial part of the products in question.

These provisions allow for individual and block exemptions. The former are dealt with by application to the European Commission and Commission decisions are subject to judicial review.

Block exemptions were introduced to speed up the process of exemption. Thus, Regulation 17/62 exempts agreements, decisions and concerted practices where the only parties involved are undertakings from one member state only and the transactions do not relate to imports and exports between member states. The same Regulation exempts resale agreements between two undertakings, but the parties involved need not be in one member state and the transaction may relate to imports and exports. Regulation 17 also exempts transactions involving no more than two parties which imposes restrictions on the rights of the user or assignee of industrial property rights. Regulation 2349/84 provides for a block exemption for certain patent licensing agreements including the transfer of know-how. Regulation 1983/83 provides a block exemption for certain exclusive distribution agreements; whilst Regulations 1984/83 provide a block exemption for certain exclusive purchasing agreements. Regulation 4087/88 provides a block exemption for certain distribution and service franchises. Regulation 418/85 exempts certain research and development agreements. Regulation 123/85 provides an exemption for certain distribution agreements in relation to motor vehicles. Regulation 3604/82 provides an exemption for certain co-operation agreements among small and medium-sized undertakings where such co-operation enables them to work more rationally and increase their productivity and competitiveness on a larger market and also specialisation agreements.

26. Sanctions for infringement

These are dealt with below in relation to Article 86.

Abuse of a dominant position

Article 86 of the Treaty of Rome provides that any abuse by one or more undertakings of a dominant position within the common market or in a substantial part of it shall be prohibited as incompatible with the common market in so far as it may affect trade between Member States. Such abuse may, in particular, consist in:

(a) Directly or indirectly imposing unfair purchase or selling prices or unfair trading conditions

(b) Limiting production, markets or technical development to the prejudice of consumers

(c) Applying dissimilar conditions to equivalent transactions with other trading parties, thereby placing them at a competitive disadvantage

(d) Making the conclusion of contracts subject to acceptance by the other parties of supplementary obligations which, by their nature or according to commercial usage, have no connection with the subject of such contracts.

It is not an offence for a firm to have a dominant position, but in *Michelin* v *Commission* (1983), the European Court stated that a firm in a dominant position 'has a special responsibility not to allow its conduct to impair undistorted competition in the common market'. In *Continental Can* (1973), the Court declared that Article 86 is 'not only aimed at practices which may cause damage to consumers directly, but also at those which are detrimental to them through their impact on an effective competition structure … Abuse may therefore occur if an undertaking in a dominant position strengthens such position in such a way that the degree of dominance reached substantially fetters competition, i.e. that only undertakings remain in the market whose behaviour depends on the dominant one'.

> *Case law* In *BRT* v *NV Fonior* (1974), the Belgian Association of Authors, Composers and Publishers, entrusted with the exploitation, administration and management of all copyrights and kindred rights of its members and associates was held to have abused its dominant position by imposing on its members obligations which encroached unfairly on the freedom of exercising their rights.

> *Case law* In *Tetra Pak I* (1988), it was held to be an abuse to take over a firm in order to acquire an exclusive licence of patents and know-how which would have the effect of excluding other operators from the market.

> *Case law* In *Decca Navigator System* (1989), the Commission held that it was an abuse to enter into an agreement with an actual or potential competitor with the intention of sharing markets or stunting the effects of competition.

> *Case law* In *Tetra Pak International SA* v *Commission* (1997), Tetra Pak was a manufacturer of cartons and carton-filling equipment. It was involved in both the aseptic and non-aseptic markets. It held a dominant position in relation to the former and was by far the largest concern in relation to

the latter. After investigation, the Commission found the company in breach of Article 86, not least because it included unfair conditions in the sale of carton-filling equipment, and because of predatory pricing. It was fined ECU 75m and an appeal to the European Court of Justice was dismissed. The Court in particular held that Article 86 applied to practices on the non-aseptic market where the company did not hold a dominant position. Such a finding was justified given the quasi-monopoly the company had on the aseptic market; and its leading position in the closely associated non-aseptic markets placed it in a situation comparable to that of holding a dominant position in the markets as a whole.

Negative clearance

Negative clearance is available in exactly the same way, and with the same effect, as in relation to Article 85 (see **24** above).

27. Dealing with infringements of Articles 85 and 86

Regulation 17/62 provides that infringements are dealt with by the Commission. It can act of its own initiative or following a complaint from an interested party. It has a discretion as to whether or not to act on a complaint, but it must advise the complainant if no action is to be taken (*GEMA* v *Commission* (1979)).

The Commission is empowered by that Regulation to impose fines ranging from 1000 to 1m ECU, or a greater sum but not exceeding 10% of turnover, for infringements of the Articles, also for the supply of false or misleading information, for submission in incomplete forms of the books or other documents required or for refusal to submit to an investigation. The European Court can affirm or annul decisions of the Commission, in whole or in part, and can cancel, reduce or increase fines imposed by the Commission. In *Polypropylene* (1986), the Commission imposed fines of 57.85m ECU for price-fixing and market sharing agreements. In *Polyethylene* (1989), fines were imposed totalling 60m ECU.

Member states may themselves deal with infringements so long as the Commission has not itself initiated proceedings. It was held in *Wilhelm* v *Bundeskartellant* (1968), that, in principle, both domestic and EU law could apply simultaneously subject to the requirement that EU law has to be implemented and that it will prevail in the case of any conflict.

4

Contract law

In this chapter, we consider the basic rules regarding the formulation and operation of contracts.

FUNDAMENTALS

1. Definition of 'Contract'

A contract is a legally binding agreement made between two or more persons, by which rights are acquired by one or more acts or forbearances on the part of the other or others.

Mere domestic or social agreements are not usually intended to be binding, and therefore are not contracts.

> *Case law* Three friends joined to enter a newspaper competition and agreed to share any winnings. It was held that they had intended to create legal relations and their agreement was therefore a binding contract: *Simpkins* v *Pays* (1955).

> *Case law* A husband promised to pay a housekeeping allowance to his wife. This was held to be a mere domestic arrangement, with no intention to create legally binding relations, therefore no contract came into existence: *Balfour* v *Balfour* (1919). However, where the spouses are legally separated it will he presumed that they did intend to create a legally binding contract: *Merrit* v *Merrit* (1970).

2. Intention to create legal relations

A binding contract is usually in the nature of a commercial bargain, involving some exchange of goods or services for a price (called the 'consideration'). But even such bargains will not be legally binding if the parties intend otherwise, i.e. do not intend to create legal relations (which, as indicated above, is normally the case with purely domestic agreements).

In considering whether sufficient intention to create a binding contract is present, two situations are possible:

(a) *Where the parties expressly deny the intention.* Here the courts will almost invariably hold that there is no contract:

> *Case law* A written commercial agreement described itself merely as an 'honourable pledge' and stated expressly that it was not 'to be subject to the jurisdiction of any court'. It was held that the parties did not intend to create legal relations, and the agreement was not a contract: *Rose & Frank Co* v *Crompton Bros.* (1923).

> *Case law* A condition imposed by a football pools company laid down that the relationship should not be legally binding. It was again held that there was no intention to create a legal relationship: *Appleson* v *Littlewoods Ltd* (1939).

> *Case law* In *Kleinwort Benson Ltd* v *Malaysia Mining Corporation* (1989), the plaintiff bank agreed with the defendants to make a loan facility of up to £10m available to the defendants' wholly owned subsidiary which traded in tin. The defendants provided the plaintiffs with two 'letters of comfort' which stated that 'it is our policy to ensure that the business of [the subsidiary] is at all times in a position to meet its liabilities to you' under the loan facility arrangement. The subsidiary later went into liquidation and the plaintiffs sought the whole amount owing from the defendants. When the defendants refused to pay, the plaintiffs brought an action against them to recover the amount owing. The Court of Appeal ruled that a 'letter of comfort' stating that it was the policy of a company to ensure that its subsidiary was 'at all times in a position to meet its liabilities' in respect of a loan made by the lender to the subsidiary did not have contractual effect if it was merely a statement of present fact regarding the parent company's future conduct. On the facts, the comfort letters were in terms of a statement of present fact and not a promise as to future conduct, and in the context in which the letters were written were not to be regarded as anything other than a representation of fact giving rise to no more than a moral responsibility on the part of the defendants to meet the subsidiary's debt.

Where the parties do not expressly deny intention to create legal relations, it is in each case a question of construction for the court to decide as to whether a contract is intended. Thus:

> *(i)* in commercial agreements there is a rebuttable presumption that a contract is intended; but

(ii) in social and domestic or family agreements (as seen above) there is a rebuttable presumption that no contract is intended.

Case law C persuaded her niece, P, to sell her own house and come and live in C's on condition that C would leave her house to P by will. After some time, C ejected P from the house, and refused to leave it to her by will. P claimed damages for breach of contract. It was held that, although this was a family agreement, there was consideration for C's promise and evidence of intention to create legal relations. P was therefore entitled to damages: *Parker* v *Clarke* (1960).

Case law B and O habitually rode in each other's cars. Neither had insurance to cover injury to passengers. While in O's car, B was injured through O's negligence and sued for damages in contract or in tort. B had contributed to petrol costs and claimed this gave rise to a contract. O claimed that: *(i)* there was no intention to create a binding contract; and *(ii)* B had consented to the risk of injury, since there was a notice in the car disclaiming liability to passengers. It was held that there was no contract, and B could not get damages either in contract or in tort: *Buckpitt* v *Oates* (1968).

It should be noted that under the Unfair Contract Terms Act 1977 liability for negligence causing death or personal injury cannot now be excluded, but this does not affect the main ruling in this case that no contract had been established.

CLASSIFICATION OF CONTRACTS

3. Contracts by deed

The law on contracts by deed ('specialty contracts') was drastically amended by the provisions of the Law of Property (Miscellaneous Provisions) Act 1989. In particular, it abolished the following three rules of law. Firstly, it abolished the rule that deeds have to be written on paper or parchment, although the requirement of writing remains. Secondly, the requirement of sealing for the valid execution of a deed by an individual is abolished, but execution by a corporation remains unaffected.

Case law It was held by the Court of Appeal in *First National Securities Ltd* v *Jones* (1978) that, as a matter of law, it was not necessary for the due execution of a deed that there should be any physical seal attached to, or impressed on, the paper. A document purporting to be a deed was capable in law of being such, even though it bore nothing more than an indication of where the seal should be. This particular document had a circle in which there were letters showing that this was where the seal should go. The signature had been placed across the circle and a witness had signed a clause saying that the document had been signed, sealed and delivered in his presence. The court ruled that it was evidence enough that the document had been executed by the party as his deed.

Finally, the Act abolished the rule that authority by a party to a deed, given to another person to deliver the deed on the party's behalf, must itself be given by deed.

The Act contains new requirements for the execution of deeds, and applies to both individuals and corporations. The instrument must make it clear on its face that it is intended to be a deed, and it must be validly executed. The first requirement would normally be satisfied by the instrument describing itself as a deed. To satisfy the requirement of valid execution, a deed is validly executed by an individual if it is signed by him in the presence of a witness who attests his signature or is signed at his direction, in his presence and the presence of two witnesses who attest the signature, and it is delivered as a deed by him or a person authorised to do so on his behalf. Signing is defined to include making one's mark.

4. Characteristics of contracts by deed

The main characteristic of a deed is that it does not require to be supported by valuable consideration, like simple contracts (see 5 below). The other main feature is that an action for breach of a specialty contract can be commenced at any time within twelve years of the breach occurring; but an action for breach of a 'simple contract' must generally, under the provisions of the Limitation Act 1980, be commenced within six years.

> *Case law* Syndicate members, whose agreements were under seal, were entitled to rely on the 12-year period, the court holding that an action under a specialty contract covered not just actions for specific performance of the contract but also actions for general damages for breach of an obligation contained in such a contract: *Aiken* v *Stewart Wrightson* (1995).

5. Simple contracts

Simple or 'parol' contracts are by far the most common and important variety. They are informal contracts and may be made in any way orally, in writing, or by implication from conduct. A person who takes a seat in a bus is entering into an implied contract to pay his fare.

6. Quasi-contracts

Sometimes the law imposes obligations of a contractual nature even where no true agreement exists between the parties. The object of such imposition is to prevent a person obtaining 'unjust enrichment' merely because there is no contract between himself and the person seeking the court's aid. The chief examples of such artificial or quasi-contracts are given below.

Money paid to the use of another

If A, at the express or implied request of B, pays to X a sum of money legally owed by B to X, the law implies a quasi-contract between A and B under which B must compensate A for the sum paid, e.g. where A pays rent owed by B to prevent the landlord seizing A's goods, which are stored at B's premises: *Edmunds* v *Wallingford* (1885).

However, this will not necessarily extend to wasted expenditure.

> *Case law* Where parties entered into negotiations with the intention of concluding a contract, but on the express terms that either was free to pull out of the negotiations at any time, the law was clear that, until such time as a binding contract was made, any costs incurred by one of the parties in preparation for the contract would be incurred at his own risk. An action in quasi-contract for the recovery of the costs accordingly failed: *Regalian Properties plc* v *London Dockland Development Corp.* (1995).

Accounts stated

Where there has been a series of transactions between A and B and they agree a balance, showing a sum payable by A to B, the agreed balance constitutes an 'account stated.' If B now has occasion to sue A for the amount so stated, he does not need to prove the details of the transactions between them but can rely on those accounts.

Total failure of consideration

Where a valid contract has been made between A and B (supported by consideration) but subsequently B fails to provide any of the promised consideration, there is said to be a total failure of consideration and A can sue for the recovery of any money he has paid.

Money had and received

If A wrongfully obtains money to which B is legally entitled, B can sue A for recovery of the money in a quasi-contractual action for money had and received, e.g. where an employee receives money on behalf of his employer and refuses to pass it on to the proper recipient.

Case law Thus where B used the authority of his army uniform to assist him in smuggling activities, it was held that the army, as his employer, was entitled to the profits he had made out of the smuggling: *Reading* v *Attorney-General* (1951).

Money paid under mistake of fact

Where money is paid under a mistake of fact it is generally recoverable by the payer, e.g. where an employer overpays wages under a mistake as to the employee's entitlement: *Lener* v *LCC* (1949).

Case law Where a local authority had overpaid an employee it was estopped from recovering amounts where the employee had, in good faith and without notice of the claim and also in reliance on the representation, so changed his position that it would be inequitable to ask him to repay the money: *Avon County Council* v *Howlett* (1983). See also *Rover International* v *Cannon Film Sales (No.3)* (1989).

Case law A local authority entered into an interest rate swap agreement with a bank. This agreement was outside the authority's powers. It was held that the authority was *prima facie* entitled to recover the payments made to the bank as money had and received on the basis that it held its money in equity as paid under a mistake of fact or on the basis that there was no consideration for the payments, since both law and equity treated the bank as unjustly enriched by the receipt of the local authority's money. The fact that the bank had made a loss on the transaction as a whole or had entered into a void agreement was immaterial. It was further held that the local authority was entitled to recover the sums paid as money had and received to the use of the local authority on the basis that there was no consideration for the payment and that it was the authority's money which was held by the bank: *South Tyneside Borough Council* v *Svenska International* (1995).

Where money is paid under a mistake of law, this is generally irrecoverable, since ignorance of the law is no excuse. This rule, however, is subject to the following exceptions:

(1) Where the payee knew of or induced the payer's mistake.

(2) Where the money was paid to an officer of the court, e.g. a trustee in bankruptcy (*ex parte James* (1874)).

(3) Where money was paid under and unjustified threat of legal proceedings against the payer.

(4) Where the payee was under a fiduciary duty to the payer, e.g. where paid by a client to his solicitor.

(5) Where the mistake of law is treated as one of fact, e.g. *(i)* mistake of foreign law; *(ii)* mistake as to private proprietary rights.

Quantum meruit

Where there is a breach of an essential condition in a contract, the injured party may either seek to enforce the contract and sue for damages by way of compensation or treat the contract as discharged, in which case he cannot sue for damages for its breach.

However, where he treats the contract as discharged, and has incurred expenses under it, he is entitled to bring a quasi-contractual action for compensation for work done. This is called a *quantum meruit* action (literally 'how much is it worth?').

In addition to providing a remedy in certain cases of breach of contract like those above, *quantum meruit* may also be used by the court to impose quasi-contractual liability where there is no contract between the parties but justice requires that some remuneration should be paid for work done.

> *Case law* A builder did certain work for D on the understanding that D would give him a contract later for some major building work. D did not give him the expected contract and the builder sued for either *(i)* damages for breach of contract or *(ii) quantum meruit* relief. It was held that there was no contract between the parties and therefore the builder could not get damages, but he was entitled to reasonable remuneration on a quasi-contract: *Lacey (William) Ltd* v *Davis* (1957).

OFFER AND ACCEPTANCE

In order to constitute a contract there must be an offer, express or implied, by one person (the 'offeror'), and unqualified acceptance, express or implied, by the person to whom the offer is made (the 'offeree'). The House of Lords has emphasised that save in exceptional circumstances, a binding contract requires an offer and an acceptance: *Gibson* v *Manchester City Council* (1979).

7. Rules governing offers

An offer may be oral, written, or implied from conduct. Thus, an implied offer is made by a bus company when it sends its buses along the street and stops them at fixed places to let people get on. Those who then get on thus accept the offer by implication. An offer may be specific, i.e. to a particular person or group of persons, or general, i.e. to the world at large. A specific offer can usually be accepted only by the person or persons to whom it was made: *Boulton* v *Jones* (1857). A general offer, in contrast, can be accepted by anyone.

Case law Thus a newspaper advertisement offering £100 to anyone who contracted influenza despite using a patent medicine in a specific way was held to be *(i)* a general offer, *(ii)* one which could be accepted by conduct, *(iii)* without previously notifying the offeror of the acceptance: *Carlill* v *Carbolic Smoke Ball Co* (1893).

8. Communication to offeree

The offer must be communicated to the offeree before it can be accepted.

Case law A seaman helped to navigate a ship home, and before sailing wrote to the owners telling them of his intention and asking a particular wage for his services. The owners did not receive the letter of offer until the ship was nearly home. It was held that the owners had no reasonable opportunity to accept or reject the offer, therefore the seaman could not compel them to pay him wages for navigating the ship: *Taylor* v *Laird* (1863).

9. Certainty of offer

The offer must be definite, not vague or illusory. Thus a promise to pay an increased price for a horse 'if it proves lucky to me' is too vague: *Guthing* v *Lynn* (1831).

10. Intention to create legal relations

The offeror must intend to create a legal relationship with the offeree, i.e. must intend that if his offer is accepted a legally binding agreement shall result (see above and the cases considered there). The House of Lords has indicated that there is an intention to create legal relations where 'free' medallions are given away with so many gallons of petrol purchased: *Esso* v *Commissioners of Customs and Excise* (1976).

11. Matters not constituting an offer

An offer must he distinguished from the following:

(a) An invitation to treat (invitation to make offers), e.g. an auctioneer's request for bids (which will themselves be offers): *Payne* v *Cave* (1789); or the display of goods in a shop window with prices marked upon them: *Fisher* v *Bell* (1961); or the display of priced goods in a self-service store:

Pharmaceutical Society of Great Britain v *Boots the Cash Chemists Ltd* (1953). Indicating that medallions are given away with the purchase of petrol is, however, probably not an invitation to treat, but is itself an offer: *Esso* v *Commissioners of Customs and Excise* (1976).

(b) A mere statement of intention, e.g. an announcement of a forthcoming auction sale. Thus a person who attends an advertised place of auction could not sue for breach of contract if the sale were cancelled: *Harris* v *Nickerson* (1873).

(c) A mere communication of information in the course of negotiations, e.g. a statement of the price at which one is prepared to consider negotiating the sale of a piece of land: *Harvey* v *Facey* (1893).

> *Case law* In discussing a possible sale of land, A wrote offering £20,000 and B replied: 'As you are aware that I paid £25,000 for this property, your offer of £20,000 would appear to be at least a little optimistic. For a quick sale I would accept £26,000 ...' A replied accepting this offer. It was held that this was an offer which A had accepted, so making a contract: *Bigg* v *Boyd Gibbons* Ltd (1971).

12. When an offer lapses

The offer lapses if one party or the other dies before acceptance: *Kennedy* v *Thomassen* (1929). But the death of the offeror may not invalidate a subsequent acceptance provided: *(i)* the offeree did not know of the death when he accepted, and *(ii)* the personalty of the offeror was not vital to the contract: *Bradbury* v *Morgan* (1862).

An offer will also lapse if not accepted within a reasonable time. If no particular time is specified, then this must be taken as a reference to a reasonable time. This is a question of fact depending on all the circumstances of the case. Five months has been held to be an unreasonable delay in accepting an offer to take shares in a company: *Ramsgate Hotel* v *Montefiore* (1866).

An offer also lapses if the offeree does not make a valid acceptance, e.g. makes a conditional acceptance; or, if a particular manner of acceptance has been requested, he accepts in some other manner, e.g. by sending a letter by mail when a reply by hand was requested: *Eliason* v *Henshaw* (1819).

Where a counter-offer is accepted, the terms of the counter-offer then form the basis of the resulting contract (and not the terms of the original offer): *Davies & Co* v *William Old* (1969).

13. Revocation prior to acceptance

An offer can be revoked at any time prior to acceptance. The revocation must be communicated. Until the offeree actually receives the revocation, he is entitled to accept the offer and so create a binding contract.

> *Case law* A sent an offer by cable to B on the 1st October requesting acceptance by the same method. B received the offer on 11th October and immediately cabled acceptance. On 8th October A had posted a letter revoking the offer, which did not reach B till after he had cabled his acceptance. It was held that B had accepted before receiving the revocation, therefore a contract was made and the revocation was ineffective: *Byrne* v *Van Tienhoven* (1880).

Indirect communication

If the offeree learns of the revocation, he cannot later accept, even though he learns indirectly, e.g. where a prospective purchaser of land learns through a reliable third party that the offeror has sold the land to someone else. He cannot then accept the offer and sue the offeror for damages: *Dickinson* v *Dodds* (1876).

An offer for shares or debentures in a public company made as a result of an advertisement or prospectus cannot be revoked until the third day after the opening of the subscription lists: Companies Act 1985, ss. 82, 86.

14. Options

An offer to keep an offer open for a specified time (an option) is not binding unless *(a)* made under seal, or *(b)* supported by valuable consideration, like any other simple contract: *Routledge* v *Grant* (1828).

In a unilateral contract, which is where A promises to give B something if B first does something for A (such as promising someone £100 if he swims a particular lake on a given day), it has been said that 'although the offeror is entitled to require full performance of the condition which he has imposed and although short of that he is not bound, once the offeree has embarked on performance of the condition [as by starting to swim the lake], there is an implied obligation on the part of the offeror not to prevent performance and he cannot revoke his offer': *Daulia Ltd* v *Four Millbank Nominees Ltd* (1978).

15. Rules governing acceptance

Manner of acceptance

Acceptance may be oral, written or implied from conduct: *Carlill* v *Carbolic Smoke Ball Co* (1893).

But if a particular method of acceptance is required the offeree must accept in the prescribed manner (see *Eliason* v *Henshaw* above).

Unqualified acceptance

Acceptance must be unqualified and must correspond with the terms of the offer.

A counter-offer or conditional acceptance operates as a rejection of the offer, and causes it to lapse. Thus where a house is offered for sale at £1000 and the offeree counter-offers £950 the offer lapses: *Hyde* v *Wrench* (1840).

Similarly, a conditional acceptance, such as making acceptance 'subject to a proper contract being drawn up', causes an offer to lapse: *Eccles* v *Bryant* (1948).

Positive conduct

There must be active acceptance: mere passive intention to accept is ineffective. Thus an offer by letter containing the words 'If I hear no more, I shall consider the horse mine' is incapable on its own of amounting to acceptance. There must be some positive communication of acceptance by the offeree; it would not be enough to show that the offeree intended to accept but died before writing a letter of acceptance: *Felthouse* v *Bindley* (1862).

It has been said, however, without the point being actually decided that, 'where the offeree himself indicates that an offer is to be taken as accepted if he does not indicate to the contrary by an ascertainable time, he is undertaking to speak if he does not want an agreement to be concluded. I see no reason in principle why that should not be an exceptional circumstance such that the offer can be accepted by silence': *Re Selectmove Ltd* (1995).

Where goods are sent unrequested to a private individual, they can become his after six months without him having to do anything positive: Unsolicited Goods and Services Acts 1971 and 1975.

16. Communication of acceptance

Normally an acceptance is ineffective unless and until communicated to the offeror. There are, however, exceptions to this statement: thus, where the offeror expressly or impliedly waives communication, e.g. where a general offer requires merely conduct as its acceptance: *Carlill* v *Carbolic Smoke Ball Co* (1893).

Similarly an offer of a reward is accepted by doing what is required, without any previous communication: *Williams* v *Carwardine* (1833). Where the contract is made by post, or the post is envisaged as the means of communication, e.g. in most commercial contracts today, acceptance is complete as soon as it is posted, provided it is properly stamped and addressed: *Household Fire Insurance Co* v *Grant* (1879).

In postal cases therefore it does not matter if the letter of acceptance is lost in the post and never reaches the offeror: the contract is complete as soon as the letter of acceptance is posted. As a matter of commercial expediency the Post Office is treated as agent for the offeror, and communication to the agent is treated as communication to the principal.

The same rule applies to telegrams, but where the method of communication is instantaneous, e.g. telex, telephone, fax, or e-mail, acceptance is not complete until it actually reaches its destination: *Entores* v *Miles Far East Corpn.* (1955). This point was confirmed by the House of Lords in *Brinkibon* v *Stahag Stahl und Stahlwarenhandelgesellschaft* (1983) where an offer was made by telex in Vienna and accepted by a telex message from London to Vienna. The House of Lords held that the contract was made in Vienna. The telex machines were in the offices of the respective parties, and the telexes were sent during business hours. The House of Lords left open the position where telexes (and hence by extension faxes and e-mail) are transmitted through agencies or outside office hours.

Where acceptance is to be by notice in writing to the offeree, mere posting of acceptance does not constitute notice – actual delivery must be proved: *Holwell Securities* v *Hughes* (1974).

17. Existence of offer unknown

No-one can accept an offer in ignorance of its existence, but provided he knows of the offer his motive for accepting is usually irrelevant.

> *Case law* C offered a reward for information leading to the arrest of a criminal. W provided the information (knowing of the offer) but saying that she did so simply 'to ease her conscience.' Therefore C refused to pay the reward. It was held that, since W knew of the offer and accepted it, her motive for doing so was irrelevant and she was entitled to the money: *Williams* v *Carwardine* (1833).

18. Tenders

A tender is a form of offer for the supply of goods or services usually made in response to a request for tenders. Tenders take the following forms:

(a) Single offer, e.g. a tender to build a factory. Acceptance of such a tender constitutes a contract.

(b) Standing offer, e.g. a tender to supply goods as and when required. Here the tenderer must supply whenever an order is made. But he cannot insist on any order being made at all.

Case law P tendered to supply goods up to a certain amount to the LCC over certain periods. The LCC's orders did not come up to the amount expected and P sued for breach of contract. It was held that each order made a separate contract and P was bound to fulfil the orders made, but there was no obligation to make any orders at all: *Percival Ltd v LCC* (1918).

(c) Sole supplier. The person seeking the tender may agree to take all his requirements for certain goods from the tenderer. This agreement does not oblige him to make any orders at all but if he does require goods within the category agreed he must take them from the tenderer: *Kier v Whitehead Iron Co* (1938).

Where a tender is made before the deadline for the receipt of tenders, a binding contract can arise to consider tenders conforming to the conditions of tender: *Blackpool and Fylde Aero Club Ltd v Blackpool BC* (1990).

STANDARD FORM CONTRACTS

There is an increasing tendency for an offeror to write out the contract entirely himself, and then demand that the offeree shall accept the detailed terms of the offer without modification. The offeror may state all his terms in one document or, as in the case, for example, of railway tickets, may simply incorporate by reference certain standard conditions contained in another document. These 'offers with terms annexed' are subject to special rules. They include most forms of transport ticket, by air, sea, or rail, many leases, and most contracts for the supply of gas, electricity and such like.

19. Contract signed by offeree

If the contract is signed by the offeree, he is bound by all the conditions contained in the document signed even if he has not read them: *L'Estrange* v *Graucob* (1934). However, if the offeree can prove he signed the document under a fundamental mistake as to its nature (not merely as to its contents), then, under the Common Law doctrine of *non est factum*, he can escape liability. The doctrine covers, for example, cases where a person is induced to sign a cheque on the mistaken assumption that it is merely a guarantee: *Foster v Mackinnon* (1869).

Where the signatory can prove that he was induced to sign as a result of a misrepresentation by the offeror, or the offeror's agent, whether innocent or fraudulent, again he can escape liability: *Curtis v Chemical Cleaning & Dyeing Co Ltd* (1951); *Mendelsohn v Normand Ltd* (1970); *Evans & Son* v *Merzario* (1976).

A signature will only be binding if the document signed is a contractual one, and this is answered by determining if the document was one which the signatory would know, or would reasonably expect, to contain relevant contractual provisions: in the matter of an arbitration between *Jayaar Impex Ltd* v *Toaken Group Ltd* (1996).

20. Contract unsigned

If the contract is unsigned, e.g. railway tickets, the offeree is bound by all the terms in the document or annexed to it:

(a) if a reasonable man would assume the document to be contractual, e.g. not merely a receipt for money: *Chapelton* v *Barry UDC* (1940)

(b) if reasonable care was taken by the offeror to bring the terms of the offer to his attention, e.g. by a notice: 'for conditions see Company's rules and regulations' clearly displayed on the face of the ticket. If the notice given is reasonable, the contract is binding whether the offeree reads the conditions or not: *Parker* v *SE Railway* (1877), or even whether the offeree is illiterate and unable to read them: *Thompson* v *LMS. Railway* (1930). If, however, it is known that the person cannot read the clause because he is not English he is not bound by it: *Geier* v *Kujawa* (1970).

(c) Notice of annexed conditions must be contemporaneous with, or prior to, the making of the contract: *Olley* v *Marlborough Court Ltd* (1949) and *Thornton* v *Shoe Lane Parking Ltd* (1971).

Case law C took a deck chair from a pile under a notice 'Hire of chairs – 3d.' Later an attendant came round to collect the money and C paid him, receiving in return a ticket which said on it, 'The Council will not be liable for any accident or damage arising from hire of chair.' C put the ticket in his pocket without reading it, thinking it was merely a receipt. The chair collapsed and he was injured and sued the Council. It was held that the Council could not rely on the exclusion clause since none of rules **(a)**, **(b)**, or **(c)** above was satisfied: *Chapelton* v *Barry UDC* (1940).

Case law O registered at a hotel by signing the visitors' book, and then went to his room where a notice was displayed excluding the hotel's liability for articles lost. It was held that he had made his contract when he signed the book, and the hotel could not rely on the exclusion clause since it was not brought to his attention contemporaneously with the making of the contract: *Olley* v *Marlborough Court Ltd* (1949).

Case law B booked a passage for P and himself on D's vessel. He later received a contract containing an exclusion clause. It was held that the contract was already made by the time its terms were received, so the exclusion clause had no validity: *Hollingworth* v *Southern Ferries* (1977).

21. Notice of unusual clauses

In *Interfoto Picture Library Ltd* v *Stiletto Visual Programmes Ltd* (1988) a photographic library provided transparencies to an advertising agency on terms which specified that, if the transparencies were held for longer than 14 days, then a charge of £7.50 per day would be made until their return. The transparencies were held for more than 14 days and the library sought to rely on the above term. The Court of Appeal ruled that this term was particularly onerous since the usual rate at the time was £3.50 per week. Where a clause was unreasonable and extortionate in this way, then it would not be held to be part of the contract unless the party seeking to enforce it could show that it had been fairly and reasonably brought to the attention of the other party. This had not been done in this case, and so the term was not part of the contract.

> *Case law* Sellers sent a confirmation of order which stated, at the bottom and in small capital letters, that: ORDERS ARE SUBJECT TO OUR CONDITIONS OF SALE – FOR EXTRACT SEE REVERSE. One of the clauses provided that: 'the purchaser shall return the defective parts at his own expense to the supplier immediately on request of the latter'. The clause as a whole excluded duties otherwise imposed on sellers by the Sale of Goods Act (see Chapter 5) and offered the buyers the sole right of returning the goods at their own expense: 'it is drafted in a way one has seen in other standard terms ... what it gives with one hand it takes away with the other ... [it] gives warranty cover. It is a very restricted warranty cover, for bad workmanship. The only way it can be taken advantage of is to send the goods back'. The clause was held to be onerous and, within the principle of the *Interfoto* case, invalid since nothing had been done to draw it to the buyers' attention: *AEG (UK) Ltd* v *Logic Resources Ltd* (1994).

EXEMPTION CLAUSES

Annexed conditions are usually aimed at exempting the offeror from some legal liability to which he would otherwise be subject, e.g. liability for negligence in carrying out the contract. Such clauses have never been popular with Parliament or the courts and each have sought to control their effectiveness, as discussed below.

22. Statutory restrictions

There are two main enactments imposing controls on exclusion clauses as well as on limitation clauses (the latter comprise clauses which accept liability in the event of a breach but not for the full amount of the loss suffered).

(a) The Unfair Contract Terms Act 1977 limits the effectiveness of exclusion clauses in contracts of sale, conditional sale and hire-purchase (see Chapter 5). In contracts made by businesses with consumers, clauses excluding the implied terms as to description, quality and fitness for purpose are void. The use of such void clauses is also unlawful by virtue of the Consumer Transactions (Restrictions on Statements) Orders 1976/1813. In contracts made between businesses, clauses excluding these terms are valid if they can be shown to be reasonable.

The 1977 Act also imposes restrictions on some exclusion clauses in contracts made on written standard terms or between a business and a consumer (i.e. whether or not on written standard terms). Clauses covered by this part of the Act are only valid if proved to be reasonable. The clauses which are covered by this part of the Act are the following: *(i)* those which seek to exclude or restrict liability for breach of contract; *(ii)* those which claim to allow a contractual performance 'substantially different' from that which was reasonably expected; *(iii)* those which claim to allow no performance at all. A contract can be on written standard terms even if subject to prior negotiation: *St Albans City and District Council* v *International Computers Ltd* (1996).

The Act states that no exclusion clause can restrict or exclude liability for negligence resulting in death or personal injury. Where negligence results in any other type of loss, such as damage to property, the clause is valid if it can be proved to be reasonable. The Act also renders void any term in a contract seeking to exempt a party from legal liability for a misrepresentation made by him before the contract was entered into (unless it is shown that the clause was reasonable).

- *Indemnity clauses*: The Act also controls clauses which require a consumer to indemnify another party for liability which the latter might incur through negligence or breach of contract. Such clauses are now only valid if they are proved to be reasonable.
- *Guarantees*: Where a guarantee is provided by a manufacturer that he will make good loss arising from negligence in the distribution or manufacture of the goods, the Act says that this guarantee cannot exclude liability for the loss or damage.
- *The reasonableness test*: Whenever the reasonableness test is imposed, the Act places the burden on the party seeking to uphold the partic-

ular clause to show that it is reasonable. Each case will fall to be judged on its individual facts and just because a clause has been found to be reasonable or unreasonable in one case does not mean that the same decision would be reached in another. For cases on the reasonableness test, see: *Smith* v *Eric S Bush* (1989); *Stewart Gill Ltd* v *Horatio Myer & Co Ltd* (1992); *Edmund Murray Ltd* v *BSP International Foundations Ltd* (1992); *W Photoprint* v *Forward Trust Group* (1993); *Lease Management Services Ltd* v *Purnell Secretarial Services Ltd* (1994); *Salvage Association* v *CAP Financial Services Ltd* (1995); *St Albans City and District Council* v *International Computers Ltd* (1996); *Monarch Airlines Ltd* v *London Luton Airport Ltd* (1996); *Omega Trust Ltd* v *Wright Son & Pepper* (1996); *Esso Petroleum Co Ltd* v *Milton* (1997).

It should also be noted that the Consumer Transactions (Restrictions on Statements) Order 1976 requires all guarantees (whether given by the manufacturer or the retailer) to be accompanied by a statement to the effect that the consumer's rights against the retailer are unaffected.

(b) The foregoing provisions have been supplemented by the Unfair Terms in Consumer Contracts Regulations 1994/3159. Apart from certain excluded contracts (dealing with employment, succession rights, family law, company law and any term required by United Kingdom law or by international convention), the Regulations apply to every contract between an individual and a business which has not been individually negotiated. The scope of the Regulations is therefore much wider than that of the Unfair Contract Terms Act. A term is not to be treated as individually negotiated where it is drafted in advance without the consumer's involvement. A term will also be regarded as not individually negotiated even though it, or certain aspects of it, have been individually negotiated if an overall assessment of the contract indicates that it is a pre-formulated standard contract.

Contracts within the Regulations must be in 'plain, intelligible language'. If not, any ambiguity will be construed against the party seeking to rely on the particular term.

If an 'unfair' term is included in a contract within the Regulations, such term is not binding on the consumer, although the contract shall continue to bind the consumer if it is capable of continuing without that term. A term will be unfair if it is contrary to the requirement of good faith and causes a significant imbalance in the parties' rights and obligations to the detriment of the consumer. An assessment of the unfair nature of a term is to be made taking account of the nature of the relevant goods or services and with regard to the circumstances prevailing when the contract was made and to all other terms of that contract or of another on which it is dependent. In determining whether a term is unfair, regard is to be had in particular to various specified matters. No assessment of the unfairness of any term can be made, however, where that term defines the main subject matter of the contract, or which concerns the adequacy of the price or charge for the particular goods or services, unless such term is not expressed in plain and intelligible language. The Director General of Fair Trading is obliged to consider any complaint that a contract term is unfair, unless he considers the complaint frivolous or vexatious. He may then bring proceedings for an injunction if he considers this an appropriate course of action. If he considers it appropriate, the Director General may take account of any undertaking offered in relation to the continued use of the particular term. He must also give reasons for any decision to apply or not to apply for an injunction. Any injunction may be directed not just to the particular term, but also to any similar term, or one having like effect, used or recommended by any party to the proceedings.

The Regulations empower the Director General to issue information on the operation of the Regulations. In one such report, the OFT found itself 'very disturbed' that unfair terms often conflict not only with the requirements of the Regulations but with consumer protection legislation that has been in place for much longer. Examples include exclusion clauses that are void under the Unfair Contract Terms Act 1977 (see above), the Consumer Arbitration Agreement Act 1988 (the provisions of which have been now repealed and replaced by the Arbitration Act 1996), and others that give rise to offences under the Consumer Transactions (Restrictions on Statements) Order 1976 (see above). This problem, the OFT said, often arose where, in dealing with consumers, businesses use contract terms originally designed for use in inter-company agreements. Where terms were drawn up for general use, including consumer contracts, they would need to be fair within the context of the Regulations. The alternative would be for firms to operate with separate forms of contract for consumers and for other businesses or to make it absolutely clear which terms do not apply to consumers.

The OFT also said that few business sectors seemed to be immune from the use of unfair terms. It pointed to its examination of consumer agreements for mobile phones and travel contracts, to wheel-clamp removal businesses and monumental masons. Potentially unfair terms seemed, according to the OFT, to be widely used in home improvement and furnishing businesses and where goods were sold in the home, including double glazing and specialist fittings and aids for the disabled. Some clauses were 'flagrantly unfair'. The OFT also pointed out that the use of all-embracing liability exclusion clauses in notices in car parks, and elsewhere, was very common. It thought this unfair and was advising the relevant trade and other organisations that such notices needed to be narrowed in scope or removed altogether.

(c) The Consumer Credit Act 1974 (see Chapter 7) makes void a term in a contract which excludes the protection afforded by the Act.

(d) The Trading Stamps Act 1964 makes void clauses seeking to avoid the warranties as to title and satisfactory quality implied into redemptions of trading stamps for goods (see Chapter 5). The use of such void clauses is also a criminal offence under the 1976 Order (see **(a)** above).

23. Judicial restrictions

The attitude of the courts can be summarised as follows:

(a) An exclusion clause will never be enforced unless adequate advance notice of it has been given to the other party: *Parker* v *SE Railway* (1877).

(b) Under the *'contra proferentem'* rule exclusion clauses are narrowly construed against the person who seeks to rely on them.

(c) Where the parties are on unequal footing, the court will more readily reject an exclusion clause designed to protect the stronger party.

> *Case law* In one case, a young song writer made an agreement with a publishing company for a five-year period. It was a particularly stringent standard form contract; for example, there was no obligation on the publishers to publish any of the songs produced. It was said by the court, when holding that the contract could not be enforced, that the courts intervene to protect those 'whose power is weak against being forced by those whose bargaining power is stronger to enter into bargains which are unconscionable': *Schroeder (A) Music Publishing Co Ltd* v *Macaulay* (1974). See also *Clifford Davis Management* v *WEA Records Ltd* (1975) and *Lloyds Bank* v *Bundy* (1975).

(d) Where the exclusion clause seeks to evade liability for breach of a fundamental term of the contract the courts will be particularly reluctant to enforce it: *Suisse Atlantique etc.* v *N. V. Rotterdamsche Kolen Centrale* (1966); *Harbutt's Plasticine Ltd* v *Wayne Tank and Pump Co Ltd* (1970); *Wathes (Western) Ltd* v *Austins Ltd* (1976).

> *Case law* Exemption clauses were held to be void where a bailee for safe custody handed the goods deposited to a stranger instead of returning them to the bailor: *Alexander* v *Railway Executive* (1951).

> *Case law* A bailee stored goods in a warehouse other than that agreed with the bailor and the goods were destroyed by fire. An exemption clause was again held to be ineffective: *Lilley* v *Doubleday* (1881).
>
> Where a bailee loses goods, the onus is on him to show he was not in fundamental breach: *Levison* v *Patent Steam Carpet Cleaning Co* (1977).

CERTAINTY OF TERMS

24. Terms must be certain

It is for the parties to make their intentions clear in their contract. The court will not enforce a contract the terms of which are uncertain. Thus an agreement to agree in the future ('a contract to make a contract') will not constitute a binding contract, e.g. a promise to pay an actress 'a West End salary to be mutually agreed between us' is not a contract, since the salary is not yet agreed: *Loftus* v *Roberts* (1902). Similarly, an agreement providing that the price will be subject to later negotiations is not a contract, since contracts to negotiate are not known to the law: *Courtney* v *Tolaini* (1975); *Walford* v *Miles* (1992).

Similarly, where the terms of a final agreement are too vague, the contract will fail for uncertainty, e.g. sale of a van 'on hire-purchase terms' was too vague, since there were several forms of hire-purchase agreement: *Scammell* v *Ouston* (1941). However, an agreement which at first sight appears to be too vague can be enforced under the following conditions:

(a) If the parties themselves have provided machinery in the contract for resolving the uncertainty, e.g. where no price was fixed for the sale of petrol, but the agreement stated that disputes should be referred to arbitration, it was held that the arbitrator could fix the prices and so resolve the uncertainty: *Foley* v *Classique Coaches Ltd* (1934). Similarly, where a five-year contract for the the supply of chickens failed to state the number of chickens, but contained an arbitration clause, it was held that the numbers could be fixed by arbitration: *F & G Sykes (Wessex) Ltd* v *Fine Fare Ltd* (1967).

(b) The deficiency can be remedied by the court implying a term, *(i)* from the course of dealing between the parties in the past (if any), or *(ii)* from trade usages in the particular trade (again, if any), or *(iii)* where certain terms are implied by statute in similar contracts, e.g. the Sale of Goods Act 1979. The court may always imply a term into a contract to save it from collapse, but will do so only where it is clearly necessary and equitable: *The Moorcock* (1889).

25. Meaningless clauses

An agreement which is definite on the whole will be enforceable notwithstanding the presence of some meaningless or unnecessary words or phrases. The court in such a case will ignore the meaningless words and enforce the contract without them (unless the parties have given such a phrase a common meaning): *Nicolene Ltd* v *Simmonds* (1953).

TERMS OF A CONTRACT

26. Express or implied terms

The parties may expressly state every term of their contract with varying degrees of precision; or they may simply agree the basic purpose of the contract and leave the detailed terms to be deduced from the surrounding circumstances.

Contractual terms are of two kinds: *(a)* conditions (main terms); or *(b)* warranties (subordinate terms). Whether a term is a condition or a warranty is a question of intention to be deduced by the court in the light of the surrounding circumstances. Mistaken use of the words 'condition' or 'warranty' by the parties will not be regarded as conclusive.

27. Conditions

A condition is an essential term which goes to the root of the contract, i.e. it may constitute the main purpose of the agreement, or one of several main purposes.

Breach of condition entitles the injured party to treat the contract as at an end: *Behn* v *Burness* (1863).

Alternatively he may treat the breach as a mere breach of warranty, claim damages and insist on the contract being performed. The Sale of Goods Act 1979, ss. 13 and 14, declares that the implied terms as to description, quality and fitness for purpose are conditions, as is the sellers's duty to have a right to sell: s. 12(1) (see Chapter 5).

28. Fundamental term

This is entirely a judicial creation. It is a condition so important that it constitutes the fundamental purpose of the contract. Where there is breach of such a term, a 'fundamental breach', the courts will not allow the contract-breaker to escape liability by relying on even an express exemption clause unless the clause clearly covers the particular breach: *Suisse Atlantique etc.* v *N. V. Rotterdamsche Kolen Centrale* (1966); *Photo Production* v *Securicor Transport* (1980).

There is no fundamental breach where breach is caused by circumstances beyond the control of the non-performing party and an exemption covers the situation: *Trade & Transport Incorporated* v *Iino Kaiun Paisha (The Angelica)* (1973).

29. Kinds of condition

(a) *Condition precedent*: a condition that the contract shall not bind one or both of the parties until such condition is fulfilled, e.g. 'this contract is not to be binding until the war ends.'

(b) *Condition subsequent*: a condition under which the contract shall cease to be binding at the option of one party on the happening of a certain event, e.g. 'this contract shall cease to be binding if war breaks out.' This is called a *determinable contract* and remains binding until the condition subsequent is fulfilled. This is to be contrasted with a voidable contract which can be made completely void at the option of one party.

(c) *Condition concurrent*: a condition under which performance by one party is made dependent on performance by the others at the same time, e.g. payment of the price upon delivery of goods ordered.

30. Warranties

A warranty is a subordinate term, subsidiary to the main purpose of the contract: Sale of Goods Act 1979, s. 61(1). Breach of warranty entitles the injured party to sue for damages, but he cannot regard the contract as at an end and must perform his part of it.

> *Case law* B promised to attend rehearsals for a concert, but arrived in London only in time for two days' rehearsals, in response to which G claimed the contract was discharged by breach of condition. It was, however, held that attendance at rehearsals was a warranty only and therefore the contract was not discharged, though G was entitled to damages for breach of warranty: *Bettini v Gye* (1876).

31. *Ex post facto* warranties

Where a breach of condition occurs the injured party can (*a*) treat the contract as discharged, or (*b*) if he prefers he may treat the breach as breach of a warranty, go on with the contract and sue for damages. In some cases he must adopt the second alternative, e.g. where in a contract for sale of goods the purchaser has accepted a substantial part of the goods, before discovering a breach of condition, he must treat the breach as a breach of warranty: Sale of Goods Act 1979, s. 11(4), though s. 35A of the Act does now provide for a right of partial rejection. This latter turns the condition into an *ex post facto* warranty.

FORMATION OF CONTRACTS

32. Implied terms

The general rule is that the parties are presumed to have expressed their intentions fully. The courts will only imply additional terms where it is strictly necessary to give effect to the clear intentions of the parties, or where custom or statute requires the implication: *The Moorcock* (1889).

When express terms are clear and unambiguous, the court will only imply a term if it is clear that the parties must have intended it to form part of the contract: *Trollope & Colls* v *NW Metropolitan Regional Hospital Board* (1973).

> *Case law* C's insurance company employed the X garage to repair C's car, damaged in an accident. The court found that there was an implied contract between C and X (contrary to X's claim that its only contract was with the insurance company). There was no term in this implied contract fixing the time to be taken for the repairs: X took eight weeks and C claimed damages for unreasonable delay. It was held that in the interests of business efficacy the court could imply that repairs must be completed in a reasonable time (in this case five weeks) and awarded damages to C: *Charnock* v *Liverpool Corporation* (1968); see also *Brown & Davis Ltd* v *Galbraith* (1972).

Occasionally, terms are implied by statute: e.g. Trading Stamps Act 1964 (stamps exchanged for goods); Sale of Goods Act 1979 (contracts of sale); Supply of Goods (Implied Terms) Act 1973 (hire-purchase); Supply of Goods and Services Act 1982 (certain contracts relating to goods and contracts for services). These are dealt with in Chapter 5.

33. Terms and representations

Frequently during preliminary negotiations one of the parties, such as the seller of goods, may make a series of statements, or representations, to help persuade the other party to enter the contract. Whether such representations become terms in the contract, and so binding the party making the representations, depends on the construction which the court puts upon them.

The test is: did the plaintiff accept the representations as mere inducements, or did he insist that he would not enter into the contract unless the representations could be regarded as binding conditions or warranties?

The following rules apply:

(a) A representation will not be regarded as a term of the contract unless the parties so agree, expressly or by implication.

(b) If a representation is treated as a mere inducement, the plaintiff cannot sue for breach of contract if it proves untrue. He may, though, under the provisions of the Misrepresentation Act 1967, or generally in the tort of misrepresentation, be able to avoid the contract and obtain damages.

(c) If a representation is agreed by the parties to be a term of the contract, the plaintiff's remedies will depend on whether it is regarded by the court as a condition or as a warranty (see above).

34. Construction of terms

In construing the terms of a contract the courts apply the following rules:

(a) Language used must be construed as far as possible in such a way as to give effect to the intentions of the parties.

(b) Words used must be presumed to have their normal literal meaning, unless the contrary is proved.

(c) Where there are two possible meanings, one legal and the other illegal, the legal meaning is to be preferred so as to render the contract enforceable (illegal contracts are void: see 61).

(d) The contract is to be construed most strongly against the party who drew it up (the *contra proferentem* rule: see **23** above).

(e) Contracts are to be construed according to their proper law, i.e. usually the law of the country in which they were made: see below.

(f) If the contract fails to express the undoubted intentions of the parties, the court will rectify it so as to make such intentions express: see below.

It should be noted that, in construing the terms of a written contract, the court cannot admit evidence of *(i)* the negotiations preceding contract, or *(ii)* the parties' intentions during negotation: *Prenn* v *Simmonds* (1971).

35. Collateral contracts

Where A and B enter into a contract the rights and duties arising will normally affect only A and B: see Privity of Contract below. Sometimes, however, if A was induced to enter into this contract by the representations of X, the court may imply a collateral contract between X and A, the consideration for which is A's agreement to enter into the contract with B.

> *Case law* X induced A to buy a car from B on hire-purchase. The hire-purchase contract was between A and B and X was not a party to it. The car was defective and injured A. X's statements as to the condition of the

car were found to be false. It was held that A had no remedy against B, by reason of an exemption clause. But there was an implied collateral contract between X and A, under which A promised to buy the car from B; X was liable in damages for his false statements: *Andrews* v *Hopkinson* (1956). See also *Evans* v *Merzario* (1976).

Under the Consumer Credit Act 1974, B would now be liable in contract for misrepresentations by his agent (see Chapter 7).

CONFLICT OF LAWS

There is an increasing tendency for mercantile contracts to be made between people in different countries and the question may then arise: which of several possible systems of law should the English court apply to resolve a dispute upon the contract? The position has been affected by the Contracts (Applicable Law) Act 1990. The major provisions of the Act, which implements the provisions of the Rome Convention, are as follows.

36. Freedom to choose

The convention, which is set out in full in a Schedule to the Act, allows the parties to make an express choice as to the proper law, or by implication. This latter will apply where the implication can be 'demonstrated with reasonable certainty by the terms of the contract or the circumstances of the case'. If, at its most basic, a contract is made between parties based in England, with the goods coming from one part of the country to another, then the contract will of course be subject to English law. Again, if a contract involves a party in this country buying goods from overseas, or from Scotland, and the contract specifies that English courts shall resolve any disputes arising between the parties, then the Act will operate to create the presumption that the English courts will apply English law.

37. Limitation on choice

This right to choose the proper law of the contract, though, is not unfettered. Thus, if a court is satisfied that, on a proper analysis, the contract really 'belongs' to a particular country, then the 'mandatory' rules (a term which awaits judicial explanation) of that country will prevail, regardless of what the contract might have said. Parties to a contract which had no connection with any country other than England, for instance, could not state that the contract was subject to the laws of France, at least so far as the 'mandatory' rules are concerned.

Then again, the law of the legal system chosen by the parties can be displaced by the law of the country in which the court deciding the matter is situated. This can occur if public policy in that country is in conflict with that of the chosen regime; or is in conflict with that country's mandatory rules.

38. Where no choice is made

Here the Act states that the contract will be governed by the law of the country 'with which it is most closely connected'. This, in fact, is in essence the test which has long been used in this country to determine the proper law of a contract. The presumption is that the contract is most closely connected 'with the country where the party who is to effect the performance which is characteristic of the contract has, at the time of the conclusion of the contract, his habitual residence or, in the case of a body corporate or unincorporated, its central administration. However, if the contract is entered into in the course of that party's trade or profession, that country shall be the country in which the principal place of business is situated or, where under the terms of the contract the performance is to be effected through a place of business other than the principal place of business, the country in which that other place of business is situated'.

The key phrase here is 'performance which is characteristic'. To give some guidance on its meaning, reference can be made to the Report on the Rome Convention reproduced in the *Official Journal* of the EC. It contains an extensive commentary on the convention and may, as the Act itself states, be considered by the UK courts when ascertaining the meaning or effect of any Convention provision. This is what the Report says: 'Identifying the characteristic performance of a contract obviously presents no difficulty in the case of unilateral contracts. By contrast, in bilateral (reciprocal) contracts whereby the parties undertake mutual reciprocal performance, the counter-performance by one of the parties in a modern economy usually takes the form of money. This is not, of course, the characteristic performance of the contract. It is the perfomance for which payment is due, i.e. depending on the type of contract, the delivery of the goods, the granting of the right to make use of an item of property, the provision of a service, transport, insurance, banking operations, security, etc. which usually constitutes the centre of gravity and the socio-economic function of the contractual obligation'. This would seem to suggest that a payment obligation can never be a performance which is 'characteristic' of the contract, a view with which some may differ. In any event, the Report is not binding, rather it is something to be taken into account when considering the meaning of the Convention.

FORM, CONSIDERATION AND CAPACITY

Generally a contract can be made in any form, but in exceptional cases the law lays down a particular requirement, e.g. that the contract shall be by deed.

All simple contracts must be supported by consideration, that is by some element of exchange which is measurable in money or money's worth, e.g. goods in return for cash, or services in return for wages or goods.

Generally, any person can make any sort of contract. Certain special classes of person, however, suffer from contractual incapacities of various kinds, e.g. minors.

39. Formal requirements

As a general rule, contracts are not required to be in any particular form. Most contracts can be made in any way chosen by the parties, that is to say, orally, by writing, by telephone, by fax, e-mail, telegram, or by deed, or by a combination of any of these. In the following special cases, however, the law requires that a particular form shall be adopted, usually to provide better evidence of the terms and so prevent disputes.

Contracts void unless made by deed

(a) Promises of gifts: *Rann* v *Hughes* (1778).

(b) Transfers of British ships or shares in British ships: Merchant Shipping Act 1995.

(c) Conditional bills of sale, as required by the Bills of Sale Acts 1879 and 1882.

(d) Certain documents creating or transferring estates or interests in land, e.g. conveyances of land, legal mortgages, and leases for more than three years: Law of Property (Miscellaneous Provisions) Act 1989.

Contracts requiring written form

(a) A bill of exchange: Bills of Exchange Act 1882, s. 3(1).

(b) Assignments of copyright: Copyright, Designs and Patents Act 1988, s. 90(3).

(c) Contracts of marine insurance: Marine Insurance Act 1906, ss 21–23. All policies of life insurance are in practice in writing, but there is no requirement that they should be.

(d) Transfers of shares in registered companies: Companies Act 1985, s. 183.

(e) Acknowledgement of statute-barred debts: Limitation Act 1980, s. 30.

(f) Articles of association of registered companies: Companies Act 1985, s. 7.

(g) Regulated consumer credit agreements: Consumer Credit Act 1974, s. 60 (see Chapter 7).

(h) Contracts of employment: Employment Rights Act 1996, s. 1 (see Chapter 2).

(i) Contracts for directory entries: Unsolicited Goods and Services Acts 1971–1975, s. 3 (see Chapter 8).

(j) Contracts for the sale or other disposition of an interest in land: Law of Property (Miscellaneous Provisions) Act 1989, s. 2. A contract to grant a put option in the form enjoyed by the defendant's predecessor is a disposition of an interest in land within the meaning of s. 2(1) of the Law of Property (Miscellaneous Provisions) Act 1989 which was required to be evidenced in writing, either in one document recording the agreement signed by both parties, or by an exchange of contracts. An exchange of letters in the particular case constituted no more than an offer and acceptance: *Commission for New Towns* v *Cooper* (1995), in correspondence, and did not record the express terms of the agreement already reached and, although the correspondence would have amounted to a sufficient note or memorandum under the Law of Property Act 1925, it did not constitute an exchange of contracts and therefore could not satisfy the more stringent requirements of s. 2 of the 1989 Act.

(k) Certain agreements under the Landlord and Tenant Act 1985, s. 4.

Company contracts

The rule that a company contract had to be by deed was abolished by the Corporate Bodies Contracts Act 1960. Companies can now make their contracts in whatever form is appropriate to private individuals. The Companies Act 1985 provides that a company contract can be made by a company in writing, under its common seal, or on behalf of the company by any person acting under its authority. A document is executed by a company affixing its common seal, but this is not essential: indeed a company might not have a seal. A document signed by the director and secretary, or by two directors, and expressed to be executed by the company, has the same effect as if executed under the common seal. A document executed by a company which makes it clear that it is intended to be a deed has effect, on delivery, as a deed.

Contracts of guarantee

Section 4 of the Statute of Frauds Act 1677 requires contracts of guarantee to be evidenced in writing. A guarantee is a contract to 'answer for the debt, default or miscarriage of another', that is a contract to discharge another's obligations if that other fails to do so himself, sometimes called a contract of secondary liability. These are to be contrasted with contracts of indemnity, which are promises to discharge another's obligation or to ensure that it is discharged, i.e. a contract in which the indemnifier accepts primary liability (indemnities do not need to be evidenced in writing).

A contract of guarantee can be made enforceable under s. 4 of the Statute of Frauds Act either by having a written agreement signed by the guarantor or his agent, or by having a note or memorandum of the agreement, which can itself be oral, signed by the guarantor or his agent. In the latter case, the intention or capacity of the person signing the memorandum is irrelevant since all that is necessary under s. 4 is the existence of a note or memorandum of a promise to answer for the debt, default or miscarriage of another person signed by the party to be charged: *Elpis Maritime Co Ltd* v *Marti Chartering Co Inc.* (1991).

It should be noted that guarantees do not need to be evidenced in writing if they are merely part of larger transactions, e.g. where, on his appointment, an agent guarantees to make good losses incurred by his employer if any of the clients introduced by the agent fail to pay their debts. Here, the guarantee is merely part of the contract of the agency and therefore the whole contract can be oral if so desired: *Eastwood* v *Kenyon* (1840).

Certain contracts of indemnity or guarantee given in relation to agreements within the Consumer Credit Act 1974 need to be in special form: s. 105 and the Consumer Credit (Guarantees and Indemnities) Regulations 1983, SI 1983/1556 (see Chapter 7).

40. Meaning of 'evidenced in writing'

The minimum of necessary written evidence suffices provided it contains all the material terms of the contract, i.e any signed note or memorandum of material terms on any scrap of paper.

The note or memorandum must contain the following:

(a) The signature of the 'party to be charged' or of his agent, i.e. the signature of the defendant in any action brought upon the contract. It need not be signed by the plaintiff in the action. Any writing by which the guarantor of a debt can be identified in a memorandum of the guarantee, and which shows an intention to adopt the guarantee, suffices as a signature for the purposes of s. 4 of the Statute of Frauds Act: *Decouvreur* v *Jordan* (1987).

(b) All material terms of the contract, i.e.

   (*i*) names of the parties or sufficient identification

   (*ii*) description of the subject matter, e.g. the address of a house being sold

   (*iii*) the price or other consideration.

It should be noted that, although, like other simple contracts, guarantees must be supported by consideration, the consideration does not need to be expressly stated in the memorandum of guarantee: Mercantile Law Amendment Act 1856.

When and how made

The note or memorandum can be made at any time after the contract is agreed, providing it is made (and signed by the defendant) before the contract is disputed in court. It may consist of several documents, provided there is sufficient evidence to connect them beyond reasonable doubt, e.g. a letter headed 'Dear Sir' might be linked to the envelope which contained it, so identifying the recipient: *Long* v *Millar* (1879).

Effect of non-compliance

If a contract required to be evidenced in writing is not so evidenced, it is unenforceable. Therefore, although it may be perfectly lawful, if one party breaks the contract, the other cannot sue him for damages for breach of contract in the normal way, although he would be entitled to keep any deposit he had obtained. The parties retain all other rights, except action in the courts. Thus, in an oral contract for the sale of land which fails through the fault of the purchaser, the vendor would be entitled to retain a deposit the purchaser had put down, and the court would not assist the purchaser to recover it: *Monickendam* v *Leanse* (1923).

An oral contract for the transfer of any estate or interest in land is invalid: Law of Property (Miscellaneous Provisions) Act 1989. Under the old law, the doctrine of part performance was available where the contract was oral, if A had performed his part of the contract, but B then refused to perform his part. The provisions of the 1989 Act now preclude the use of the doctrine.

41. Valuable consideration

The courts will not enforce a simple contract unless it is supported by valuable consideration, which is therefore an essential element in most contracts.

Meaning of 'valuable consideration'

This has been defined as 'the price for which a promise is bought'. Consideration itself means 'some right, interest, profit, or benefit accruing to one party or some forbearance, detriment, loss of responsibility given, suffered or undertaken by the other': *Currie* v *Misa* (1875).

Consideration therefore means the element of exchange in a bargain, and in order to satisfy the requirements of English law it must be valuable consideration, i.e. something which is capable of being valued in terms of money or money's worth, however slight. It may take the form of money, goods, services, a promise to forbear from suing the promisee, and many other forms.

Kinds of consideration

(a) *Executory consideration*, i.e. where the consideration consists of a promise to do something in the future (such as to render a service at a future date).

(b) *Executed consideration*, i.e. where the act constituting the consideration is wholly performed. Thus if X pays a shopkeeper now for goods which are promised to be delivered later, X has executed his consideration, but the shopkeeper is giving executory consideration, i.e. a promise to be executed in the future.

(c) *Past consideration*, i.e. where one party agrees to reward someone for something the latter has already done. Past consideration, however, has no effect.

> *Case law* A party brought an action on an alleged contract, stating that 'in consideration that the plaintiff at the request of the defendant had bought of the defendant a certain horse at and for a certain price, the defendant promised the plaintiff that the said horse was sound and free from vice'. The plaintiff sued for breach of this promise. The court ruled that the express promise was made after the sale was over and unsupported by any fresh consideration. The plaintiff could only show 'past' consideration and the action therefore failed: *Roscorla* v *Thomas* (1842).

42. Rules relating to consideration

Every simple contract must be supported by valuable consideration, otherwise it is normally void. An exception exists, however, in the case of a gratuitous bailment. A bailment arises where goods are delivered to a person for some limited purpose or period, and usually for reward, such as a rental payment. It seems, though, that even an entirely gratuitous bailment can give rise to an enforceable contract: *Bainbridge* v *Firmstone* (1838).

Legality of consideration

The consideration must be legal, e.g. not some illegal act, such as paying someone to commit a crime. If the consideration is illegal, the contract is void.

Consideration must move from the promisee

This means that a person seeking to enforce a simple contract in court must prove that he himself has given consideration in return for the promise he is seeking to enforce.

> *Case law* D had supplied goods to a wholesaler, X, on condition that any retailer to whom X resold the goods should promise X not to sell them to the public without fulfilling stated conditions. X supplied goods to S upon this condition, nevertheless S sold them in breach of those conditions. It was held that there was a contract between D and X, and a contract between X and S, but none between D and S. D therefore could not obtain damages from S. The main reason for this decision was the fact that D could not show that he himself had given any consideration for S's promise to X: *Dunlop Pneumatic Tyre Co* v *Selfridges Ltd* (1915) (affirmed in *Scruttons Ltd* v *Midland Silicones Ltd* (1962)).

It is also the case that valuable consideration must be something more than the promisee is already bound to do for the promisor. This means that the person seeking to enforce the promise must show that he himself has undertaken some obligation to the promisor beyond what he is already bound to do either as part of his legal duty as a citizen, or as part of a private contractual duty owed to the promisor.

> *Case law* If a seaman deserts his ship, thus breaking his contract, and is induced to return to duty by the promise of extra wages, he cannot later sue for the extra wages since he has only done what he was already contracted: *Stilk* v *Myrick* (1809).

It has been held, however, that performance by A of an existing duty owed to B will suffice to support a promise by C to A. Thus where A was engaged to marry B, and C promised A a sum of money to carry out this promise to B, it was held that A could sue C for the money as soon as he had performed his promise and married B: *Shadwell* v *Shadwell* (1860).

In contrast, where one party to a contract agreed, in the absence of economic duress or fraud, to make a payment to the other party to the contract over and above the contract price in order to secure completion of the contract by the other party on time, and thereby obtained a benefit in that a penalty clause was avoided, it was held that the obtaining of that benefit could amount to consideration for payment of the additional sum: *Williams* v *Roffey Bros & Nicholls (Contractors)* Ltd (1990).

The courts have confirmed that a promise to perform an existing obligation can amount to good consideration so long as there were practical benefits to the promisee, but this is confined to cases where the obligation involved a supply of goods or services: it is contrary to precedent to hold that this principle can be extended to 'an obligation to make a payment', in this case tax and national insurance: *re Selectmove Ltd* (1995).

Consideration must be real

This means that consideration must not be vague, indefinite, or illusory, e.g. a son's vague promise to 'stop being a nuisance' to his father: *White* v *Bluett* (1853).

Although the consideration must be real, it need not be adequate. It is up to the parties to fix their own prices, and providing there is some definite valuable consideration, the court will not set a contract aside merely because the price is inadequate. If, though, the consideration is ridiculously inadequate, this may be prima facie evidence of misrepresentation or coercion (see below).

> *Case law* A bought a guarantee contract from B which later turned out to be unenforceable. It was held that A had got what he wanted and could not later rescind the contract merely because it turned out to be worth less than he thought: *Haigh* v *Brooks* (1839).

Consideration must not be past

This means that a a promise made in return for some past service is unenforceable, as where, having bought a horse, the purchaser promised to give the seller an extra sum because of his satisfaction with the purchase. It was held that the promise was unenforceable since it related to a past sale, and the purchaser was therefore receiving no new benefit as consideration for his new promise: *Roscorla* v *Thomas* (1842).

Past consideration can, exceptionally, suffice in certain cases:

> (*i*) To revive a statute-barred claim, a mere written acknowledgment is enough without any fresh consideration: Limitation Act 1980 (for further detail on limitation of actions, see below).
>
> (*ii*) A bill of exchange can be supported by any antecedent debt or liability: Bill of Exchange Act 1882, s. 27.

(iii) Where the past consideration was rendered in response to an earlier request by the person who subsequently promises to pay for the service rendered. This is the so-called rule in *Lampleigh* v *Braithwaite* (1615). In this case, the promisor's request is held to imply a promise to pay a reasonable sum later and the subsequent promise to pay merely fixes the sum: *Stewart* v *Casey* (1892).

Case law A asked B to use his influence to obtain a royal pardon for A, who had committed a crime. B did as he was asked, and later, in consideration of this past service, A promised to pay B £100. It was held that B could enforce payment: *Lampleigh* v *Braithwaite* (1615).

Payment of a smaller sum will not discharge a liability to pay a larger sum. This is the rule in *Foakes* v *Beer* (1884). Thus if A owes B £100 and B agrees to accept £50 in complete discharge of the debt, there is nothing to stop B later changing his mind and suing for the remaining £50.

Case law The plaintiff and defendant were engaged in a transaction involving the sale of a knitting machine. The parties met and agreed that a commission should be paid. They later disagreed whether the commission should be 10 per cent as the plaintiff claimed, or 5 per cent as the defendant claimed. The parties met again, and the plaintiff accepted 5 per cent in 'full and final settlement'. The court ruled that, since there was no consideration for the plaintiff's agreement to accept only 5 per cent commission, and since there was no accord between the parties when the reduced commission was negotiated, it would not be inequitable to allow the plaintiff to receive the remaining 5 per cent: *Tiney Engineering Ltd* v *Amods Knitting Machinery Ltd* (1986).

It is, however, possible for payment of the smaller sum to suffice if it is paid in a form or manner not originally envisaged as where the smaller sum is paid earlier than the debt was due, or where a money debt is settled in goods, or is paid by handing over 'a horse, hawk, or robe': *Pinnel's Case* (1602).

It is, however, important to note that the creditor's acceptance of the smaller sum must be voluntary. Thus where a debtor put pressure on his creditor to accept a smaller sum, it was held that the acceptance was not binding: *D & C Builders Ltd* v *Rees* (1966). A further exception arises where the creditor promises to accept a smaller sum intending his position to be relied upon and the debtor alters his financial position in reliance on the promise. In such a case, the creditor may be estopped from going back on his promise, even though it was unsupported by consideration.

Case law A leased property to B at a rent of £2500 p.a. but promised to accept half this sum during the war years, and B relied on this promise, making no attempt to earn the money necessary to pay the full rent. If

121

later A went back on his promise and sued for the full rental, the court would exercise its equitable discretion and estop A from retracting his promise: *The High Trees Case (Central London Property Trust* v *High Trees House* (1947)).

This is an application of the principle of equitable estoppel, whereby a person may be prevented from denying any promise unconscionably even though it was unsupported by consideration. The *High Trees* rule can, however, only be raised as a defence, and not as a cause of action by the debtor. Where a creditor retracted his promise to accept a smaller sum and forced the debtor to pay him the full amount, the debtor could not use the *High Trees* rule as the basis of an action to recover the extra money paid: *Combe* v *Combe* (1951). It has also been held that, where a company failed to honour a promise to pay tax as it fell due, it was not inequitable or unfair for the Revenue to demand payment of all arrears, nor, in the light of further late payments by the company, was it unfair or inequitable to serve a statutory demand under the Insolvency Act 1986 and present a winding up petition to enforce the debt: *re Selectmove Ltd* (1995).

43. Contractual capacity

The general rule is that all persons have full capacity to make binding contracts, but there are exceptions.

Aliens

Aliens residing in countries at war with Britain are classed as enemy aliens, whatever their nationality. They cannot sue in British courts during wartime, but can be sued; and if sued they can defend the action, appeal, and lodge counter-claims in the normal way, either personally or through agents: *Porter* v *Freudenberg* (1915).

Foreign sovereigns and diplomats

These have diplomatic immunity and cannot be sued in British courts, unless they voluntarily submit to the jurisdiction: Diplomatic Privileges Act 1964. It should be noted that diplomatic immunity does not arise until the diplomat's appointment has been accepted by the Government: *R* v *Pentonville Prison Governor, ex parte Teja* (1971).

The State Immunity Act 1978 provides that there is no immunity in respect of commercial contracts, or contracts to be performed wholly or partly in this country.

Married women

They now have full contractual capacity, can sue or be sued in their own names and can be bankrupted for their debts: Law Reform (Married Women and Tortfeasors) Act 1935.

Mental patients and drunkards

Contracts made by such parties are voidable, if they were so drunk or mentally unbalanced as not to understand what the contract was about, and the other party was aware of this: *Imperial Loan Co* v *Stone* (1892). Such voidable contracts can be ratified during lucid or sober intervals.

The Sale of Goods Act 1979, s. 2, lays down that lunatics, drunkards, and minors are bound to pay a reasonable price for necessaries (see further Minors below).

Corporations

A corporation is an artificial personalty recognised by the law. Consequently it can only contract through human agents. Under the *ultra vires* doctrine a statutory or registered corporation could only contract validly within the powers conferred upon it. However, the Companies Act 1989 has effectively abolished this doctrine, so any question of whether or not a company has acted beyond its powers in making a contract is now purely one for its internal administration.

CONTRACTS BY MINORS

44. Capacity of minors

The Family Law Reform Act 1969 defines a minor as one who has not reached the age of 18. Much of the old law on the binding nature of contracts by minors was considerably affected by the Minors Contracts Act 1987.

The position is that contracts are not generally binding on minors. The basic principle is that contracts made by a minor with an adult are binding on the latter only. The contract will bind the minor only if, after reaching his majority, he ratifies the contract.

Although a contract may not bind a minor, this does not mean that it is void. Money paid or property transferred under the contract can be recovered by the minor only if he can show that there has been a total failure of consideration. For instance, a minor's action to have her name removed from a register of shareholders succeeded but she was not allowed to recover money already paid since she had got the thing bargained for: *Steinberg* v *Scala Ltd* (1923).

45. Contracts for necessaries

The principal exception to the common law rule that a contract does not bind a minor is where that contract is for 'necessaries'. Section 3 of the Sale of Goods Act 1979 states that 'where necessaries are sold and delivered to a minor ... he must pay a reasonable price for them'. The section defines 'necessaries as goods suitable to the condition in life of the minor ... and to his actual requirements at the time of sale and delivery'.

A widow who was a minor was held liable to an undertaker for work in connection with the funeral of her late husband: *Chapple* v *Cooper* (1844). However, if the minor has more than enough of the articles in question, then more cannot be necessary. An undergraduate was not liable to pay for clothing, including eleven fancy waistcoats, when his father gave evidence that his son was already amply supplied with clothes: *Nash* v *Inman* (1908). It is to be noted that the minor is liable to pay for necessaries, not at the agreed price, but whatever amounts to a 'reasonable' price.

46. Beneficial contracts of service

If a service contract entered into by a minor is to his benefit, then it is binding. Where a minor entered into a contract of employment as a railway porter, he was required to forgo claims under current legislation in return for joining an insurance scheme. Although that particular scheme might not have been to his benefit, the contract as a whole was, and so it was binding: *Clements* v *L&NWR* (1894).

Other examples of contracts held to be binding are: *(a)* a contract by a professional boxer, a minor, to observe the rules of the sport: *Doyle* v *White City Stadium* (1935); and *(b)* a contract to write a book and assign the copyright: *Chaplin* v *Leslie Frewin* (1966).

47. Restitution

The Minors Contracts Act 1987 affords a limited measure of redress to the adult who may otherwise find that the minor may obtain property without having to pay. The Act provides that where a contract is unenforceable against a defendant because he was a minor when it was made, the court may 'if it is just and equitable to do so, require the defendant to transfer to the plaintiff any property acquired by the defendant under the contract, or any property representing it'. There is in addition the equitable doctrine of restitution to allow recovery of property from a minor in relation to property obtained by deception: *Leslie* v *Sheill* (1914).

48. Guarantees of minors' contracts

Section 2 of the 1987 Act provides that a guarantee of a minor's contract is not unenforceable merely because he is a minor. Before the Act, the guarantee would be a nullity since there was in effect nothing to guarantee.

VOID, VOIDABLE AND ILLEGAL CONTRACTS

This category includes contracts invalidated because they rest upon some fundamental mistake of fact (void), contracts induced by misrepresentation or coercion (voidable), and contracts which are contrary to some statute or to common law (void and illegal).

49. Mistake

Effect of mistake

The general common law rule is that mistake made by one or both parties in making a contract has no effect on the validity of the contract, e.g. where a person pays an excessive price for goods under a mistake as to their true value: *Leaf* v *International Galleries* (1950). Again, if a mistake is to have any effect, it exists at or before the time when the contract was made. Thus, there is no relevant mistake where parties to a contract for the sale of a building believe it is not listed if the listing occurs after they have made their contract: *Amalgamated Investment and Property Co Ltd* v *John Walker & Sons Ltd* (1976).

However, mistake can have an effect on the contract and, though it is often difficult to deduce consistent principles from the cases, the effects of mistake are generally dealt with as below.

1. Common mistake

Common mistake as to existence of subject-matter applies when, unknown to both parties, the subject-matter has been destroyed before the contract is made. Instances include: the sale of a life insurance policy on the life of a person who, unknown to purchaser or seller, is already dead: *Scott* v *Coulson* (1903): the sale of goods which, unknown to the contractors, have already been destroyed: *Couturier* v *Hastie* (1856), and Sale of Goods Act 1979, s. 6.

> *Case law* L paid a senior employee £50,000 compensation for loss of office, when dismissing him before his contract had expired. Later L discovered that the employee had committed breaches of duty which would have entitled L to dismiss him without compensation. It was held

that L could not recover the money on discovering the truth, since the House of Lords considered that the mistake related only to the quality of what was purchased, namely release from the contract of employment: *Bell* v *Lever Bros* (1932).

Case law L bought from C a painting which both mistakenly believed to be by Constable and of great value. Later, L discovered it was by an unknown artist and comparatively worthless. It was held that L could not avoid the contract, as his mistake related only to the quality of the subject-matter of the contract: *Leaf* v *International Galleries* (1950).

Case law A party concluded a sale and leaseback transaction with the plaintiff in respect of four machines which were defined by serial numbers. The obligations assumed by him as lessee of the machines were subsequently guaranteed by the defendant bank. The lessee paid the first rental but subsequently defaulted. It was then discovered that the machines did not exist. The plaintiff then sued on the contract of guarantee. The defendant contended that it was not liable on the guarantee, either because it was an express or implied condition precedent to the guarantee that the machines existed, or because the guarantee was void because of common mistake. The Commercial Court held that, given that the terms of the guarantee referred to the leasing of four identified machines and stipulated that any substitution of those machines could only be done with the consent of the guarantor, the only sensible construction was that the guarantee was subject to a condition precedent that there was a lease in respect of existing machines. Alternatively, there was an implied condition precedent to the guarantee that the machines existed, having regard both to the fact that both parties were informed that the machines existed and to the express terms of the guarantee. The plaintiff's claim was dismissed. The court said that, except where a party seeking to rely on a mistake has no reasonable ground for his belief, a contract will be void for common mistake where both parties share the same mistake as to facts existing at the time the contract is made and the mistake renders the subject-matter of the contract essentially and radically different from the subject-matter which the parties believed to exist: *Associated Japanese Bank (International) Ltd* v *Credit du Nord SA* (1988). See also *Citibank NA* v *Brown Shipley* (1991).

It should be noted that mistakes as to the quality of the subject-matter generally have no effect. The maxim of English law is: buyer beware. If a person mistakenly pays an unduly high price for something, that person has only himself to blame for the bad bargain.

126

2. Mutual mistake

Where the parties misunderstand each other as to the terms of the offer, the contract will be void if the mistake is sufficiently fundamental. Here there is no real concurrence of offer and acceptance, since the offeree is accepting on a mistaken understanding of what the offeror intended.

> *Case law* A and B contracted to ship a cargo on The Peerless from Bombay. Unknown to either party there were two ships of the same name, and both were at Bombay and were due to sail on different dates. A had in mind one of the two ships, and B had in mind the other. It was held that the the the contract was void: *Raffles* v *Wichelhaus* (1864).

Mistake as to the identity of the subject-matter can also lead to the contract being declared void.

> *Case law* At an auction X, misled by the catalogue, bid an absurdly high price for some tow (thinking it was hemp) and the auctioneer accepted the bid thinking that X was merely mistaken as to the value of tow. It was held that the contract was void: *Scriven* v *Hindley* (1913).

3. Unilateral mistake

Where there has been a unilateral mistake as to the identity of the person contracted with, the mistake will only operate to void the contract where the identity of the person contracted with is of fundamental importance; and this is made clear by the party mistaken before or at the time of contracting, so that the other party knows of the mistake.

Where the parties contracted 'face to face' the presumption is that there can be no mistake as to identity: *Lewis* v *Averay* (1973). This presumption may be rebutted by clear evidence to the contrary: *Ingram* v *Little* (1960).

> *Case law* X entered a jewellers and offered to buy goods. His offer was accepted, and he then offered to pay by cheque. The jeweller accepted the cheque, but said delivery would be delayed until the cheque was cleared. X then said he was a well-known person and asked to take some of the jewels immediately. Deceived as to his identity, the jeweller agreed. X took the goods and sold them to a pawnbroker, and the cheque proved worthless. It was held that the contract was made before the identity became important, therefore it was not void on the ground of mistake: *Phillips* v *Brooks* (1919). The contract was, however, almost certainly void on the ground of misrepresentation.

> *Case law* L advertised his car for sale and B answered, describing himself as a well-known film-star. L was impressed and accepted B's cheque after B had produced a film-studio admission card as proof of identity. B

then took the car and sold it to A, a *bona fide* purchaser. When L discovered the fraud he sued A to recover the car. It was held that L had intended to contract with the man he met 'face to face' and the contract was therefore not void for mistake, but merely voidable for misrepresentation: *Lewis* v *Averay* (1973).

4. Mistake as to nature of document

Generally a person who signs a contract is bound by it, even if he has not read it: *L'Estrange* v *Graucob* (1934). A person, however, who signs a document under a fundamental mistake as to its nature may have it avoided. For example, A might be induced to sign a negotiable instrument believing it is merely a guarantee: *Foster* v *Mackinnon* (1869). It is essential for the mistake to relate to the fundamental legal nature of the document, and not merely to its contents.

> *Case law* A, who was senile, was persuaded to sign a bill of exchange under the misapprehension that it was a guarantee. It was held that the bill was void for mistake: *Foster* v *Mackinnon* (1869).

> *Case law* A executed a transfer of land under a misapprehension as to its contents and effect. It was held that the contract was not void. The mistake was not sufficiently fundamental: *Howatson* v *Webb* (1907).

> *Case law* G, an elderly lady, signed without reading a document which L informed her was a gift transferring her house to her nephew P. In fact it was a transfer on sale to L for £3000. G sought to have the sale annulled. It was held that she failed on the facts of the case because: the document was not radically different in type from what she thought she was signing; she was careless; and she had failed in her evidence to show that she would not have signed had she known the true facts: *Saunders* v *Anglia Building Society* (1971).

> *Case law* An individual signed a form in blank addressed to a finance house, believing it to be a hire-purchase agreement. It was, in fact, a loan agreement. It was held that a binding contract existed between the signatory and the finance house. The signatory was under a duty of care to ensure that the completed document represented his true intention. He had not shown he had acted carefully, so he was bound by his signature: *United DominionsTrust* v *Western* (1975).

5. Mistake in equity

The rules relating to mistake stated above are those rules developed by the courts of common law. Certain rules have also been developed by the courts of equity which fused with the courts of common law under the provisions of the Judicature Acts 1873–1875. The rules of equity prevail over the rules of the common law, where they conflict, and certain equitable principles have been established to mitigate some of the harsher aspects of the common law. Accordingly, equity will thus intervene for the following purposes:

(a) *To rectify, or amend, a written instrument containing patent errors of expression.*

Case law On 15 August 1986 the defendant's predecessor in title (EHL), as tenant of commercial premises underlet by the plaintiff's predecessor, made four agreements by deed with the underlessor. The deeds comprised: *(i)* a building works deed, by which the plaintiff was to undertake certain remedial work; *(ii)* a put option deed, by which the tenant agreed to take an assignment of option relating to the lease of larger premises; (iii) an option relating to the lease of larger premises; and *(iv)* a side land option, by which the plaintiff granted an option to acquire the lease of an adjacent site. Both the put option and the larger premises option were expressed to be personal to EHL. The defendant acquired the unexpired residue of the terms of the underlease by assignment in 1988. The business however made losses and in 1990 the defendant's parent company analysed the costs of closing the business, including the penalty payable on surrender of the lease. It decided instead to try to obtain the put option previously enjoyed by EHL from the plaintiff without revealing its intention to use the option to enable it to reduce its liquidation costs by avoiding the penalty payment for termination of the lease. The parties met on 11 January 1991 with no formal agenda; the defendant did not mention the put option at all but indicated that, as part of a comprehensive settlement, it expected to obtain the rights previously enjoyed by EHL, and specifically mentioned the side land option.

A provisional agreement was reached at the meeting under which the defendant agreed to make a payment to settle the building works issues and the plaintiff agreed to treat the defendant 'in all respects as having the same rights and benefits under the original documentation' as its predecessor had had and to grant to the defendant a fresh side land option. The plaintiff later confirmed the agreement (as set out in the defendant's letter of 11 January 1991) and annexed a copy of the recommendation which it had sent to its executive committee for approval. The executive committee approved the agreement and on 16 January 1991 the defendant sought a further letter confirming the accuracy of the 11 January letter, which the plaintiff duly gave. As soon as agreement had been reached, the defendant wrote to the plaintiff with notice of its intention to exercise the put option in August 1991 so as to require the plaintiff to take an assignment of the underlease. The plaintiff denied that it had granted a put option and sought, *inter alia*, rectification of the agreement.

The judge held *(i)* that on the true construction of the agreement the plaintiff had granted a put option to the defendant, *(ii)* that the plaintiff was not entitled to rectification of the agreement on the ground of unilateral mistake, since the defendant's representatives did not have actual knowledge of the mistake, and that *(iii)* the plaintiff's representatives had authority to agree to the grant of the put option, but *(iv)* that the two letters of 16 January 1991 confirming the agreement were insufficient to satisfy the requirements of s. 2 of the Law of Property (Miscellaneous Provisions) Act 1989 that contracts for the sale or disposition of an interest in land should be in writing. He accordingly concluded that there was no enforceable agreement to grant the put option. The defendant appealed from the judge's decision on the fourth issue, and the plaintiff cross-appealed against his decisions on the first, second and third issues.

It was held that the cross-appeal would be allowed and the appeal would be dismissed for the following reasons. The contract contained in the letters of 16 January 1991 (which referred to the letter of 11 January) was to be construed against the factual context in which it was made and any ambiguity in the wording was to be construed both *contra proferentem* the defendant and in the light of the agenda for discussion at the meeting. It was clear from the correspondence and dealings between the parties prior to the meeting of 11 January that the topics for discussion at the meeting did not include the put option but were limited to the specific matters in dispute, being the remedial work still to be carried out and payment for extra building work carried out under the building works deed, together with the extension of the side land option. Accordingly, when construed in its proper context, the reference in the letter of 11 January to the plaintiff treating the defendant in all respects as having the same rights and benefits under the original documentation as EHL could not be extended to include the grant of a put option. In addition, para 2 of that letter was deliberately ambiguous and, on any fair construction, the references to the defendant continuing to have all the rights previously granted to its predecessor related only to the rights under the building works deed and the side land option and did not include the put option. It followed that, on its true construction, the agreement did not grant a put option to the defendant.

Rectification could be granted on the basis of unconscionable conduct in circumstances where one of the parties to a contract intended the other to be mistaken as to the terms of their agreement and diverted his attention from discovering the mistake by making false and misleading statements, with the result that he in fact made the very mistake intended, notwithstanding that the former did not actually know but merely suspected that the latter was mistaken and that it could not be shown that the mistake was induced by any misrepresentation. In the absence of any express misrepresentation, where a false representation was made for the purpose of inducing the other party to adopt a certain course of conduct and the representation was such as to influence a person behaving reasonably to adopt that course of conduct, that representation did have that effect. On the facts, it was clear *(a)* that the defendant had actual knowledge of the plaintiff's mistake in the sense that it had wilfully shut its eyes to the obvious or wilfully and recklessly failed to make such inquiries as an honest and reasonable man would have made, *(b)* that, although there was no express misrepresentation, the references to the side land option were made for the purpose of concealing from the plaintiff's representatives the fact that the language used was wide enough to cover the put option and *(c)* that the conduct of the defendant's representatives in raising the side land issue was dishonest and intended to deceive. It followed that, if the contract had been construed to include the grant of the put option, equity required that the contract be rectified on the basis of the defendant's unconscionable conduct: *Commission for New Towns* v *Cooper* (1995).

(b) *To refuse to order specific performance of a contract against a defendant who is labouring under a mistake such that it would be grossly unjust to compel him to perform his contract*, as where A, by a slip of the pen, writes offering to sell land to B for '£1250' when he meant to write '£2250'. Here if B tries to enforce a contract at the lower price, equity will refuse to help him and will protect A against the consequence of his mistake: *Webster* v *Cecil* (1861).

(c) *To set aside an agreement on terms fair to all parties, where common law will not declare it void: Solle* v *Butcher* (1949).

Case law The sale of a house was held voidable on grounds of common mistake as to value, which was not sufficient to render the contract void at law: *Grist* v *Bailey* (1966).

This discretionary power to rescind a contract operates only if: the contract is not void at common law and is merely voidable in equity: *Lewis* v *Averay* (1973); there is a fundamental mistake common to both parties; and the party seeking rescission is not at fault.

50. Rectification

Where a written contract does not accurately express the intentions of the parties, the court will amend or rectify it to make it express the true intentions. The party seeking rectification must prove that: the mistake to be rectified lies only in the words used; there is a complete and final contract between the parties; there is clear oral or written evidence of the true intention of the parties; and the mistake is common to both parties: *Craddock Bros* v *Hunt* (1923).

51. Misrepresentation and fraud

In English law a person is generally under no duty to disclose all facts in his possession to the other contracting party. Each must protect his own interests unaided. Keeping silent therefore is generally not actionable, even though it causes damage to the other party.

> *Case law* H sold pigs 'with all faults' to W, knowing that they had swine fever and that W was unaware of this. It was held that W could not have the contract set aside: *Ward* v *Hobbs* (1878).

Where, however, one party makes a positive false statement which deceives the other, this may amount to misrepresentation which renders the contract voidable at the option of the party misled. The deceived party may also be entitled to damages: for deceit, if he can prove fraud, or, under the provisions of s. 2(1) of the Misrepresentation Act 1967, for negligent misrepresentation, unless the defendant can show that he had reasonable grounds for believing that what he said was true.

An actionable misrepresentation consists of a false statement of material fact, made by a party to the contract or his agent and which induces the other party to enter into the contract.

Misleading conduct may also amount to misrepresentation if it presents a misleading picture about material facts and induces another to enter into a contract.

For a misrepresentation to be actionable, the particular statement must be of fact, not of law or opinion, although an opinion expressed by a person who might be expected to know the facts, such as a technical expert when speaking on his subject, may amount to a statement of fact: *Brown* v *Raphael* (1958). An actionable misrepresentation must also be of material importance to the transaction. For example, in the sale of a car, a statement that the car is in good working order: whereas a representation relating to trivial matters, such as the condition of the windscreen wipers, would not amount to an actionable misrepresentation. It is also necessary that the misrepresentation complained of must have been made by the party to the contract or his agent. Thus where A invests money in a company in reliance on a false statement by the company's auditor in the company's balance sheet, A cannot sue the company for misrepresentation because the contract is between him and the company, and the auditor is not an agent for the company for the purpose of making statements to lure investors: *Candler* v *Crane Christmas* (1951). It is, however, possible that an action might lie against the auditor for the tort of negligence: *Hedley Byrne & Co* v *Heller & Partners Ltd* (1964). It is also the case that the misrepresentation in question must have been relied upon, and induced the other party to enter into the contract.

> *Case law* A sold a broken gun to B and patched the barrel with clay to conceal the crack. B did not examine the gun and therefore was not deceived by the patch. It was held that the misrepresentation was not actionable, since it had no effect on B: *Horsfall* v *Thomas* (1862).

A further condition for an actionable misrepresentation is that it must be by positive words or conduct, not by mere silence unless the silence amounts to active concealment of facts, or where silence about some facts puts those revealed into a false and deceptive light.

> *Case law* A company's prospectus showed that it had paid dividends for several years, without disclosing that these had been paid out of reserves as the company was trading at a loss. It was held that the omission was deceptive and amounted to misrepresentation: *R* v *Kylsant* (1932).

As a final point, a statement which was true when made, but which subsequently becomes false before the contract is made, must be corrected.

> *Case law* R arranged to sell a business to Y and estimated annual profits at £2000. By the time the sale was completed the profits had fallen considerably. It was held that A's failure to disclose the change amounted to an actionable misrepresentation: *With* v *O'Flanagan* (1936).

52. Innocent misrepresentation

If a person makes a misrepresentation believing what he says is true he commits innocent misrepresentation, provided he had reasonable grounds for his belief. The party misled may affirm the contract and treat it as binding or may rescind the contract by notifying the other. He may also sue for damages under the Misrepresentation Act 1967. If he obtains damages under the Act, he is prohibited from rescinding the agreement. Prior to the Act, the victim of an innocent misrepresentation was restricted to recovering those costs and expenses directly imposed by the contract he had entered into on the basis of such misrepresentation: *Whittington* v *Seale-Hayne* (1900).

53. Negligent misrepresentation

Where a misrepresentation was made negligently, the innocent party can sue either at common law, under the principles established in *Hedley Byrne v Heller & Partners Ltd* (1964) or under the 1967 Act. It is easier to bring proceedings under the Act since, once an allegation of negligence is made, the defendant can only escape liability for it if he can show that he had reasonable grounds for believing what he said was true at the time the contract was made. In *Banque Financière* v *Westgate Insurance* (1988), the court pointed out that the Act uses the words 'where a misrepresentation has been made...'. It therefore held that where a failure to disclose had been made in circumstances where disclosure should have been made (see below), no action could lie under the Act since no representation had been made. The court said that if it had been the intention of the legislature that a mere failure to discharge the duty of disclosure was to be treated as the 'making' of a representation within the meaning of the 1967 Act, it would have said so.

Damages for negligent misrepresentation are to be assessed on the basis of the measure of damages in tort for fraudulent misrepresentation, with the result that the innocent party is entitled to recover any loss which flowed from the misrepresentation, even if the loss could not have been foreseen: *Royscott Trust Ltd* v *Rogerson* (1991). It has been held that, where an article bought as a result of a misrepresentation could have been sold immediately after the sale for the price paid, but, by the time the misrepresentation has been discovered, its value had fallen by reason of a defect which by then had become apparent, the appropriate measure of damages could be the difference between the purchase price and its value at the time the misrepresentation was discovered, and not the difference between the purchase price and its value at the time of purchase, provided that the article purchased was altogether different from that which had been expected. The case itself concerned a horse whose pedigree had been misrepresented, and this was held to be the purchase of something 'altogether different': *Naughton* v *O'Callaghan* (1990).

54. Fraudulent misrepresentation

The long-accepted definition of a fraudulent misrepresentation is that it is an 'untrue statement made knowingly, or without belief in its truth, or recklessly, careless whether it be true or false': *Derry* v *Peek* (1889). In order to establish fraudulent misrepresentation, it has to be shown that any recklessness in making a false representation is such as to amount to a disregard of the truth to the extent that it should be regarded as fraudulent: *Witter Ltd* v *TBP Industries* (1996).

Thus if the maker believes that his representation is true, he cannot be guilty of fraud, even if he was negligent or unreasonable in saying what he did: *Akerheim* v *De Mare* (1959). (He may, however, be liable for damages for the tort of negligence: *Hedley Byrne & Co* v *Heller & Partners Ltd* (1964) and for negligent misrepresentation.)

Remedies for fraudulent misrepresentation

The plaintiff may sue for damages for the tort of deceit or fraud. Damages for deceit or fraudulent misrepresentation are awarded on the basis that the plaintiff is to be compensated for all the loss he has suffered, so far as money can do it: *Doyle* v *Olby* (1969); *Royscott Trust* v *Rogerson* (1991); *East* v *Maurer* (1991).

> *Case law* On 21 July 1989 the plaintiff company, SNC, purchased a parcel of ordinary shares in company P at a price of 82.25p per share, totalling over £23m. The first defendant company, SVAM, sold the shares to SNC as broker on behalf of the second defendant company, C, to which they had been charged by way of security. In September 1989 there was a serious decline in the market price of P shares as a result of a fraud (which was unrelated to the transaction involving the sale of shares to SNC) perpetrated on P which dramatically reduced the company's net worth. SNC eventually sold its holding of P shares at a significant loss and subsequently issued proceedings against SVAM, claiming that it had been induced to purchase the shares by one or more fraudulent misrepresentations made on behalf of C. The judge found that two of the representations had been made in circumstances which entitled SNC to recover damages equivalent to the difference between the price paid and the true value of the shares on 21 July, that, by reason of the unconnected and then undiscovered fraud, the value of each share on the date of sale was only 44p and, further, that it was on the basis of that value and not the price at which the shares would have changed hands in the market that SNC was entitled to recover. The judge awarded SNC damages of £10,764,005, being the difference between the purchase price (£23,146,321) and the value of the shares at 44p each (£12,382,226). C appealed, contending *inter alia* that SNC was only entitled to recover on the basis of the price at which the shares would have changed hands, being 82.25p or at all events not less than 78p each, rather than the price which would have been paid if the market had known about the fraud which had been revealed. SNC challenged that part of the judge's ruling that not all the alleged incidents of fraud had been proven. It was held that where a party had been induced to purchase shares by fraudulent misrepresentation on the part of the vendor, the court would assess the damages

135

recoverable by the innocent purchaser as the difference between the price paid and the price which, in the absence of the misrepresentation, the shares would have fetched on the open market and not on the price which would have been paid if the market had known about the fraud. The assumption that the market knew everything it actually knew on the date of sale, without being influenced by the misrepresentation itself, was clearly a rational principle on which to calculate the loss which directly flowed from the representation on the relevant date, in contrast to the assumption that the market was omniscient (in the sense that it knew everything material to the price of the shares which was in fact the case), which was entirely arbitrary and allowed the damages to be increased or diminished by any fact or event which, unknown to anyone, actually existed or occurred before the relevant date, provided that it had emerged before the trial. It followed that the correct measure of damages was the difference between what SNC paid for the shares (82.25p per share) and the price which, in the absence of fraudulent misrepresentation, the parcel of shares would have fetched on the open market on the date of sale. Since 78p was the market price on the date in question, the loss was 4.25p per share and therefore the damages which SNC was entitled to recover, on the broader basis that all the incidents of fraud had been made out, would have to be reduced from £10,764,005 to £1,196,010. C's appeal would accordingly be allowed to that extent: *Smith New Court Securities Ltd* v *Scrimegour Vickers (Asset Management) Ltd* (1994).

55. Further remedies

The plaintiff may repudiate the contract or have it rescinded by the court, with or without claiming damages for deceit. He may also affirm the contract and still claim damages for deceit. Certain restrictions exist, however, on the right to rescind.

Limits on right to rescind

The party who is the victim of any kind of misrepresentation does generally have the right to rescind the contract brought about because of the misrepresentation. This right is, however, lost in the following cases:

- Affirmation of the contract. This arises where the innocent party has expressly or by implication indicated that he wishes to continue with the contract, the misrepresentation notwithstanding.
- Restitution has become impossible. In such a case, the parties can no longer be restored to their original position: *Witter Ltd* v *TBP Industries* (1996). The contract, for example, might have related to the supply of fuel which was consumed before the misrepresentation was discovered.

- Third parties would be prejudiced. This would arise, for example, where an innocent third party has acquired an interest in or title to the subject matter of the contract. In the case of *Phillips* v *Brooks* (1919) (see **49** above), the innocent purchaser of the jewels from the fraudulent person was held entitled to retain them since he had obtained them in good faith before the initial contract had been rescinded.
- Undue delay. This will arise where the party seeking to rescind delays beyond what in the circumstances is a reasonable time: *North Ocean Shipping Co* v *Hyundai Construction Co* (see **58** below).

Rescinding a contract will generally take some form of notice to the party who was responsible for the misrepresentation. This need not, however, always be the case.

> *Case law* The owner of a car was induced by fraud to sell it to a person who later absconded and who could not be traced. On discovering the fraud, the owner notified the police and the Automobile Association and asked them for help in recovering the car. It was held that this was enough to rescind the contract, so that an innocent third party who had acquired the car obtained no title: *Car & Universal Finance Co Ltd* v *Caldwell* (1965).

If a misrepresentation has become a term of the contract, the innocent party will have available to him the remedies available generally for breach of contract (see below). The innocent party will also have the rights of rescission for misrepresentation open to him.

Damages as an alternative to rescission

Under s. 2(2) of the Misrepresentation Act 1967, damages may be awarded in lieu of rescission, except in the case of fraud, if the court considers this equitable. This power to award damages does not depend on the right to rescind still being in existence but on a plaintiff having had the right in the past: *Witter Ltd* v *TBP Industries* (1996). The same case decided that damages could be awarded under s. 2(2) even if damages were not available under s. 2(1) (see above).

Section 2(3) provides that any damages so awarded shall be set off against any damages awarded under the Act for negligent misrepresentation (see above).

56. Contracts of the utmost good faith

The general rule is that neither party to a contract is ever under a duty to make a positive disclosure to the other side: each generally has the right to remain silent on matters they would rather not disclose. There is, however, a group of contracts, often involving insurance, which are known as 'contracts of the utmost good faith' (sometimes also described by the Latin tag of 'contracts *uberrimae fidei*'). Silence on the relevant points in the case of such contracts has the status of an actual misrepresentation and thus renders the contract voidable at the option of the other party. The duty of disclosure does not, however, of itself provide a right to damages: *Banque Financière* v *Westgate Insurance Co* (1988).

Examples of the duty actively to disclose are as follows:

(a) *Contracts of insurance.* The insured must disclose all the facts which might influence the judgment of the prudent insurer in deciding whether or not to accept the risk. In the *Banque Financière* case, the court stated that the obligation to disclose material facts was a mutual and absolute obligation which imposed reciprocal duties on both contracting parties. In the case of the insurer, this required him to disclose all facts known to him which were material either to the nature of the risk for which cover was sought or to the recoverability of a claim under the policy which a prudent insured party would take into account when deciding whether to place the risk with the insurer.

The duty of disclosure placed on the party seeking insurance is that of honesty: he is not under any duty of care. It is enough that he believed in what he disclosed. He need not have reasonable grounds for that belief: *Economides* v *Commercial Union* (1997).

(b) *Contracts of family arrangement.* In the case of settlement of family property, for example, each member of the family must disclose any portion already received without the knowledge of the others.

(c) *Company prospectuses.* Sections 67–69 of the Companies Act 1985 provide that directors and promoters must make a full disclosure of material facts in any prospectus which invites the public to subscribe for shares in the company. Failure to do so renders a contract voidable and gives a right to damages.

(d) *Contracts for the sale of land.* A vendor must disclose all known defects in his title, but not in relation to other matters, such as the physical condition of the property.

(e) *Suretyship and partnership contracts.* In these cases, the parties must disclose to one another all material facts coming to light once the contract has been made.

57. Exclusion and limitation clauses

The Misrepresentation Act 1967, and the Unfair Contract Terms Act 1977, provide that a term in a contract seeking to exclude or limit any liability for misrepresentation is valid only if shown to be reasonable. Furthermore, any such clause may also be invalid under the provisions of the Unfair Terms in Consumer Contracts Regulations 1994 (see **22** above).

DURESS AND UNDUE INFLUENCE

58. Duress

Duress can be the use of threats or actual violence and any contract obtained by such means is voidable at the option of the party coerced: *Cummings* v *Ince* (1847).

Economic duress can also amount to duress such as to render a contract voidable.

> *Case law* Shipbuilders, without any justification, demanded an additional 10% on the contract price, this being reluctantly agreed to by the other party in order to avoid delay in delivery. Any delay could have had serious financial consequences. The court found that there was consideration for the promise to pay the extra 10% because the builders, in return, had complied with a request to increase by 10% the letter of credit which they had opened to provide security for repayment of instalments in the event of their default in performance of the contract. The court further held, however, that the threat to break the contract was economic duress which rendered the contract voidable. Since the other side had waited 8 months after delivery before making any claim, they must be taken to have affirmed the contract and hence to have lost the right to rescind: *North Ocean Shipping Co* v *Hyundai Construction Co* (1979).

> *Case law* K, a small company, secured and was ready to fulfil a large contract to supply goods to Woolworths. K made a contract with A, a national road carrier, to distribute the goods to Woolworths' shops at an agreed price per carton. K had underestimated the size of the cartons, so the price quoted and agreed was uneconomically low. After the first delivery, A realised this. They then sent an empty vehicle to K, the driver carrying a document amending the contract in favour of A. The driver's instructions were to take his vehicle away unloaded unless the amended contract was accepted. It was essential to K's commercial survival that he met the delivery dates, and K signed the amendment. The court held that they were not bound by the amendment because it was procured by

139

economic duress and there was no consideration for it: *Atlas Express Ltd v Kafco* (1989).

Case law A company ran a cash and carry business. It purchased cigarettes from the defendants. Each sale was under a separate contract. The defendants had also arranged credit facilities for the plaintiffs which could be withdrawn at any time. In November 1986, an order was placed for cigarettes which, by mistake, were delivered to the wrong address. The parties agreed for the consignment to be delivered to the correct address but it was stolen before this could take place. The defendants believed in good faith that the goods had been at the plaintiffs' risk and invoiced them accordingly. The plaintiffs at first refused payment but later agreed after being threatened with the loss of their credit facilities. The court ruled that although, in certain circumstances, a threat to perform a lawful act coupled with a demand for payment might amount to economic duress, it would be difficult, though not impossible, to maintain such a claim in the context of arm's length commercial dealings between trading companies, especially where the party making the threat *bona fide* believed that the demand was valid. Any extension of the categories of duress to encompass 'lawful act duress' in a commercial context in pursuit of a *bona fide* claim would be a radical move with far-reaching implications and would introduce a substantial and undesirable element of uncertainty in the commercial bargaining process. On the facts of the present case, the defendants were entitled in law to vary the terms on which they contracted with the plaintiffs by withdrawing credit facilities and they had made their demand for payment in good faith, believing that they were owed the sum in question: *CTN Cash and Carry Ltd v Gallaher Ltd* (1994).

59. Undue influence

Undue influence differs from duress in that no form of threat is involved. Undue influence accordingly covers all types of pressure not constituting duress, such as moral pressure, taking advantage of someone's dependent position and such like.

Case law A mother coerced her daughter into making a moneylending contract with a party who knew of the mother's actions. It was held that the contract was voidable at the instance of the daughter: *Lancashire Loans Ltd v Black* (1934).

The court will presume that undue influence has existed in certain cases, particularly where the parties are in a fiduciary relationship, meaning that one party is able to exert unfair influence over the other. Undue influence will be presumed with such relationships as parent and child, trustee and beneficiary, solicitor and client, doctor and patient, employer and junior employee and so forth. The presumption of undue influence can be displaced by showing that full disclosure of all material facts was made; that the consideration provided by the other side, where consideration is relevant, was adequate; and that the weaker party had the opportunity of independent advice.

Case law A bank manager knew that an elderly farmer relied on him for his advice. The manager allowed the farmer to mortgage his house to the bank as a guarantee for a loan to help his son's failing business. It was held that a fiduciary relationship had been established between the manager and the farmer and that the bank was therefore under a duty to advise the latter to receive independent advice. This had not been done and the guarantee could thus be set aside: *Lloyds Bank Ltd v Bundy* (1975).

Case law A client of a bank acted on the advice of her bank manager and gave her house as security for a mortgage. She had no independent advice. The court, however, declined to set the transaction aside since it was not satisfied that the relationship between the client and the manager went beyond a normal business relationship or that the transaction was disadvantageous: *National Westminster Bank plc v Morgan* (1985). See too: *Inche Noriah v Shaik Allie Bin Omar* (1929); *Hodgson v Marks* (1971); *Coldunell Ltd v Gallon* (1986); *Midland Bank v Shephard* (1988); *Barclays Bank v O'Brien* (1994); *CIBC Mortgages plc v Pitt* (1993); *TSB Bank plc v Camfield* (1995); *Halifax Mortgage Services Ltd v Stepsky* (1995); *Massey v Midland Bank plc* (1995); *Banco Exterior Internacional v Mann* (1995); *Dunbar Bank plc v Nadeem* (1997).

Where a bank, as mortgagee of a property jointly owned by husband and wife, brings proceeedings for possession on the husband's default, and the wife alleges that her share was free of the bank's legal charge on the ground that her husband had induced her to sign the charge by a misrepresentation, the burden is on the bank to plead and to prove that it did not have constructive notice of the misrepresentation, and not on the wife to prove that it did: *Barclays Bank plc v Boulter* (1997).

Relief for undue influence may be lost in circumstances where the right to rescind generally is lost (see above). The courts have, however, stated that relief will be granted even if the parties could not be restored to their original position since the court will look at all the circumstances and do what is fair and just in practical terms. In the relevant case, the undue influence had been exercised in relation to a house purchased by plaintiff and defendant, the plaintiff contributing more than the defendant. The agreement had been reached because of the undue influence of the defendant, but when the transaction came to be set aside, the house had fallen in value. The court held that the plaintiff could recover only such sum as represented the proportion he had paid of the original price: *Cheese v Thomas* (1993). A court also has power to award fair compensation in equity to a plaintiff who had trusted a defendant and who succeeded in persuading the court to set aside an unfair agreement induced by reliance on that trust in circumstances where the taking of an account would not do practical justice between the parties: *Mahoney v Purnell* (1996).

ILLEGALITY

60. Meaning of illegality

An illegal contract is one which has an illegal purpose in mind, or which is contrary to some rule of public policy.

> *Case law* A pilot was engaged to recover certain aircraft in Nigeria. He was advised that his life, and that of his wireless operator, were in danger and that the Nigerian Government could offer no protection. He flew from Nigeria without obtaining air traffic control clearance, this being in breach of Nigerian law. The court ruled that a contract is not normally enforced if this would mean a party benefiting from his criminal conduct. In this case, however, the public conscience would not be offended if the criminal conduct was designed to free the relevant parties, as here, from pressing danger: *Howard v Shirlstar Container Transport Ltd* (1990).

If a contract has several independent purposes in view, some of which are legal and some illegal, the courts will, so long as the respective parts are not interdependent, sever the illegal parts and leave the legal parts in operation: *Pickering v Ilfracombe Rail Co* (1868); *Napier v National Business Agency* (1951).

> *Case law* One party remitted to another £3m for the purchase of shares pursuant to various investment management agreements between the parties. A month later, following a fall in the market, the latter party sold the shares at the direction of the purchaser for a loss of just under £1m. The purchaser brought proceedings to recover his loss on the ground that, while the other party was licensed under the Prevention of Fraud (Investments) Act 1958, the individual who made and signed the contract did not hold a representative's licence as required by that Act and that, in consequence, the investment management agreements were a nullity since the Act, by prohibiting unlicensed persons from dealing in securities, rendered void any purported contract that such an individual

made. The court held that the public interest under the Act was fully met by the imposition of criminal sanctions and neither the words of the Act, nor the type of prohibition imposed (which was directed not against the deals themselves or the contracting parties but against the servant or agent making the deals), showed any intention by Parliament that deals made through an unlicensed agent should be rendered void, nor was there any consideration of public policy in support of such an interpretation: *Hughes* v *Asset Managers plc* (1995).

61. Consequences of illegality

Except as far as the contract can be severed (see above), the illegality renders it entirely void. Any negotiable securities, such as cheques and other bills of exchange, which are transferred between the parties are void as between them. An innocent party, however, who acquires the securities in good faith and for value can normally enforce them. It is also the case that a party who seeks the assistance of the court cannot base his claim on his own illegal or immoral act.

> *Case law* A rented a flat to R for £1200 a year. To avoid tax, the parties agreed to divide this up as £450 for rent and the balance for 'services'. Later, R sought to cheat A by refusing to pay the balance on the ground that he had received no services. The court held that the contract was illegal as an attempt to defraud the Revenue and so A could not recover the balance. At the same time, and to prevent R from benefiting from the illegality, the court terminated the tenancy on the grounds of the illegality, and offered him a new lease at the full rent: *Alexander* v *Rayson* (1936).

Money or property transferred under an illegal contract cannot normally be recovered. There are, however, exceptions to this rule. For example, the party seeking recovery might not have the same degree of guilt as the party from whom the transfer is sought. The former might, for instance, have been induced to make an illegal contract by the fraud of the other party: *Shelley* v *Paddock* (1978). Again, the transferee might be a person under a fiduciary duty to protect the interests of the transferor, and might have abused that duty by making the illegal contract. It might also be the case that the transferor is a member of a class protected by an enactment which makes the particular contract illegal. It would be a consequence of that protection that money or property paid or transferred under the contract could be recovered.

CONTRACTS SUBJECT TO A DISABILITY

62. Business names

Under the Business Names Act 1985, all orders, invoices and business letters must disclose the true surname of all owners of the business, whether individuals or companies, as well as the addresses at which they can be contacted. Such information must also be displayed on a notice in a prominent position at the business premises. A customer must, on demand, be supplied with a written list of the required information. Actions in contract by a person in breach of these requirements can be dismissed if the party against whom the action is brought can show that he has a claim against the person bringing the action because of his failure to comply, or if he can show that such failure caused him damage. The court can, however, allow the action if it considers it just and equitable so to do.

63. Consumer credit

Under the Consumer Credit Act 1974, all those providing credit or hire to consumers by way of business must have the appropriate licence from the Office of Fair Trading. An unlicensed business cannot enforce its contracts without the consent of the Office.

64. Financial services

A broadly similar position exists under the terms of the Financial Services Act 1986. Investment businesses need authorisation unless exempt from such requirement. A contract made in breach of this requirement is enforceable only on a court order. The Act also provides for restrictions on the issue of investment advertisements and contracts resulting from advertisements not complying with these requirements are again enforceable only on a court order.

65. Wagering and gaming contracts

A wagering contract has been defined as 'one by which two persons, professing to hold opposite views touching the issue of a future uncertain event, mutually agree that, dependent upon the determination of that event, one shall win from the other, and that the other shall pay, or hand over to him, a sum of money or other stake; neither of the contracting parties having any other interest in that contract than the sum or stake he will win or lose, there being no other real consideration for the making of such contract by either of the parties': *Carlill* v *Carbolic Smoke Ball Co* (1893).

'Gaming' means the playing of a game for money or money's worth: *Ellesmere* v *Wallace* (1926). The Gaming Act 1968 also defines 'gaming' in s. 52(1) as 'the playing of any game of chance for winnings in money or money's worth, whether any person playing the game is at risk of losing money or money's worth or not'. A bet on the movement of a stock market index is not a wagering contract: *City Index Ltd* v *Leslie* (1991). An interest rate swap contract has potentially a speculative character deriving from the fact that the obligations of the floating rate payee were to be ascertained by reference to a fluctuating market rate, and which was therefore capable of being entered into by two parties with the purpose of wagering on future interest rates. In the context of interest rate swap contracts, however, when entered into by parties involved in the capital market and in the making or receiving of loans, the normal inference would be that such contracts were not gaming or wagering, but were commercial or financial transactions to which the law will, in the absence of some other consideration, give full recognition and effect. The inference will be rebutted only if the purpose and interest of both parties was to wager, in which case the consequence of legal invalidity and enforceability would follow. Since the main purpose and interest of the relevant party in making the particular contract was not wagering, the fact that there was an element of wagering, as a subordinate element and not as the substance of the transaction, did not affect its validity or enforceability. Moreover, whatever might have been the purpose or intent of one party in entering the contract, the contract was not one of wager because the purpose and intent of the other party was in no way directed to or concerned with wagering: *Morgan Grenfell* v *Welwyn Hatfield DC* (1995).

Many kinds of gaming and wagering are regulated by statute, notably the Betting, Gaming and Lotteries Act 1960, the Gaming Act 1968 and the Lotteries and Amusements Act 1976.

Contracts of gaming and wagering are not enforceable. The resultant position is complex but the following basic rules apply:

- Money earned as commission on bets and wagers cannot be recovered by virtue of the Gaming Act 1892. An agent is, therefore, unable to recover commission from his principal, but the latter can recover any winnings received on his behalf by the former: *De Mattos* v *Benjamin* (1894).
- The Gaming Act 1835 provides that negotiable instruments given for a bet are given for an illegal purpose and are void as between the parties. An innocent third party, however, who becomes a holder in due course of such an instrument may be able to enforce it in full. This follows from the provisions of s. 29 of the Bills of Exchange Act 1882 as to the holder in due course.

145

- Money lent to a loser to pay his bets is recoverable: *Re O'Shea* (1911). This is, however, not the case if the lender himself pays the winner, since he is then himself participating in a void transaction: *Macdonald v Green* (1951).
- The winner of a wager cannot sue the loser for his winnings, even though the loser later makes a fresh promise to pay and this promise is supported by fresh consideration: *Hill v William Hill Ltd* (1949). This is the case even though gaming in some contexts is lawful under the provisions of the Gaming Act 1968.
- Money paid to a stakeholder for him to retain pending the result of a wager can be recovered from him by the party giving him the money at any time before the money has been handed over to the other party to the wager: *Burge v Ashley & Smith Ltd* (1900).

Section 63 of the Financial Services Act 1986 says that the following contracts will not be void by reasons of the provisions of the Gaming Act 1835 or the Gaming Act 1892: any contract entered into by either or each party by way of business and the making or performance of which by either party constitutes an activity which, broadly, amounts to an investment business.

CONTRACTS ILLEGAL AT COMMON LAW

66. Immorality

A contract will be void if, to the knowledge of the parties, its ultimate purpose is immoral. For example, a contract for the lease of premises would be void if it was known that it would be used as a brothel.

> *Case law* A hired a carriage to a woman knowing that she was a prostitute and that the carriage was to be used for the purposes of soliciting. It was held that the contract was void and that the lessor could not recover the hire charges: *Pearce v Brooks* (1866).

67. Sanctity of marriage

A contract tending to interfere with the sanctity of marriage is void, as for example a promise by a married man to marry another woman once his wife was dead: *Wilson v Carnley* (1908). It should perhaps be noted, though this does not affect the principle just stated, that the right to sue for breach of promise was abolished by the Law Reform (Miscellaneous) Provisions Act 1970.

Contracts prejudicial to the freedom of marriage are also void. A promise by a widow to pay £100 if she marries is void, as is a promise not to marry anyone but X: *Baker* v *White* (1690); *Hartley* v *Rice* (1808); *Lowe* v *Peers* (1768). Contracts to arrange marriages for reward are also void: *Hermann* v *Charlesworth* (1905).

68. Champerty and maintenance

Maintenance is the giving of financial or other assistance to a party to a law suit where the maintainer has no sufficient legal or moral interest in the case. Champerty is maintenance with a view to sharing the profits of the action. The Criminal Law Act 1967 provides that neither champerty nor maintenance can any longer be treated as crimes or torts, but does provide that a contract can still be treated as contrary to public policy or otherwise illegal.

> *Case law* The plaintiffs retained the defendants as their solicitors under an agreement which provided for a 20 per cent reduction from costs where any case was lost. The agreement was later terminated when some £257,000 was owed under the retainer. It was held that a contingency fee for conducting litigation which was champertous and unenforceable as contrary to public policy was not confined to a direct or indirect share of the spoils and included a differential fee dependent on the outcome of the litigation, and so the arrangement in the instant case was champertous and unenforceable: *Aratra Potato Co Ltd* v *Taylor Joynson Garrett* (1995).

The assignment of a *bona fide* debt in accordance with the provisions of the Law of Property Act 1925 (see below) was not invalid even if the need for litigation to recover it had been contemplated before the assignment: the debt did not become unassignable merely because the debtor chose to dispute it. Suing on an assigned debt was not contrary to public policy even if the assignor retained an interest; what was contrary to public policy and ineffective was an agreement which had maintenance or champerty as its object and such a consequence would not be avoided by dressing up a transaction which had that character and intent as an assignment of a debt. However, because the assignment of a debt of itself included no element of maintenance and was permitted by statute, any objectionable element alleged to invalidate the assignment had to be provided separately and distinctly: *Camdex* v *Bank of Zambia Ltd* (1996).

An agreement between a car hire company and a potential plaintiff whose car needed repairs as the result of an accident for which he was not to blame, and where the negligent defendant was insured, whereby the potential plaintiff received a free car in return for agreeing that the car hire firm could bring an action for damages, including the company's charges, in the plaintiff's name against the insured defendant, did not amount to champerty. It could not be said that the car hire company was intermeddling in the dispute between the plaintiff and defendant with a view to dividing the spoils: *Giles* v *Thompson* (1944).

69. Public offices and titles

A contract is void if it is for the sale of a public office, title or honour. Thus, a promise to use influence to obtain a title or a commission in return for payment is void: *Parkinson* v *College of Ambulance Ltd* (1925). Furthermore, the Honours (Prevention of Abuses) Act 1925 makes the parties to such a contract guilty of a criminal offence. A contract by a Member of Parliament is void if it is an agreement to vote in accordance with the wishes of some body outside Parliament: *ASRS* v *Osborne* (1910).

70. Crimes or torts

A contract to commit a crime or tort, whether at home or abroad, is void, such as a contract to smuggle goods into the USA: *Foster* v *Driscoll* (1929).

> *Case law* A contract was made for the export of Indian jute to Italy, with a view to re-export to South Africa. The court refused to enforce the contract as it contravened Indian law forbidding the export of goods produced in India to South Africa, as it could only be performed by making false declarations in India: *Regazzoni* v *KC Sethia (1944) Ltd* (1958).

71. Trading with the enemy

Contracts involving trading with the enemy are void at common law and also under the provisions of the Trading with the Enemy Act 1939.

72. Deceiving the public authorities

A contract to deceive the public authorities, such as the Revenue, is void: *Alexander* v *Rayson* (1936) (see **61** above). Similarly, a contract by which an employee receives expenses in excess of the expenses actually incurred is void: *Napier* v *National Business Agency Ltd* (1951). The same is true where part of an employee's actual pay is concealed from the Revenue to avoid paying tax: *Corby* v *Morrison* (1980).

73. Administration of justice

A contract is void if it tends to impede the administration of justice, such as an accused person agreeing to indemnify someone who stands bail for him: *Herman* v *Jeuchner* (1885).

74. Restraint of trade

All contracts for the restraint of trade are *prima facie* void, though they may be valid if they seek no more than to protect a legitimate commercial interest. In contrast, a restraint which seeks simply to prevent competition will always be void: *Morris* v *Saxelby* (1916). For convenience, restraints of trade can be divided into restraints on employees and restraints imposed on the sale of a business. Agreements between traders are dealt with in Chapter 3.

Restraints of trade, whether imposed on employees or in relation to the sale of a business, are *prima facie* contrary to public policy and hence are void. This presumption can, however, be displaced if:

(i) the party imposing the restraint can show that is reasonable as between the parties; and

(ii) if the party accepting the restriction cannot show that it is unreasonable: *Nordenfelt* v *Maxim Nordenfelt Guns and Ammunition Co* (1894); *Morris* v *Saxelby* (1916).

Case law A tailor's assistant agreed not to open a competing business within 10 miles of his former employer's business. This was held to be void because the employee had no confidential relationship with the customers and the restriction was simply aimed at restricting competition: *Attwood* v *Lamont* (1920). A similar view was taken in *Home Counties Dairies Ltd* v *Skilton* (1970), a case involving a milk roundsman.

Case law S was an estate agent with offices in Dartmouth and Kingsbridge. J was employed at the Kingsbridge office and agreed not to open a competing business within 5 miles of either office within 3 years of leaving the employment. It was held that the restraint was too wide, in that J had never worked at Dartmouth, but was valid so far as it related to Kingsbridge. The agreement could therefore be severed, leaving part of it valid: *Scorer* v *Seymour-Johns* (1966).

Case law A salaried partner in a medical practice agreed not to practice in the practice area, which was physically defined, within a period of 3 years in the event of the agreement being terminated. The partner later decided to set up in General Practice about 100 yards away and well within the defined area. It was held that this restraint was valid: *Clarke* v *Newland* (1991).

Case law K, an inventor of guns, sold his world-wide business to M and promised not to manufacture guns anywhere in the world for 25 years. This was held to be reasonable and hence binding: *Nordenfelt* v *Maxim Nordenfelt Guns and Ammunition Co* (1894).

Case law S sold his localised business to C, who already had branches all over the country, and promised not to open a competing business anywhere within 10 miles of any of C's branches. This restraint was held to be void since it was more than was necessary to protect the goodwill of the small local business purchased: *British Concrete Co* v *Schelff* (1921).

An employer is entitled to restrain an employee from making use of trade secrets, whether during the employment or following his departure: *Robb* v *Green* (1895); *Amber Size and Chemical Co* v *Menzel* (1913); *Thomas Marshall (Exports) Ltd* v *Guinle* (1978).

It is, however, the case that not all confidential information can be protected. It has been ruled that an employer cannot restrict the use or disclosure of confidential information by means of a restrictive covenant unless the information is subject to the restraint as a trade secret or equivalent to a trade secret. In order to determine if information fell within this category, it was necessary to have regard to the nature of the employment, the nature of the information itself, whether the employer had stressed the confidentiality of the information to the employee, and whether the information could be easily isolated from other non-confidential information which was part of the same package of information. In the case itself, the court held that sales information and prices charged did not come into the category of information which could not be used or disclosed once the employment had ceased: *Faccenda Chicken Ltd* v *Fowler* (1986).

The categories of case in which covenants in restraint of trade were enforceable are not rigid or exclusive.

Case law The plaintiffs and the defendants were engaged in a joint venture. The contract between them imposed on the defendants an obligation not to compete with the plaintiffs, not to solicit business from their customers and not to solicit or entice away staff employed by the plaintiffs for one year from the date when the relationship of the defendants with the plaintiffs ended. The court said that it was not the law that covenants in restraint of trade could never be upheld outside the established categories of vendor and purchaser, and employer and employee. The fact that the plaintiffs were neither the purchasers of a business from the defendants nor their employers did not mean that the covenants could not be enforced. The court upheld the covenants, saying that the agreement gave the plaintiffs a clear commercial interest in safeguarding themselves against competition from the defendants, individually or collectively for the agreed period. The plaintiffs were entitled to protection where and to the extent that protection was reasonably necessary: *Dawnay Day & Co Ltd* v *D'Alphen* (1997).

A party who has been freed from an invalid restraint of trade in an employment contract can enforce the remainder of the contract provided that the invalid element had not constituted the real or main consideration for the contract. A party was therefore entitled to renewal commission under a contract of employment even though a proviso to the payment of the commission was an unlawful restraint of trade: *Marshall* v *NM Financial Management Ltd* (1997).

DISCHARGE OF CONTRACTS

75. Complete performance

In order to effect a complete discharge of a contract, performance must be complete and exactly in accord with the terms of the contract. Substantial performance will not suffice.

> *Case law* A sailor, having signed on to receive a lump sum payment for a complete voyage, died before completion of the voyage. Since he was entitled to payment only on completion of the voyage, his widow could claim nothing: *Cutter* v *Powell* (1795).

There are, however, a number of exceptions to the basic rule that only complete performance operates as a discharge.

76. Acceptance of partial performance

If the other party agrees to accept less than complete performance, he must pay for the value of the work done, providing his agreement was entirely voluntary.

> *Case law* A agreed to erect a building for B. When the job was half done, A abandoned the job. B completed the work himself and A sued for the work done. It was held that B need pay nothing as he had not freely chosen to complete the work, but had been forced to by reason of the breach: *Sumpter* v *Hedges* (1898).

77. Divisible contracts

If performance is to be by instalments, payment can be recovered for each instalment, unless the intention of the parties was that there should be payment only for complete performance.

78. Substantial performance

Payment can be demanded for a performance which is as complete as a reasonable person could expect, even though not strictly in accord with every aspect of the contract.

> *Case law* A decorated B's flat for £750 but, because of faulty workmanship, B had to pay an extra £250 to complete the job. B refused to make any payment. It was held that A was entitled to receive £750 less the £250 to make good the poor workmanship: *Hoenig* v *Isaacs* (1952).

> *Case law* A installed a central heating system for B, charging £560. The installation was defective and B had to spend £174 to have a third party put it into working order. It was held that this had not amounted to substantial performance, so B did not have to pay anything: *Bolton* v *Mahadeva* (1972).

79. Tender of performance

If a party makes a valid offer of performance of his contractual obligations, and the other party wrongfully refuses to accept performance, the other party is freed from liability for non-performance: *Startup* v *Macdonald* (1843). Section 29(5) of the Sale of Goods Act 1979 provides that a tender of delivery at an unreasonable hour, this being a question of fact, has no effect.

If a party makes a valid tender of payment, and this is wrongfully refused, this does not discharge the debt, but there is no obligation to make a further tender. If an action for non-payment is later brought:

- The costs of the action must be borne by the other party: *Griffiths* v *Ystradyfodwg School Board* (1890).
- A right of lien is generally extinguished.
- A claim for interest on the debt subsequent to the tender of the debt is barred: *Norton* v *Ellam* (1837).

This means that a creditor who refuses a valid tender can only recover the amount tendered and the debtor who had made a valid tender is not prejudiced by the refusal to accept.

80. Appropriation of payments

Where there are several debts outstanding between the same parties, it is important to ascertain the debts to which payment, if not entire, is to be appropriated. The debtor can himself decide on the manner of appropriation but, if he fails so to do, then the creditor can make the decision for him. If there is a current account between the parties which is subject to movement, then the rule in *Clayton's Case* (1816) applies to the effect that, if neither party makes an appropriation, then the first payment is made in discharge of the earliest debt. There are statutory rules for the apportionment of debts arising under regulated consumer credit and consumer hire agreements, as laid down in s. 81 of the Consumer Credit Act 1974.

81. Discharge by agreement

Where the contract is entirely executory, that is to say each party has something to do in the future, the contract is discharged simply by each releasing the other from his performance. Consideration is provided by each agreeing not to sue the other for non-performance. Similarly, the parties to an executory agreement can agree to substitute it with another contract.

If, however, one side has wholly or partly performed his side of the contract, different provisions apply if the contract is to be treated as discharged. A deed of release is effective, even if no consideration is provided.

Alternatively, the parties may agree to discharge the contract through accord and satisfaction. This is essentially one agreeing to partial performance, and the party providing such performance offering some consideration in return.

> *Case law* Buyers of machinery sued the supplier for damages. An agreement was made by which the buyers withdrew the claim and the sellers agreed to repair the machines, partly at their expense. The buyers later sued on the original contract. The court, however, held that there was an accord which was supported by satisfaction, in this case the promise to repair the machines; *Elton Cop Dyeing Co Ltd* v *Robert Broadbent & Son Ltd* (1919).

82. Variation and waiver

If there is an agreement to vary a contract, as opposed to discharging it, then the agreement must be supported by consideration. Variations can generally take any form except that a contract unenforceable unless evidenced by writing can only be varied in writing: *Morris* v *Baron* (1918).

Section 82 of the Consumer Credit Act 1974 imposes certain formalities in the case of a variation of a regulated consumer hire or consumer credit agreement.

A waiver, in contrast to a variation, can be valid even in the absence of consideration or a deed. The legal basis of waiver is not entirely clear, but it is probably based on the notion of estoppel. Whatever its precise legal basis, the validity of a waiver has been well estabished.

> *Case law* A buyer of goods sued for non-delivery on the conrtact date. The seller was held to have a defence since it was the buyer himself who had requested postponement of delivery: *Levey & Co* v *Goldberg* (1922).

A waiver also binds the party granting it and he may not withdraw it without first giving reasonable notice: *Hartley* v *Hymans* (1920); *Panoutsos* v *Raymond Hadley Corpn of New York* (1917). There is also authority for the proposition that a waiver will be permanently irrevocable if the party who grants it leads the other to believe that he will never enforce the strict contractual rights which he has waived: *Brikom Investments Ltd* v *Carr* (1979).

83. Discharge by operation of law

If the contract is one of personal services, such as that between employer and employee, the contract is discharged by the death of the party providing such services: *Farrow* v *Wilson* (1869). In other cases, the Law Reform (Miscellaneous Provisions) Act 1934 provides that all causes of action subsisting against or vested in the deceased survive for the benefit of the estate.

In the event of bankruptcy, the trustee in bankruptcy is generally in the position of an assignee of all the contractual rights of the bankrupt. The trustee has the power to disclaim any executory contract on the ground that it is onerous or unprofitable; and, on discharge from bankruptcy, the former bankrupt is discharged from all provable debts existing at the date.

84. Expiry of limitation periods

The Limitation Act 1980 provides that actions for breach of contract will automatically lapse after a given period. It should be noted, and will be explained further below, that the right of action does not lapse, rather it cannot be enforced.

The more important periods of time laid down by the Act are:

(i) 6 years for actions for breach of a simple contract.
(ii) 12 years for actions on a contract contained in a deed.
(iii) 30 years in actions concerning land where the Crown is the plaintiff: 12 years in other cases.

(iv) 3 years where the claim is for personal injury. Section 14 of the Act, however, provides that this period begins to operate only when the injured party discovers certain relevant facts, in particular the seriousness of his injury and the fact that it can be attributed to a particular party. The limitation period begins to run when the potential plaintiff first has knowledge of the nature of his injury which justifies him in taking the first steps towards instituting proceedings against the person whose act or omission had caused the significant injury concerned: *Nash v Eli Lilly & Co* (1993).

(v) Section 11A of the Act provides that actions under Part I of the Consumer Protection Act 1987, which provides for claims to be brought against the producer of defective products, regardless of negligence (see Chapter 8) expire after 10 years.

(vi) In cases of negligence, except cases involving personal injury or death, the limitation period is 6 years. Section 14A of the Act, however, provides that this can be extended by allowing a further 3 years from the date when the damage was discoverable. A party seeking to claim the further period must show that he did not possess, before the 3 year period prior to the date on which proceedings commenced, sufficient knowledge of the material facts to enable him to commence proceedings. It has been held that s. 14A is limited to actions for damages for negligence where the duty of care, breach of which constitutes the negligence relied on, arises solely in tort, and does not apply to actions framed in contract: *Iron Trades Mutual Insurance Co Ltd* v *JK Buckenham* (1990); *Société Commerciale de Reassurance* v *ERAS (International) Ltd* (1992).

Section 33 of the Act gives the court a discretion to allow an action in respect of personal injury or death to proceed, despite the expiry of the limitation period, if it considers it fair to do so having regard to the degree to which the parties would be prejudiced: *Donovan* v *Gwentoys Ltd* (1990); *Ramsden* v *Lee* (1992); *Hartley* v *Birmingham City DC* (1992). When considering whether to exercise its discretion, the court is to consider all the circumstances of the case and to balance the prejudice to the respective parties. There are no grounds for limiting the exercise of the court's discretion for reasons of public policy where the particular case involved a group action: *Nash* v *Eli Lilly & Co* (1993). In the case of a personal injury claim, the court will not exercise its discretion, having regard to the potentially serious prejudice to the defendant if the action was permitted to proceed after a long delay, by reason of the inability to locate relevant medical records and witnesses, the fading of memories, the difficulty for expert witnesses of placing themselves into the standard of medical practice of 14 years before, and the fact that the plaintiff's case was supported by scanty evidence and had only modest prospects of success: *Forbes* v *Wandsworth Health Authority* (1996).

85. When time runs

The limitation period under the Act is generally calculated from the time when the particular breach occurs. Where, however, the potential plaintiff was under some form of disability at the date of the breach, such as minority or mental incapacity, ss 23 and 31 provide that time runs only from the time when the disability ceases, or death if the disability persisted, whichever comes first.

It is further provided by s. 32 that if the action is based on fraud, concealment or mistake, then time will only start to run when the particular fraud, concealment or mistake is discovered, or could with reasonable diligence have been discovered. If a plaintiff relies on mistake, he must show that it was a mistake as to the facts, and not, for example, a mistake or ignorance as to his rights in law: *Central Asbestos Co Ltd* v *Dodds* (1972).

> *Case law* Eight years after his house was built, A discovered that, in breach of contract, the builder had laid defective foundations. He could not have discovered the real state of affairs since these had been concealed by the builder. It was held that the right of action was not time-barred: *Applegate* v *Moss* (1971).

Section 14B further provides that no action can be brought once 15 years have elapsed from the date when any action or omission occurred which is alleged to be the cause of the action.

86. Acknowledgement and part payment

It was noted above that, when a claim becomes time-barred, this means only that a right of action cannot be pursued: the right of action is not of itself destroyed. Thus, the right of action can be revived under s. 29 of the Act by a written acknowledgment which constitutes an express or implied admission of liability.

FRUSTRATION OF CONTRACTS

The general rule is that contractual obligations are absolute, so that any undertaking must be performed, failing which there will be a breach of contract.

> *Case law* A tenant was held bound to pay 3 years' arrears of rent even though, throughout that period, he had been expelled from his premises by Prince Rupert and his army. The court distinguished between duties imposed by law and those imposed by contract. In the former, perfor-

mance might be excused by circumstances; in the latter, however, performance would only be excused if this were provided for in the contract, for '...though the land be surrounded, or gained by the sea, or made barren by wildfire, yet the lessor shall have his whole rent': *Paradine* v *Jane* (1647).

Case law A contract to build houses for £92,000 within a period of 8 months took 22 months and cost an extra £17,000 because of unexpected shortage of skilled labour and building materials. These supervening circumstances were no answer to an action for breach of contract: *Davis Contractors Ltd* v *Fareham Urban District Council* (1956).

87. The doctrine of frustration

The doctrine of frustration was developed to meet the hardship which the above and other cases had revealed. Although it is not always easy to discern the precise basis on which the doctrine of frustration rests, the following instances of when a contract will be frustrated by some supervening event explain how the courts tend to approach the matter. A contract has been judged frustrated when:

(a) It depends on the continued existence of something which was destroyed, such as a theatre: *Taylor* v *Caldwell* (1863).

(b) There is the non-occurrence of an essential event. Thus, the hire of rooms to see the Coronation procession was cancelled when the Coronation itself was postponed: *Krell* v *Henry* (1903). Where, however, a steamboat was hired to see the naval review at Spithead, and the review itself was cancelled because the Coronation was postponed, the contract was held not to be frustrated because the fleet was still there and could be seen: *Herne Bay Steam Boat Co* v *Hutton* (1903).

(c) A person who has contracted to supply personal services dies or falls ill. Whether illness will frustrate a contract will often depend on its duration, so that the illness of a concert pianist for the first day might well frustrate a three day engagement: *Robinson* v *Davison* (1871).

(d) Performance is inhibited by the Government. If the Government bans performance for a particular period, the contract is frustrated if it would be unreasonable to expect performance once that period had passed: *Metropolitan Water Board* v *Dick, Kerr Ltd* (1918).

(e) There is a change in the relevant law. A contract is frustrated if, legal when made, it subsequently becomes illegal: *Avery* v *Bowden* (1856).

(f) Where the mode of performance becomes impossible, where that mode of performance is essential: *Jackson* v *Union Marine Insurance Co Ltd* (1874); *Tsakiroglou & Co Ltd* v *Noblee and Thorl GmbH* (1962).

Case law The headmaster of a school was suspended after criminal charges had been laid against him. He was subsequently acquitted. It was held that his enforced absence from work did not frustrate the contract since his presence as headmaster was not vital to the continued running of the school: *Mount* v *Oldham Corporation* (1973).

Case law Property was advertised as being suitable for redevelopment. On the day when the parties entered into the contract, they were unaware that the Department of the Environment was proposing to give the property listed buildings status. This was done the next day. The development value of the property was accordingly reduced from £1.7m to £200,000. The court ruled that listing was an inherent risk which a purchaser had to bear and that listing did not make the contract radically different from what had been originally contemplated. There had, therefore, been no frustration: *Amalgamated Investment and Property Co Ltd* v *John Walker & Sons Ltd* (1976).

It had at one time been thought that contracts for the lease of real property could never be frustrated, but this view, if ever correct, was overruled in *National Carriers Ltd* v *Panalpina (Northern) Ltd* (1981).

88. Express provision

The doctrine of frustration does not apply if the parties have made provision in the contract to deal with the frustrating event which has occurred, except where the supervening event is the illegality of the venture: *Ertel Beiber & Co* v *Rio Tinto Co Ltd* (1918).

If the risk of the frustrating event was foreseen or foreseeable by one of the parties to the contract, the doctrine is inapplicable. It is up to that party to provide against the risk of that event, and he will be liable for breach of contract if the relevant event occurs and he has not so provided: *Walton Harvey Ltd* v *Walker and Homfrays Ltd* (1931). If, on the other hand, both parties are aware of the risk of the particular frustrating event, but make no provision for it, the doctrine of frustration can apply: *The Eugenia* (1964).

89. Self-induced frustration

A party cannot rely on a frustrating event which he himself brought about or induced.

Case law Plaintiffs chartered to the defendants a trawler fitted with an otter trawl. Both parties knew that this was illegal in the absence of a licence. The defendants applied for licences for five trawlers which they were operating, including the plaintiffs'. Three licences were granted and they were asked to specify the vessels to which they were to be allocated. They specified three but did not include the plaintiffs'. They subsequently claimed that they were no longer bound by the charter since the contract had been frustrated. The court ruled that the frustration was due to the deliberate act of the defendants in not specifying the plaintiffs' vessel for a licence, with the result that the doctrine of frustration did not apply: *Maritime National Fish Ltd* v *Ocean Trawlers Ltd* (1935).

90. Effect of frustration

Section 1(2) of the Law Reform (Frustrated Contracts) Act 1943 provides as follows:

(i) All sums payable under the contract prior to the frustrating event cease to be payable whether or not there has been a total failure of consideration.

(ii) All sums paid under the contract before the frustrating event are recoverable, again whether or not there has been a total failure of consideration.

(iii) The court has a discretionary power to allow the payee to set off against sums paid or payable a sum not exceeding the value of any expenses incurred before the frustrating event, in, or for the purpose of, performance of the contract. There is no scope for adding something extra to represent the time value of money: *BP Exploration Co (Libya) Ltd* v *Hunt (No 2)* (1983).

Money payable under the contract after the frustrating event is not recoverable by the party to whom it was due since it is the essence of frustration that all obligations cease at the point of frustration.

Case law The owner of the flat could not recover a sum payable for the hire of the flat because it was not due until a time after the Coronation procession had been postponed: *Krell* v *Henry* (see **87** above).

91. Award for benefits obtained

Section 1(3) of the Act provides that compensation is available to either party where a valuable benefit is conferred on the other. The compensation is to be such sum as the court considers just having regard to all the circumstances of the case. From the compensation to be awarded, s. 1(3)(a) provides that there must be deducted any expenses incurred by the benefited party before the contract was frustrated, including any sums payable by him under the contract and retained or recoverable by the other party under the provisions of s. 1(2).

Section 2(3) of the Act provides that where a contract contains a provision intended to have effect in the event of circumstances which would frustrate the contract, a court must have regard to such provision and give effect to s. 1(2) and (3) to such extent, if any, as is consistent with that contractual provision.

92. Areas not covered by the Act

The Act states that it does not apply to the following:

(i) Charterparties, except a time charterparty.

(ii) Contracts, other than charterparties, for the carriage of goods by sea.

(iii) Contracts of insurance.

(iv) Any contract to which s. 7 of the Sale of Goods Act 1979 applies. This provides that, where there is an agreement to sell specific goods, and subsequently, without the fault of either party, the goods perish before the risk passes to the buyer, the agreement is thereby avoided. Where a contract is avoided under s. 7, the common law rules as to the effects of frustration will apply (see above).

The Act binds the Crown. It may be excluded by the parties in the sense that, if their contract contains a provision to meet the event of frustration, that provision applies to the exclusion of the Act.

BREACH OF CONTRACT AND REMEDIES

93. Breach of contract

A party may breach his obligations at the time for performance, or he may indicate in advance that he is not going to perform when the time comes. This latter is known as *anticipatory breach*.

> *Case law* A hired B to act as a courier, the employment to begin on 1 June. A wrote to B in May repudiating the agreement. It was held that B had an immediate right to sue and did not have to wait until 1 June for his right of action to accrue: *Hochster* v *De la Tour* (1853).

A party can, however, ignore another party's anticipatory repudiation, perform his own side, and then claim damages for the breach: *White & Carter Ltd* v *McGregor* (1962).

> *Case law* Buyers entered into a contract with sellers for the purchase of propane. The contract provided that the cargo was to be shipped from

Houston and that delivery was to be between 1 and 7 March, 1991. The contract also required the tender of a bill of lading by the sellers promptly after the loading of the cargo. On 8 March, the buyers telexed the sellers saying that the vessel would not complete loading until 9 March and that, in view of this breach of the agreed dates, they would have to reject the cargo and repudiate the contract. The vessel completed loading and thereafter neither party took any further step towards performing the contract. The sellers subsequently sold the cargo on 15 March at a lower price than that agreed with the buyers. The sellers claimed damages based on the difference in prices. It was held that, as a matter of law, mere failure to perform a contractual obligation was capable of amounting to aceptance by the innocent party of an anticipatory repudiation, depending on the particular contractual relationship and the circumstances of the case. In the present case, the arbitrator had inferred an election by the seller to treat the contract as at an end, and communication of it, from the tenor of the rejection telex and the failure to tender the bill of lading. That was an issue of fact within his exclusive jurisdiction: *Vitol SA* v *Norelf Ltd* (1996).

94. Effect of breach of condition

A condition is a major term of the contract. In the event of a breach, the injured party is entitled to rescind the contract and to claim damages: *Wallis Sons and Webb* v *Pratt & Haynes* (1910). The right to rescind is lost in the same way as in cases of misrepresentation (see **51–54** above). It should also be remembered that, in certain cases of what might be a breach of condition, the Sale of Goods Act 1979 will prevent the exercise of the right to rescind (see Chapter 5).

The innocent party is always entitled to affirm the contract. In such a case, he will still be entitled to damages, but not to treat the contract as at an end.

> *Case law* A hired B's ship to carry cargo from Russia. Later, B repudiated the contract. A delayed a decision as to whether to treat the contract as at an end or sue for damages, hoping that B would change his mind. War then broke out between Britain and Russia before the performance date, thus frustrating the contract (see **87** above). It was held that A had kept the contract alive by his actions and, given the frustrating event, had thus lost his right of action: *Avery* v *Bowden* (1856).

95. Effect of breach of warranty

A warranty is a minor term of the contract, breach of which entitles the innocent party only to claim damages: s. 61(1) of the Sale of Goods Act 1979.

96. Breach of 'middle term'

The division of contract terms into conditions and warranties has been eroded in recent years by the courts being prepared to accept that, unless statute or some binding precedent decides that a contract term is one or the other, a more flexible approach will be adopted. In such cases, attention will be concentrated on the effect of a breach, so that a serious breach will lead to termination of the contract and a claim for damages, while a less serious breach will provide only for damages: *Hong Kong Fir Shipping Co Ltd* v *Kawasaki Kishen Kaisha Ltd* (1962); *Cehave* v *Bremer* (1975).

97. Assessing damages

Damages for breach of contract are assessed by reference to the principles laid down in *Hadley* v *Baxendale* (1854) to the effect that a person who breaks a contract is entitled to recover damages for such loss as he contemplated as a probable consequence of the breach. He will be assumed to contemplate any loss which is properly regarded as a natural consequence of his breach. If, however, the loss is not to be so regarded, then the innocent party must be able to show that the party in breach had special knowledge at the time the contract was made which would have led him to expect the particular special loss. These principles were specifically enacted in ss. 50, 51 and 54 of the Sale of Goods Act 1979.

> *Case law* A contracted to supply a boiler to B's laundry and was 5 months late. It was held that B could recover for loss of general business profits, but not damages for the loss of profit under a lucrative and exceptional contract of which A had not been told in advance: *Victoria Laundry* v *Newman Industries* (1949). See too *Parsons* v *Uttley Ingham* (1978).

> *Case law* A building society wrongfully dishonoured an account holder's cheque. In an action for breach of contract, liability was admitted and damages were awarded as general damages for the injury done to the plaintiff's credit. The award included a small amount for the alleged injury to the plaintiff's reputation and credit in Nigeria of which the plaintiff was a native. The dishonoured cheque was for goods which were required by him for shipment to Nigeria. The plaintiff appealed,

contending that he was also entitled to recover special damages for trading losses sustained by reason of the delay in the shipment in question and further shipments. The defendants cross-appealed contending that damages should be nominal on the ground that they did not know that the account was to be used for trading purposes. It was held that a person who was not a trader could recover substantial damages rather than nominal damages for loss of credit or business reputation, so the award was consistent with the correct approach to an award of general damages in the circumstances. However, the special damage which the plaintiff had sought to recover was too remote, since there was nothing to indicate that a one-delay in payment, which was what had occurred, would cause the loss of a transaction or a substantial trading loss for the plaintiff, and the defendants could reasonably have expected that they would have been given special notice of the need for immediate clearance so that, if they were willing, a special arrangement could be made. The appeal and cross-appeal were therefore dismissed: *Kpohraror v Woolwich Building Society* (1996).

The basic principle behind these cases is that the innocent party is to be compensated for his loss. While he might be able to recover his own loss of profit, he cannot recover the profit made by the other party from the breach.

Case law A local authority sold a site for development. The developer increased his profit by building additional houses in breach of contract. The authority sought damages in the amount equal to the payment that it might have obtained in return for modifications to the contract to authorise the more profitable development which had in fact been carried out. It was held that the remedy at common law for breach of contract was the award of damages to compensate the innocent party for his loss, not to transfer to that party, if he had suffered no loss, the benefit obtained by the party in breach. That meant that, in the present case, only nominal damages would be awarded: *Surrey County Council v Bredero Homes Ltd* (1993).

Case law A local authority entered into a contract for the supply of a computer system to be used in the collection of the community charge. An error in the software overstated the local population with the result that the charge per head was set too low with a resulting loss of income. It also had to pay an additional sum to the county council by way of increased precept payments. It was held that the local authority had the right to recover damages for breach on behalf of the inhabitants of its area since it had to administer its funds for their benefit and owed them a duty to collect all sums which were owed to it. The authority could therefore recover damages for the increased precept payments which would otherwise be recovered from those inhabitants, but it could not recover damages in respect of the reduced receipts since the additional cost thereby caused to the inhabitants the following year was the same as the sum which, but for the breach, would have been charged in the year in question: *St Albans City and District Council v ICL* (1996).

98. Defective building work

In assessing damages for defective building work, where the court takes the view that it would be unreasonable for the plaintiff to insist on reinstatement because the cost would be out of proportion to the benefit obtained, the plaintiff will be confined to the difference in value. The plaintiff's intentions as to reinstatement would be relevant to the issue of reasonableness since, if the plaintiff does not intend to rebuild, he had lost nothing except the difference in value, if any. However, where the diminution in value was nil, it would not be correct to award the cost of reinstatement as an alternative, since it could not be right to remedy the injustice of awarding too little by unjustly awarding too much. The cost of reinstatement and diminution in value are not the only available measures of recovery for breach of contract in relation to effective building works and a court is not confined to opting for one or the other. Where there had been a breach of performance resulting in loss of expectation of performance, satisfaction of a personal preference or a pleasurable amenity, but there had been no diminution in value, a court can award modest damages as compensation: *Ruxley Electronics and Construction Ltd v Forsyth* (1995).

A victim of a breach of contract is not entitled to recover damages from the other party by way of loss of profit which he would have incurred as a result of the breach had not some supervening event caused greater damage: *Beoco Ltd v Alfa Laval Co Ltd* (1994).

99. Contributory negligence

Section 1 of the Law Reform (Contributory Negligence) Act 1945 provides that, where any person suffers damage as the result partly of his own fault and partly of the fault of any other person, a claim in respect of that damage shall not be defeated by reason of the fault of the person suffering the damage, but the damages recoverable shall be reduced to such extent as the court thinks just and equitable. Prior to this Act, fault on the part of the innocent party eliminated his claim to damages altogether. After some doubt, it has now been settled that contributory negligence on the part of the innocent party is not a defence to a claim for damages founded on a strict contractual obligation. Accordingly, where a party's liability arose from breach of a contractual provision which did not depend on a failure to take reasonable care, contributory negligence did not apply, even though the defendant might at the same time have a parallel liability in tort. In the particular case, the defendant had breached two strict contractual terms, namely the requirement to execute works in an expeditious, efficient and workmanlike manner and to comply with any statutory provisions applicable to the work, which were independent of its failure to exercise reasonable care. This meant that there was no defence based on contributory negligence to the claim in damages: *Barclays Bank* v *Fairclough Building* (1995).

100. Penalties and liquidated damages

Instead of leaving it to the courts, the parties to a contract can and often do provide in the contract the damages to be paid in the event of breach. The courts have, however, distinguished between liquidated damages, which will be enforceable, and penalties, which are not.

Liquidated damages represent a genuine pre-estimate of the measure of loss which is likely to follow a breach: *Dunlop Pneumatic Tyre Co* v *New Garage* (1915).

> *Case law* A lease for a computer provided that, in the event of a default in payment, the lessors were entitled to all arrears and to all future instalments which would have fallen due if the contract had not been terminated. It was held that this was an unforceable penalty since, in the absence of repudiation by the lessee, it obliged him, regardless of the gravity or otherwise of the breach, to make payments in respect of future instalments: *Lombard North Central* v *Butterworth* (1987).

> *Case law* The plaintiffs were members of the committee of an association formed to co-ordinate and finance the prosecution of claims by Lloyd's names. Under its rules, the association could levy additional subscriptions from members so long as this was approved by members. A proposal to this effect was carried at the annual general meeting. Written notices were then sent to members requiring payment of the additional sums. A number of members failed to pay. The committee exercised its powers under the rules of the association to declare them 'defaulting members'. As such, they were precluded from the distribution of any proceeds which might be recovered. The actions brought by the association were later compromised by an agreement under which it was to receive £116m. The association brought proceedings seeking a declaration that it was entitled to exclude the defaulting members from the distribution. The court had to decide whether the powers to declare a

165

member who failed to make the additional payments defaulting members and thus to exclude them from distributions was a penalty and hence unenforceable. It was held that the essence of the contract between the members of the association was that the burden and benefit of enforcing their claims should be shared between them. There was a pooling of all such claims and of contributions in the form of subscriptions for the purposes of financing the contemplated litigation, and it was an essential part of the arrangement that, if a member ceased to contribute to the cost of pursuing the claims, there should be power for the committee to contribute to the cost of pursuing the claims on behalf of all the members to determine that he should cease to share in the pool of benefit represented by the proceeds of such claims. Accordingly, the power in the rules to deprive a member who failed to pay his share of financing the litigation was not a penalty for breach of contract, but an essential part of the scheme of pooling the benefits and burdens of the contemplated litigation: *Nutting* v *Baldwin* (1995).

If a sum is held to be a penalty, the court will not award it, but will instead make its own assessment of damages. There is no distinction between a penalty which requires the payment of money and a penalty which requires the transfer of property: *Jobson* v *Johnson* (1989).

101. *Quantum meruit*

A claim for *quantum meruit* (or 'how much is it worth') will arise where a claim is brought for the value of work done, even though that work was not the entire work required under the contract. Such a claim can be made where, for example:

- a defendant repudiates a contract for a series of articles before all the articles have been written: *Planché* v *Colburn* (1831)
- a contract is void but one party has done work and the other has received the benefit of it: *Craven-Ellis* v *Canons Ltd* (1936)
- the parties have agreed to terminate the contract but the plaintiff has performed a substantial part of his own side of the bargain: *Dakin* v *Lee* (1916)
- one party has obtained a benefit which he could not reasonably expect to get without paying, as where a builder leaves building materials on another's land, and that other uses the materials: *Sumpter* v *Hedges* (1898).

102. The duty to mitigate

The victim of a breach of contract is not entitled to sit back and allow the loss deriving from the breach to accumulate. He is under a duty to take reasonable steps to mitigate the loss. If he fails so to do, he is not entitled to recover any damages which he could reasonably have prevented: *British Westinghouse Electric & Manufacturing Co Ltd* v *Underground Electric Rail Co Ltd* (1912). If an employee is wrongfully dismissed, he can recover damages for loss of wages, but he must reduce his loss as much as he can by seeking alternative employment: *Brace* v *Calder* (1895).

103. Specific performance

Specific performance is a court order compelling a party to perform his side of the contract. It is, however, a discretionary remedy and is generally only given when damages would not be an adequate remedy.

> *Case law* Under a contract made in March 1970 the plaintiff agreed to buy all its petrol and diesel fuel from the defendant for at least 10 years. The latter sought to terminate the contract when the market for oil was in an exceptional state. It was held that the court could grant an order of specific performance, even though the contract was not for specific or ascertained goods, because damages would not have been an effective remedy: *Sky Petroleum Ltd* v *VIP Petroleum Ltd* (1974).

It is generally the case that specific performance will not be granted if the contract is not equally enforceable by both parties. Thus, a minor could not obtain specific performance of a contract which would not be enforceable against himself: *Lumley* v *Ravenscroft* (1895). Similarly, if the defendant agrees to form a company for the purpose of working the plaintiff's patent, and the latter agrees to devote all his time to the interests of the company, there can be no specific performance since the plaintiff cannot himself be compelled to provide personal services (see below): *Stocker* v *Wedderburn* (1857). As indicated immediately above, the courts will not issue a decree of specific performance in relation to contracts of personal services because of the undesirability of compelling a party to maintain a personal relationship with another: 'the courts have never dreamt of enforcing agreements strictly personal in their nature, whether they are agreements of hiring and service, being the common relation of master and servant, or whether they are agreements for the purpose of pleasure, or for the purpose of scientific pursuits, or for the purpose of charity or philanthropy': *Rigby* v *Connol* (1880). This principle has been extended to contracts of agency; of partnership and of apprenticeship: *Chinnock* v *Sainsbury* (1861); *Scott* v *Rayment* (1868); *Webb* v *England* (1860).

It is also the case that the courts will not generally order specific performance if constant supervision is required to ensure compliance with the order by the defendant: *Ryan* v *Mutual Tontine Westminster Chambers Association* (1893).

If an order for specific performance is obtained, and it becomes impossible to perform it, the party who obtained the order has the right to ask the court to discharge the order and to award damages instead. On such an application, he can be awarded damages at common law for breach of contract since the contract had not been terminated but remained in existence until terminated by the court. The court will, however, not discharge the decree and order damages if to do so would be unjust to the other party: *Johnson* v *Agnew* (1979).

104. Injunctions

An injunction may be prohibitory or mandatory. A prohibitory injunction is granted only to restrain a breach of a negative obligation, such as an obligation not to sell beer other than beer brewed by the plaintiff: *Clegg* v *Hands* (1890). A mandatory injunction directs the defendant to take positive steps to undo what he has done in breach of contract, such as compelling a party to demolish a building which he has erected, or to remove a road which he has constructed if what has been done was in breach of contract: *Lord Manners* v *Johnson* (1875); *Charrington* v *Simons & Co Ltd* (1970). The courts will refuse to grant an injunction if its inevitable result would be to enforce a contract where a decree of specific performance would not be granted, such as a contract for personal services (see above). If, however, that would not be the effect then, even in relation to such a contract, an injunction can be awarded.

> *Case law* A agreed to serve B as an actress and not to act for any other film company. It was held that an injunction could compel her not to breach this undertaking, since there would be other ways in which she could earn her living: *Warner Bros Pictures Inc* v *Nelson* (1937).

PRIVITY, ASSIGNMENT AND NEGOTIABILITY

105. Privity of contract

The doctrine of privity of contract means that only parties to the contract acquire rights and obligations under it (for the special provisions relating to agency, see Chapter 6).

Case law B sold his business to C on condition that C pay a weekly sum to B for life and a weekly sum to his widow after his death. After B's death, C refused to pay the sum to the widow. It was held that, as she was not a party to the contract, she was unable to bring an action on it. Separately, however, as administratrix of her husband's estate (which was a party to the contract), she could enforce the contract: *Beswick v Beswick* (1968). See too *Tweddle v Atkinson* (1861); *Scruttons Ltd v Midland Silicones Ltd* (1962); *New Zealand Shipping Co v Satterthwaite* (1975).

106. Exceptions: benefits on third parties

There are, however, a number of exceptions to this strict doctrine of privity.

Constructive trust

If A can be regarded as the constructive trustee of B, and there is a contract between B and C which is then broken by C, B can sue C and join A as a co-defendant.

> *Case law* W, as broker, had negotiated a charterparty between the owners of a particular vessel and another party. A clause in the charterparty obliged the owners to pay W a commission. The broker brought an action against the owners to obtain his commission. Holding in the broker's favour, the court said that 'in such cases charterers can sue as trustees on behalf of the broker': *Les Affreteurs Reunis SA v Walford* (1919). See too *Gregory and Parker v Williams* (1817).

The courts, however, have generally been reluctant to allow the notion of a constructive trust to make much of an inroad into the doctrine of privity of contract, and it seems clear that a trust will not be inferred simply because A and B have made a contract for the benefit of C.

> *Case law* S was employed by two companies. By a contract made between him and them, one of the companies agreed in certain circumstances to pay £5500 to his widow and daughter. It was held that the contract did not create a trust in favour of the widow and daughter: '...unless an intention to create a trust is clearly to be collected from the language used and the circumstances of the case ... the court ought not to be astute to discover indications of such an intention ... in the present case both parties (and certainly the debtor) intended to keep alive their common law right to vary consensually the terms of the obligation undertaken by the company, and if circumstances had changed in the debtor's life-time injustice might have been done by holding that a trust had been created and that those terms were accordingly unalterable': *Re Schebsman* (1944). See too *Green v Russell* (1959).

169

Resale Prices Act 1976

Section 26 of the Act allows a supplier to enforce a condition as to the minimum resale price of exempted goods and as to the maximum resale price of any goods, whether exempted or not. The only goods currently exempted are medicaments and certain related goods: *Re Medicaments Reference* (1971), but readers should be advised that this is currently under review. The right to enforce a condition as to resale price maintenance against a person acquiring the goods requires satisfaction of the following conditions:

(i) The goods were sold to the supplier subject to a condition as to the price at which those goods might be resold, either generally or by or to a specified class of persons.

(ii) The person against whom it is sought to enforce the condition acquired the goods for the purpose of resale in the course of business.

(iii) The goods had not, whether immediately or not, reached the person against whom it is sought to enforce the condition through a person who had acquired them otherwise than for the purpose of trade.

(iv) The person against whom it is sought to enforce the condition had acquired the goods with notice of the condition.

(v) The resale of the goods was not pursuant to any order of any court, or by way of execution or distress, or by any person who had acquired goods, whether immediately or not, after such resale.

(v) The condition was not imposed in pursuance of any restrictive practice which had been declared by an order of the Restrictive Practices Court to be contrary to the public interest (see Chapter 3).

Law of Property Act 1925

Section 56 states that a person may take 'an immediate or other interest' under a contract, provided it is in writing. In *Beswick* v *Beswick* (above), the Court of Appeal held that a promise in writing by A to B to pay a sum of money to C would be within this provision and hence entitle C to bring an action. The House of Lords, however, rejected this view, principally on the ground that the contract did not involve 'property' within the definition of the Act. As for the precise application of s. 56, this remains somewhat unclear, but the House of Lords appeared to indicate that it applies only: to real property; to covenants running with the land; to cases where the instrument is not merely for the benefit of a third party but purports to contain a grant to or conveyance to him; and to deeds strictly between the parties. There appear to be just two cases in which the section has been applied. *Re Ecclesiastical Commissioners' Conveyance* (1936) is consistent with all of these points; while *Stromdale and Ball Ltd* v *Burden* (1952) is consistent with just the last two. The third limitation was regarded as the operative one in both decisions.

Life insurance

Section 11 of the Married Women's Property Act 1882 provides that, where a man insures his life for the benefit of his wife or children, or where a woman insures her life for the benefit of her husband or children, the policy shall 'create a trust in favour of the objects therein named'. This provision only applies where a person insures his or her own life and not where the policy is on the life of the beneficiary; and it is restricted to policies for the benefit of spouses and children, so it does not apply in favour of other beneficiaries.

Motor insurance

Section 148(7) of the Road Traffic Act 1988 provides that a person driving a motor vehicle with the consent of the owner can take the benefit of a provision in his favour in the owner's insurance policy without having to prove that the owner intended to constitute himself trustee. Sections 151, 152 of the Act further provide that persons specified in a third party car insurance policy can bring proceedings against the insurance company for their own benefit.

Fire insurance

Section 83 of the Fire Prevention (Metropolis) Act 1774 provides that, where an insured house is destroyed by fire, 'any person ... interested' may require the insurance money to be laid out towards reinstating the house. This means that a tenant could claim under the landlord's insurance, and vice versa: *Lonsdale & Thompson Ltd* v *Black Arrow Group plc* (1993).

Solicitor's indemnity insurance

Section 57 of the Solicitors' Act 1974 provides for the establishment by the Law Society of a compulsory insurance scheme to cover solicitors against liability for professional negligence or breach of duty. The scheme takes the form of a contract between the Society and insurers, whereby the latter undertake to provide indemnity insurance to solicitors. It has been held that the scheme gives rise to reciprocal rights and duties between insurer and solicitors 'by virtue of public law, not the ordinary English private law of contract': *Swain* v *Law Society* (1982).

Land Charges Act 1972

Section 4 of the Land Charges Act provides that a purchaser of land will be deemed to have notice of a duly registered land charge.

Defective premises

Section 3(1) of the Occupiers Liability Act 1957 provides that an occupier of premises who is bound by contract to permit persons who are not party to the contract to enter or use the premises owes them, not just the common law duty of care, but also any stricter obligation he may undertake towards the other contracting party.

Similarly, s. 1 of the Defective Premises Act 1972 provides that the duties imposed on a person who takes on work in connection with the provision of a dwelling are owed not only to the person to whose order the dwelling is provided, but also to any person who acquires an interest in the dwelling.

107. Exceptions: liabilities on third parties

Restrictive covenants

A restrictive covenant, which binds a purchaser not to perform certain acts of ownership on the land he has acquired, may be enforced against third parties who later acquire the land.

> *Case law* The plaintiff, the owner of several plots of land, sold the garden in the centre to E, who agreed not to build on it but to preserve it in its existing condition. After a number of conveyances, the garden was sold to the defendant who, though he knew of the restriction, proposed to build on the property. An injunction was granted to prevent him, the decisive factor being his knowledge of the restriction: *Tulk* v *Moxhay* (1848).

It has since been established that more than mere notice to the third party is required. In particular, it is essential that the original vendor, who was the first to impose the restriction, should have retained other land in the neighbourhood for the benefit and protection of which the covenant was first imposed: *Formby* v *Barker* (1903); *LCC* v *Allen* (1914).

The position with regard to land charges is subject to the Land Charges Act 1972 (see above),

Sale of ships

The question whether a restriction on use could bind a third party in relation to the sale of a ship is also one to have come before the courts.

> *Case law* A chartered a ship from X. While the charterparty was still in existence, X mortgaged the ship to B, who knew at the time of the existence of the charterparty. A alleged that B, as mortgagee, proposed to sell the ship in disregard of his contract rights and applied for an injunction to restrain B. This was agreed to in principle, but ultimately refused

because, on the facts, B had not interfered with the peformance of the charterparty: *De Mattos* v *Gibson* (1858).

However, this case cannot be taken as an example of a more wide-ranging principle. It has been said that 'it is not true as a general proposition that a purchaser of property with notice of a restrictive covenant affecting the property is bound by the covenant': *LCC* v *Allen* (1904).

Notwithstanding this observation, however, a wider view of the law has been adopted.

Case law B chartered his vessel to A on terms that A should be free to use her on the St Lawrence river for the summer season and then should return her to B each November. During the currency of the charterparty, and while B was in possession of the vessel, B sold and delivered it to C who resold it to D. D, although he knew of the charterparty, refused to deliver the ship to A for the summer season. An injunction was granted: *Lord Strathcona SS* v *Dominion Coal Co* (1926).

This was a ruling of the Privy Council and hence is not binding on English courts, though it does have persuasive authority. The position at the moment is unclear, with the cases giving no precise guidance.

Case law The plaintiffs chartered a ship from X, the owner, for 30 months. The ship was to remain in X's possession, but to be at the disposition of the plaintiffs. Some 11 months later, X sold the ship to the defendants who chartered it back to X so that it was always in the latter's possession. The plaintiffs knew of the sale and agreed to it since the ship was to remain available under their own charter. The charter between X and the defendants provided that 'if the ship is requisitioned, the charter shall thereupon cease'. There was no such clause in the plaintiffs' charter. The defendants, when they bought the ship, knew of the plaintiffs' charter, but not its terms. The ship was later requisitioned. The plaintiffs sued the defendants to obtain the compensation which had been paid to the defendants as owners.

The court refused the claim, saying that the Strathcona judgment was not good law. It pointed in particular to absence of any proprietary interest in this case (see the developments following *Tulk* v *Moxhay* discussed above). In any case, the court said that, even if that case had been correctly decided, the defendants in the present case had no knowledge of the terms of the particular charter. The position has become more confused with the decision in *Swiss Bank Corpn* v *Lloyds Bank Ltd* (1981) which endorsed both the *Strathcona* case and *De Mattos* v *Gibson*. It thought that two lines of reasoning might be applicable. One is that a purchaser who takes expressly subject to the terms of an earlier

173

contract as to the use of the property may be held to be a constructive trustee (see above). The other, to which more weight was given, arises out of the tort of inducing a breach of contract. The court thought that the grant of the injunction in *De Mattos* v *Gibson* was 'the counterpart in equity of the tort of knowing interference with contractual rights': *Port Line Ltd* v *Ben Line Steamers Ltd* (1958). See too *Sefton* v *Tophams* (1967).

108. Assignment of contracts

As a general rule, neither party to a contract can assign his rights and duties under the contract to another party.

> *Case law* S hired a carriage to D for a period of 5 years. The contract was with S alone, though R was a partner of S. After 3 years, S retired and D was informed that R would henceforth be responsible for the contract and would receive the payments. S refused to deal with R and returned the carriage. The court held that he was entitled to do so: 'Now the defendant may have been induced to enter into this contract by reason of the personal confidence which he reposed in [the other contracting party], and therefore have agreed to pay money in advance. The latter, therefore, having said it was impossible for him to perform the contract, the defendant had a right to object to its being performed by any other person, and to say that he contracted with [the other contracting party] alone, and not with any other person': *Robson and Sharpe* v *Drummond* (1831).

This does not, however, prevent what might be called 'vicarious performance' by a third party of the duty imposed on one of the contracting parties. If one party undertakes work for another in circumstances where it does not seem that his special skill and personal qualifications are essential to the task in hand, B cannot complain if A obtains another party to do the work. In such a case, however, A remains a party to the contract, so that he alone is liable and he alone can receive payment.

> *Case law* The PW Company agreed to let railway waggons to the defendants and to keep them in repair. The company went into liquidation and assigned the benefit of and the liabilities under the contract to BWC. It was held that this was properly done. The court said that the defendants could not have attached any special importance to the repairs being done by the PW Company: it was 'a rough description of work which ordinary workman conversant with the business would be perfectly able to execute': *British Waggon Company* v *Lea & Co* (1880). See too *Davies* v *Collins* (1945).

If, however, the person employed has been selected with reference to some personal factor, performance must be by that person. It has been held that personal skill and care is an ingredient in a contract by a warehouseman for the storage of furniture; and also in the contract by a publishing firm for the publication of a book: *Edwards* v *Newland & Co* (1950); *Griffith v Tower Publishing Ltd* (1897).

Another way to assign a contract is of course with the agreement of the original contracting parties. This is a rescission of one contract and its substitution for another, sometimes called a *novation*.

109. Statutory assignment

Section 136 of the Law of Property Act 1925 provides that, so long as certain conditions are observed, the assignee has a right in law to sue in his own name and take an assignment of any debt or 'legal thing in action'. This is a reference to all personal rights of property which can only be claimed or enforced by action: *Master* v *Miller* (1793). This will include contractual rights. The requirements of s. 136 are dealt with below.

Absolute

The Act says that the assignment must be 'absolute' and not 'by way of charge', meaning that the assignment must not be subject to any condition.

> *Case law* A firm of builders wrote to the plaintiffs: 'In consideration of money being advanced from time to time we hereby charge the sum of £1080, being the price ... due to us from [name of party] on the completion of the [named] buildings as security for the advances, and we hereby assign to you our interest in the above-mentioned sum until the money with added interest is repaid to you'. This was held to be conditional, since the debt was transferred only until the advances were repaid: *Durham Bros* v *Robertson* (1898).

An assignment is by way of charge, and outside the Act, if it merely gives a right to payment from a fund without transferring the whole of the fund.

> *Case law* K agreed, in consideration of a loan, to assign so much and such part of his income, salary and other emoluments from his employers as should be necessary and requisite for the repayment of sums borrowed, with interest, of such further sums as he might become indebted. This was held to be a mere security by way of charge: *Jones* v *Humphreys* (1902). The assignment of a definite part of an existing debt is not absolute, but a charge on the whole debt: *Williams* v *Atlantic Assurance Co* (1933).

175

Writing

The assignment must be in writing and signed by the assignor.

Notice

The Act requires that express notice in writing should be given to the other side. This is so even though that party is unable to read: *Hockley* v *Goldstein* (1920). No form is required for the notice, it being enough that it indicates the fact of the assignment, and the notice takes effect when received by the party to whom it is addressed: *Denny, Gasquet & Metcalfe* v *Conklin* (1913); *Holt* v *Heatherfield Trust Ltd* (1942).

Consideration

Consideration is not required for there to be a valid assignment.

110. Equitable assignment

An assignment not complying with the provisions of the Act may nonetheless be a valid equitable assignment. No particular form is required for such an assignment. It need not be in writing, except where the interest assigned is an equitable interest or trust within s. 53 of the Act. It may be addressed to the other party to the contract or to the assignee: *Brandt's Sons & Co* v *Dunlop Rubber Co Ltd* (1903); *Thomas* v *Harris* (1947). No notice to the other contracting party is required, the assignment being effective between assignor and assignor the moment it is made: *Brandt's Sons* v *Dunlop Rubber Co Ltd* (1905). Notice is, however, advisable since assignment does not bind the debtor until he has received notice. If, therefore, a debtor pays the assignor before receiving notice, that is a discharge of the debt: *Stocks* v *Dobson* (1853). Notice is also necessary to establish priority (see below).

Consideration

It has been said that for 'every equitable assignment … there must be consideration. If there be no consideration, there can be no equitable assignment': *Glegg* v *Bromley* (1912). It is, however, generally the view that this statement is too wide, As far as the other party to the contract is concerned, the presence or otherwise of consideration between assignor and assignee would appear to be immaterial: *Walker* v *Bradford Old Bank* (1884).

As between assignor and assignee, the position appears to be that consideration is necessary for an agreement to assign, but not for the actual assignment: *Tailby* v *Official Receiver* (1888).

111. Title of assignee

Whether the assignment is conducted under the Act or is an equitable assignment, the assignee takes 'subject to equities', that is subject to all such defences as might have prevailed against the assignor. This means, for example, that although the assignee might be entirely free of any blame and have paid value for the rights assigned, the debtor can rescind the original contract on the ground that he was induced to enter it by the fraud of the assignor, or set off a claim for damages for breach of the contract by the assignor: *Graham* v *Johnson* (1869); *Young* v *Kitchin* (1878). The debtor cannot, however, set up against an innocent assignee a claim for a strictly personal nature which he may have against the assignee. He is restricted to claims arising out of the contract itself.

> *Case law* A party was fraudulently induced to buy a particular newspaper for £1000, of which £200 was to be paid immediately, the balance by instalments. The seller assigned this £800 to a party who took in good faith without knowledge of the fraud. When sued by the assignee, the purchaser claimed that they had lost more than £800 and that no money was therefore owed. The court held that the purchaser's claim was purely personal and did not come within the 'category of claims arising out of the contract upon which the person is sued by the assignee ... may set up for his protection': *Stoddart* v *Union Trust* (1912). It is, however, not easy to justify this decision which appears to draw a distinction between a claim for damages in fraud and a similar claim for breach of contract, and it may be that the case is explicable on the ground that the debtor had counterclaimed for damages for fraud against the assignee instead of setting up the fraud by way of defence.

112. Priorities

It may happen that an assignor makes two or more assignments of the same matter to different assignees. If it is the case then not all assignees can be satisfied. The so-called rule in *Dearle* v *Hall* (1828) is that successive assignees rank in order of notice to the other contracting party and not according to the date of assignment. This rule will, however, operate only if the subsequent assignee has no knowledge of the earlier: *Re Holmes* (1885). It is not relevant that he knew of that assignment when he gave notice: *Mutual Life Assurance Society* v *Langley* (1886).

> *Case law* A debt due to a firm was assigned by one partner to the defendants in writing and afterwards by the other partners to the plaintiff by deed. The plaintiff gave notice to the debtor before the defendants. It was

held that there was a valid equitable assignment to the plaintiffs in priority to the defendants: *Marchant* v *Morton, Down & Co* (1901).

113. Form of notice

In general, notice need not be formal. Any kind of notice suffices so long as the fact of assignment is brought to the attention of the other contracting party. A letter stating that the writers had 'authority to collect freight against which we have made payments' was held to be good notice: *Smith* v *SS Zigurds* (1934). Again, oral notice acquired in the ordinary course of business has been held to suffice, even though no notice was given by the assignee: *Re Worcester* (1868).

114. Non-assignable rights

Despite the existence of the provisions of the Law of Property Act 1925, the assignability of contractual rights in any given case is governed by the rules as to what could be assigned by the rules established prior to the Judicature Act 1873, which contained the forerunner to s. 136 of the 1925 Act: *Tollhurst* v *Associated Portland Cement Manufacturers Ltd* (1903).

Assignment prohibited by the contract

If rights arising under a contract are stated not to be assignable, any purported assignment will be invalid as against the other party to the contract.

> *Case law* The benefits of building contracts were purportedly assigned by lessees of the properties on which the building work was being carried out to assignees of the leases. The building contract specified that there was to be no assignment of the contract by either party without the other's consent. No consent was obtained. It was held that the assignment of the benefit of the contract, as opposed to vicarious performance (see above), was barred: *Linden Gardens Trust Ltd* v *Lenesta Sludge Disposals Ltd* (1993).

It does, however, seem that a prohibited assignment can be effective as between assignor and assignee: '[A] prohibition on assignment normally only invalidates the assignation as against the other party to the contract so as to prevent a transfer of the chose in action; in the absence of the clearest words it cannot operate to invalidate the contract as between the assignor and assignee and even then it may be ineffective on public policy grounds': *Linden Gardens Trust Ltd* v *Lenesta Sludge Disposals Ltd*. See *Tom Shaw & Co* v *Moss Empires Ltd* (1909).

Assignment prohibited by statute or public policy

Assignment may be prohibited by statute, as for example the assignment of certain benefits is prohibited by s. 187 of the Social Security Administration Act 1992. An assignment of a salary by a public offer has been held to be void on grounds of public policy: *Re Mirams* (1891).

Assignments savouring of maintenance or champerty

A chose in action is not assignable if it savours of maintenance or champerty (see **68** above for the meaning of these terms): *Dawson v Great Northern & City Rly* (1905); *Glegg v Bromley* (1912); *Defries v Milne* (1913); *Giles v Thompson* (1944).

The scope of this prohibition, however, is relatively limited: 'If the assignment is of a property right or interest and the cause of action is ancillary to that right or interest, or if the assignee had a genuine commercial interest in taking the assignment, [there is no reason] why the assignment should be struck down as an assignment of a bare cause of action or as savouring of maintenance': *Trendtex Trading Corporation v Credit Suisse* (1982). It has been held that rights of action which are incidental and subsidiary to property rights may be assigned when the property is transferred; and that a claim to a simple debt can be assigned even though the debtor has refused to pay, and even though this may be said to be an assignment of a right to litigate: *Dickenson v Burrell* (1866); *County Hotel and Wine Co Ltd v London & North Western Rly* (1921); *Comfort v Betts* (1891). It is, however, the case that a purported assignee has no legitimate commercial interest in a purely personal claim, the result being that such a claim cannot be assigned: *Trendtex Trading Corporation v Credit Suisse* (1982). Obvious examples would be the right to damages for a personal tort such as assault or defamation.

It should be noted that trustees in bankruptcy and liquidators are to some extent permitted to assign bare rights to litigate by the provisions of ss. 167, 314, 436, Scheds 4 and 5 of the Insolvency Act 1986.

115. Personal contracts

The benefit of a contract can only be assigned in 'cases where it can make no difference to the person on whom the obligation lies to which of two persons he is to discharge it': *Tollhurst v Associated Portland Cement Manufacturers Ltd* (1903). As a general rule, contractual rights to, for example, the payment of money, to the sale or occupation or use of land, or to building work, do not involve personal considerations and can be assigned: *J Miller Ltd v Lawrence & Bardsley* (1966); *Charlotte Thirty Ltd and Bloom Ltd v Croker Ltd* (1990). The benefit of a car insurance policy, however, involves personal considerations and cannot be assigned: *Peters v General Accident, etc. Ltd* (1938). The right to employ someone is also clearly unassignable: *Nokes* v *Doncaster Amalgamated Collieries Ltd* (1940).

116. Negotiable instruments

Negotiable instruments, such as cheques and bills of exchange, differ in a number of ways from assignable contracts. Thus:

(*i*) They are transferable by delivery (or in some cases by delivery and endorsement).

(*ii*) No notice need be given to the debtor.

(*iii*) The right or contract embodied in them cannot be transferred without the instrument.

(*iv*) A *bona fide* transferee for value may obtain a good title even though the title of his transferor was defective.

5

Sale and supply of goods and services

In this chapter, we consider the law as it relates to the sale and supply of goods and services. To a high degree, the law has been codified in a number of enactments, notably the Sale of Goods Act 1979 and the Supply of Goods and Services Act 1982. Similarly, the law relating to exclusion clauses and disclaimers is almost entirely to be found in the Unfair Contract Terms Act 1977 and the Unfair Terms in Consumer Contracts Regulations 1994.

CONTRACT OF SALE

1. What constitutes a contract of sale

The Sale of Goods Act 1979, s. 1, defines a contract of sale as one 'whereby the seller (a) transfers, or (b) agrees to transfer, the property in the goods to a buyer for a money consideration called the price'. Section 61 of the Act says that 'property' means 'general property' and not merely a 'special property'. In effect, the reference to 'general property' is a reference to the full rights of ownership. 'Goods' in turn is defined by s. 61 as meaning all chattels and choses in possession, but not things in action or money (unless the money is traded as goods and not as money, such as an antique). 'Goods' also means (a) 'industrial growing crops', once they have been severed from the land; until severance, they are classed as part of the land and are not goods; and (b) 'future goods', i.e. goods to be made or acquired after the contract has been made.

2. Sale and agreement to sell

When the property in goods is to be transferred immediately, the contract is known as a 'sale'. If property is to be transferred at some future time, s. 2 of the 1979 Act provides that the contract is known as 'an agreement to sell'. All contracts relating to future goods (see above) are agreements to sell: s. 5(3). A common form of an agreement to sell is the conditional sale under which a buyer agrees to buy goods with the price payable in instalments.

3. Contracts not within the 1979 Act

Work and materials

The Sale of Goods Act does not apply to contracts in which the purchaser is buying the skills of a craftsman and not merely the goods produced by him. Instead, they are governed by the Supply of Goods and Services Act 1982 (see **62** below). The test usually applied is: is the essential object of the agreement the provision of goods or the exercise of skill?

> *Case law* In *Robinson* v *Graves* (1935) the employment of an artist to paint a portrait was held to be a contract for the supply of work and materials, since the artist's skill is the main constituent of the contract.

Barter

The 1979 Act lays down that a contract for the sale of goods is one where money is exchanged for goods, hence it does not apply to contracts of barter. Here the transaction is governed instead by the Supply of Goods and Services Act 1982. However, where a contract is one of part-exchange (a typical example being an old car plus cash in exchange for a new car), that is probably a contract for the sale of goods, certainly where a specific sum is allocated to the trade-in. If a contract of part-exchange is not a contract for the sale of goods, it will be covered by the Supply of Goods and Services Act. In fact, the distinction is largely academic, since, in terms of the obligations imposed on the seller or supplier, there is no material difference between the Sale of Goods Act and the Supply of Goods and Services Act, the latter covering such transactions if the former does not.

Sale and loan on security

The Act is expressly stated in s. 62(4) not to apply to any transaction in the form of a contract of sale which is to operate by way of mortgage, pledge, charge or other security. These are governed by the Bills of Sale Acts 1878–1882.

4. Capacity to contract

Capacity to contract is stated by s. 3 of the Act to be governed by the ordinary rules as to making a contract. The Act provides that where necessaries are supplied to someone under the age of 18, to a drunkard or someone lacking full mental capacity, that person must pay a 'reasonable price' for them. By virtue of the Minors' Contracts Act 1987, a court, where it considers it fair to do so, can order a minor against whom a contract cannot be enforced to return the property which he has acquired. Prior to the Act, the minor could keep the property even if he could not be made to pay for it, as where the contract was not for necessaries (*Nash* v *Inman* (1908)). Similarly, that Act also changed the law by providing that an adult guarantor could be made liable where the minor could not be held to the contract.

5. Form of contract

Section 4 of the 1979 Act provides that any form suffices, written or oral, and a contract may be implied from conduct. This is a clear distinction from contracts for the sale of land where, under the provisions of the Law of Property (Miscellaneous Provisions) Act 1989, the contract must at the very least be in writing and signed by the relevant parties.

6. The price

Section 8(1) of the 1979 Act provides that the price:

(i) may be fixed at the time of contracting by the parties themselves, *or*
(ii) may be left to be determined in the course of dealings between the parties, *or*
(iii) may be left to be fixed by some third party.

Where the contract states that the price is to be fixed by a third party, and he fails to do so, s. 9 states that the contract is void. If, however, the purchaser has by then taken the benefit of the goods, he must pay a reasonable price for them. If the third party's failure to fix the price is due to the fault of one of the parties, s. 9(2) provides that such party is liable in an action for damages. Where no price is fixed in any of the ways listed above, the buyer must pay a reasonable price. Section 8(3) says that this is a question of fact to be judged on the circumstances of the particular case.

7. Agreement in the absence of agreement on price

The price is so basic to a contract that, if the parties have expressly left it over for later agreement, a court could well conclude that the parties did not intend to make, and have not made, a contract.

Case law In *May & Butcher* v *R* (1934), an agreement for the purchase of government tentage provided that the price, the manner of delivery and dates of payment were to be agreed upon from time to time. If the

183

contract had simply failed to mention these items, they could have been resolved by applying the provisions of the Sale of Goods Act. However, the contract expressly left them over for later agreement. That being so, and the items being so basic, the House of Lords held that the parties had not intended to make a contract but had simply agreed to agree. There was therefore no contract.

If, however, a relatively minor matter is left over for later agreement it does not necessarily follow that there is no contract. It is perfectly possible in law for parties to make an interim agreement for the sale of goods which requires further negotiation to iron out the less important details of the transaction (*Pagnan* v *Food Products* (1987)). All the circumstances must be examined to see if the parties intended to leave over the entire agreement or whether they intended to make a binding contract, albeit one with some details still outstanding.

> *Case law* In *Foley* v *Classique Coaches Ltd* (1934), the defendants bought some land from the plaintiff and it was a condition of the purchase that the defendants agreed to buy petrol (for their coach business) only from the plaintiffs. The agreement provided for the price of the petrol 'to be agreed by the parties from time to time' and, failing agreement, to be settled by arbitration. It was held there that the parties had made a binding contract, albeit with the price still outstanding.

As in *May & Butcher* v *R*, no price is payable and s. 8 is irrelevant. If there is a contract the price is ascertained by the relevant method in s. 8. In *Foley's* case, this was by arbitration, the manner agreed in the contract as provided for in s. 8(1).

8. Deposits and part payment

It is not uncommon for the buyer to pay part of the price at the time of making the contract to buy. This payment could be either a deposit or mere part payment. The effect of a deposit or mere part payment is a matter of agreement between the parties. In the absence of any agreement to the contrary, a deposit is generally forfeited by the buyer if the sale falls through because of his fault. A mere part payment, however, is returnable. A deposit is, in the words of Lord Macnaughten in *Soper* v *Arnold* (1887), 'a guarantee that the purchaser means business'.

It is a security for the completion of the purchase. As so often, the law endeavours to discover the intention of the parties. It examines all the circumstances to see whether they intended the money to be a deposit or merely a payment on account. If the parties actually used the word 'deposit', then unless there is evidence to the contrary it will be assumed that that is what they meant: *Elson* v *Prices Tailors Ltd* (1963).

TERMS IMPLIED BY THE 1979 ACT

9. Conditions and warranties

The terms implied by the Sale of Goods Act 1979 are described in the Act as being either 'conditions' or 'warranties'. The former is not defined in the Act, but a warranty is as something 'collateral' to the main purpose of the Act, upon breach of which the injured party may claim only damages but not repudiate the contract: s. 61. In effect, these terms bear their conventional meaning so that a 'condition' is a major term of the contract, while a 'warranty' is a minor term . There is no definition of 'condition' in the Act, but it has been judicially defined to mean a term which goes 'directly to the substance of the contract, or, in other words, [is] so essential to its nature that [its] non-performance may fairly be considered by the other party as a substantial failure to perform the contract at all ... usage has consecrated the term 'condition' to describe an obligation of [this] class' (*Wallis Sons & Webb* v *Pratt & Haynes* (1910)). The importance of the distinction lies in the remedies available on breach. Where a warranty is broken the position is as stated above. Where the breach is of a condition, the injured party may claim damages and elect to terminate the contract.

10. Assessment of terms: innominate terms

If the Act states specifically that a particular term is a condition or a warranty, that necessarily determines the issue. There will be many cases, however, where nothing is said specifically in the Act. In such cases, the courts will look to other relevant Acts, case law and the intentions of the parties. The courts have, though, said that the use of one term or the other will not necessarily conclude the matter if the facts showed that what the contract called a 'condition' was, on analysis, really a 'warranty': *Schuler AG* v *Wickman Maritime Tool Sales Ltd* (1974).

In recent years, the courts have also developed the theory of the 'innominate term'. If there is no clear guidance as to whether a term is a condition or a warranty, the effects of a breach of this innominate term will depend on whether or not it goes to the root of the contract: *Cehave N.V.* v *Bremer* (1975); *Hong Kong Fir Shipping Co Ltd* v *Kawasaki Kishen Kaisha Ltd* (1962). See too the preceding chapter.

11. *Ex post facto* warranties

The buyer is always entitled to treat any breach of condition as a breach of warranty: s. 11(2). This means that he will be able to claim damages but will lose his right to terminate the agreement. In some cases (unless otherwise agreed in the contract), the buyer has to treat a breach of condition as a breach of warranty. This arises where the contract is non-severable and the buyer has accepted any part of the goods: s. 11(4). Section 14(1) of the Supply of Goods (Implied Terms) Act 1973, however, provides that this does not apply where the buyer is not a trade buyer and the agreement is a conditional sale agreement. In such cases, s. 14(2) of the 1973 Act further provides that a condition is to be treated as a warranty when it would have been treated in such a way in a hire purchase agreement.

12. Terms and mere representations

It used to be of considerable importance to determine whether some statement made in the course of contractual negotiations was a term of the contract or a mere representation inducing the other party to make the contract. The difference could affect the remedies available if the statement was false. If it was a representation, and was made innocently, then the contract could be terminated, but damages were unavailable. If, on the other hand, the same statement were a term of the contract, the victim would always be able to claim damages and terminate the contract.

Now, however, the Misrepresentation Act 1967 has considerably reduced the relevance of the distinction because (a) it no longer matters that a representation has become a term of the contract: and (b) damages and termination are allowed for a negligent misrepresentation and damages can be awarded at the court's discretion for an innocent misrepresentation as an alternative to termination of the contract.

13. Implied terms as to title

Section 12 of the Sale of Goods Act provides as follows:

> In every contract of sale, other than one to which subsection 3 applies (see 'Circumstances showing limited title' below), there is:
> (a) an implied condition that the seller has the right to sell or, in an agreement to sell (see above), the right to sell at a time when the property is to pass and
> (b) an implied warranty that the goods shall be free of any undisclosed charge or encumbrance and that the buyer shall enjoy quiet possession (subject to any encumbrance or charge disclosed known to him).

For 'conditions' and 'warranties', see 9 above.

Case law A purchased a car from B and resold it to C. A then discovered that the car had never belonged to B who had bought it in good faith from someone having no title. The car was reclaimed by the original owner and A paid off C by refunding him the £400. He sued B for the return of £334 and was upheld in the Court of Appeal: *Rowland* v *Divall* (1923).

Case law In another case, the buyer was entitled to disturbance of quiet possession when a third party validly claimed that he had patent rights over the machine sold by the seller. This was so even though the seller did have title in the goods: *Microbeads AC* v *Vinhurst Road Markings Ltd* (1975).

14. Circumstances showing limited title

Where it appears from the contract, or can be inferred from the circum-stances, that the seller is transferring only such title as he or a third person may have, there is:

(a) an implied warranty that all known charges or encumbrances have been disclosed to the buyer, and

(b) an implied warranty that neither *(i)* the seller, nor *(ii)* any third person to whose claims the sale is subject, nor *(iii)* any person claiming under the seller or such third person, will disturb the buyer's quiet possession (subject to any encumbrance or charge disclosed or known to him).

Case law In *Greenwood* v *Bennett* (1973). the seller sold a car which he had stolen. The buyer spent over £200 on repairs. When it was discovered, the police commenced proceedings to determine the rightful owner. In these proceedings, the car was ordered to be returned to its true owner, but compensation was to be paid to the buyer for the cost of repairs.

The principle of this case was subsequently consolidated in s. 6 of the Torts (Interference with Goods) Act 1977.

15. Avoiding the terms as to title

The Unfair Contract Terms Act, s. 6, provides that terms as to title cannot be excluded, whether the contract is with a business or a private consumer. Furthermore, the Consumer Transactions (Restrictions on Statements) Order 1976 provides that if such an exclusion clause were to be incorpo-rated into a consumer contract, a criminal offence would be committed.

Such exclusion clauses would also be unfair and unenforceable in consumer contracts under the provisions of the Unfair Terms in Consumer Contracts Regulations 1994, but this in effect adds nothing to the above (these Regulations are discussed in detail in the preceding chapter).

187

16. Correspondence with description

In every sale of goods by description, in accordance with s. 13 of the Sale of Goods Act, there is an implied condition (see **9** above) that the goods shall correspond with their description.

Case law Pinnock v *Lewis* (1923): A contract described the product as copra cake, which was to be used as a cattle feed. The goods delivered combined copra cake with castor beans. The court held that the quantity of beans so changed the nature of the product that it no longer fitted the description 'copra cake'.

Case law Raynham Farm v *Symbol Motor Corporation* (1987): A car sold as 'new' had, some months previously, been damaged by fire in the Netherlands after being exported from the United Kingdom. It was returned to this country where a great deal of repair work was done. The court accepted that a certain amount of very minor damage could be sustained by a car which could still properly be described as 'new'. The damage suffered in this case, however, however good the quality of the repairs, prevented such a description being made, not least because there would always be a lurking doubt that the fire had caused additional damage which had not been detected.

There will, however, be cases where, although there might be some admixture or alteration in the substance or the character of the product, it retains enough of its identity for it not to have been misdescribed.

Case law Ashington Piggeries Ltd v *Christopher Hill* (1972): Herring meal was contaminated with a substance which made it unsuitable for feeding to mink, the purpose for which it had been bought. It was ruled that the product had been correctly described as 'herring meal' even though not suitable for its intended purpose

The requirement that goods must conform to their description is stated by the Act to apply only when goods are sold by description.

Case law Harlingdon & Leinster v *Christopher Hull Fine Arts Ltd* (1990): A firm of art dealers was asked to sell certain paintings described in a catalogue as being the work of a certain German painter. They themselves only specialised in British paintings and took them to an auction-house which expressed an interest. They also contacted the plaintiffs who specialised in German paintings, telling them that they did not know much about the German school. An employee of the plaintiffs examined the paintings and agreed to buy the paintings without seeking further details. The paintings were forgeries.

The court held that the goods had not been sold by description. For that to happen, the buyer had to rely on the description, and the facts showed that this had not been the case. The plaintiffs had not relied on the description and so, although the goods might have been misdescribed, there was no breach of s. 13.

Section 13(3) provides that, just because goods are selected by the buyer from goods exposed for sale, this does not prevent the sale from being a sale by description. This provision ensures that when, for example, goods are selected from a supermarket shelf, those goods can still be sold by description even though no words are ever exchanged.

The provision as to conformity with description is one of strict liability (see **22** Strict liability below).

17. Avoiding the term as to description

The Unfair Contract Terms Act 1977 states that, where the buyer is a consumer, the seller cannot exclude his duty to provide goods which conform to their description. If the buyer is a business buyer, the 1977 Act states that s. 13 can be excluded only if the seller can prove that the exclusion is a reasonable one (see the discussion of this Act in the preceding chapter). In addition, it is a criminal offence under the Consumer Transactions (Restrictions on Statements) Order 1976 to include in a consumer contract a clause excluding s. 13.

It would almost certainly be the case that a term seeking to exclude the condition as to description would be unfair and unenforceable under the Unfair Terms in Consumer Contracts Regulations 1994, but this adds nothing to the above.

18. Satisfactory quality

Under the provisions of the Sale of Goods Act 1979, in its original form, a seller was under a duty to supply goods which were of *merchantable quality*. This requirement has now been changed by the provisions of the Sale and Supply of Goods Act 1994 which instead imposes a 'condition' (see **9** above) that goods must be of a *satisfactory quality*. It further provides that they will meet this standard if they are such 'that a reasonable person would regard as satisfactory, taking account of any description of the goods, the price (if relevant) and all the other relevant circumstances'. It goes on to say that 'quality' includes state or condition and that the following matters, among others, are in appropriate cases aspects of the quality of goods:

- fitness for all the purposes for which goods of the kind in question are commonly supplied

- appearance and finish
- safety
- durability.

Although there is considerable overlap between 'merchantable quality' and 'satisfactory quality', many of the cases dealing with the former requirement cannot be safely accepted as precedents for the new law. It is likely, however, that the following cases would be decided the same way now.

Case law Bernstein v *Pamson Motors (Golders Green) Ltd* (1987): A new car broke down when the buyer had had it for just three weeks and when he had driven only some 220 km. It was held that the car was not of merchantable quality. This was because, while the car had been repaired to 'good as new', there would always be doubt as to the area of potential damage caused by the seizing up of the engine; second, the fact that the engine had seized while being driven on a motorway meant that the car had been unsafe. It is certain that this car would also have been held not to have been of satisfactory quality.

Case law Rogers v *Parish (Scarborough) Ltd* (1987): A new Range Rover was purchased for about £16,000. It proved unsatisfactory and it was replaced by another which turned out no better. Although drivable, it had faulty oil seals and defects in the engine, gearbox and bodywork. Despite several attempts at repair, problems persisted with the engine and gearbox. The court ruled that the car was not of merchantable quality, since consideration had to be given not merely to drivability, but also to comfort, ease of handling and pride in the vehicle's outward appearance. There can be no doubt that this finding would be the same under the new law.

In the *Harlingdon & Leinster* case (see **16** above), the court ruled that the painting was still of merchantable quality, even though not by the painter ascribed to it. The point was that it could still be resold, albeit at a lower price, and was still capable of aesthetic appreciation. Again, it is likely that the painting would now be judged to be of satisfactory quality.

The provision as to satisfactory quality is stated only to apply to business transactions, so that purely private transactions (such as a sale through the classified sections of a newspaper) will not be within the Act. Avoiding the term as to satisfactory quality the Unfair Contract Terms Act 1977 states that where the buyer is a consumer, the seller cannot exclude these provisions. If the buyer is a business buyer, they can be excluded only if the seller can prove that the exclusion clause is a reasonable one (see generally the preceding chapter). In addition, it is a criminal offence under the Consumer Transactions (Restrictions on Statements) Order 1976 to include in a consumer contract a clause excluding the provisions as to satisfactory quality.

It would almost certainly be the case that a term seeking to exclude the condition as to description would be unfair and unenforceable under the Unfair Terms in Consumer Contracts Regulations 1994, but this adds nothing to the above.

However, the Sale of Goods Act itself does indicate that, outside the case of exclusion clauses, it may be possible for a buyer, consumer or business to lose his rights to goods of satisfactory quality. This will come about when any matter making the quality of the goods unsatisfactory is:

(a) specifically drawn to the buyer's attention before the contract is made; *or*

(b) the buyer has examined the goods before the contract was made which that examination ought to reveal.

There has been no case law on **(a)** but it is not thought that it is necessary for a seller specifically to refer to 'defects'. It would be enough that he pointed out facts which were defects.

In the case of **(b)**, the buyer must actually have examined the goods. It is not enough that he was offered the chance to examine the goods and declined it. It is, furthermore, only the examination which was actually made which is relevant, not some different or more rigorous examination which could have been made, but which was not.

The provision as to satisfactory quality is one of strict liability (see **22** Strict liability below).

19. Fitness for particular purpose

Where the seller sells goods in the course of a business and the buyer, expressly or by implication, makes known to the seller any particular purpose for which the goods are being bought, s. 14(3) lays down an implied condition that the goods are reasonably fit for that purpose, whether or not it is a purpose for which such goods are commonly supplied, except where the circumstances show that the buyer did not rely, or that it was unreasonable for him to rely, on the seller's skill or judgement.

Where the goods have only one normal purpose, a seller will be taken to know the purpose for which the goods are wanted.

Case law In *Priest* v *Last* (1903), a hot water bottle was held to be bought for a particular purpose although it had only the one purpose.

If the goods have a special purpose, this must be disclosed to the seller.

Case law In *Griffiths* v *Peter Conway Ltd* (1939), a buyer of a coat contracted dermatitis. This was, however, because of an abnormally sensitive skin. It was held that the buyer should have advised the seller of the special use in advance. Since this had not been done, and although the coat was not fit for this buyer's purpose, there was no breach of the statutory requirement.

Case law The correctness of the decision in the preceding case was upheld by the House of Lords in *James Slater and Hamish Slater* v *Finning Ltd* (1996). The dispute itself involved the installation by the respondents of a camshaft in a motor fishing vessel owned by the appellants. Satisfactory sea trials were held, but, following fishing trips of some 50 hours, noises were heard from the engine. A cam lobe was found to be badly worn and the newly installed camshaft was replaced. Even so, further trouble was encountered and the followers on the exhaust valves were found to be worn, and they were replaced. For the next four months, the vessel was trouble-free, but then tapping noises reappeared in the engine. An exhaust follower was found to be badly worn. This was replaced, but then it was decided to replace the whole camshaft with its followers and cam blocks, with the same model. Again, however, after a four-week period at sea, noises were once more heard coming from the engine. It was the view of a marine surveyor that the vessel was unseaworthy. The appellants rejected the offer of a free overhaul of the engine and insisted that a new engine be installed. Eventually, a new engine of a different design was installed.

The old engine was overhauled and installed in another vessel. No trouble was ever experienced by that boat and there was evidence that such camshafts had been installed in hundreds of other engines without causing any problems. It was held at first instance, and this was not challenged before the House of Lords, that excessive torsional resonance caused the damage to the camshafts, and this was produced by some unascertained force which was external to both engine and camshaft. It was argued by the appellants that the provisions of s. 14(3) were to be applied to a vessel having such characteristics; that they had made known to the respondents the fact that the camshaft was to be installed in that vessel; and that, in consequence, the respondents had taken the risk that the vessel might have some characteristic which would subject the camshaft to excessive wear.

The appellants had relied on *Cammell Laird & Co Ltd* v *The Manganese Bronze and Brass Co Ltd* (1934) where the contract had been for the supply of two propellers for ships then under construction. The House of Lords in that case had found there to be a breach of the Act, but the present House distinguished it on the grounds that the problem which had arisen lay with the propellers themselves, whereas in the present case it lay with some external feature peculiar to the particular vessel.

Lord Keith applied the Griffiths ruling as 'directly applicable' to the case in hand. He noted that the abnormality in this case was the tendency of the vessel to create excessive torsional resonance in camshafts, a fact of which the respondents had not been made aware and hence in relation to which they were in no position to exercise any skill or judgment. As a matter of principle, he said 'a buyer who purchases goods from a seller who deals in goods of that description there is no breach of the implied condition of fitness where the failure of the goods to meet the intended purpose arises from an abnormal feature or idiosyncrasy not made known to the seller, in the buyer or in the circumstances of the use of the goods by the buyer'. Lord Keith also stated that this would be so even if the buyer was himself unaware of such feature or idiosyncrasy. Lord Steyn agreed, saying that, on the facts of the case, the seller was entitled to assume that the camshaft was to be used in an ordinary vessel, and that the duty imposed by the Sale of Goods Act was accordingly limited in its scope. To argue that *Griffiths* v *Peter Conway* should have been decided on the absence of any reliance by the buyer on the seller's skill and judgment was wrong. It was the failure of that buyer to disclose as a particular purpose the fact that the coat was to be worn by a person with sensitive skin which was fatal to the claim. He concluded with the observation that, to uphold the present claim, 'would be to allow *caveat vendor* to run riot'.

By s. 14(4) an implied condition or warranty as to fitness for a particular purpose may be annexed to a contract of sale by usage, e.g. trade custom.

The instructions accompanying goods are part of the goods themselves. So if the instructions are misleading the goods will not be reasonably fit for their purpose, nor will they be of satisfactory quality: *Wormell* v *RHM Agriculture (East) Ltd* (1987).

20. Avoiding the term as to fitness for purpose

The Unfair Contract Terms Act 1977 states that where the buyer is a consumer, the seller cannot exclude the provisions as to fitness for purpose. If the buyer is a business buyer, these provisions can be excluded only if the seller can prove that the exclusion clause is a reasonable one (see generally the preceding chapter). In addition, it is a criminal offence under the Consumer Transactions (Restrictions on Statements) Order 1976 to include in a consumer contract a clause excluding these provisions.

It would almost certainly be the case that a term seeking to exclude the condition as to description would be unfair and unenforceable under the Unfair Terms in Consumer Contracts Regulations 1994, but this adds nothing to the above.

It should, however, be remembered that the implied condition will not apply when the buyer did not rely on the seller's skill or judgment, or was unreasonable in any such reliance.

> *Case law* *Baker* v *Suzuki* (1993): The buyer of a motor cycle was injured in an accident involving the motor cycle. The court ruled that the machine was, in fact, reasonably fit for its purpose but added that the term was inapplicable since the buyer had not relied on the seller's skill and judgement. The buyer 'knew what he wanted when he came in, and chose one of the two vehicles the seller had of that description for ... reasons that he arrived at on his own'.

21. Sales by sample

In a sale by sample, there is a condition implied by s. 15 of the Act that:

(a) the bulk shall correspond with the sample in quality, and

(b) the buyer shall have a reasonable opportunity to compare the bulk with the sample, and

(c) the goods shall be free of any defect rendering them unsatisfactory, and which would not be apparent on reasonable examination of the sample.

Section 15(1) provides that a contract is by way of sample where there 'is an express or implied term to that effect in the contract'.

Avoiding the term as to samples

The Unfair Contract Terms Act 1977 states where the buyer is a consumer, the seller cannot exclude the above implied condition. If the buyer is a business buyer, s. 15 can be excluded only if the seller can prove that the exclusion clause is a reasonable one. It is also, under the provisions of the Consumer Transactions (Restrictions on Statements) Order 1976, a criminal offence to include in a consumer contract a clause excluding s. 15. It is also likely to be the case that an exclusion clause would be unfair and hence unenforceable under the provisions of the Unfair Terms in Consumer Contracts Regulations 1994, but this adds little to the foregoing.

22. Strict liability

The above implied conditions impose duties of strict liability. That is to say, the seller is liable merely because the goods do not match the particular condition, even if the seller is totally free of blame.

Case law In *Frost* v *Aylesbury Dairy Co Ltd* (1905) a bottle of milk was contaminated by the presence of a bacillus. The seller was held to be in breach of the Act even though the presence of the bacillus was not then discoverable by the use of any care or diligence.

23. Trivial breaches

Section 15A of the 1979 Act provides that where the breach of ss. 13, 14 or 15 is so slight that rejection of the goods would be unreasonable, the breach of the condition is to be treated as a breach of warranty unless the contract provides to the contrary (for the right to reject, see **48** below). This provision does not, however, apply where the buyer deals as consumer. A person deals as consumer if, in accordance with s. 12 of the Unfair Contract Terms Act 1977, he neither makes the contract in the course of a business nor holds himself out as so doing, and the other party does make the contract in the course of a business: the goods must be of a type ordinarily supplied for private use or consumption.

PASSING OF OWNERSHIP AND RISK

24. Conditions of assessment

The transfer of the legal property in the goods is important for assessing who bears the risk of loss or deterioration, damage and such like. The position depends *(a)* on whether the contract is a sale or an agreement to sell (see **2** above) and *(b)* on whether the goods are specific and ascertained, or unascertained (see **25** below).

25. Specific and ascertained goods

Specific goods are defined in s. 61(1) of the Sale of Goods Act as goods identified and agreed upon at the time of making the contract and includes an undivided share, specified as a fraction or percentage of goods agreed on and identified at the time the contract is made. Goods are not specific merely because the source of supply has been agreed, e.g. '500 tonnes of coal from stack no. 2'.

Ascertained goods, though not specifically defined in the Act, will be those goods identified and agreed upon after the making of the contract. Unascertained goods, again not specifically defined in the Act, will be

195

goods not yet identified and agreed upon, but merely described, e.g. the coal in the example given above.

When the property passes:

(a) Specific and ascertained goods: the property in them passes whenever the parties intend it to pass. The intention of the parties may be *(i)* stated in the contract or *(ii)* left to be ascertained by the court from the circumstances: see below.

(b) Unascertained goods: the property passes only when they become ascertained, i.e. no property can pass in unascertained goods. There is, however, an exception to this introduced by s. 20A of the Sale of Goods Act as inserted by the Sale of Goods (Amendment) Act 1995. These rules apply to a contract to sell a specified quantity of unascertained goods out of a specified bulk and provide for a special kind of proprietary interest to pass even before the goods have become ascertained. These special provisions are dealt with below.

26. Tests of intention

Where the contract does not state when the property is to pass, the court will apply the following tests, referred to in the Act as Rules to ascertain the intend of the parties.

Rule 1

Where there is an unconditional contract for sale of specific goods in a deliverable state (defined under Rule 2) the property passes when the contract is made (even if delivery is postponed): s. 18(1).

> *Case law   Dennant* v *Skinner & Collom* (1948): Goods were knocked down at auction to the highest bidder. Payment was made by cheque and the goods taken away. The cheque was not honoured. It was ruled that property had passed when the bid was accepted, so that a term in a document signed subsequently to the effect that property only passed when the cheque was met had no effect. The risk (see below) then passes to the buyer, even though the seller retains a lien for unpaid purchase money.

Rule 2

In the case of a sale of specific goods not in a deliverable state, the property does not pass until *(i)* the seller puts them into a deliverable state, and *(ii)* the buyer is notified thereof: s. 18(2). Section 61(1) says that goods are in a 'deliverable state' when they are in such a condition that, under the contract, the buyer would be bound to take delivery.

Case law Underwood Ltd v Burgh Castle Brick and Cement Syndicate (1922): An engine was sold when bolted to a factory floor. It was held that property had not passed when the contract had been made.

Rule 3

Where there is a sale of specific goods in a deliverable state, but requiring some additional act such as weighing, measuring, testing to fix the price, the property does not pass until *(i)* the seller has done the required act, and *(ii)* the buyer is notified thereof: s. 18(3).

Case law Nanka Bruce v Commonwealth Trust Ltd (1926): Cocoa was sold to a buyer who resold to a third party. This party was to weigh it to determine how much the buyer owed the seller. It was held that the Rule did not apply because it was not the seller who did the weighing.

Rule 4

This deals with the case of goods delivered on approval or on sale or return, or similar terms. In such a case, the property does not pass until *(i)* the buyer signifies acceptance, or adopts the goods (e.g. by using them), or *(ii)* the buyer retains the goods for an unreasonable time or beyond any agreed time limit: s. 18(4). What is a reasonable time is a question of fact in each case: s. 59.

Case law Poole v Smith's Car Sales (Balham) Ltd (1962): A car was left with dealers, but no time limit given. It was unsold for three months. During this period, the owner made several requests for the car's return. It was held that property had price.

Rule 5

Rule 5(1) deals with contracts for the sale of unascertained or future goods: the property passes when *(i)* the seller unconditionally appropriates goods of the required description to the contract, *(ii)* puts them in a deliverable state (see above), and *(iii)* notifies the buyer: s. 18(5). Rule 5(2) states that appropriation by the seller includes delivery to the buyer or to a carrier on behalf of the buyer, provided the seller has not reserved a right of disposal. Section 19(1) states that if a right of disposal is reserved, property does not pass until the seller's conditions are satisfied. Where the goods are shipped on a bill of lading to the order of the seller or his agent, it is presumed that a right of disposal is reserved: s. 19(2).

Case law Pignataro v Gilroy (1919): 140 bags of rice were sold, the bags being unascertained. The buyer paid by cheque and asked for a delivery order which was sent for 125 bags. The seller said that the balance was awaiting delivery at his place of business. These were stolen. It was held that property had passed since the seller had appropriated the balance to the contract and the buyer had agreed to this by his conduct.

Case law Wardar's (Import & Export) Co Ltd v *W Norwood & Sons Ltd* (1968): The seller sold 600 boxes of frozen kidneys from a consignment of 1500. The buyer's carrier took delivery the next day of the 600 boxes when the delivery note was handed over. It was held that property had passed since there had been an unconditional appropriation.

27. Ascertainment by exhaustion

Rules 5(3) and 5(4) were added by the Sale of Goods (Amendment) Act 1995. The former gave statutory expression to the rules on ascertainment which had been previously recognised by the courts in cases such as *Karlshamns Oljefabriker* v *East Port Navigation Corp.* (1982). The principle involved is that of ascertainment and appropriation by exhaustion. Rule 5(3) applies where there is one contract and one buyer. It means that a buyer's undivided share in the bulk at any time should be such a share as the quantity of goods paid for and due to the buyer at that time bears to the quantity of goods in the bulk at that time. Rule 5(4) extends its application to cases where there are two or more contracts in which the buyer is the same person and the bulk is reduced to less than the total of goods covered by those contracts.

The buyer's interest before ascertainment by exhaustion, section 20A as added by the 1995 Act, has the effect that, once the buyer pays the price, or a part of it, he acquires property in an undivided share of the bulk, becoming thereby an owner in common of the bulk. His share is 'such share as the quantity of goods paid for and due to the buyer out of the bulk bears to the quantity of goods in the bulk'. It is provided that, where a buyer has paid for only some of the goods, any deliveries to him from the bulk are to be ascribed in the first place to the prepaid goods. To allow trading to continue normally in the goods comprised in the bulk, s. 20B as inserted by the 1995 Act provides that each co-owner is deemed to have consented to deliveries to the other co-owners of the quantities due to them. It is made clear that each co-owner can deal with goods coming within his share without the need to obtain the consent of the others.

It is also expressly provided that nothing in s. 20A or B imposes any obligation on a buyer who takes delivery from bulk to compensate others who receive short delivery because of a shortage; affects any contractual arrangements between the buyers for adjustments amongst themselves; or alters or diminishes any contractual rights of the buyer against the seller.

28. Perishing of specific goods

If, before the contract is made, specific goods perish (see **25** above for the meaning of 'specific'), s. 6 provides that the contract is void. In the case of an agreement to sell specific goods (that is to say, a contract where property is to pass at some future date), and the goods perish before risk passes to the buyer, then s. 7 provides that the agreement is avoided so long as neither party was at fault for the perishing. If either party was at fault, the other party would thus be able to sue for breach of contract. It does not appear possible to reconcile the various cases on what amounts to perishing. In *Asfar and Co Ltd* v *Blundell* (1896), dates saturated in sewage were held to have perished, while in *Horn* v *Minister of Food* (1948), potatoes which had so rotted as to be worthless were held still to be potatoes and so not to have perished.

29. Frustration

The above are instances of the wider doctrine of frustration, but are applicable only to the stated cases, that is to say the goods must be specific and the frustrating event must have come about through the perishing of the goods. At common law, a contract for the sale of specific goods can be frustrated by events other than perishing, and this will be so where the particular event destroys the whole basis of the contract. A contract for the sale of unascertained goods can also be frustrated, as where the sale is of so much of a crop as is grown on specific land (see *Howell* v *Coupland* (1876)).

Effect of frustration

If the contract is frustrated within the meaning of s. 7 above, then the effect of frustration is regulated by the common law. This provides as follows:

(*i*) Both parties are discharged from obligations which have not yet accrued.
(*ii*) If the price, or any part of the price, has been paid, it can be recovered if there has been a total failure of consideration.
(*iii*) If there is a total failure of consideration, no part of the price can be retained for expenses incurred.
(*iv*) Payments made cannot be recovered if there has been only a partial failure of consideration.
(*v*) It is not possible to compel one party to pay for a benefit received where the contract was to perform one indivisible service and nothing had been received.

Case law In *Fibrosa Spolka Akcyjna* v *Fairbairn Lawson Combe Barbour Ltd* (1943), an agreement was made in 1939 to sell and deliver to a company in Poland. Part of the price was paid in advance. The contract was frustrated by the outbreak of war. The Polish company requested the return of part of the advance payment. This was refused on the ground that considerable work had already been performed on the goods. It was held that the advance payment could be recovered because there had been a total failure of consideration. The principle of this case only operates where there has been a total failure of consideration. It does not allow for the recovery of an advance payment if there has been only a partial failure of consideration. Again, the recipient of the payment will be obliged to return it, but without any set off for expenses incurred.

If, on the other hand, the contract is frustrated when it is not within s. 7, the position is regulated by the Law Reform (Frustrated Contracts) Act 1943, which provides:

(*i*) All sums paid under the contract before discharge may be recovered.
(*ii*) If the person who received payment under the contract has incurred expenses in its execution, he may retain or recover from the payer all or part of his expenditure if the court considers it just so to do.
(*iii*) All sums payable under the contract cease to be payable
(*iv*) Any valuable benefits obtained from the other party's actions under the contract must be paid for if the court thinks this just.

The Act also states that its provisions can be excluded by the express terms of the agreement.

30. Risk passes with property

Section 20 of the Act provides that the party who has property in the goods takes the risk of any damage or deterioration in them. If, therefore, property has passed to the buyer under the contract, or by virtue of the operation of any of the above Rules, then he must take the risk of anything happening to them, even if happening before he takes possession.

Case law In *Mitchinson* v *Otaihape Farmers' Meat and Produce Co Ltd* (1920), the buyer selected 280 sheep from a flock of 1100. These were put into a separate pen. Property thereby passed to the buyer. Later that day, the sheep were destroyed by fire. It was held that the buyer had to pay the price since the risk had passed to him with the property. See too *Wardar's* case discussed above under Rule 5.

Section 20 also says that the parties can provide in the contract that risk and property need not go together. It is therefore always possible for the contract, expressly or by implication, to provide that the buyer takes the risk, even though the property is still with the seller. Conversely, it can also state that the risk remains with the seller, even though property has passed to the buyer. Section 20(2) says that where delivery of the goods is delayed by the fault of one of the parties, that party bears the risk in relation to any loss arising because of such fault.

> *Case law* In *Demby* v *Bardon* (1949), the buyer was at fault in not taking apple juice at agreed times. The juice went bad and it was held that the buyer was to bear the risk.

Section 32(3) provides that where delivery involves a sea journey, the goods remain at the risk of the seller unless he gives the buyer reasonable notice to allow him to insure those goods. Section 33 further provides that, where delivery is to a place other than where they are sold, and the seller agrees to deliver at his own risk, the buyer still has to accept the risk of any loss which is incidental to the journey.

SALES WITHOUT TITLE

There is a general rule of law, often described under the Latin tag of *Nemo Dat Quod Non Habet* – No one can give what he has not got. As applied to the sale of goods, this rule means that a seller of goods cannot give a better title to the purchaser than he himself possesses. Thus to take a simple case a purchaser who buys stolen goods from a thief can get no valid title to them, since the thief himself has no title and hence no title to give.

This is the basic rule and, though it remains intact, there are many exceptions to the rule as discussed below. The Sale of Goods Act 1979 lays down important exceptions to this general rule and these are stated below.

31. Estoppel

Section 21(1) of the Sale of Goods Act 1979 accepts that there may be circumstances when the true owner of goods is 'estopped' from setting up his title, thus allowing the seller to pass a good title, even if without authority to sell.

> *Case law Eastern Distributors* v *Goldring* (1957): A, as part of a plan to deceive a hire purchase company, signed and delivered forms to B which enabled the latter to represent that he had A's authority to sell a car which belonged to him. A was thereby estopped from setting up his title against the party who had bought the car from B.

Case law Central Newbury Car Auctions Ltd v *Unity Finance Ltd* (1957): A person offered to buy a car on hire purchase terms. He gave a car in part-exchange, which was itself subject to a hire purchase contract, and drove away in the new car. His proposal to buy this car on hire purchase was, however, rejected by the finance company. The new car was later found in the possession of a party who had bought it in good faith. The case for estoppel was based on the fact that the owner had allowed the new car to be driven away complete with its registration book. This argument was, however, rejected because the registration book was not a document of title and even contained a warning that the person in whose name the car is registered may not be the owner.

Case law Shaw v *Commissioner of Police of the Metropolis* (1987): The owner of a car entrusted it to a third party to find a buyer. The owner signed a letter stating that he had sold the car to the third party. In reliance on the letter, a purchaser took the car in good faith under a conditional contract which did not pass property until the third party was paid.

The court held that s. 21(1) applied where goods were 'sold' by parties such as the third party here and hence did not apply where the third party only entered into an 'agreement to sell' (see above).

32. Orders for sale

Where a person not the owner sells goods *(a)* under a court order, or *(b)* under a legal power of sale, e.g. the power of sale given to a legal mortgagee, the purchaser gets a good title under the provisions of s. 21(2)(b). There are, for instance, statutory powers of sale under the Innkeepers Act 1878 and the Torts (Interference with Goods) Act 1977.

The High Court has significant powers to order sale if goods are perishing or fast losing value while subject to litigation: Rules of the Supreme Court 1965 Order 27, r. 4; County Courts Act 1984, s. 38. Furthermore, rules of court allow for the sale of goods seized in execution where a claimant alleges that he is entitled to the goods by way of security for a debt: RSC Ord 17, r. 6; County Courts Act 1984, s. 100.

33. Writs of execution

If a person fails to pay a debt when ordered by the court, a writ may be issued empowering the sheriff to seize his chattels and to sell them in satisfaction of the debt. The sheriff then has power to give a good title, although he is not the owner of the goods sold: Supreme Court Act 1981, s. 138.

34. Factors Act 1889

The purchaser will get a good title under the Factors Act if he buys in good faith from a factor, who is in possession of the goods with the consent of the owner even though the factor may have no actual authority to sell. A factor is defined by the Act as a party, in the ordinary course of business, authorised to sell or buy goods, or to raise money on the security of goods. This includes such businesses as that of car dealer and auctioneer. Under the Act, possession is deemed to be with the consent of the owner unless the contrary is proved.

The courts have further read it as implied into the Act that the mercantile agent obtained possession in his capacity as such an agent. The owner 'must consent to the agent having [the goods] for a purpose which is in some way or other connected with his business as a mercantile agent. It may not actually be for sale. It may be for display, or to get offers, or merely to put in his showroom; but there must be consent to something of that kind before the owner can be deprived of his goods' (*Pearson* v *Rose & Young* (1951)). See too *Cole* v *North Western Bank* (1875). If, therefore, the owner is unaware that the party to whom he gives the goods is a mercantile agent, the latter does not obtain possession under the provisions of the Act (*Henderson* v *Prosser* (1982)).

> *Case law Astley Industrial Trust* v *Miller* (1968): A car was provided to a self-drive car hire business. As an ancillary activity to this business, they also sold second-hand cars. They re-sold this car before title had passed. It was held that the Factors Act did not apply as they had obtained possession as operators of a car hire business and not as mercantile agents.

It will be recalled that the Factors Act will apply only when the mercantile agent is selling in the ordinary course of his business. This means 'acting in such a way as a mercantile agent in the ordinary course of business as a mercantile agent would act, that is to say, within business hours, at a proper place of business, and in other respects in the ordinary way in which a mercantile agent would act, so that there is nothing to lead the [other party] to suppose that anything is done wrong, or to give notice that the disposition is one which the mercantile agent has no authority to make' (*Oppenheimer* v *Attenborough* (1908)). Thus, a transaction whereby payment is made, not to the mercantile agent, but to one of his creditors, may well be outside the ordinary course of business (see the *Oppenheimer* case). Whether a transaction has taken place in the ordinary course of business is a question of fact which depends on the circumstances of the particular case.

35. Seller in possession

Section 24 of the Sale of Goods Act (and, in virtually identical terms, s. 8 of the Factors Act) provides that, where the seller remains in possession following sale, any further sale to a second purchaser taken in good faith gives title to that second purchaser.

> *Case example Pacific Motor Auctions Pty Ltd* v *Motor Credits (Hire Finance) Ltd* (1965): Dealers in vehicles sold a number to another party under a 'display agreement' whereby the dealers remained in possession for display. The dealers were paid 90% of the price and were authorised to sell the vehicles as agents for that other party. The dealers fell into financial difficulties and their authority to sell was revoked. However, the dealers still sold a number of the vehicles to purchasers who took in good faith. It was held that these purchasers obtained a valid title from a seller in possession. See too *Worcester Works Finance Ltd* v *Cooden Engineering Co Ltd* (1972).

However, if the seller resumes possession after having released the goods to the buyer, as where he borrows them back, his possession will not be as a seller in possession and therefore the above provisions will not apply (*Mitchell* v *Jones* (1905)).

It should be noted that the second buyer must take actual or constructive possession of the goods if he is to obtain a good title. Thus, if a person sells goods to A, retaining possession, and then sells to B, and still retains possession, A has a better claim to the goods (see *Forsythe International (UK) Ltd* v *Silver Shipping Co Ltd* (1994) discussed in **37** below). The transfer of possession must also be voluntary (see again the *Forsythe* case below).

36. Buyer in possession

Section 9 of the Factors Act, and s. 25(1) of the Sale of Goods Act, provide that where a person has bought or agreed to buy goods, obtains possession of goods, or the documents of title to goods, with the seller's consent, any delivery or transfer by the buyer to a third party taking in good faith and without notice of any rights of the original seller 'shall have the same effect as if the person making the delivery or transfer were a mercantile agent in possession of the goods or documents of title with the consent of the owner' (for a 'factor' or 'mercantile agent', see **34** above)

> *Case example Lee* v *Butler* (1893): Goods were bought under the terms of a conditional sale agreement. The goods were sold before title had passed. The person who took under this sale was in good faith and so title passed to him.

It must be remembered that a conditional sale agreement is different from a hire purchase agreement (see above). Under the latter, a person is not committed to making the purchase. For that reason, the rules as to a buyer in possession have no application to hire purchase contracts (see *Helby* v *Matthews* (1895)). The position is further complicated by the fact that the Consumer Credit Act 1974 provides that, where the amount of credit extended to a person buying under a conditional sale agreement does not exceed £25,000, and the buyer is an individual or a partnership or any other unincorporated body of persons not consisting entirely of bodies corporate, then the agreement is to be treated as a hire purchase agreement. Readers should be aware that the £25,000 figure can be altered at any time, and they should always check for the latest figure (£25,000 effective 1 May 1998).

37. Dispositions by a thief

One particular problem which had arisen in the interpretation of the provisions relating to the buyer in possession is this. Suppose a thief steals goods from the owner, and then sells them to a third person. The thief is not a buyer in possession, so that third person could not acquire a good title under these provisions. But suppose that the third party then sells to a fourth party. It could be argued that the third party is a buyer in possession, and that he can therefore pass a good title to the fourth party.

> *Case law National Employers Mutual General Insurance Association Ltd* v *Jones* (1990): The court ruled that, because the thief never had title to the goods, he could not be said to have 'sold' the goods to the third party who was therefore not a buyer in possession. The absence of a genuine contract of sale on the part of the thief would mean, the court said, that however many further sales of the stolen goods there might be, none of the buyers could be classified as buyers in possession.

It will be recalled that the provisions relating to the buyer in possession are to apply as if the buyer in possession were a mercantile agent in possession with the consent of the owner. The provisions relating to mercantile agency (see **34** above) prescribe that an unauthorised sale by a mercantile agent only has effect if he is selling in the ordinary course of his business. The problem in relation to the buyer in possession provisions is that, if the buyer in possession is not a mercantile agent, he cannot be said to be acting in the ordinary course of business. The problem has not been resolved, but the better approach would be to treat the relevant words as meaning that the sale by the buyer in possession has effect as if he were a mercantile agent acting in the ordinary course of his business; and not as meaning that he must be judged as though he were such an agent and whether he was or was not acting in the ordinary course of his business: *Jeffcott* v *Andrew Motors Ltd* (1960); *Lambert* v *G&C Finance Corporation Ltd* (1963); *Newtons of Wembley Ltd* v *Williams* (1965); *Forsythe International (UK) Ltd* v *Silver Shipping Co Ltd* (1994).

As with the position regarding the seller in possession, the provisions as to the buyer in possession only apply when the third party obtains actual or constructive possession Furthermore, the transfer of possession must be voluntary.

> *Case example   Forsythe International (UK) Ltd* v *Silver Shipping Co Ltd* (1994): A party contracted with charterers to supply bunker oils to a vessel which was on a time charter from the owners. The vessel was withdrawn from charter by the owners ahead of time because of non-payment of hire. At that time, the vessel was carrying bunker oil supplied by that party but not paid for. The owners contended that title had passed to them because the charterers were buyers in possession, and they had obtained possession. The court held that the delivery to the owners had to be voluntary. In this case, the transfer was involuntary since it had come about by virtue of the owners' termination because of non-payment of hire and not because of any act of the charterers.

38. Sale under voidable title

Section 23 of the Sale of Goods Act provides that the purchaser from a seller whose own title is voidable will get a good title, provided *(a)* he had no knowledge of any defect in the seller's title and *(b)* the seller's title had not been avoided at the time of the sale.

> *Case law Phillips* v *Brooks* (1919): A third party obtained jewels on credit from P by fraud and sold them to B before P discovered the fraud. It was held that P could avoid the third party's title to the jewels on the grounds of fraud, but since he had not done so before B bought the jewels B got a good title. See too *Cundy* v *Lindsay* (1878); *Ingram* v *Little* (1961); *Lewis* v *Averay* (1973).

It appears that where the fraudulent third party cannot be found, rescission can be made effective by, for example, reporting what has happened to the police or the motoring organisations: *Car & Universal Finance Co* v *Caldwell* (1964); *Newtons of Wembley Ltd* v *Williams* (1965).

39. Market overt

The former exception to the *nemo dat rule* for sales in market overt was abolished by the Sale of Goods (Amendment) Act 1994.

40. The Hire Purchase Act 1964

The Hire Purchase Act 1964 covers those cases where a motor vehicle is being bought under either hire purchase or conditional sale terms. Where a motor vehicle being obtained in such circumstances is sold to a private consumer (i.e. someone not buying in the course of a trade or business) and he takes in good faith and without notice of the seller's defect in title, he obtains a good title in that motor vehicle.

> *Case law Dodds* v *Yorkshire Finance* (1992): The purchaser of a car had stipulated that the receipt for her payment was to contain a declaration that the car was not the subject of an existing hire-purchase agreement. The Court of Appeal said that good faith was to be equated with honesty. The purchaser's evidence was that, when this declaration had been given, 'I was not suspicious any more'. It was held that she had been a purchaser in good faith.

PERFORMANCE OF THE CONTRACT

41. Delivery

Section 27 of the Sale of Goods Act makes it the duty of the seller to deliver the goods, and of the buyer to accept and pay for them. Unless otherwise agreed, s. 28 states that payment and delivery are normally concurrent conditions. Section 61(1) defines 'delivery' as the voluntary transfer of possession from one person to another. It may be actual or constructive, e.g. by handing over documents of title, or authority for the buyer to obtain the goods from some person in whose possession they are (*Central Newbury Car Auctions* v *Unity Finance* (1957)).

Delivery may also be by the seller agreeing to hold the goods as agent for the buyer, a process known as *attornment*.

42. Time and place of delivery

Section 29 of the Act lays down a number of rules, as below, relating to the time and place of delivery as above defined.

Where the seller is to send the goods to the buyer but no time is fixed, they must be sent within a reasonable time and delivery must be at a reasonable hour: s. 29(3). Section 61(1) states that what constitutes a 'reasonable time' is a question to be determined on all the facts of the case. Section 29(3) applies the same test for determining a 'reasonable hour'.

Section 29(6) provides that it is the seller who, subject to any agreement to the contrary, who is to bear the expense of putting the goods into a deliverable condition, and he must take reasonable care to see that they reach the right person. If, on arrival, the seller hands the goods over to someone he reasonably assumes to be authorised to receive them, he has carried out his duty of delivery (*Galbraith and Grant* v *Block* (1922)).

It is also provided by s. 29(2) that, unless otherwise agreed, delivery is to be at the seller's place of business, or if he has none then his residence. If the sale is of specific goods known by both parties to be lodged at some other place, then delivery is to be made at that place.

43. Delivery to a carrier

Where the seller is to send the goods, s. 32(1) provides that delivery to a carrier, whether named by the buyer or not, is *prima facie* proper delivery to the buyer. In such cases the seller must, under the provisions of s. 32(2), make a reasonable contract with the carrier. If he fails to do so, and the goods are lost or damaged in transit, the buyer is entitled to decline to treat delivery to the carrier as delivery to himself, or, in the alternative, he may accept delivery but hold the seller liable in damages.

44. Delivery of wrong quantities

Section 30 of the Sale of Goods Act, as amended by the Sale and Supply of Goods Act 1994, lays down what is to happen when the wrong quantity is delivered.

If less than the amount ordered is delivered, the buyer may reject the entire quantity delivered or he may accept the goods delivered. In this latter case, he must pay a proportionately reduced price. If more than ordered is delivered, the buyer may reject the lot, or may accept the agreed quantity only. Section 30(2A) provides that where the buyer is not dealing as consumer, he is compelled to ignore any slight excess or shortfall, if rejection would be unreasonable, the burden of proof lying on the seller. Although a consumer buyer is not caught by these provisions, however, it has been established that in any case minimal shortfalls or excesses will be overlooked, as where 4950 tons were ordered and an extra 55 lbs were delivered (*Shipton, Anderson* v *Weil Bros* (1912)). A person deals as consumer if, in accordance with s. 12 of the Unfair Contract Terms Act 1977, he neither makes the contract in the course of a business nor holds himself out as so doing, and the other party does make the contract in the course of a business: the goods must be of a type ordinarily supplied for private use or consumption.

There used to be provisions, contained in s. 30(4) of the 1979 Act, dealing with the position where the contract goods were delivered mixed with other goods, but these were repealed by the 1994 Act.

45. Delivery by instalments

Section 31 provides that, unless otherwise agreed, a buyer is not bound to accept delivery in instalments.

If instalments are to be paid for separately on delivery, s. 31 provides that it is a question of fact whether failure to deliver one instalment justifies repudiation of the whole contract.

The test as laid down in the courts is: is the breach regarding one instalment such as can be regarded as a repudiation of the whole contract?

Case law Maple Flock Co Ltd v *Universal Furniture Products* (1934): The seller delivered too great a quantity of rag flock in one instalment. This was held not to be a repudiation of the whole contract since it was unlikely to recur. The court took note of the quantitative ratio of the breach to the contract as a whole; and the degree of probability that it would be repeated.

Case law Regent OHG v *Francesco of Jermyn Street* (1981): The plaintiffs were manufacturers of menswear. They agreed to sell 62 suits to the defendants, who owned a retail shop. Delivery was to be by instalments. The number and size of the instalments was to be left to the plaintiffs' discretion. The defendants later informed the plaintiffs that they wished to cancel the order but the plaintiffs insisted on delivery of the suits which were in production. Because of shortage of cloth, one consignment was delivered one suit short, the plaintiffs having previously advised the defendants of the fact. The defendants, consistent with their wish to cancel the entire order, rejected delivery of all the consignments. The plaintiffs were forced to sell the suits elsewhere at a much lower price and brought an action against the defendants for non-acceptance. The defendants contended short delivery of one instalment amounted to short delivery on the whole contract, and the plaintiffs having delivered a quantity of goods less than they contracted to sell, they were entitled under s. 30 Sale of Goods Act to reject all the goods even though the parties had agreed on delivery in instalments. The plaintiffs contended that the contract was divisible into separate instalments and that, under s. 31, whether the short delivery was of the whole contract or merely a severable breach depended on the terms of the contract and the relevant circumstances. The court held that the plaintiffs were entitled to damages for the following reasons. First, on its true construction, the contract was divisible even though the number and size of the individual deliveries were not fixed in advance but were left to the plaintiffs' discretion. It followed that s. 30 (see above) did not apply to the contract and that the defendants were not entitled to cancel the contract under s. 30 because of short delivery of one suit. Second, in any event, where the nature of the delivery of goods was short delivery in one instalment, the more flexible provisions of s. 31 were to apply in preference to those of s. 30. Applying s. 31, the short delivery of one suit, in all the circumstances, could not be said to go to the root of the whole contract and did not entitle the defendants to repudiate the whole contract.

46. Delivery by sea

In contracts for the carriage of goods delivered by sea, various special terms are usual. These may be expressly agreed between the parties, but more often they rely on one of the established customary agreements with the implied terms that these contain. The most common of these standard agreements are set out below.

F.O.B (free on board)

Under such a contract, the seller's duties (unless otherwise agreed) are as follows:

- To deliver the goods to a named port of shipment.
- To put the goods on board ship at his own expense.
- To negotiate a reasonable bill of lading or other contract of carriage, and forward it to the buyer (who pays the freight).
- To notify the buyer of shipment, so as to enable him to insure the goods at sea. If the seller fails to do this the goods will travel at his risk; otherwise the goods will be at the buyer's risk.

Once the goods are shipped the property in them (and usually the risk) passes to the buyer. If the seller is prevented from putting the goods on board, e.g. by a strike, the property and risk remain with him (*Colley* v *Overseas Exporters* (1921)).

C.I.F. (cost, insurance, freight)

Here the seller's duties go further than in an f.o.b. contract and are as follows:

- To deliver the goods to the port of shipment at his expense, and to see them safely on board.
- To insure the goods during transit.
- To negotiate a suitable bill of lading or other contract of carriage and

to forward this to the buyer to enable him to claim the goods on arrival at the port of destination. (Purchase money is not normally paid until the documents of title reach the buyer.)

Once the goods are delivered to the ship the risk passes to the buyer (and should be covered by his insurance). The property in the goods passes to the buyer when the goods are shipped, unless the seller reserves a right of disposal in which case property does not pass until the price is paid.

The buyer is entitled to reject the documents of title and/or the goods. Acceptance of one does not bind him to accept the other. But the buyer must pay the price when he receives the documents of title, even though he has not yet examined the goods. It is also the buyer's responsibility to pay unloading charges and transport from the port of destination to any further inland destination.

Ex-ship

Here the seller is bound to arrange the shipment of the goods to the port of destination, and to such further inland destination as the buyer may stipulate. The buyer is not bound to pay for the goods until they are unloaded from the ship and all freightage charges paid. The goods travel at the seller's risk, but he is not bound to insure them.

EXAMINATION AND ACCEPTANCE BY THE BUYER

47. Examination

The buyer is by s. 34 entitled to examine goods not previously seen before accepting them. Generally, the place of delivery is the place of examination, unless otherwise agreed.

> *Case law M&T Hurst Consultants Ltd* v *Grange Motors Ltd & Rolls Royce Ltd* (1981): It was held that it was reasonable for a buyer of a second-hand car to wait until four months from the date of purchase before having serious defects investigated as 'until that date the plaintiff had not had any reasonable opportunity of ascertaining whether the vehicle conformed with the contract'.

48. Acceptance

Under s. 35 of the Act, acceptance of the goods will take one of three forms. The buyer will be taken to have accepted goods: when he so informs the seller; or except where he was unable to exercise his right to examine the goods, the buyer does some act of ownership, e.g. sells the goods. In neither case, however, will the buyer be taken to have accepted the goods if he has not first had a reasonable opportunity of determining if the goods conform to the contract, or, in the case of a sale by sample, of comparing the bulk with the sample. The right to examine cannot be lost where the buyer deals as consumer (see above).

Section 35 further provides that acceptance takes place if the buyer keeps the goods for more than a reasonable time without notifying the seller that he wishes to reject them. Section 59 says that this is something to be determined on the facts of the particular case, but s. 35 adds that, in determining the issue, attention must be paid to whether the buyer had a reasonable opportunity to examine the goods to see if the goods conform to the contract, or, in the case of a sale by sample, of comparing the bulk with the sample.

> *Case law* In *Bernstein* v *Pamson Motors* (1987), a buyer of a new car had it for approximately three weeks during which time he drove some 140 miles. The High Court ruled that enough time had run against him with the result that he was unable to reject the car. Since this decision, the Act was amended to provide that, as indicated above, account must be taken as to whether the buyer had a reasonable opportunity of examining the goods to see if they are in conformity with the contract. It must therefore be considered doubtful if this case remains good law. (See *Addendum*.)

RIGHTS OF AN UNPAID SELLER AGAINST THE GOODS

49. An unpaid seller

The seller is unpaid, by virtue of s. 38(1), as long as any part of the purchase price is outstanding. Sub-section (2) adds that payment by a negotiable instrument is conditional only, meaning that it is not effective until the negotiable instrument has been honoured.

However, payment by means of a credit card is unconditional. If the credit card company goes into liquidation before it has paid the suppliers who took the particular card, the suppliers have no right of recourse against the customers. The company can, however, pursue the debts as can any third party to whom the company may have sold its receivables (*Re Charge Card Services* (1989)).

50. Effect of property passing

The rights of an unpaid seller will differ according to whether the property in the goods has passed or not (see **24** above for passing of property).

If property has not passed to the buyer, the seller may withhold delivery if the price is unpaid or not tendered, or if the buyer is insolvent; or if part of the goods have been delivered, he may, under s. 39, withhold the remainder.

51. Retention of title

It has become common, starting with the decision in *Aluminium Industrie BV* v *Romalpa Aluminium Ltd* (1976) for sellers to insert retention of title clauses into the agreement. Under such a clause, which can take one of several forms, a seller stipulates that property remains his until all sums outstanding under the contract have been paid. In the so-called 'all monies' clause, the seller goes a stage further and retains title in particular goods until all sums are paid both under the particular contract and all other contracts between them. Such clauses were upheld in *Thyssen* v *Armour Edelstahlwerke AG* (1991). There have been many cases on aspects of retention of title (see for example *Re Bond Worth* (1980); *Clough Mill* v *Martin* (1985); *Compaq Computer Ltd* v *Abercorn Group Ltd* (1991); *Modelboard Ltd* v *Outer Box Ltd* (1993)).

Where property has passed to the buyer, the seller has the following rights:

- Lien (see **52** below).
- Stoppage in transit (see **53** below)
- Resale (see **55** below).

52. Lien: s. 41

Under s. 41. the seller's lien is a right to retain possession of goods until payment or tender of payment. A lien arises when:

(a) goods have been sold without any agreement as to credit; *or*

(b) goods have been sold on credit, but the period of credit has expired; *or*

(c) goods have been sold on credit and the buyer has become insolvent (whether the period of credit has expired or not).

A lien is lost when

(a) goods have been delivered to a carrier for transmission to the buyer, without the seller reserving a right of disposal; *or*

(b) the buyer or his agent lawfully obtains possession of the goods; *or*

(c) the seller waives his lien (s. 43).

213

The seller may exercise a lien

(a) when in possession merely as agent for the buyer

(b) where part delivery has taken place (the lien extends over the remainder of the goods)

(c) if the seller breaks his contract while the buyer is solvent, he will still be entitled to claim a lien if the buyer subsequently becomes insolvent.

53. Stoppage in transit

A right to stop goods in transit is provided by s. 44. It means a right to stop the goods when they are on their way to the buyer (and after they have left the possession of the seller). The right arises when:

(a) the goods are in transit *and*

(b) the buyer becomes insolvent. (The buyer is insolvent if he has ceased to pay his debts as they fall due in the ordinary course of business or he cannot pay debts as they become due: s. 61.)

Goods are in transit until the buyer accepts them, i.e. if in the hands of a carrier prior to delivery, or if rejected by the buyer when delivered: s. 45.

Where goods are in the possession of a carrier, the position depends on whether he is agent for the seller or for the buyer (a question of fact in each case). If he is agent for the seller, then the goods are still in the possession of the seller and his right is one of lien, not stoppage. If he is agent for the buyer, transit is over, and the seller has no right of stoppage. The carrier may become agent for the buyer either by appointment as such, or by notifying the buyer that he holds the goods on his behalf, i.e. that they await collection.

Transit ceases when the goods reach their ultimate destination, but not some intermediate destination (unless further instructions are conveyed to the carrier to send them on, in which case transit has ceased).

Stoppage in transit is effected by the seller *(a)* taking possession of the goods or documents of title thereto, or *(b)* giving notice to the carrier of his exercise of the right of stoppage. If the seller wrongfully stops the goods, e.g. where the buyer is solvent, he is liable for damages for the tort of conversion if the property has passed to the buyer, or for damages for breach of contract if the property has not yet passed to the buyer. If a carrier wrongfully delivers stopped goods to the buyer, he is liable for damages to the seller. And if he wrongfully obeys the seller's instructions to stop transit, he is liable for damages to the buyer.

54. End of transit

Transit ceases when

(a) Goods reach their destination and possession is transferred to the buyer or his agent.

(b) The buyer or his agent obtains delivery before they reach their destination.

(c) A carrier wrongfully refuses to deliver the goods to the buyer or his agent.

(d) The goods have reached their destination and the carrier has notified the buyer that he holds them as his agent.

(e) Goods are delivered to the master of the buyer's ship, or of a ship which the buyer has chartered.

It should be noted that sale by the buyer does not affect the seller's right of stoppage, unless the seller has consented thereto.

55. Resale

Section 48 provides that the contract is not necessarily rescinded by the exercise by the seller of his rights of lien or stoppage, nor does the seller automatically thereby acquire a right to resell the goods to another purchaser.

The seller has a right of resale after exercise of his rights of lien or stoppage in transit where:

(a) the goods are perishable; *or*

(b) the price has not been paid within a reasonable time after notice was given by the seller of his intention to resell; *or*

(c) such right was expressly reserved by him in the contract.

In addition to the above, the seller may also have a right of action for damages for breach of contract: *Ward* v *Bignall* (1967).

ACTIONS FOR BREACH OF CONTRACT

56. By the seller

Section 49 gives the seller the following rights of action:

(a) *For the price.*
   (i) Where the property in the goods has passed to the buyer (see above) and he has failed to pay for them.

215

(ii) Where the price is payable on a certain day and has not been paid, the seller can sue for the price notwithstanding that the property has not passed to the buyer (see above) or the goods have not yet been appropriated to the contract (see above).

(b) *Damages for non-acceptance.* This action lies, under s. 50(1), where the buyer has refused to accept the goods and the property has not passed to him.

The measure of damages is the estimated loss directly and naturally resulting to the seller: s. 50(2). Where there is an available market for the goods, s. 50(3) provides that the measure of damages will therefore normally be the difference between the contract price and the market price at the date of breach.

In determining whether there was an available market, if the seller actually offered the goods for sale there was no available market unless there was one actual buyer on that day at a fair price.

If, on the other hand, there was only a hypothetical sale, there would be no available market unless on the relevant day there were in the market sufficient traders potentially in touch with each other to evidence a market in which the seller could, if he wished, sell the goods. The market price on a hypothetical sale is the fair market price for the total quantity of the goods if they have to be sold on the relevant day, but taking into account the price which might be negotiated within a few days with other potential buyers who were not part of the market on that day only because of difficulties in communications: *Shearson Lehman* v *Maclaine Wilson (No.2)* (1990). Where there is no available market, the seller is entitled to damages for loss of his bargain: *Thompson* v *Robinson* (1955) and *Lazenby Garages Ltd* v *Wright* (1976).

57. By the buyer

(a) *For non-delivery.* The buyer can recover damages under s. 51(1) calculated in the same manner as in an action by the buyer, that is to say by reference to the difference between the contract and market price (see above)

The buyer is also entitled under the so-called second rule in *Hadley* v *Baxendale* (1854) and also by virtue of s. 54 to recover special damages where the particular loss was in the seller's contemplation as a probable consequence of the breach.

> *Case law* In *Parsons (Livestock) Ltd* v *Uttley, Ingham & Co Ltd* (1978) the sellers sold a pig hopper. When installing it, they left the ventilator closed with the result that the pig feed became mouldy. The animals

became ill, triggering off a serious illness. The value of the affected animals was in the region of £10,000. It was held that, although the extent of the loss could not have been contemplated, the seller could still have reasonably expected that illness would occur, so he was liable for the full extent of the loss.

(b) *For recovery of the price,* where this has been paid and the goods have not been delivered.

(c) *For specific performance,* where the contract is for sale of specific or ascertained goods (see above). But such an order is discretionary, and the court may, under s. 52, award damages instead.

Case law Société des Industries Metallurgiques SA v Bronx Engineering Co Ltd (1975): The court refused to order a seller to deliver a machine, although it was over 220 tonnes in weight, cost some £270,000, and could only be bought in the market with a 9 to 12 months delivery date.

Case law Sky Petroleum Ltd v VIP Petroleum Ltd (1974): A buyer sought specific performance of a contract under which the seller had agreed to supply all its requirements for 10 years. Because of the unusual state of the oil market at the time the order was sought, damages would not be adequate compensation for failure to deliver and specific performance was awarded.

(d) In the tort of conversion if the property has passed to the buyer and the seller has wrongfully detained or disposed of the goods.

(e) For breach of condition the buyer can reject the goods, or, if he chooses, accept them and sue for damages for breach of an *ex post facto* warranty (see **11** above).

(f) For breach of warranty, the buyer can only sue for damages; he cannot reject the goods (see above).

CONTRACTS FOR THE SUPPLY OF GOODS AND SERVICES

58. The relevant Acts

As regards hire-purchase agreements, the Supply of Goods (Implied Terms) Act 1973 implies conditions and warranties which are identical to those implied in contracts for the sale of goods. The position with regard to exclusion clauses is also identical. With regard to conditional sales, these are contracts of sale covered by the Sale of Goods Act 1979.

The Supply of Goods and Services Act 1982, which deals only with implied terms, applies to many contracts where ownership or possession of goods passes but where the contract is not a contract of sale or hire-purchase. A typical case covered by the 1982 Act is a contract for work and materials. For example, if a plumber is employed to install a tap, the contract is for work (the service of installing the tap) and materials (the tap itself) and is governed by the Act.

59. Implied terms

Where ownership of goods passes, the supplier of the goods is under identical obligations as to title, description, satisfactory quality, fitness for purpose and sample as the seller of goods under a contract of sale (see above).

Exclusion clauses

The implied terms as to title cannot be excluded: Unfair Contract Terms Act 1977, s. 7(3A). In relation to the other implied terms, these cannot be excluded in contracts with consumers. The provisions of the Unfair Terms in Consumer Contracts Regulations 1994 would also apply but would add little if anything to the provisions of the Act. In business to business contracts the terms can be excluded provided the particular exclusion clause is reasonable as provided in s. 7(2),(3) of the Act.

60. Contracts of hire

The 1982 Act provides that the owner of goods which are hired out is subject to a condition that he has a right to transfer possession, or will have that right where possession is to be transferred, at a date later than the contract itself: s. 7(1). There is also an implied warranty that the person taking the goods on hire will have quiet possession except insofar as that possession is disturbed by the owner of the goods or some other person entitled to the benefit of a charge or encumbrance disclosed or known to the hirer before the contract was made. In addition, there are conditions as to description, sample, satisfactory quality and fitness for purpose identical to those in contracts for the sale of goods.

Exclusion clauses

The terms as to description, sample, satisfactory quality and fitness for purpose cannot be excluded in contracts with a consumer: Unfair Contract Terms Act 1977, s. 7(2). The Unfair Terms in Consumer Contracts Regulations 1994 is to like effect.

In contracts between businesses, those terms can be excluded if the exclusion clause is a reasonable one: s. 7(3). The terms as to transferring possession and the assurance of quiet possession can be excluded in consumer and business contracts if the exclusion clause is reasonable: s. (4).

61. Trading stamps

Under the Trading Stamps Act 1964, where a consumer exchanges his stamps for goods, s. 4 of that Act provides that the promoter of the trading stamps scheme provides a warranty that he has the right to give the goods in exchange; that the goods are free from undisclosed charges or encumbrances and that the consumer will have quiet possession of the goods; and that the goods are of satisfactory quality except as regards defects specifically drawn to the consumer's attention and as regards defects which ought to have been seen by the consumer if he had examined the goods in advance. It should be noted that these provisions are all warranties, and that there is no requirement as to reasonable fitness for purpose.

Exclusion clauses

The Act states that the foregoing terms will apply regardless of any term to the contrary and the same result would no doubt be reached under the provisions of the Unfair Terms in Consumer Contracts Regulations 1994. A criminal offence is committed under the provisions of the Consumer Transactions (Restrictions on Statements) Order 1976 if the contract does contain a term rendered void by the 1964 Act.

62. Supply of services

Where services are supplied under a contract, whether or not the ownership or possession of goods is also transferred:

(a) The supplier must provide his services with reasonable care and skill: Supply of Goods and Services Act, s. 13 (*Wilson* v *Best Travel Ltd* (1993); *Society of Lloyds* v *Clementson* (1994)).

(b) Where the time for carrying out the service is not fixed by the contract, left to be determined in a way agreed in the contract or determined by the course of dealing between the parties, the supplier must carry out the service in a reasonable time: s. 14.

(c) Where no charge is agreed in advance, left to be determined in a way agreed in the contract, or determined by the course of dealing, only a reasonable charge can be made: s. 15.

219

Exclusion clauses

Liability for any act of negligence resulting in death or personal injury cannot be excluded: Unfair Contract Terms Act s. 2(1). The provisions of the Unfair Terms in Consumer Contracts Regulations 1994 have the same effect where the victim is a private individual and not a business. Where the negligence results in any other category of loss, such as damage to property, liability can be excluded or limited if the relevant clause can be shown to be reasonable. Again, the Regulations will have much the same effect in relation to consumers.

Where the infringement is of the duty to exercise reasonable care and skill liability can also be excluded if the term is reasonable; in business to business contracts, the reasonableness test will be imposed, however, only if the contract is on written standard terms: s. 3 of the 1977 Act. Again, as far as consumer contracts are concerned, the 1994 Regulations will have broadly the same effect.

OTHER TYPES OF CONTRACT

63. A contract of hire

Such a contract arises where a person agrees to hire goods for a particular or indeterminate period. Such contracts are sometimes called *contracts of bailment*.

A contract of hire-purchase is one where a person hires goods for a specified period and has an option to purchase the goods hired, often at the end of the period of hire. During the period of hire, he is a mere bailee of the goods.

Such a contract must be distinguished from contracts of conditional sale where the buyer agrees to pay off the price in instalments, but commits himself at the outset to making the purchase.

64. Auction sales

An auction is a sale at which the auctioneer (as agent for the seller) invites persons present to bid (offer) for goods sold. The bidder is the offeror, and can, under normal contractual principles, withdraw his bid at any time before the auctioneer accepts it, usually by knocking with a hammer.

The general rules laid down by the Sale of Goods Act apply to sales of goods by auction; therefore if the sale is of specific goods the property in them will pass to the buyer as soon as the hammer falls, i.e. as soon as the contract is made: s. 57(2).

Each lot put up for sale becomes the subject of a separate contract.

65. Position of auctioneer

Auctioneers require to be licensed annually under the Auctioneers Act 1845. The auctioneer is primarily agent for the seller, but on accepting a bid he becomes also agent for the buyer. Thus his signature on a memorandum of sale would be binding on both seller and buyer: *Cohen v Roche* (1927). The auctioneer has a lien on the goods for his charges and has a right of action for the price against a buyer who has taken delivery and has failed to pay. He has implied authority to receive payment in cash, but no implied authority to sell on credit.

Auctioneer's warranties

Independently of any liability as agent, the auctioneer impliedly warrants on his own behalf:

(i) that he has authority to sell the goods
(ii) that he knows of no defect in the seller's title
(iii) that he will give possession upon payment of the price, and that the purchaser's possession will not be disturbed by the seller or by himself.

He does not warrant the seller's title in a sale of specific goods, unless he fails to make it clear he is merely acting as agent (*Benton v Campbell, Parker & Co. Ltd* (1925)).

66. Auctions with and without reserve

An auction 'with reserve' is an auction which is announced as being *(i)* subject to a reserve price being reached, and/or *(ii)* subject to the seller himself reserving a right to bid.

If a reserve price has been announced and the auctioneer inadvertently accepts a bid at a lower price, the buyer cannot enforce the sale.

An 'auction without reserve' is an auction in which the seller cannot legally bid, either personally or through an agent. If he does so, the buyer can, under the provisions of s. 57(4),(5) of the Sale of Goods Act, treat the sale as fraudulent.

67. Bidding rings

It is a criminal offence for any dealer to make an agreement supported by consideration to abstain from bidding at any sale which he attends: Auctions (Bidding Agreements) Acts 1927–1969. A 'dealer' is any person who makes it his business to attend auctions for the purpose of buying goods for resale.

If a dealer is convicted under these enactments, the buyer can claim damages for fraud against any person who is a party to the agreement, provided the buyer himself is innocent of any complicity. In addition, the seller can avoid the sale, unless the goods were bought by an innocent purchaser.

The 1969 Act itself must be displayed at auctions.

68. Mock Auctions Act 1961

It is a criminal offence under the Mock Auctions Act 1961 to promote or conduct a 'mock auction', i.e. an auction at which:

(a) articles are sold to a bidder for a sum lower than his highest bid, or where part of the price is refunded; *or*

(b) the right to bid is restricted to persons who have already agreed to buy one or more other articles; *or*

(c) an article is offered as a gift by way of inducement.

6

Agency law

1. Definition of agency

An agent is a person who is employed to bring the person appointing him agent, the principal, into a contractual relationship with a third party: *Towle v White* (1873). The agent is not a party to the contract and can only enforce it on his own behalf against the third party if he has a personal interest in it, such as a lien on the proceeds of a sale, as is the case with an auctioneer: *Chelmsford Auctions Ltd v Poole* (1973).

2. Categories of agency

Except for the case of commercial agents (see below), the categories of agency are not defined in any particular statute, but the various categories referred to below are the commonly accepted formulations.

(a) A *universal* agent, rarely encountered, is an agent appointed to handle all the affairs of his principal.

(b) A *general* agent is appointed to represent his principal in all business of a certain kind. A partner is a general agent for the partnership.

(c) A *special* agent is one appointed for a particular purpose. A bank is a special agent of its customers for the clearance of cheques.

(d) A *del credere* agent is an agent employed to sell goods and who promises his principal that he will be paid. If the buyer does not pay, the principal can look to the *del credere* agent for payment.

(e) A *commercial* agent is one within the Commercial Agents Regulations 1993: a self-employed intermediary who has continuing authority to negotiate the sale or purchase of goods on behalf of another person (the principal) or to negotiate and conclude the sale and purchase of goods on behalf and in the name of that principal. The position with regard to commercial agents is set out below.

(f) A *professional* agent is one not within the definition of commercial agency and who deals in services, such as travel agents and solicitors.

METHOD OF APPOINTMENT

3. Express appointment

The general rule is that no particular form of appointment is required, and that appointment may be oral, in writing, or a combination.

There are, however, exceptions. Thus, ss. 53 and 54 of the Law of Property Act 1925 stipulate that an agent is to be appointed in writing if he is appointed to create or dispose of an interest in land. Similarly, an agent who is to execute a deed must himself be appointed by deed unless the principal is present at the execution of the deed and consented to his agent entering into the deed: *Ball* v *Dunstonville* (1791); *Berkeley* v *Hardy* (1826).

It is also possible to give a power of attorney under the Powers of Attorney Act 1971 in which case the agent must be appointed in the form prescribed by the Act. The document must be signed and witnessed, but, by virtue of the Law of Property (Miscellaneous Provisions) Act 1989, the document need not be sealed. If it is intended that the agency powers should continue beyond the incapacity of the principal, the procedures set out in the Enduring Powers of Attorney Act 1985 must be followed.

4. Implied appointment

An appointment to act as agent may be implied from all the circumstances of the case.

> *Case law* In *Hely-Hutchinson v Bray Head Ltd* (1968), the chairman of a company acted as managing director, though never formally appointed as such and had made a number of contracts on behalf of the company. One such contract was a guarantee of a third party debt. It was held that the board of directors, by allowing him to act as managing director, had by implication given him the authority to enter into the contract as agent of the company.

> *Case law* A company secretary hired a Rolls Royce in the name of the company but, in fact, for his own personal use. The company refused to pay. It was held that if a person who was a company secretary could be expected to have the authority to hire such a car, then the company would be liable: *Panorama Developments Ltd* v *Fidelis Furnishing Fabrics Ltd* (1971).

Agencies may also be implied by law. Thus, s. 56(2) of the Consumer Credit Act 1974 provides for the 'negotiator' in the course of the preliminary discussions designed to lead to a credit or hire agreement to be deemed the agent of the creditor or owner (see Chapter 7). Similarly, s. 5 of the Partnership Act 1890 provides that all general partners are agents both for the firm and of one another in relation to the normal business of the firm.

5. Agency by estoppel

If one party allows third parties to believe that another is acting as his authorised agent, then he will be prevented, or 'estopped', from subsequently denying that other's authority to act on his behalf. The conditions under which an agency by estoppel will arise were established in *Rama Corporation Ltd* v *Proved Tin and General Investments Ltd* (1952) as:

- a representation is made by the principal to the third party
- the third party relies on the representation; and
- the third party as a consequence of his reliance on the representation alters his position.

Thus, a husband, partner or master who allows his wife, co-partner or servant, as appropriate, to act as his agent, cannot later avoid liability on contracts made through that agent even after revocation of the agency unless and until he has expressly notified third parties with whom the agent has habitually dealt: *Scarf* v *Jardine* (1882)

> *Case law* L owned a house and allowed his wife to induce S to buy it, though he did not give her authority to sell. S commenced doing repairs to the house, but L then decided he did not wish to sell. S claimed specific performance and L denied his wife's authority to sell. It was held that L had allowed S to believe that his wife was his properly authorised agent and was therefore estopped from denying her authority to contract on his behalf: *Spiro* v *Lintern* (1973).

6. Apparent authority

Apparent authority may apply to create the relationship of agent and principal, even though there is no formal relationship between the parties. It may in many ways be regarded as a species of agency by estoppel as discussed above.

The nature of this category of agency has been explained as follows: "an 'apparent'... authority ... is a legal relationship between the principal and the contractor created by the representation made by the principal to the contractor, intended to be and in fact acted upon by the contractor, that the agent has authority to enter on behalf of the principal into a contract of a kind within the scope of the 'apparent' authority, so as to render the principal liable to perform any obligations imposed on him by such contract. To the relationship so created the agent is a stranger. He need not be (although he generally is) aware of the existence of the representation. The representation, when acted on by the contractor by entering into a contract with the agent, operates as an estoppel, preventing the principal from asserting that he is not bound by the contract. It is irrelevant whether the agent had actual authority to enter into the contract': *Freeman and Lockyer* v *Bucklehurst Park Properties (Mangal) Ltd* (1964).

In this judgment, the court referred to 'ostensible' authority as being an alternative mode of expression for 'apparent' authority. This approach was endorsed in *Armagas Ltd* v *Mundogas SA* (1986), when the court said: 'Ostensible authority comes about where the principal, by words or conduct, has represented that the agent has the requisite actual authority, and the party deals with him in reliance on that representation. The principal in these circumstances is estopped from denying that actual authority existed'.

Case law Where an employee of A had had discussions with a potential purchaser, and had then left to join B but had continued those discussions and then entered into a contract, the employee could not be said to have fixed any liability on B since not only had he no actual authority, but he had no apparent authority: *Discount Kitchens* v *Crawford* (1988).

Case law Where there is a change in the ownership of a property, a request by the owners to previous suppliers, who are unaware of the change, to deliver further goods to the same address, does not amount to a representation that would form the basis of an estoppel on which the concept of ostensible authority could be founded and under which the former owner could be held liable for payment: *Charrington Fuel Oil* v *Parvant* (1988).

7. Usual authority

The usual authority of an agent is closely linked to his implied authority. Where an agent carries on a particular trade or profession, such as auctioneer or estate agent, he has an implied authority to perform such acts as are usual in that trade or profession. What is 'usual' will often be a matter for expert evidence.

Case law P appointed A as manager of P's business carried on under the name of A & Co. A was forbidden to accept bills of exchange, an act which was incidental to his duties. He did, however, accept a bill in the name of A & Co, and it was held that P was liable on it. The court said that 'if a person employs another as agent in a character which involves a particular authority, he cannot by secret reservation divest him of that authority': *Edmunds* v *Bushell & Jones* (1865).

Case law P appointed A as manager of his public house, but the licence was taken out in A's name. A's name duly appeared over the door. A bought cigars on credit. Although such purchases appeared to be within the usual authority of a manager, P had in fact forbidden A so to act. It was held that P was liable. It was said to be reasonable for an innocent third party to rely on the authority usually held by a person with the status of a public house manager to order bar supplies: *Watteau* v *Fenwick* (1893).

This case has been criticised as the third party did not know of the agency. It has not been formally overruled but it has been said to be a case 'which a court should be wary of applying': *Rhodian River Shipping Co* v *Halla Maritime Corporation* (1984).

8. Agency of necessity

There are limited occasions when the law will allow someone to act as another's agent in cases of urgency or necessity even though there was no question of any appointment as agent.

Case law A sent a horse by rail. On arrival at the due destination, there was no one to collect it. The railway company sent it to local stables, but S refused to pay the charges. It was held that the railway company had acted reasonably since they could not let the horse starve: *GNR* v *Swaffield* (1874).

Case law S contracted with the railway company for the carriage of tomatoes from Jersey to Weymouth by ship and then to London by rail. The vessel was delayed at Weymouth and, when finally unloaded, the railway company, fearing that the tomatoes would soon perish, sold them locally without attempting to contact S. Since there had been no such attempt, the railway company had to compensate S for the difference between the sale price and the higher price prevailing in London: *Springer* v *GWR* (1921). See too *The Choko Star* (1990).

Agency of necessity also requires an emergency.

Case law M had agreed to store S's furniture. He later decided he needed the storage space himself, but was unable to contact S. He then sold the furniture claiming to be S's agent. The court held that there was no

227

agency of necessity as there was no commercial emergency: *Sachs* v *Miklos* (1948).

9. Agency by ratification

It is always open to a party, expressly or by implication, subsequently to adopt, or ratify, an act of agency purported to have been carried out on his behalf. It is, however, necessary that the agent informed the third party that he was acting as agent.

> *Case law* A was authorised by P to buy wheat at a particular price. A, however, went beyond his authority by buying at a higher price. A bought in his own name, although he intended the purchase to be on behalf of P. P then told A that he would take the wheat at the purchase price, but later refused to accept delivery. It was held that P was not liable to A as an undisclosed principal could not ratify the acts of a purported agent: *Keighley, Maxstead & Co* v *Durant* (1901).

Ratification also requires the principal to be in existence at the time the agent purported to act on his behalf, and that the principal had contractual capacity when the contract was made and when he sought to ratify that contract. Under the Minors' Contracts Act 1987, a minor, when reaching full age, may ratify an earlier indebtedness.

> *Case law* The principal, at the date the contract was entered into, was an enemy alien. Subsequent ratification was held to be invalid: *Boston Deep Sea Fishing and Ice Co* v *Farnham* (1888).

> *Case law* A contract to buy wine on behalf of a company which was yet to be registered could not be ratified once the company had been registered: *Kelner* v *Baxter* (1886). While the principle established by this case remains valid, its effect has been modified by s. 36(c) of the Companies Act 1985, which provides that, in such circumstances, the purported agent is personally liable on the contract.

A principal can, after the expiry of the relevant limitation period, ratify the commencement or conduct of legal proceedings in an action which had been commenced without authority within the limitation period. If, however, a time is fixed for doing a particular act, the doctrine of ratification will not apply if it had the effect of extending that time, nor can a principal ratify an act of the agent if such ratification would adversely affect rights of property in either real or personal property, including intellectual property, which had arisen in favour of a third party or others claiming through him since the unauthorised act of the agent: *Presentaciones Musicales SA* v *Secunda* (1994).

It is also the case that ratification must take place within a reasonable time, this being a question of fact dependent on all the circumstances of the case: *Re Portuguese Consolidated Copper Mines Ltd* (1890).

Once an agency has been ratified, ratification is back-dated to the purported act of agency.

> *Case law* A purported to accept an offer from L to buy property belonging to P, although A did not have the relevant authority. L later tried to withdraw his offer claiming that, since P had never previously accepted the offer, no contract had existed. P ratified the actions of A and insisted that the sale contract be honoured. It was held that P's ratification related to the time when A had accepted the offer and not to the time of ratification: *Bolton Partners* v *Lambert* (1889).

Ratification can be express or implied: *Waithman* v *Wakefield* (1807).

DUTIES AND AUTHORITY OF PRINCIPAL AND AGENT

10. Duties of principal

The principal is under a duty to pay any agreed commission or remuneration and not to hinder the agent from earning this: *Rhodes* v *Forwood* (1876): *Alpha Trading Ltd* v *Dunnshaw-Patten Ltd* (1981). If, however, where the contract negotiated by the agent is for the sale of land, and the seller refuses to sign the contract, or the buyer signs 'subject to contract' and the seller refuses to complete, then the agent is not entitled to his commission, unless the agency contract specifies otherwise: *Luxor (Eastbourne) Ltd* v *Cooper* (1941).

If no sum is agreed for payment, then the provisions of s. 15 of the Supply of Goods and Services Act 1982 would apply and thus entitle the agent to payment of a reasonable sum. Where, however, the agency agreement provides for payment to be at the discretion of the principal, and he declines to exercise that discretion, the agent is unable to enforce any right to payment: *Re Richmond Gate Property Ltd* (1965). An unpaid agent, as a matter of general law, will have a lien over any property of the principal in his possession: *Taylor* v *Robinson* (1818).

A principal is also bound to indemnify the agent against all liabilities properly incurred in the discharge of his duties, unless the agency contract specifies to the contrary: *Christoforides* v *Terry* (1924). The agent must, however, have been acting properly, otherwise the principal can properly refuse to provide an indemnity.

Case law Agents who failed to pay customs duties failed to claim an indemnity for a fine which had to be paid, since it was their breach of their duty which had led to the fine being imposed: *Lage* v *Siemens Bros & Co Ltd* (1932).

The principle of vicarious liability means that the principal will be liable for the tortious acts of the agent, if committed in the course of the agency.

Case law The defendants were solicitors who employed a managing clerk to carry out property transactions. He fraudulently induced L to transfer two properties which the managing clerk sold, absconding with the proceeds. The defendants, as principals, were held liable as, by holding out the clerk as being authorised to transfer property, they had given him the apparent authority to act as he had. Even though the managing clerk's act was fraudulent and for his own benefit, he was nonetheless within the scope of his authority: *Lloyd* v *Grace, Smith & Co* (1912). See too *Armagas Ltd* v *Mundogas SA* (1986).

11. Duties of agent

The agent is required by s. 13 of the Supply of Goods and Services Act 1982, and at common law, to act with reasonable care and skill on behalf of the principal: *Keppel* v *Wheeler* (1927).

Case law P asked a close friend to seek out a car for her to buy, saying that it must not have been involved in an accident. The friend, who had some knowledge of cars, found one which he thought to be in good condition, though he did notice that the bonnet had been crumpled and perhaps straightened. He recommended that she purchase it, which she did. It later became apparent that the car had been badly damaged in an accident, poorly repaired and was unroadworthy. It was held that even a gratuitous agent owed a duty to exercise reasonable care and skill, such care and skill to be measured objectively, and that this agent had been in breach of such duty: *Chaudhry* v *Prabhakar* (1988).

The agent is also required promptly to disclose to the principal any relevant information he receives relevant to the contract he is to execute.

Case law P leased premises and instructed A to sell the remaining period of the lease. P believed that the owner of the freehold would not allow the premises to be used for business purposes. A contacted the owner and obtained his permission for the premises to be so used. P was not informed who sold the remaining period of the lease for less than he would otherwise have done. It was held that A was not entitled to his commission since he was in breach of his duty of disclosure: *Heath* v *Parkinson* (1926).

An agent must not disclose any confidential information entrusted to him by the principal or which he obtains in the course of the agency: *Faccenda Chicken Ltd* v *Fowler* (1986).

The agent must not allow there to be a conflict of interest between himself and his principal. He should not, for example, accept a commission from the third party as well as the principal without first obtaining the approval of the principal: *North & South Trust Co* v *Berkeley* (1971).

> *Case law* P instructed his stock-broker, A, to buy shares in a particular company. A pretended to buy them on the open market, but actually made use of his own shareholding in that company. Although the price was in fact the same as on the open market, A did not inform P of the source of the shares. P had the transaction set aside with A being ordered to repay all the money paid by P: *Armstrong* v *Jackson* (1917).

An agent must obey the lawful instructions of the principal

> *Case law* An agent was instructed by his principal to insure the latter's vessel but failed to do so. On the loss of the vessel, the agent had to compensate the principal: *Turpin* v *Bilton* (1843).

The agent must not make a secret profit or accept any bribe.

> *Case law* P owned property which A offered to purchase. Before contracts had been exchanged, A made an application for planning permission in the name of P and which he signed as 'agent' for P. Unknown to P, planning permission was granted before completion. It was held that P was entitled to the profits which had accrued to A. He had acted as a self-appointed agent and had placed himself in a fiduciary position with the result that the application for planning permission should have been disclosed: *English* v *Dedham Vale Properties Ltd* (1978).

> *Case law* A were auctioneers engaged by P. They paid for the printing of advertisements and received, and kept, a trade discount from the printers. They later said that trade custom allowed them to keep this discount. P was charged the full cost and, on discovering the discount, refused to pay A agency commission. It was held that A were entitled to their commission as it related to the sale of P's goods and the secret performance did not affect the performance of the sale. A were, however, in breach of the duty not to make a secret profit and had to hand the discount over. They could keep the commission since they had acted in good faith: *Hippisley* v *Knee Bros* (1905).

A bribe has been defined as a commission or other inducement given by a third party to an agent and kept secret from the principal: *Arrangel Atlas Compania Naviera SA* v *Ishika Wajima-Harima Industries Co Ltd* (1990). See too *Industries and General Mortgage Co Ltd* v *Lewes* (1949).

Case law M had a controlling shareholding in the defendants as nominee for J, who was the defendants' chairman. He negotiated the grant of a licence for the plaintiffs to operate a market on the defendants' land. M, in reaching that agreement, failed to disclose to the defendant's board that their solicitors had advised against that agreement or that, acting on J's instructions, he had required the plaintiffs to pay £70,000 to an offshore company which he controlled. Subsequently, M disclosed the payment and accounted for most of that sum. The defendants served a notice to determine the licence. The plaintiffs claimed the return of the £70,000 for damages, and the defendants counterclaimed for rescission. The court gave judgment for the defendants and said that a principal who discovered that his agent had either obtained or arranged to obtain a bribe from the other party to the transaction was entitled to treat the transaction as void from the very beginning. He was also entitled to rescind where, to the knowledge of the other party, the agent had placed himself in a position where his interests and duties conflicted so that he could no longer give impartial advice; but that in these circumstances, the other party had to have actual knowledge or be wilfully blind to the fact that the agent intended to conceal his dealings from his principal. Since the plaintiffs knew that M was concealing his dealings from his principal, the defendants were entitled to rescind the contract and it was immaterial that the plaintiffs, who had the requisite knowledge, did not know whether M's concealment of his dealings was for his personal interest or not. The court said that, where an agent received a bribe, the principal was entitled to affirm or rescind the contract. In recovering the money, there was no implication that he had adopted the transaction: *Logicrose* v *Southend United Football Club* (1988).

The remedies available to the principal on the agent making a secret commission are to: dismiss the agent without notice or compensation; sue the agent for the secret commission; terminate the contract with the third party, but only where the third party had actual knowledge of what the agent was doing, or deliberately closed his eyes; and sue the third party for damages: *Salford Corporation* v *Lever* (1891). Should a bribe be involved, then, in addition to these remedies, the principal may choose between recovering the bribe and claiming damages: *Mahesen* v *Malaysia Government Officers' Co-operative Housing Society Ltd* (1978).

The giving and taking of bribes and secret commissions may also involve offences under the Prevention of Corruption Acts 1901-1916.

An agent is also under a *prima facie* duty to act as the agent himself and not to delegate his role to anyone else. This is because the agent has normally been selected because of his own qualities and skill. There are, however, a number of exceptions to the rule, as below:

- Where the principal consents to the delegation when the relationship was created: *Quebec and Richmond Railway Ltd* v *Quinn* (1858).
- consent to delegation may be presumed from the circumstances: *De Bussche* v *Alt* (1878).
- Where delegation is the usual practice in the agent's trade or profession, such as a country solicitor being enabled to delegate complicated legal work to a specialist: *Solley* v *Wood* (1852).
- Where an emergency makes performance impossible: *De Bussche v Alt* (1878).
- Where no special skill is required, as where the duties of the agent are purely clerical: *Allam & Co Ltd* v *Europa Poster Services Ltd* (1968).

Normally, the principal will have no contract with the sub-agent and has therefore no right of action against him, though he could sue the agent for appointing an incompetent sub-agent: *Balsamo* v *Medici* (1984).

An agent is under a duty to provide to his principal an accurate record of transactions conducted on behalf of the principal. This duty arises by reason of the fact that the principal, having entrusted to the agent the making of transactions binding on the principal, is entitled to know what his personal contractual rights and duties were both in relation to third parties and the agent. The existence of such a duty is not affected by whether or not the agency is founded on contract. In the absence of an agreement to the contrary, the agent s duty to prove pre-existing records relating to authorised transactions continued notwithstanding termination of the agent s authority to enter into further transactions. Furthermore, the documents which the principal is entitled to see can include computer documents and an agent cannot deny access on the ground that these records contain irrelevant or confidential material when the difficulty of separating out such information was caused by the agent s own maladministration: *Yasuda Fire and Marine Insurance Co of Europe Ltd* v *Orion Marine Insurance Underwriting Agent Ltd* (1995).

12. The agent and the third party

The general rule is that the agent can neither sue, nor be sued, on the contract concluded on behalf of his principal: *Paquin Ltd* v *Beauclerk* (1906). There are, however, a number of exceptions:

(a) Where the agent agrees to accept personal liability. An agent who is described as a party to a written contract and who signs it without qualification is liable under it, even though the third party knew he was acting as agent: *Basma* v *Weekes* (1950).

(b) At common law, an agent who executed a deed was personally liable even though the deed might say that it was executed on behalf of his principal: *Appleton* v *Binks* (1804). This appears, however, to have been reversed by s. 7(1) of the Powers of Attorney Act 1971.

(c) Where the agent signs a bill of exchange in his own name. Here, he can escape liability by adding words to the bill to show that he was acting as an agent: s. 26(1) Bills of Exchange Act 1882.

(d) Trade custom can make an agent personally liable.

> *Case law* Agents signed 'as agents for principals'. There was a custom that the agents were personally liable unless the name of the principal was forthcoming within a reasonable time. It was held that evidence of this custom was admissible: *Hutchinson* v *Tatham* (1873).

(e) If the agent is in fact the principal, he is liable on the contract. A person described in a charterparty as 'agent for the freighters' was personally liable on proof that he was himself the freighter: *Schmalz* v *Avery* (1851). If the agent purports to act for a named principal, he can only enforce the contract after giving due notice to the third party that he acted on his own behalf: *Bickerton* v *Burrell* (1816). Even here, however, the agent will not be allowed to sue if this would prejudice the third party: *Fellowes* v *Gwydyr* (1829).

(f) If the alleged principal does not exist, it may be easier to infer that the agent intended to assume personal responsibility: *Kelner* v *Baxter* (1886). Section 36 of the Companies Act 1985 provides that an agent acting on behalf of a company which is not yet formed will escape personal liability if there is a clear exclusion of such liability.

13. The undisclosed principal

If the third party is unaware that he is dealing with an agent, the principal can sue and be sued on authorised contracts made on his behalf: *Scrimshire* v *Alderton* (1743); *Thomson* v *Davenport* (1829). The agent can also sue and be sued: *Saxon* v *Blake* (1861). The third party can sue either party: *Clarkson Booker Ltd* v *Andjel* (1964).

An undisclosed principal, however, cannot sue:

(a) If he did not exist or lacked contractual capacity at the time the agent made the contract. This follows from the basic provisions as to capacity to contract (see Chapter 4).

(b) If the contract specifically prohibits the intervention of an undisclosed principal: *United Kingdom Mutual SS Assurance Ltd* v *Nevill* (1887).

(c) If the contract by implication excludes the intervention of an undisclosed principal.

> *Case law* When making a contract with the defendant, an agent described himself as 'the owner of the ship or vessel called the Ann'. It was held that the undisclosed principal could not sue on the contract, since the agent, in describing himself as the owner, had implied that he was the sole contracting party: *Humble* v *Hunter* (1848).

(d) If the third party can show that he had some reason for wishing to deal with the agent on a personal basis, as where the agent was a man of reputation and skill and the contract relied on such matters: *Collins* v *Associated Greyhound Racecourses Ltd* (1930). The same would apply where the third party would not wish to deal with the undisclosed principal.

> *Case law* B had banned S from attending first night performances. To get around this, S got a friend to buy tickets for him. B refused S admission on the ticket thus obtained. S was held to be an undisclosed principal who could not take over the contract since he knew that, had B known the truth, he would not have sold a ticket to the friend: *Said* v *Butt* (1920).

If, however, the contract is not one of a personal nature, the undisclosed principal can sue even though the third party would not have dealt with him directly, provided there was no misrepresentation as to the principal's identity: *Dyster* v *Randall & Sons* (1926).

(e) If the third party would have a defence to an action by the agent, as for example where he has a right of set-off against the agent. This rule, however, only prevents the principal from suing when it is his own conduct which enabled the agent to appear to be dealing for himself: *Cooke* v *Eshelby* (1887).

(f) If the third party's legal position would be materially worse as a result of the intervention of the undisclosed principal: *Collins* v *Associated Greyhound Racecourses Ltd* (1930).

> *Case law* Where a person became a protected tenant of a flat, it was held that evidence could not be brought to show that she had made the lease as agent for an undisclosed principal since that would increase the number of people who would be entitled to protection under the Rent Act 1974: *Hanstown Properties Ltd* v *Green* (1977).

14. The agent's warranty of authority

Every agent purporting to act as agent warrants that he has the authority to make a binding contract on behalf of his principal: *Collen* v *Wright* (1857).

Case law Solicitors, acting as agents, were instructed by a client to defend him against threatened legal proceedings. Prior to the proceedings taking place, the client, unknown to the solicitors, became insane. This meant that the solicitors lost their authority to act. They delivered a defence after learning of the insanity. The plaintiffs demanded that the defence be struck out as being invalid. It was held that the solicitors had impliedly warranted that they had authority to act when they had not, and that they were liable for the plaintiffs' costs: *Yonge* v *Toynbee* (1910).

It should be noted in this particular context that, if the agent was appointed under the Powers of Attorney Act 1971, s. 5(1) of the Act will free an agent of any responsibility if unaware that his power to act has been revoked

The agent will not be liable if his lack of authority is known to the third party when the contract was made, or if the third party agrees to exclude liability for breach of warranty of authority: *Lilly* v *Smales* (1892). Such an exclusion clause would, however, now be subject to the Unfair Contract Terms Act 1977 and, if appropriate, to the Unfair Terms in Consumer Contracts Regulations 1994 (see Chapter 5).

15. Termination of agency

Like any other contract, a contract of agency can be terminated by mutual agreement, performance, breach or by frustration. Insanity and death also terminate the agency: *Yonge* v *Toynbee* (1910); *Campanari* v *Woodburn* (1854). The principal's bankruptcy terminates the agency, and so does that of the agent if it makes him unfit to perform: *Elliott* v *Turquand* (1881); *McCall* v *Australian Meat Co Ltd* (1870).

16. Revocation of authority

An agent's authority can be determined by notice from the principal. If the agency contract was for a specific period, and notice is given before this period has been reached, the revocation remains effective, though the principal can be sued for breach of contract: *Page One Records Ltd* v *Britton* (1967).

If no term of notice is specified, nor any term for the agency, the contract is terminable on reasonable notice, which will be a question of fact dependent on the circumstances of the particular case: *Martin-Baker Aircraft Co Ltd* v *Canadian Flight Equipment Ltd* (1955); *Richardson* v *Koefod* (1969).

It is important to remember that, even though the agent's authority might be validly revoked, the agent's ostensible authority might still be intact. It is therefore prudent for the principal to give notice of the revocation otherwise he might remain liable for further contracts entered into by the former agent: *Summers* v *Salomon* (1857).

17. Irrevocable agencies

An authority coupled with an interest cannot be revoked. Such an authority occurs where the agency was created to protect an interest of the agent.

Case law The defendant was appointed by a power of attorney to take possession of an estate and to manage it for the principal. The estate was mortgaged to a third party and, to support this, the defendant gave a personal guarantee that the mortgage would be paid. The power of attorney made no mention of the guarantee. When the plaintiff later revoked the defendant's authority and demanded possession of the estate, the court held that the authority, as it was coupled with an interest, was irrevocable: *Frith* v *Frith* (1906). See too *Raleigh* v *Atkinson* (1840); *Smart* v *Saunders* (1848).

An agency can also be irrevocable if made under the Powers of Attorney Act 1971. If a power of attorney is expressed to be irrevocable and given to secure a proprietary interest of the donee, s. 4 provides that this power can be revoked neither by the donor without the consent of the donee, nor by the death, insanity or bankruptcy of the donor. The Enduring Powers of Attorney Act 1985 makes provision for powers of attorney contained in a prescribed form and expressed to continue despite the donor's supervening mental incapacity. Such an enduring power is not revoked by such incapacity but, when such incapacity occurs, the power is suspended until registered by the court. Once the enduring power has been registered, it can only be revoked with the consent of the court.

A problem may arise where a principal, without actually revoking the agency, effectively brings it to an end by, for example, closing down the business to which it relates. An agent would need to show that the principal's action was a breach of an express term of the contract, or of a term implied to give the contract business efficacy.

Case law A colliery owner appointed brokers as sole agents for sale of his coal for 7 years, or for as long as he did business in Liverpool. After 4 years, the colliery was sold. It was held that the owner had not agreed, expressly or by implication, to keep the brokers supplied with coal for sale and so he was therefore not in breach: *Rhodes* v *Forwood* (1876). See too *French & Co Ltd* v *Leeston Shipping Co Ltd* (1922)

Case law A shirt manufacturer expressly agreed to employ an agent for 5 years, but the factory was destroyed after 2 years. It was held that the manufacturer was not released from his obligations to provide the agent with a chance to earn commission, so the agent was therefore entitled to damages: *Turner* v *Goldsmith* (1891).

18. Accrued rights

Rights which accrued prior to termination are not affected by it, so the agent retains his right to commission already earned: *Chappell* v *Bray* (1860).

19. Various types of agent

Advertising agents

Although advertising agents are almost invariably referred to as such, they have for a long time been independent parties who do not act as agents in the legal sense. It is for this reason that their trade association is the Institute of Practitioners in Advertising.

Auctioneers

An auctioneer is someone engaged to sell goods or property as agent for another party. Occasionally, following a sale, they can act as agent for the purchaser.

Bankers

A banker is the agent of a customer in relation to paying out, on and receiving the proceeds of, cheques.

Estate agents

Although it is common to use the term 'estate agent', he does not normally act as an agent in the strict sense and normally has no power to make a contract between a client and prospective purchaser. He is usually an independent person: *Sorrell* v *Finch* (1977). The position of an estate agent is not unlike that of the advertising agency (see above).

Factors

The position of the factor, or mercantile agent, is regulated by the Factors Act 1889 (see Chapter 5).

There are two commonly termed 'agents' who are not in fact agents in law.

Canvassing, or marketing, agents

Their authority does not extend to the creation of a binding contract on behalf of a principal, but is limited to introducing customers. Their authority may, however, allow them to make representations about goods or services and, in this respect, the 'principal' may be bound by what they have said.

Commission agents

Here, the principal appoints a person to deal on his behalf but on the understanding that, when dealing with third parties, they deal in their own name. The contract between 'principal' and 'agent' is analogous to that of agency, but, as the 'agent' does not bring the 'principal' into a contractual relationship with the third party, there is no true agency.

20. Commercial agents

The Commercial Agents (Council Directive) Regulations 1993/3053, as amended by 1993/3173, implement in the United Kingdom the provisions of Council Directive 86/653 on the law in relation to self-employed commercial agents. The Regulations set out the rights and obligations as between commercial agents and their principals, and deal with remuneration and the conclusion and termination of the agency contract. The main details of the Regulations are set out below.

Agents covered by the regulations

The regulations only apply to a 'commercial agent' who is defined as: a self-employed intermediary who has continuing authority to negotiate the sale or purchase of goods on behalf of another person or to negotiate and conclude the sale and purchase of goods on behalf of and in the name of that principal.

Despite the term 'self-employed intermediary' it is believed that a company as well as individuals are covered. A number of agents are excluded, notably distributors who buy and sell goods in their own right and sellers of goods from mail-order catalogues who sell to friends or families. 'Goods' is interpreted to be 'substances, growing crops and things comprised in land by virtue of being attached to it and any ship, aircraft or vehicle'. 'Services' are excluded.

The form of the agreement

Both the principal and the agent have the right, on request, to a signed document from the other setting out the terms of the agency agreement, including any later variation of it. This right cannot be excluded.

The obligations of an agent

The regulations impose an obligation on the agent to look after the interests of the principal and to act dutifully and in good faith. Three particular examples of this duty are provided. The agent must:

- make proper efforts to negotiate and, where appropriate, conclude those transactions they are instructed to take care of
- communicate to the principal all the necessary information available to them
- comply with the principal's reasonable instructions.

The obligations of a principal

As with an agent the principal must act dutifully and in good faith towards the agent. In particular a principal must:

- provide the agent with necessary documentation relating to the goods concerned, e.g. sales literature, training manuals and the like
- notify the agent of pertinent matters, for example that he or she expects that the volume of transactions is likely to be lower than that which the agent could normally have expected
- inform the agent within a reasonable period of his or her acceptance or refusal of any commercial transaction negotiated or concluded by the agent.

The agent's remuneration or commission

The regulations provide that, in the absence of any agreement as to remuneration between the parties: a commercial agent shall be entitled to the remuneration that commercial agents ... are customarily allowed, and if there is no such customary practice, a commercial agent shall be entitled to reasonable remuneration taking into account all the aspects of the transaction. 'Commission' means any part of the remuneration which varies with the value of the business transactions. The agent also has the right to demand all information and extracts from the principal's financial records in order to check the amount of the commission due. This right to information cannot be excluded.

Payment of commission

Commission becomes due to the agent as soon as either the principal or the third party has performed its obligation under the contract of sale. The agent is entitled to the commission if the principal fails to perform the contract but not if the third party fails to perform. The commission shall be paid not later than on the last day of the month following the quarter in which it became due. The provisions concerning payment of commission cannot be contracted out of to the detriment of the agent.

After the termination of an agency agreement

Under the regulations an agent will be entitled to commission, notwith-standing the termination of the agency, provided that the transaction was mainly attributable to the agent's efforts and that it was concluded within a reasonable period after the agency agreement was terminated.

Information concerning commission

The regulations impose a duty on the principal to supply their commercial agent with a statement of commission due, showing the method of calcula-tion, not later than the end of the month following the quarter in which the commission was earned.

The termination of the agency contract

Where an agency contract is entered into for an indefinite period and the agreement does not specify notice periods, either party may terminate it on notice. Such notice shall expire at the end of a calendar month and shall be:

- one month during the first year of the contract
- two months during the second
- three months during the third and each subsequent year.

Where the agency agreement was entered into for a fixed term then it auto-matically terminates at the end of that period.

Compensation at termination of the agreement

Compensation is payable on the termination of the agency agreement whether it was for an indefinite period or fixed term. Therefore, if an agency agreement is not renewed compensation is payable even though there is no breach by the principal. To claim compensation the agent must notify the principal that they intend to claim within one year following ter-mination. Compensation is based upon damage suffered by the agent and the agent will have the burden of proof to establish this. While damages are not fully defined in the regulations they are deemed to have been suffered if:

(a) Termination has deprived the agent of commission which the proper performance of the agency agreement would have processed for them while providing substantial benefit for the principal.

(b) Where termination prejudiced the agent's ability to be reimbursed for expenses incurred in the performance of the contract on the principal's advice.

Non-competition covenants

Any post-termination restraint of trade clause in a commercial agency must:

- be concluded in writing
- relate to the geographical area, group of customers and goods entrusted to the commercial agent under the agency agreements
- last for no more than two years from the date of termination.

7

The regulation of the provision of credit and hire

In this chapter, we examine the statutory framework provided by the Consumer Credit Act 1974 for the regulation of all aspects of obtaining goods, services and financial accommodation by means of credit or hire agreements.

1. Regulating hire and hire purchase and credit businesses

The Consumer Credit Act 1974 creates a system for controlling regulated consumer hire and consumer credit agreements. These are defined as follows (please note that all the figures and amounts quoted below are liable to change and readers should always check for themselves if they are still correct).

(a) A regulated consumer hire agreement is an agreement with a non-corporate hirer where the agreement must run for at least three months and the rental does not exceed £25,000: s. 15.

Goods hired from the public utilities such as British Gas or British Telecom are not covered by the definition: s. 16(6).

(b) A regulated consumer credit agreement is an agreement with a non-corporate borrower for any kind of financial accommodation (and includes hire-purchase agreements) provided the accommodation does not exceed £25,000: s. 8.

Exempt agreements

Agreements will be outside the above definitions, even if within the financial limits, if they are classed by the Act, and Regulations made under it, as 'exempt'.

An agreement is not regulated if it is exempt. Generally, agreements are exempt if they cover mortgage loans made by local authorities, friendly societies, banks and insurance companies: s. 16(1).

There are also exemptions for agreements where the number of payments does not exceed a specified number or the rate of interest does not exceed a particular percentage: s. 16(5) and the Consumer Credit (Exempt Agreements) Order 1989.

2. Licensing of businesses

A business providing any kind of regulated agreement must be licensed by the Office of Fair Trading: s. 21(1). A local authority, however, does not need to apply for a licence nor does a body corporate empowered by a public general Act naming it to carry on a business: s. 21(2),(3).

Type of licence

A licence issued by the OFT is either standard or group: s. 22(1). Standard licences cover individual applications and last for ten years. Group licences cover a particular group where the OFT feels that this would be better than having members of the group apply individually for a licence: s. 22(1)(b). The Law Society has a licence covering solicitors in practice. Where a licence, group or standard, is refused an appeal may be made to the Secretary of State for Trade and Industry, and from him to the High Court: ss. 41, 42.

Unlicensed trading

An offence is committed by a business which needs a licence but which does not have one: s. 39. In addition, agreements made by an unlicensed trader cannot be enforced by him unless he has been granted an order by the OFT: s. 40. Appeals against refusals are the same as in a case of refusal to issue a licence (see above).

3. Form and content of agreements

Agreements which are regulated consumer hire and regulated consumer credit agreements have to be in the specified form: ss. 60, 61 and the Consumer Credit (Agreements) Regulations 1983. If the prescribed formalities are not observed, then the agreement is 'improperly executed' and it can only be enforced on a court order: ss. 61,65.

Copy requirements

The customer under a regulated consumer hire or consumer credit agreement is entitled to copies of the agreement within strictly controlled time limits: ss. 62–64. The contents of these copies must also conform to the Consumer Credit (Cancellation Notices and Copies of Documents)

Regulations 1983. If these requirements are not observed, then the agreement is improperly executed with the consequences referred to above.

4. Statutory right of cancellation

If the negotiations leading up to a regulated consumer hire or consumer credit agreement included oral representations made in the presence of the customer, the agreement may be cancelled by the customer for any reason. His right to cancel lasts in most cases for five days from the day following his receipt of his copy of the agreement (see above).

An agreement cannot be cancelled if (i) the credit extended is a mortgage loan or a bridging loan, or (ii) the agreement was signed by the customer on the other party's business premises, or (iii) the agreement is secured on land.

5. Statutory right to withdraw

The customer has a right to withdraw from any regulated consumer credit or consumer hire agreement before it is made: s. 7(2). In addition, where the agreement is to be secured on land, certain formalities must be followed: ss. 58(1), 61(2). The details as to what information must be given to a consumer as regards the right to cancel are set out in the Consumer Credit (Cancellation Notices and Copies of Documents) Regulations 1983. If these requirements are not observed, then the agreement is improperly executed with the consequences as set out above: ss. 61(2), 65.

6. Statutory right of termination

The customer under a hire-purchase or conditional sale agreement can, if the agreement is regulated (see **1** above), terminate it at any time. His liability is to bring his payments up to at the most one half of the total price and any installation charges: ss. 99, 100.

If the agreement is a regulated consumer hire agreement the customer can terminate the agreement at any time when it has lasted 18 months: s. 101(1), (3).

There are certain categories of agreement which cannot be terminated:

(a) A conditional sale agreement for the purchase of land cannot be terminated after the property has passed to the customer: s. 99(3), and a conditional sale agreement for the purchase of goods cannot be terminated if the property has passed to the customer who has transferred it to a third party: s. 99(4).

245

(b) A hire agreement cannot be terminated if *(i)* the goods are hired out for business purposes, or *(ii)* if the goods are selected by the customer and then acquired by the other party from a third party, or *(iii)* if the rental payments exceed £900 a year: s. 101(7).

7. The relationship of the parties to an agreement

In many hire-purchase or conditional sale transactions, there are in fact three parties involved. Thus, A wishes to buy a car and arranges to take one stocked by B, a dealer, who offers to arrange terms through C, a finance company. B then sells the car to C who lets it out to the customer, A. A therefore has no direct contract with B. However, it has been ruled that A has a right to sue B for any misrepresentation or breach of the 'collateral' contract between himself and B (i.e. a contract whereby A agrees to hire or buy the car from C in return for B arranging a hire-purchase or conditional sale): *Andrews* v *Hopkinson* (1956). The contract between A and C will be governed by the Sale of Goods Act 1979 or the Supply of Goods (Implied Terms) Act 1973 depending on whether it is a contract of hire purchase or conditional sale. Furthermore, anything said by the dealer in the negotiations preceding the contract with the finance company is said by him as agent of the finance company who must therefore take responsibility for what is said: Consumer Credit Act 1974, s. 56. The Act only applies, however, to regulated consumer hire or regulated consumer credit agreements.

8. Joint and several liability

In certain circumstances, a customer will buy goods direct from a dealer with credit extended to him by a third party. A typical case is the purchase of goods from a retailer by means of a credit card provided by a bank. In such cases his contract for the supply of the goods, unlike the position discussed above, will be directly with the dealer. If the customer has any claim against the dealer for misrepresentation or breach of contract under a regulated consumer credit agreement, he has the same claim against the party who extended the credit who is therefore 'jointly and severally' liable with the dealer so long as there was some kind of business tie-up between the dealer and the party providing the credit: Consumer Credit Act 1974, s. 75(1). This means that each is responsible to the customer for the full amount of his loss. The foregoing provisions will not apply if the cost of the particular item was £100 or less or was more than £30,000: s. 75(3)(l).

If the creditor is sued directly by the customer, the creditor will be able to seek compensation from the dealer, subject to any agreement made between them: s. 75(2).

If the breach or misrepresentation entitles the customer to rescind the agreement, he will also be entitled to rescind the credit agreement: *UDT* v *Taylor* (1980).

9. Advertisements

A false or misleading advertisement gives rise to a criminal offence under s. 46 of the Act. For example, an advertisement for mortgages offering small fixed rate mortgages for a limited time and therefore showing a low annual percentage rate of charge can be misleading if it is likely that the rate will rise once the fixed rate period is over (see *National Westminster Bank* v *Devon County Council* (1993), *R.* v *Munford and Ahearne* (1995) and *Scarborough Building Society* v *Humberside Trading Standards Dept* (1996)).

The form and content of consumer credit and consumer hire advertisements is governed by the Consumer Credit (Advertisements) Regulations 1989. There are three permitted categories of advertisement: simple, intermediate and full. It is the latter category which is the most detailed and will require such items to be included in the advertisement as the annual percentage rate of charge (the APR), and an example of repayment terms.

10. Supply of information

Customers under regulated agreements are entitled, on payment of 50p, to a copy of the agreement and to a statement of account. This information must be supplied within 12 working days of receiving a request in writing: Consumer Credit (Prescribed Period for Giving Information) Regulations 1983. If this is not done the agreement cannot be enforced while the default continues. If default in supplying the information extends for a month, a criminal offence is committed: Consumer Credit Act, ss. 77,78.

Customers who have 'running account' credit agreements (whereby they have a credit limit and can keep borrowing up to that limit, such as a bank overdraft or a credit card) are also entitled to regular information without having to make a separate request: s. 78(4).

11. Default notices

No action can be taken to enforce or terminate a regulated agreement unless due notice has been given in the prescribed form giving a minimum of seven days' notice: Consumer Credit Act, ss. 76, 87, 88 and 98. The form and content of such notices are prescribed by the Consumer Credit (Enforcement, Default and Termination Notices) Regulations 1983. It is not necessary to prove that a notice actually reached the consumer: *Lombard North Central plc* v *Power-Hines* (1995).

12. Statutory rebate

The customer under a regulated consumer credit agreement has a right to pay off the agreement early. If he does so, he is entitled to a rebate of credit charges: ss. 94, 95. The manner of calculation is set out in the Consumer Credit (Rebate on Early Settlement) Regulations 1983. If the contract provides for a figure higher than would be reached by application of the Regulations, the consumer is entitled to the higher figure: *Home Insulation Ltd* v *Wadsley* (1988).

13. Protected goods

When the customer under a regulated hire-purchase or conditional sale agreement has paid all the installation charges and at least one-third of the total price, the other party cannot recover the goods in the event of a breach of contract without a court order.

If he does recover the goods without a court order, the agreement is terminated and all sums paid in the past can be recovered: ss. 90, 91.

14. Extortionate credit bargains

The rules relating to extortionate credit bargains apply to all agreements for the provision of credit, whether or not regulated.

If the court finds that the bargain is extortionate, it can reopen matters to do justice between the parties: s. 137.

A bargain is extortionate if:

(a) it requires the customer or a relative to make payments which are grossly exorbitant; *or*

(b) it otherwise grossly contravenes ordinary principles of fair dealing: s. 138.

These provisions do not apply to hire agreements.

However, where goods hired out under a regulated consumer hire agreement are repossessed, the customer can apply to the court for relief from sums paid or to be paid: s. 132.

15. Ancillary credit businesses

The Consumer Credit Act 1974 also lists five 'ancillary credit businesses'. These are: credit-brokerage, debt-adjusting, debt-counselling, debt-collecting and the operation of a credit reference agency. The licensing provisions described above apply equally in such cases.

16. Credit reference agency files

An individual, on payment of £1, is entitled to see a copy of a file held on him by a credit reference agency and, if appropriate, to have the file corrected. Any disputes are settled by the Office of Fair Trading: ss. 158, 159. A consumer is also entitled to be advised of the name and address of any credit reference agency consulted in the course of his seeking to enter a regulated consumer credit or consumer hire agreement: Consumer Credit (Conduct of Business) (Credit References) Regulations 1977.

17. Powers of the court

On application the court has the power to issue time orders (time to pay or remedy a breach); protection orders (for protecting property subject to the particular agreement); return orders (for the handing over by the customer of goods to which a regulated consumer hire purchase or conditional sale agreement relates); and transfer orders (passing of title to the customer under regulated hire-purchase or conditional sale agreement of some of the goods, return to other party of balance): ss. 129, 131, 133.

In exercising its discretion under the Act to make a time order, a court must take account of the following (*Southern & District Finance plc v Barnes* (1995):

(*i*) Whether it is just to make the order bearing in mind the position of both parties

(*ii*) That, when a time order is made, it should normally be made for a stipulated period on account of temporary financial difficulty

(*iii*) The sum owing means every sum which is due and owing, and where possession proceedings have been brought, that will normally comprise the total indebtedness

(*iv*) That, if a time order is made when the sum owed is the whole of the outstanding balance, there will inevitably be consequences for the term of the loan, or the rate of interest, or both

(*v*) That, when making a time order, the court should suspend any possession order that it also makes so long as the terms of the time order are complied with.

Where there has been a long history of default on the part of a debtor, it would not be just to require the creditor to accept the figure offered by the debtor and make a time order if the instalments which he can afford will not meet the accruing interest, and if there is no realistic prospect of his financial position improving: *First National Bank v Syed* (1991).

8

Consumer protection and fair trading

There are a number of enactments, mainly imposing criminal penalties, which are generally regarded as measures of consumer protection. Some of the more important of these enactments are dealt with below.

TRADE DESCRIPTIONS

1. Goods

Section 1 of the Trade Descriptions Act 1968 provides that no one in the course of a business may apply a false trade description to goods, or supply goods to which a false trade description has been applied. A 'trade description' is defined in the Act as being exclusively any of the following (anything not in the list is not a trade description):

(a) Quantity, size or gauge

(b) Method of manufacture, production, processing or reconditioning

(c) Composition

(d) Fitness for purpose, strength, performance, behaviour or accuracy

(e) Any physical characteristics not included in the previous paragraphs

(f) Testing by any person and the results thereof

(g) Approval by any person or conformity with a type approved by any person

(h) Place or date of manufacture, production, processing or reconditioning

(i) Person by whom manufactured, produced, processed or reconditioned

(j) Other history including previous ownership or use.

It has been laid down that the offences created by the Act are offences not requiring any proof of *mens rea*: *Alec Norman Garages Ltd* v *Phillips* (1985); *Chilvers* v *Rayner* (1984). It has, however, been held that it is a basic principle that' it was a necessary ingredient of the offence that the offender should have knowledge at the time of the supply or offer to supply goods that a trade description is applied to them': *Cottee* v *Douglas Seaton (Used Cars) Ltd* (1972); *Fletcher* v *Budgen* (1974).

The Act has been held to apply to a person a who, in the course of a trade or business, applied a false trade description to goods which he was buying and was not necessarily limited to false trade descriptions applied by seller of goods: *Fletcher* v *Sledmore* (1973). In *Roberts* v *Leonard* (1995), the Act was held to apply to a veterinary surgeon who signed certificates relating to calves even though he was not the supplier of the calves. This last case decided that the Act also applied to false trade descriptions made in the course of a profession.

In the context of the car trade, it has become common to apply disclaimers which seek to disclaim the accuracy of the mileometer reading. False mileometer readings are false trade descriptions and hence infringements of the Act. The rule laid down in *Norman* v *Bennett* (1974) is that a disclaimer will have effect only if the disclaimer is as 'bold, precise and compelling' as the false description (i.e. the reading on the mileometer) which it seeks to disclaim.

> *Case law* The defendants applied a disclaimer by means of sticker which read: 'Trade Descriptions Act 1968. Dealers are often unable to guarantee the mileage of a used car on sale. Please disregard the recorded mileage on this vehicle and accept this as an incorrect reading'. This was held to be an adequate disclaimer: *Newham London Borough Council* v *Singh* (1987).
>
> A statement in a sales invoice alongside an odometer reading stating that the reading had not been confirmed and must be considered incorrect meant that the figure thus qualified could not be considered a false trade description: *R* v *Bull* (1993). Where a trader sold counterfeit goods but posted disclaimer notices and told customers that the goods were copies, these actions were held to avoid the commission of an offence: *Page* v *Kent County Council* (1993).

2. Defence to a charge

It was pointed out above that the offence under s. 1 of the Trade Descriptions Act is one of strict liability. This is, however, not the same as absolute liability since, under the Act, the person charged does have a defence, but the burden is on him to prove that he comes within the defence.

Section 24 provides for what is often called the 'due diligence' defence. A person charged with an offence under the Trade Descriptions Act 1968 has a defence if he can prove both that he took all reasonable precautions and exercised all due diligence to avoid commission of the offence by himself or anyone under his control, and that the commission of the offence was due to any of the following: a mistake; reliance on information supplied to him; an act or default of another; an accident or some other cause beyond his control.

> *Case law* A company imported pencils which broke United Kingdom law because of excessive lead in the paint coating. The company had obtained assurances that the products complied with the law and had indeed obtained written assurances to that effect. It was held that this did not show due diligence since a company of the size of these defendants could have sampled the products to determine whether or not they complied with the law: *Boots* v *Garrett* (1980).

Where a person is charged with the offence of supplying or offering to supply goods to which a false trade description is applied a defence lies if he can show that he did not know, and could not with reasonable diligence have ascertained, that the goods did not conform to the description or that the description had been applied to the goods.

A defence also lies to a person on a charge under the Act committed by the publication of an advertisement if he can show that it was part of his business to publish or arrange for the publication of advertisements, and if he can also show that he received the advertisement for publication in the ordinary course of business and did not know, and had no reason to suspect, that publication would amount to an offence. This defence is available to publishers but will rarely be available to advertising agencies, if only because they do not receive advertisements for publication.

3. Services, facilities, accommodation

Section 14 of the Act makes it an offence to make in the course of a trade or business a false statement as to:

(a) The provision of any services, accommodation or facilities

(b) The nature of any services, accommodation or facilities so provided

(c) The time at which, manner in which or persons by whom any services, accommodation or facilities are provided

(d) The examination, approval or evaluation by any person of any services, accommodation or facilities so provided

(e) The location or amenities of any accommodation so provided.

No definition is given in the Act of a 'service' or 'facility', but this omission has been largely made good by the courts. *Service* constitutes doing something for someone, while a *facility* means the opportunity or provision of the wherewithal for someone to do something for himself: *Newell* v *Hicks* (1984); *Kinchin* v *Ashton Park Scooters Ltd* (1984); *Dixons Ltd* v *Roberts* (1984). Where a person guaranteed a refund of the price of a book containing instructions on a gambling system, he made a statement as to the nature of services provided in the course of a trade or business: *Ashley* v *Sutton London Borough Council* (1995).

This offence differs significantly from that contained in s. 1, however, in that the latter, as pointed out, is an offence of strict liability. The offence created by s. 14, however, is of the more traditional type in that an offence can only be committed if the statement was known to be false or was made recklessly. The Act defines 'reckless' to mean a statement made careless of whether it is true or false.

> *Case law* An advertisement indicated that certain items were available carriage-paid. The advertisement was later amended to refer to additional items, stating also carriage paid. However, the intention was that carriage would be paid only if both the original and the later items were ordered. One person who ordered just the one item was charged carriage. It was held that the statement in the advertisement had been made recklessly in that no care had been taken to determine whether the advertisement was ambiguous: *MFI* v *Nattrass* (1973).

4. Defences

The various defences discussed above in relation to s. 1 of the Act apply in relation to s. 14 also.

5. The 'bypass' provision

This applies equally to s. 1 and s. 14 offences.

Section 23 allows the prosecution to charge the person whose 'act or default' caused the commission of an offence, whether or not this latter is himself also charged. If, therefore, a manufacturer were to supply a retailer with a product bearing a false label, any offence committed by the retailer could be said to have been caused by the manufacturer who could, therefore, be prosecuted under s. 23 as well as or instead of the retailer: *Cadbury Ltd* v *Halliday* (1975).

The courts have also ruled that a person can be charged under s. 23 even though he did not act in the course of a trade or business: *Olgeirsson* v *Kitching* (1986).

6. Penalties

If a case is taken before the magistrates, the current maximum penalty is a fine of £5000. If the case is taken before the Crown Courts (which will happen only in the more serious cases), then the penalty is a maximum sentence of 2 years, or a fine, or a combination. The fine can be set at such level as the court chooses.

The Act provides that a contract for the supply of goods shall not be void or unenforceable by reason only of a contravention of any provision of the Act. It is quite likely that, when there has been a breach of the Act, the injured party will have in any event remedies in contract, for misrepresentation and under the Sale of Goods Act 1979 (see Chapter 5).

A magistrates' court or Crown Court before which a person is convicted of an offence is empowered to make a compensation order requiring him to pay compensation for any personal injury, loss or damage resulting from that offence or any other offence which was taken into consideration by the court in determining sentence under the provisions of the Powers of Criminal Courts Act 1973.

If subsequent civil proceedings are brought, damages are assessed without regard to any compensation order, but the plaintiff may only recover an amount equal to the aggregate of any amount exceeding the compensation; and a sum equal to any portion of the compensation which he fails to recover. He may not enforce the judgment relating to the latter sum without the leave of the court.

No prosecution for an offence may be made after the expiration of three years from the commission of the offence, or one year from its discovery by the prosecutor whichever is the earlier. A magistrates' court may try an offence if the information is laid at any time within 12 months from the commission of the offence.

ADVERTISING AND PROMOTION

7. Misleading advertising

False or misleading advertisements will very often fall within the provisions of the Trade Descriptions Act. In addition, the Director General of Fair Trading can obtain an injunction to restrain the publication of misleading advertisements under the Control of Misleading Advertisements Regulations 1988, SI 1988/915. An injunction was obtained in *Director General of Fair Trading* v *Tobyward* (1989).

Case law The High Court imposed an interim ban on a company's misleading advertisements about the availability of European Community and other grants. It granted an *ex parte* interlocutory injunction to the Director General of Fair Trading, under the Control of Misleading Advertisements 1988. This prevents the continuation of advertisements, in the form of telephone cold-calling and personal visits, by Tyler Barrett and Co. Ltd and its director, Peter Kemp. The interim injunction against Tyler Barrett and Co and Mr Kemp was granted after the court was presented with evidence that these advertisements were misleading and false in a number of respects. Personal visits were made by company representatives to the premises of small local businesses, following telephone cold-calling about the service offered by the company. The sales representative offered to obtain business grants from the EEC/EU for a search fee of £350 plus 10 per cent of any grant obtained. Clients were led to believe that the company would assist them in obtaining grant funding for a variety of business purposes. The availability of such grants and the likelihood of success in obtaining such funding was greatly exaggerated by the company. Clients were reassured that, should no grants be obtained for them, they would receive a full refund of their search fee. The information given to clients in relation to the availability of grants was incorrect, as was the statement that fees were refundable if no grants were forthcoming. What clients actually received was a standardised list of grant-making bodies, most of which was wholly irrelevant to the client's needs. When clients realised the very limited nature of the service, and that they had been deceived, they sought to obtain the refund but without success. The information provided by the company to small businesses and its failure to provide a refund of the search fee has been the subject of a high level of complaints to trading standards departments and other bodies, such as local business link offices.

In order to comply with the injunction Tyler Barrett and Co Ltd and Mr Kemp will have to stop making misleading statements about what they offer to their clients. They will have to attend a further hearing if they wish to try and get the injunction lifted: *Director General of Fair Trading Ltd* v *Tyler Barrett & Co Ltd* (1997).

Only a handful of injunctions have been obtained, though undertakings have been obtained in place of injunctions.

Certain categories of financial advertisement fall outside the Regulations, and the Director's remit does not extend to broadcast advertising. Before dealing with a complaint, he must consider whether or not the person making the complaint should first take that complaint to any established means of dealing with such complaints. He must also have regard to the desirability of encouraging the control of advertisements by self-regulatory bodies. In the exercise of his functions, the Director has power to obtain and disclose information. He may also for the purpose of controlling misleading advertisements refer any complaint about an advertisement to any person.

With regard to advertisements broadcast over commercial radio and television, the Regulations allow the Radio Authority, the Independent Television Commission or the Welsh Authority, as appropriate, to refuse to broadcast an advertisement which it considers misleading.

8. Trading stamps

The main features of the Trading Stamps Act 1964 in relation to the warranties implied when stamps are exchanged for goods have been dealt with above (see 5:**61**). Here we will note that, under the 1964 Act, all trading stamps must bear on their face the name of the promoter and the cash value. No sum is prescribed but many stamps show a face value of 0.001p. When a person has collected 25p worth, he is entitled to redeem the stamps for cash.

In any shop in which trading stamps are available, a notice must be displayed indicating how much has to be spent to obtain one stamp, stating the cash value of that stamp.

The Act makes it an offence for any advertisement to convey the cash value of any stamp by means of a statement which associates the worth of any trading stamp with what a customer must pay to obtain them; or to advertise a cash value in terms which are misleading or deceptive.

9. Catalogues

If the particular trading stamps scheme provides for the redemption of stamps for goods (which is normally the case), there is no requirement in law to publish any catalogue. However, if one has been published, the Act provides that it must contain the name of the promoter and the address of his registered office. Similarly, there is no obligation to issue a stamp book but, if one is issued, this must also contain that information. In addition, a copy of a current catalogue must be placed in every shop where trading stamps are available in a place where it can be 'conveniently consulted' by customers.

FAIR TRADING

10. Office of Fair Trading

This section deals only with those parts of the Fair Trading Act 1973 which are properly considered as referring to consumer protection. There is therefore no discussion of those parts of the Act which deal with monopolies and mergers (see instead Chapter 3).

The 1973 Act provides for the Secretary of State to appoint a Director General of Fair Trading whose renewable term of appointment is for five years.

At present, the Office of Fair Trading is divided into a Consumer Affairs Division, a Competition Policy Division, a Legal Division, an Economics Branch, an Administration Branch and an Information Branch. The officers include a Deputy Director General, a Director of Consumer Affairs and a Director of Competition Policy, a Director of Legal Affairs, a Head of Economics, a Chief Information Officer and a Principal Establishment and Finance Officer.

11. Duties of Director General

The Director General of Fair Trading is required to keep under review the carrying on of commercial activities in the United Kingdom which relate to goods or services supplied to consumers in the United Kingdom or to goods produced with a view to their being so supplied, and also to collect information with respect to such activities, and the persons by whom they are carried on, with a view to his becoming aware of, and ascertaining the circumstances relating to, practices which may adversely affect the economic interest of consumers in the United Kingdom. The Director General must receive and collate evidence becoming available to him with respect to the foregoing activities and which appears to him to be evidence of practices which may adversely affect the interests of consumers in the United Kingdom, whether those interests are economic interests, or interests with respect to health, safety or other matters. It should be noted from this that the active functions of the Director General, where he is required to keep the relevant matters under review, relate just to the economic interests of consumers; but in his passive function, where he is required to receive evidence, he is required to take into account matters affecting all the interests of consumers.

It is the duty of the Director General, so far as appears practicable, to keep under review the carrying on of commercial activities in the United Kingdom, and to collect information with respect to those activities, and the persons by whom they are carried on, with a view to his becoming aware of, and ascertaining the circumstances relating to, monopoly situations or uncompetitive practices. Further, he is under a duty to have regard to evidence becoming available to him with respect to any course of conduct on the part of a person carrying on a business which appears to be conduct detrimental to the interests of consumers in the United Kingdom and, in accordance with his additional functions for the protection of consumers under the Act, to be regarded as unfair to them, with a view to considering what action should be taken thereunder.

12. Role of Secretary of State

It is the duty of the Director General, where either he considers it expedient to do so, or he is so requested by the Secretary of State, to give the latter information and assistance as to any of the matters in respect of which the Director General has any duties as set out in the preceding paragraph. The Director General must also have regard to evidence becoming available to him with respect to making recommendations to the Secretary of State as to any action which, in his opinion, it would be expedient for the Secretary of State, or any other Minister, to take in relation to any of the matters in respect of which the Director General has any such duties as are laid down in the preceding paragraph. This particular obligation is made subject to the provisions of the 1973 Act dealing with references to the Consumer Protection Advisory Committee. The Secretary of State has the power to give general directions to the Director General indicating considerations to which he should have particular regard in determining the order of priority in which matters are to be brought under review in the performance of his active and passive duties as described in the preceding paragraph. He may give such general directions which indicate:

(a) Considerations to which, in cases where it appears to the Director General that a practice may adversely affect the interests of consumers in the United Kingdom, he should have particular regard in determining whether to make a recommendation to the Secretary of State.

(b) Considerations to which, in cases where it appears to the Director General that a consumer trade practice may adversely affect the economic interests of consumers in the United Kingdom, he should have particular regard in determining whether to make a reference to the Consumer Protection Advisory Committee.

The expression 'consumer trade practice' is exhaustively defined by the 1973 Act as any practice carried on in connection with the supply of goods or services to consumers and which relates to:

- The terms or conditions, whether as to price or otherwise, on or subject to which goods or services are supplied
- The manner in which those terms or conditions are communicated to persons to whom goods or services are supplied
- The promotion, by advertising, labelling or marking of goods, canvassing or otherwise, of the supply of goods or services
- Methods of salesmanship employed in dealing with consumers
- The way in which goods are packed or otherwise got up for sale
- Methods of demanding or securing payment for goods or services.

Though this list is wide, it would appear to have some gaps; for example, no mention is made of the non-availability of goods, nor of quality. In addition, by limiting itself to supplies, the Act appears to exclude those who purchase from consumers, such as antique dealers or car dealers, unless it could be argued that the valuation they provide is the supply of a service.

The Secretary of State, on giving any such directions, must arrange for those directions to be published in such manner as he thinks most suitable in the circumstances.

13. References to the Consumer Protection Advisory Committee

The Consumer Protection Advisory Committee is established by the 1973 Act and consists of between 10 and 15 people appointed on a full or part-time basis by the Secretary of State. In making the appointments, the Secretary of State is required to appoint at least one person from the following categories: persons qualified to advise on practices relating to particular goods or services by virtue of their knowledge or experience in the supply of such goods or services; persons qualified to advise on such practices by virtue of their knowledge or experience in the enforcement of the Trade Descriptions Act 1968 or the Weights and Measures Act 1985; persons qualified to advise on such practices by virtue of their knowledge or experience in organisations established, or carried on, for the protection of consumers.

The provisions for references to be made to the Committee are contained in Part II of the Act. There are provisions in the Act for 'study references' to be made to the Committee. Such references may be made by the Secretary of State, any other Minister or the Director General of Fair Trading, and will ask the Committee to determine whether a specified consumer trade practice (see above) so specified adversely affects the economic interests of consumers in the United Kingdom.

259

It will then be the task of the Committee to prepare a report on the question and to submit the report to the person who made the reference. If that person was not the Secretary of State, a copy must be sent to him; similarly a copy must be sent to the Director General of Fair Trading if he was not the party who made the reference. It is also the duty of the Director General to assist the Committee, on request, by providing any information which is in his possession and relates to matters falling within the scope of the investigation, and any other assistance which the Committee may require and which it is within his power to give in relation to such matters.

14. Follow-up action on a report

There are two categories of reference which may be made to the Consumer Protection Advisory Committee. If the reference is one (sometimes called a 'study reference') which contains no proposals from the Director General in relation to the particular practice, the Act contains no follow up provisions to enforce whatever conclusions the report might have reached. The precise significance of such references cannot be determined because there have been none so far. However, if a reference is made by the Director General (and it would appear only if it has been made by the Director General), the reference can include proposals which must have regard to the particular respects in which it appears to him that the consumer trade practice specified in the reference may adversely affect the interests of consumers in the United Kingdom, and to the class of relevant consumer transactions, or the classes of such transactions, in relation to which it appears to him that the practice may affect those consumers.

The Director General's proposals must be for the making of an order providing, in relation to the relevant consumer transactions, for modification or ending the particular practice. Further, without in any way prejudicing the foregoing provisions, the Director General's proposals may in particular recommend the imposition in such an order of certain prohibitions or requirements specified in the Act.

These are:

- Prohibition of the specified consumer trade practice, either generally or in relation to specified consumer transactions
- Prohibition of specified consumer transactions unless carried out at specified times or at a place of a specified description
- Prohibition of the inclusion in specified consumer transactions of terms or conditions which purport to exclude or limit the liability of a party to such a transaction in respect of specified matters
- A requirement that contracts relating to specified consumer transactions shall include specified terms or conditions

- A requirement that contracts or other documents relating to specified consumer transactions shall comply with specified provisions as to lettering (whether as to size, type, colouring or otherwise)
- A requirement that specified information shall be given to parties to specified consumer transactions.

However, before the Director General seeks to exercise these rights, it must first appear to him that a consumer trade practice has the effect of:

(a) Misleading consumers as to, or withholding from them adequate information as to, or an adequate record of, their rights and obligations under relevant consumer transactions otherwise misleading or confusing consumers with respect to any matter in connection with relevant consumer transactions

(b) Subjecting consumers to undue pressure to enter into relevant consumer transactions, *or*

(c) Causing the terms or conditions, on or subject to which consumers enter into relevant consumer transactions, to be so adverse to them as to be inequitable.

The reference to the Consumer Protection Advisory Committee must identify which of these effects is relevant. In addition, the reference must be published in full in the London, Edinburgh and Belfast Gazettes. Once a reference has been made, the Committee must report before the end of three months beginning with the date of the reference. However, extensions may be granted by the Secretary of State of up to three months' duration, it being expressly allowed that two or more such extensions can be granted. Every report on such a reference must be made to the Secretary of State and must set out in full the reference on which it was made. There is no requirement that a copy of the report be given to the Director General.

When the Committee makes its report, it must give its conclusions as to whether the consumer trade practice does adversely affect the economic interests of consumers, and whether it does so by reason, or partly by reason, that it has one or more of the above-described effects. It would appear that the Committee could in fact specify an effect in its report not specified by the Director General in his reference. If they find that the consumer trade practice specified in the reference does adversely affect the economic interests of consumers, and does so wholly or partly because it has one or more of the above-described effects, the Committee must state whether they agree with the Director General's proposals or would agree with them if modified in the manner specified in the report, or disagree with the proposals and do not wish to suggest any modification. Where the

261

Committee has agreed to the proposals, or agreed to them if modified in the way suggested in the report, the Secretary of State is then empowered to make an order by statutory instrument which embodies the original proposals, or the proposals as modified. He is also able not to make an order at all. If, however, he does decide to make an order, a draft of that order must be approved by a resolution of each House of Parliament.

The Committee is required to take representations and to consider excluding from the report private or business matters. To date, there have been four such references. The first three produced the following orders: Mail Order Transactions (Information) Order 1976, SI 1976/1812; Consumer Transactions (Restrictions on Statements) Order 1976, SI 1976/1813 (as amended by SI 1978/127); Business Advertisements (Disclosure) Order 1977, SI 1977/1918. No order resulted from the reference on VAT-exclusive Prices although the Committee did accept the proposals contained in the reference with suggested modifications. The position with regard to indicating VAT is now covered by the Price Marking Order 1991, SI 1991/1382. It is an offence, punishable summarily or on indictment, to contravene an order made under these provisions.

15. The 'bypass' provision

The provisions relating to offences due to the act or default of another in the Fair Trading Act 1973 are the same as in the Trade Descriptions Act 1968 (see 1 above).

16. Defences

The defences provided by the Fair Trading Act 1973 are the same as in the Trade Descriptions Act 1968 (see 2 above). The provisions relating to innocent publication are also the same as in the 1968 Act.

17. Assurances as to future conduct

Where it appears to the Director General that a person carrying on a business has persisted in a course of conduct which is detrimental to consumers and is to be regarded as unfair under the statutory criteria, he must use his best endeavours to obtain a satisfactory written assurance that the person will refrain from continuing that course of conduct and from carrying on any similar course of conduct. 'Unfair' in this context means a course of conduct involving breach of the criminal law, whether or not the law in question relates to consumers as such, and whether or not the person carrying on the particular business has been convicted in respect of any such contravention. Of course, if he has been tried and acquitted, then the conduct will not consist of infringement of any relevant enactments. A course of conduct is also to be regarded as unfair if it consists in breaches of contract or civil duty, enforceable by civil proceedings, whether such proceedings have been brought or not.

A considerable range of criminal and civil offences can be considered under this definition of 'unfair'. The Office of Fair Trading, in relation to the former, refers to breaches of food safety legislation, currently contained for the main part in the Food Safety Act 1990 (see below), the Trade Descriptions Act 1968, the Food Safety (General Food Hygiene) Regulations 1995, safety regulations, unroadworthy cars in breach of the Road Traffic Act 1988, the Consumer Credit Act 1974 and the Trading Representations (Disabled Persons) Act 1958.

With regard to breaches of the civil law, the Office of Fair Trading gives the following examples:

1. Failing to return to consumers money to which they are legally entitled (e.g. for goods not supplied, goods lawfully rejected).
2. Failing to deliver goods in breach of contract.
3. Failing to ensure that cheques given to consumers are met when properly presented for payment.
4. Failing to comply with terms of a guarantee given in respect of parts and labour at the time of purchase of the goods.
5. Inducing consumers to pay money in advance or to enter into contracts for the provision of services by knowingly, recklessly or negligently making false statements about the nature of the services it is intended to give.
6. Inducing customers to enter into contracts for the purchase of goods by making false statements about the description and availability of goods.

As stated the above-described provision only applies where the trader has engaged in a 'persistent' course of conduct. The Office of Fair Trading states that whether the requirements of the Act are met will vary considerably and that it is necessary to look at all the relevant facts, such as the trader's attitude to his conduct, the nature and scale of the business, the period over which the individual breaches took place, the degree of repetition and the seriousness of each of the breaches and whether the trader had followed or allowed a policy or practice in relation to the business which had the effect of causing the breaches of the law. Whilst noting that no hard and fast rules can be laid down, the Office says that an approach for an assurance could be made in the case of a small trader, with well-documented evidence, over a short period of time, with deliberate behaviour concerning serious breaches of the law, about three or four incidents. Where the case is not strong, there would need to be a minimum of ten incidents; in a less well-documented case, over a long period of time, with less deliberate behaviour and/or less serious breaches of the same aspect of the law, 20 to 30 incidents. In the case of a larger trader, with well-documented evidence, over a short period of time, with deliberate behaviour and serious breaches of the same aspect of the law, 20 to 30 incidents. In a less well-documented case, over a longer period of time and with less deliberate behaviour and/or less serious breaches of the same aspect of the law, 30 to 50 incidents.

18. Powers of the Restrictive Practices Court

If the Director General of Fair Trading is unable to obtain an assurance, he may bring proceedings before the Restrictive Practices Court. The case may be brought in the county court where the trader does not have a share capital in excess of £10,000 and the proceedings are not of such general application as to justify reservation for determination by the Restrictive Practices Court. When an action is so brought under the foregoing provisions the proceedings are, for evidential purposes, to be taken to be civil proceedings. Where proceedings are so brought, and the Director General alleges unfair conduct by reference to a breach of contract or duty, a judgment of any court to that effect is admissible and must, unless the contrary is proved, be taken as proof that the particular breach was committed. However, for the present purpose, no account is to be taken of a judgment given in civil proceedings if it was reversed on appeal, or was varied on appeal in such a way as to negative the finding.

Where, in any proceedings before the Restrictive Practices Court, the Court finds that the person against whom the proceedings are brought (the respondent) has persisted in such a course of conduct as is mentioned above, and he does not give an undertaking to the court which is accepted, and it appears to the court that, if no order is made, he is likely to continue with the same or a similar course of conduct, the Court may make an order against the respondent. An order of the court, if made, must indicate the nature of the course of unfair conduct. It must also direct the particular party to refrain from continuing that course of conduct and to refrain from carrying on any similar course of conduct.

The court may accept an undertaking instead of making an order if it thinks fit to do so. That undertaking must be to refrain from the particular course of conduct and any similar course of conduct, or to take particular steps which, in the court's opinion, would prevent a continuation of the particular course of conduct to which the complaint relates and to prevent the carrying on of any similar course of conduct. Where an undertaking has been given to the court, or a court order has been made, any breach of that undertaking or order will amount to contempt.

The position with regard to breach of an assurance is identical to the position above set out with regard to the refusal to give an assurance.

An appeal lies from a decision or order of a court on fact or law to the Court of Appeal.

19. Pyramid selling

The Fair Trading Act 1973 imposes controls on pyramid selling and similar marketing schemes. The essence of such schemes is that the focus is on participants securing other participants, and not actually on selling the particular goods or services. The controls imposed by the Act were supplemented by the Pyramid Selling Schemes Regulations 1989, SI 1989/2195 (as amended).

However, these controls were generally felt to be ineffective (particularly to cover what became known as 'money-circulation schemes') so fresh controls were introduced under the Trading Schemes Act 1966 supplemented by the Trading Schemes Regulations 1997/30 and the Trading Schemes (Exclusions) Regulations 1997/31.

None of these provisions make pyramid selling illegal, so long as it is carried out in the manner authorised by the respective enactments.

Defences

The Fair Trading Act 1973 provides for the defence of innocent publication of an advertisement in certain proceedings relating to pyramid selling and similar trading schemes. This defence is similar to that provided by the Trade Descriptions Act 1968 (see above).

20. Publications

The Director General of Fair Trading may arrange for the publication in such form and in such manner as he considers appropriate of such information and advice as it appears to him expedient to give to consumers with respect to his duties. In addition, he must consult with the Directors General of Telecommunications, Gas Supply, Water Services, and Electricity Supply before publishing any advice or information which the latter might have power to publish under their respective powers.

21. Codes of Practice

The Director General is under a duty to encourage relevant trade associations to prepare and to disseminate to their members codes of practice for guidance in safeguarding and promoting the interests of consumers in the

United Kingdom. The stated policy of the Office of Fair Trading is only to endorse codes which set standards for marketing, quality, provision of information, publicity for the code, complaints handling and enforcement of compliance. All endorsed codes will contain an independent system as an alternative to court action for the settlement of disputes. A trade association will be required to publish an annual report on the operation of the code. The codes are not legally enforceable in that there are no direct civil or criminal sanctions for failure to comply with them.

Codes have been negotiated in relation to: antiques; credit; double glazing; domestic laundry and cleaning services; electrical appliances; footwear; funerals; furniture; selling, siting, letting holiday caravans; list and data suppliers; mail order trading; direct marketing; mechanical breakdown insurance; motorcycles; the motor industry; travel agents; vehicle body repairs; shoe repairs; the photographic industry; postal services and party plan selling. In *Lewin* v *Rotherthorpe Road Garage Ltd* (1983), a defendant made out a successful defence under the Trade Descriptions Act 1968 by showing that he had adopted the Code of Practice for the motor industry, had instructed salesmen in the operation of the code and had emphasised the importance of observing the code.

22. Annual and other reports

The Director General, as soon as practicable after the end of the calendar year, must report to the Secretary of State on his activities and those of the Consumer Protection Advisory Committee and of the Monopolies and Mergers Commission. This is not to apply to those activities of the Commission on which the Directors General of Telecommunications, Gas Supply, Water Services, or Electricity Supply are required to report.

Every such report is to include a general survey of developments in respect of matters falling within the scope of the Director General of Fair Trading's duties under any enactment and must set out any directions given under the Consumer Credit Act 1974. The Secretary of State is to lay every annual report before each House of Parliament and to arrange for the publication of every such report in such manner as he considers appropriate. In addition, the Director General may also prepare such other reports as appear to him expedient with respect to matters falling within his duties under any enactment, and may arrange for the reports to be published in such manner as he considers appropriate.

CONSUMER SAFETY – THE CRIMINAL LAW

The penal provisions relating to consumer safety are presently contained in the Consumer Protection Act 1987 and the General Product Safety Regulations 1994.

23. Safety regulations

The Consumer Protection Act 1987 gives the Secretary of State the power to make safety regulations. These regulations may make such provision as is considered appropriate for the purposes of the general safety requirement and for the purpose of securing that:

1. The goods to which the Act applies are safe.
2. The goods to which the Act applies and which are unsafe, or would be unsafe in the hands of particular persons, are not made available to persons generally or to those persons.
3. Appropriate information is, and inappropriate information is not, provided in relation to goods to which the section applies.

The Act states that safety regulations may contain certain provisions but this is expressly stated to be without prejudice to the generality of the foregoing. These provisions cover any goods other than growing crops and things comprised in land by being attached to it; water, food, feeding stuff and fertiliser; gas supplied by a person authorised under the Gas Act 1986; controlled drugs and licensed medicinal products.

The Act specifies that breach of the safety regulations is an offence. Furthermore, any breach of the safety regulations is actionable on the part of any person affected as on a breach of statutory duty, subject to any relevant provision in the particular safety regulation. This right cannot be limited or excluded by any notice, contract term or other provision. Apart from the right to an action as on a breach of statutory duty, no other civil rights accrue on behalf of the affected party except in relation to his rights in a product liability action. Breach of the regulations, subject to any provision in the agreement itself, does not of itself affect the agreement.

24. Prohibition notices and notices to warn

Prohibition notices are addressed to individual traders, requiring them to cease the supply of the goods designated in the notice, being goods which the Secretary of State considers to be unsafe. The Consumer Protection Act 1987 contains a consultation procedure in relation to such notices, but there is no provision for by-passing this procedure in cases considered as emer-

267

gencies. Since prohibition notices are not made in the form of a statutory instrument, it is difficult to keep an exact tally of how many have been made, but it is a small number. There is no provision for the automatic lapse of such a notice.

A *notice to warn* requires a person on whom it is served at his own expense to publish warnings (in a form and manner and on occasions specified in the notice) that he supplies or has supplied unsafe goods. Provision is made for consultation without there being any provision for an emergency procedure.

Notices are not made in the form of statutory instruments and there is no provision for automatic lapse. There have, to date, been no notices to warn.

The position on criminal liability is the same as for a breach of safety regulations (see above), but civil liability differs in that there is no right of action as on a breach of statutory duty.

25. Suspension notices

Enforcement authorities are empowered by the 1987 Act to issue suspension notices when they have reasonable grounds to suspect that there has been a breach of any of the safety provisions. A safety provision is a reference to the general safety requirement, the safety regulations or a suspension notice itself and the requirements of the General Product Safety Regulations (see below). The maximum duration of a suspension notice is six months, and during the period of the notice, the recipient of the notice cannot offer to supply, agree to supply or expose for supply the particular goods without the consent of the enforcement authority. The suspension notice must identify the goods, indicate the grounds for suspecting a breach of the relevant provisions, and set out the appeals procedure. Breach of a suspension notice is an offence, the penalty for which is the same as for breach of the safety regulations except that there is no right of action for breach of statutory duty.

Where a suspension notice has been served, compensation is to be paid when it is established that there has been no breach in relation to the goods covered by a suspension notice, provided the suspension notice was not issued because of any neglect or default on the part of the relevant trader. Any disputes as to the amount of compensation are to be settled by arbitration.

Any person with an interest in goods subject to a suspension notice is given the right to apply for an order setting it aside. The application may be made in any magistrates' court in which proceedings have been brought for an offence under any of the relevant provisions, or which relate to proceedings for a forfeiture order. If no such proceedings have been commenced, the application may be made to a magistrates' court.

The Consumer Protection Act 1987 states that the court shall set aside a suspension notice only if it is satisfied that there is no breach of any safety provisions.

26. Forfeiture orders

Enforcement authorities may apply for forfeiture orders on the grounds that there has been a contravention of a safety provision (i.e. breach of a safety regulation, the general safety requirement, a prohibition or suspension notice or the requirements of the General Product Safety Regulations). The courts are empowered to infer that there has been a breach of these provisions where there has been a breach in relation to goods which are 'representative' of the goods in relation to which forfeiture is requested. The application for forfeiture may be made when proceedings have been commenced for a contravention of any safety provision in relation to some or all of the goods or when an application has been made against a suspension notice or detention in relation to some or all of the goods and may be made directly to a magistrates' court. The court may order the forfeiture of the goods only if it is satisfied that, in relation to the particular goods, there has been a breach of a safety provision.

The order made by the court must provide for the destruction of the goods. However, the court may instead direct that the goods be released to a person specified by the court provided that that person only supplies them to a trader whose business is repairing or reconditioning such goods or who supplies them as scrap. If the court does make this alternative order, the person specified in the order must also comply with any order to pay costs or expenses which has been made against that person in the proceedings for the forfeiture order. An order made by the court may contain provisions for delaying its coming into force pending the outcome of an appeal.

27. The general safety requirement

The general safety requirement is imposed by both the Consumer Protection Act 1987 and the General Product Safety Regulations 1994/2328.

The Consumer Protection Act 1987 provides that an offence is committed by the offer to or agreement to supply, supply, or exposure or possession for supply of goods which fail to comply with the 'general safety requirement'.

Goods will fail to meet this standard if they are 'not reasonably safe having regard to all the circumstances', including the manner in which, and the purposes for which, the goods are being or would be marketed, the get-up of the goods, the use of any mark in relation to the goods and instructions or warnings which are given or would be given with respect to the keeping, use or consumption of the goods; any published safety standards; and the existence of any means by which it would be reasonable, taking account of cost, likelihood and extent of any improvement, for the goods to have been made safer. There will, however, be no breach of the 'general safety requirement' in respect of anything attributable to compliance with any statutory obligations, including those imposed by the EU. Nor will there be a breach from the failure to do more than is required by or under any safety regulations; or the provisions of any legislation imposing requirements with respect to the relevant matter as are designated by safety regulations.

The duty applies only to 'consumer goods'. However, there are express exclusions in relation to: growing crops or things comprised in land by virtue of being attached to it; water, food, feeding stuff or fertiliser; gas supplied by a person authorised under the Gas Act 1986; aircraft (other than hang gliders) or motor vehicles; controlled drugs or licensed medicinal products; tobacco.

The offence created by the foregoing is not an absolute offence: no offence will arise if the person charged reasonably believed that the goods were not for use or consumption in this country; if it was made clear that the goods were not supplied as new and the terms of the supply provided for the acquisition of an interest in the goods by the person supplied; or if, in the case of a retail business, the person charged neither knew nor had reasonable grounds for believing that the goods failed to comply with the general safety requirement. In the latter case, goods are supplied at retail, whether or not supplied for private use or consumption, if they are supplied in the course of carrying on a business of making a supply of consumer goods available to persons who generally acquire them for private use or consumption, and the descriptions of goods the supply of which is made available in the course of that business do not, to a significant extent, include manufactured or imported goods not previously supplied in the United Kingdom. This would appear to mean that, if the limit as to a 'significant extent' is breached, the retailer defence will be unavailable in respect of all the goods he supplies.

Breach of the 'safety requirement' is a summary offence.

The General Product Safety Regulations also provide that no producer shall place a product on the market unless the product is a safe product. Goods are 'safe', under normal or reasonably foreseeable conditions of use, including duration, if they do not present any, or only the minimum, risk compatible with the product's use, considered as acceptable and consistent with a high level of protection for the safety and health of persons, taking into particular account:

1. The characteristics of the product, including its composition, packaging, instructions for assembly and maintenance.

2. The effect on other products, where it is reasonably foreseeable that it will be used with other products.

3. The presentation of the product, the labelling, any instructions for its use and disposal and any other indication or information provided by the producer.

4. The categories of consumers at serious risk when using the product, in particular children. The fact that higher levels of safety may be obtained or other products presenting a lesser degree of risk may be available shall not of itself cause the product to be considered unsafe.

A product shall be presumed to be safe if it complies with domestic law laying down health and safety requirements which must be satisfied before the product is marketed. If there are no such rules, conformity with the general safety requirement shall be assessed taking account of:

1. Voluntary national standards giving effect to a European standard; *or*

2. Community technical specifications; *or*

3. (Where there are no such standards or specifications), standards drawn up in the United Kingdom, or codes of good practice in respect of health and safety in the particular product standard, or the state of the art and technology; *and*

4. The safety which consumers may reasonably expect.

The products covered by the Regulations are those intended for consumers, or which are likely to be used by consumers, supplied in the course of a commercial activity, and whether new, used or reconditioned; except that a product which is used exclusively in the context of commercial activity, even if used by a consumer, shall not be regarded as a 'product' unless actually supplied to a consumer. The Regulations do not apply to second-hand products which are antiques; products supplied for repair or reconditioning before use, provided the supplier clearly so informs the person to whom the product is supplied; or any products where there are specific provisions in rules of Community law governing all aspects of the safety of the product.

CONSUMER SAFETY – THE CIVIL LAW

The foregoing provisions apply only to impose criminal sanctions in respect of certain unsafe or dangerous goods. The law also imposes, however, and quite separately from any criminal offences which might simultaneously be committed, various civil obligations in respect of such goods, breach of which can give rise to personal actions by the party injured.

28. Liability

Under the provisions of the Consumer Protection Act 1987, where any damage is caused wholly or partly by a defect in a product, each of the following is liable for the damage:

- The producer of the product
- Any person who imported the product into the EU in the course of his business for the purpose of supply to another
- Any person who has held himself out to be the producer of the product, as by putting his name on the product or by using a trade mark or other distinguishing mark in relation to the product.

This last definition is intended to catch the 'own brander', a common feature of supermarket sales. In addition, liability is imposed on the supplier of a defective product for damage caused wholly or partly by a defective product, regardless of the party to whom the supply was made. However, this liability will only operate when the following conditions are met:

- The person who suffered the damage requests the supplier to identify the party liable under the first-mentioned provisions, whether that person is still in existence or not.
- That request is made within a reasonable period after the damage occurred and when it was not reasonably practicable for the injured person to identify all those persons.
- And the supplier fails, within a reasonable period after receiving the request, either to comply with the request or to identify the person who supplied the product to him.

It appears that if the party making the request can identify only some of those covered in the above-described provisions, then the supplier is still personally liable, unless he can satisfy the other conditions.

None of the above provisions will apply in relation to game or agricultural produce if it was supplied at a time when it had not undergone an industrial process. The Act gives no guidance as to what constitutes such a process. It is doubtful if it covers the mere wrapping of a product, though it probably does cover freezing, cutting and washing. In the case of goods which are subject to a process while still growing, such as crops which are sprayed, it is likely that these do not constitute produce because they are yet to be harvested.

29. Meaning of defect

The Act says that a product is defective if its safety is not such as persons generally are entitled to expect. In making a decision on this point, the court must take all circumstances into account, including: the manner in which, and the purposes for which, the product has been marketed, its get-up, the use of any mark in relation to the product, and any instructions for, or warnings with respect to, doing or refraining from doing anything with or in relation to the product; what might reasonably be expected to be done with or in relation to the product; and the time when it was supplied by its producer to another.

A product is not to be judged defective simply because a safer version is later put on the market.

The above definition of 'defective' clearly covers goods which, while not of themselves defective, are marketed with, for example, misleading instructions, or without instructions when these could reasonably be expected, or without warnings when these too could reasonably be expected. Again, if goods are advertised as being used in a particular location, when in fact they cannot safely be so used, then they will be defective for the purposes of the Consumer Protection Act 1987 even if not defective in themselves.

30. Defences

The Consumer Protection Act 1987 creates strict liability in relation to defective products, not absolute liability. The Act provides a number of defences.

It will be a defence if the person proceeded against can show that the defect is attributable to compliance with any requirement imposed by any enactment or Community obligation. Typical requirements will be those found in safety regulations made under the Act. To establish this defence, it will not be enough to show that the requirements of the relevant enactment or obligation were complied with. The person proceeded against will have to show that the defect was attributable to that compliance. If it had been possible to comply without leaving the product with the defect in question, then the defence cannot be established.

A defence can be made out if the person proceeded against can show that he did not at any time supply the product to another. Anyone who makes an article for his own use will qualify for this defence if during that use the defect causes damage to someone else. Again, the defence will be available where an employee of the producer is harmed before it leaves the producer's control, and it will be available in relation to stolen goods and drugs undergoing clinical trials prior to marketing.

A defence can be made out if the following conditions are met:

1. That the only supply was otherwise than in the course of a business of the supplier; and

2. That the person proceeded against was not within the categorised classes of persons who are, under the Act, liable for defective products or was within those categorised classes otherwise than with a view to profit. Activities can be carried on otherwise than for profit although profits are made. The types of situation covered here are private sales or gifts of second-hand goods such as toys, or cakes as gifts for friends or for sale, for example at a charity stall; or where a person privately imports goods into the Community and then sells them.

The person proceeded against has a defence if he can show that the defect did not exist in the product at the 'relevant time'. In relation to electricity, this means the time at which it was generated, being a time before it was transmitted or distributed. In relation to other products, it means the time when any of the categorised classes of persons supplied the product to another. If the person proceeded against falls outside the categories, then the relevant time means the time when the product was last supplied to a person who does fall within them. This definition means that the electricity-generating companies could use the defence in relation to any damage caused by voltage surges or falls due to distribution faults.

For a defendant falling within the categorised classes of persons, he will not be liable for defects caused further down the distribution chain, as for example when a retailer wrongly removes instructions or warning labels. Nor would he be liable for alterations or adaptations of products which made them defective, or for any subsequent deterioration of perishable products such as foodstuffs. For defendants who are liable as suppliers within the meaning of the Act, the defence will mean that a supplier will not be liable if the product was not defective when supplied by the producer, own brander or importer into the Community. This will mean that where a product becomes defective by a retailer removing instructions or warning notices, the producer will have a defence, as will the retailer since the product was defective when it left the producer. In such circumstances, the injured party will be forced to rely on an action in negligence and an action in contract against the retailer. The person proceeded against has a defence if he can show that the state of scientific and technical knowledge at the 'relevant time' was not such that a producer of products of the same description as the defective product might be expected to have discovered the defect if it had existed in his products while they were under his control. This is commonly called the 'development risks' defence, and it is a defence made available in the Directive on which the Act was based as an option which the member states were free to choose if they so wished. The test is an objective one, so that the skills and capabilities of the individual producer will not be relevant. This would appear to mean that if the person proceeded against had good cause for suspecting that the product was defective, he would be able to make use of the defence if producers generally would have no such cause. Equally, if the particular producer had no reason at all to suspect that his product was defective, but producers generally did, then the defence would not be available. The European Commission has indicated that it intends to remove the defence.

The person proceeded against may show that the defect was a defect in a product which contained his product as a component and that the defect was wholly attributable to the design of the product containing the component or to his compliance with instructions given by the producer of the product containing the component. For example, brake linings supplied to a car manufacturer might fail on use, thus rendering the car defective. The supplier of the linings would not be liable in a product liability action brought against him if he could show that the failure was due to the design of the car or because the supplier was acting in compliance with the manufacturer's instructions. If the supplier of the component ought to have known that the instructions were incorrect, or that the design of the car could cause problems, it would seem that he could still plead the defence, though he would of course be liable in negligence to the injured party.

31. Damage covered by the Act

No liability attaches for loss of, or any damage to, the product itself or for any loss of or damage to the whole or any part of any product which contained the defective product as a component. If a car has a faulty carburettor and a fire breaks out as a consequence, there is no liability for damage to the car or the carburettor. However, any injury to the occupants of the car or to personal property in the car is recoverable as compensation.

There is no liability in relation to property which, when lost or damaged, was not of a description ordinarily intended for private use, occupation or consumption; and which was intended by the injured party mainly for his own private use, occupation or consumption. Where business property is damaged, therefore, there can be no claim.

In the case of damage to, or loss of, property when the amount of the loss does not exceed £275 no claim can be brought, but if the claim is in excess of that sum, all the loss can be claimed. Liability cannot be excluded or limited by reference to any notice, contract term or other provision.

32. Forum shopping

The Civil Jurisdiction and Judgments Act 1982 provides for a degree of forum shopping among the member states of the EU. In essence, the position in product liability litigation is that the claimant may sue in any member state where any of the defendants are domiciled, or in any member state where the harmful event occurred. If the defendant is not domiciled in a member state, the question of jurisdiction over him will be determined by the national court applying its own laws. The possibilities opened up by the Convention will be useful to a plaintiff who, for example, wishes to sue in a member state where the development risks defence does not apply.

33. Unsolicited goods and services

Right to treat unsolicited goods as gift

As against the sender, the recipient of unsolicited goods may treat them as an unconditional gift in the following circumstances:

- The goods were sent or delivered for the purpose of their being acquired by the recipient
- The recipient had no reasonable cause for believing that they were sent for acquisition in the course of a trade or business
- The recipient had agreed neither to acquire nor return the goods and either of the following further conditions is met:
- During the six months from receipt of the goods, the sender did not take possession of them nor was he unreasonably refused permission to do so
- Before 30 days were left to run of the six month period, the recipient sent a notice to the sender, and during the 30 days beginning with the day when the notice was given, the sender did not take possession of the goods, and the recipient did not unreasonably refuse to permit the sender to do so.

To take advantage of this the notice must give the recipient's name and address, the address of the goods (if different) and a statement that the goods are unsolicited. The notice may be sent by post. It should be noted that the above provisions operate only as between sender and recipient. This means that if the sender is not the true owner and the owner is not a 'sender' within the meaning of the Unsolicited Goods and Services Act 1971, the true owner will not forfeit his title.

Illegally asserting a right to payment

An offence arises if a person in the course of a trade or business, in relation to what he knows are unsolicited goods sent for the purposes of acquisition, makes a demand for payment, or asserts a present or prospective right to payment, if he has no reasonable cause for believing that he has a right to payment. In contrast with the position of a recipient of unsolicited goods who, in certain prescribed circumstances under the Unsolicited Goods and Services Act 1971, has a right, as between himself and the sender, to the goods, it does not appear that the recipient who might acquire the goods for business purposes is outside the above-described provisions.

For the purposes of the 1971 Act, any invoice or similar document stating the amount of any payment shall constitute an assertion of a right to payment if it does not comply with any applicable regulations. Further, if a person without reasonable cause to believe there is a right to payment, in the course of a trade or business and with a view to obtaining payment for goods he knows to be unsolicited goods sent to another person, for the purpose of acquisition: threatens legal proceedings; places or causes the name of any person (not necessarily the recipient of the goods) to be placed on a list of defaulters or debtors, or threatens to do so; or invokes or causes to be invoked any other collection procedure, or threatens to do so, he commits an offence. It does not appear to matter if the goods were sent for the purposes of acquisition in the course of a trade or business.

34. Directory entries

There is no liability to pay for a directory entry, and any money paid can be recovered, except where the person on whose behalf the entry is made has signed an order or a note of his agreement to the charge. In the case of a note, a copy must have been supplied to him or someone on his behalf before the note was signed. Further, the order form or note must be in a specific form if there is to be any liability to payment.

An order for an entry must be on an order form or other stationery of the relevant party which bears, in print, the name and address of that person. In the case of a note, there must be a statement of the amount of the charge immediately above the place for signature. In addition, the note must identify the directory and state: the proposed date of publication or of the issue in which the entry is to be included and the name and address of the person producing it if the directory or that issue is to be put on sale, the price and the minimum number of copies for sale; if it is to be distributed without charge, whether also put on sale or not, the minimum number of copies which are to be distributed without charge. The note must also set out or give reasonable particulars of the entry.

Where payment is demanded for an entry not complying with the above requirements and the person so demanding neither knows nor has reasonable cause to believe that the entry did so comply, an offence is committed which may be tried summarily or on indictment.

35. Offensive material

An offence arises if a person sends, or causes to be sent, any book, magazine or leaflet (or advertising material for any such publication) which he knows or ought reasonably to know is unsolicited and which describes or illustrates human sexual techniques. Prosecutions can only be instigated by or with the consent of the Director of Public Prosecutions.

THE PRIVATISED UTILITIES

36. The regulators

Following the privatisation of certain nationalised industries, a number of regulators were established, namely: The Director General of Telecommunications; The Director General of Office of Gas Supply; The Director General of Electricity Supply; The Director General of Water Services; and the Rail Regulator.

These parties have in general terms the broad remit of keeping their particular area under review, to publish information and advice and to investigate complaints.

37. Consumer representation

Under the Telecommunications Act 1984, the Secretary of State for Trade and Industry is required to establish advisory bodies whose members must, *inter alia*, include persons representing the consumer interest. The Director General of Telecommunications may establish such bodies consisting of such members as he thinks fit.

The Gas Act 1986 established a Gas Consumers' Council which has certain duties and powers of investigation and a duty to advise the Director General of Gas Supply as to certain matters.

The Electricity Act 1989 established consumers' committees for particular areas which have a general duty to advise the Director General of Electricity Supply and to refer certain matters to him. The Act also establishes a National Consumers' Consultative Committee charged with a duty of keeping matters of consumer interest under review and of facilitating the exchange of information relating to such matters.

The Water Industry Act 1991 requires appointed water companies to be allocated to a customer service committee which has a general duty to keep consumer matters under review and to liaise in relation to such matters with the particular company and the Director General of Water Services.

The Railway Act 1993 requires the establishment of a Central Rail Users

Consultative Committee which must look into any matter relating to the provision of railway passenger services or the provision of station services.

38. Standards of performance

The Competition and Service (Utilities) Act 1992 places a series of common responsibilities, some of which were contained in earlier legislation, on the regulators and the utilities in relation to the protection of consumer interests:

- A power to make regulations prescribing standards of performance in individual cases together with a power to determine disputes between the supplier and the customer about failed service and compensation.
- A power to determine and enforce standards of overall performance.
- A power to collect information on the levels of performance achieved by suppliers and the compensation paid by them in respect of failure to meet the target level set and a further power to give directions as to the information to be provided by the suppliers.
- A power to direct a supplier to publicise information to consumers about overall performance and the content and method of publication.
- An obligation on each supplier to establish a complaints handling procedure to be vetted by the regulator, who can give directions to a supplier to review procedures and the manner in which they operate.
- Powers for each regulator to resolve disputes.
- A power for the Secretary of State to make regulations conferring powers on the regulators to determine billing disputes.

In addition, specific powers are given to the Directors General in relation to specific utilities, such as powers to prevent disconnection of services where there is a genuine dispute between supplier and customer.

TIMESHARE

39. Scope of the Timeshare Act 1992

The Timeshare Act 1992 is principally concerned with 'timeshare accommodation'. This is defined as any accommodation, in the United Kingdom or elsewhere, which is to be used wholly or partly for leisure purposes by a class of persons ('timeshare users') who have the right to use the accommodation, or accommodation within a pool of accommodation, for intermittent periods of short duration. The Act further defines 'timeshare rights' as the rights by virtue of which a person becomes, or will become, a timeshare user where those rights are exercisable during a period of not less than three years. A 'timeshare agreement' is defined as an agreement under which timeshare rights are conferred or purported to be conferred on any person, although this will not include an agreement which is cancellable under the Consumer Credit Act 1974 (see Chapter 7). Subject to the same exception, the Act defines a 'timeshare credit agreement' as an agreement which is not a timeshare agreement, under which a creditor provides credit to a person seeking to enter a timeshare agreement and who knows or has reasonable cause to believe that all or some of the credit will finance the timeshare agreement.

The Timeshare Act applies to any timeshare agreement or timeshare credit agreement where the agreement is to any extent governed by the law of the United Kingdom, or if, when the agreement was entered into, either of the parties was in the United Kingdom.

40. Rights of cancellation

The party who is making a contract for the timeshare agreement with a consumer must provide the latter with a document setting out the terms of the agreement, or their substance, along with a notice of his right to cancel. This notice must give at least 14 days' notice of cancellation starting from the day after the day on which the agreement was entered into and must also indicate that cancellation will free the consumer from his obligations under the contract and entitle him to recover any sums paid under or in contemplation of the agreement. The cancellation notice must be accompanied by a blank notice of cancellation and both it and the notice of cancellation rights must be in the form prescribed and comply with the requirements laid down: see the Timeshare (Cancellation Notices) Order 1992, SI 1992/1942.

Contravention of this provision will not invalidate the agreement but it will give rise to an offence triable summarily or on indictment. The obligation to give notice as to the right to cancel a timeshare credit agreement follows the above, except that the notice accompanying the notice of the right to cancel must indicate the position as to the repayment of credit and interest. An agreement is not automatically invalidated by a breach of these requirements. When a consumer has received his notice of cancellation rights under a timeshare agreement, the agreement cannot be enforced against him before the cancellation period has expired. Where no such notice has been provided, the agreement cannot be enforced at any time and the agreement may be cancelled at any time. If, in this latter case, the consumer affirms the agreement after the expiry of 14 days beginning with the day on which the agreement was entered into, then the agreement may be enforced against him and he cannot subsequently give notice of cancellation.

Where notice of cancellation is given, this has the effect of cancelling the agreement or withdrawing any offer to enter into the agreement, as appropriate. In the former case, the agreement ceases to be enforceable, and in either case any sums paid become repayable at the time notice of cancellation is given, but no sum may be recovered from the consumer. If the timeshare agreement includes provision for allowing the consumer credit, cancellation does not affect the repayment of credit and interest and notice of this must be given in the notice of cancellation rights.

Broadly comparable provisions in relation to cancelling a timeshare credit agreement also apply. The agreement continues in force insofar as it relates to the payment of credit or interest.

None of the foregoing provisions applies where the consumer is entering into the contract in the course of a business.

41. Repayment of credit and interest

The provisions relating to the repayment of credit and interest where a timeshare credit agreement has been cancelled, or the consumer has withdrawn from or cancelled a timeshare agreement which provides for credit, are parallel to those provisions which apply on the cancellation of agreements under the terms of the Consumer Credit Act 1974 (see Chapter 7).

For the prescribed form in which the request for repayment of credit and interest must be made, see the Timeshare (Repayment of Credit on Cancellation) Order 1992, SI 1992/1943.

42. Powers of enforcement and offences

Local weights and measures authorities are enforcement authorities for the purposes of the Timeshare Act 1992. Similar provisions to those found in the Trade Descriptions Act are made for the defence of due diligence and offences due to the default of another (see above).

43. Timeshare regulations

The Timeshare Regulations 1997, SI 1997/1081 implement EU law. The Directive requires Member States to provide measures for the protection of purchasers of timeshare rights in immovable properties. The Regulations provide for new rights in respect of timeshare rights in buildings. The protection of purchasers of timeshare rights in caravans and mobile homes remains unchanged save for some very minor adjustments. To benefit from the new protection a purchaser must be an individual who is not acting in the course of a business. Timeshare rights acquired as the result of share ownership and timeshare rights under collective investment schemes formerly excluded by the 1992 Act are no longer excluded from the application of the 1992 Act. The application of the 1992 Act has also been extended to cover timeshare rights where the accommodation is situated in the United Kingdom and timeshare rights where the accommodation is situated in another EEA state (i.e. the 15 EU countries, Iceland, Norway, Liechtenstein and Switzerland) and the purchaser is ordinarily resident in the United Kingdom.

A vendor of rights to timeshare accommodation in a building is required to provide any person on request with a document containing information on the property. Such information will become a term of the agreement if an individual not acting in the course of a business, who receives such information, subsequently enters into an agreement to purchase timeshare rights in the property. Subsequent changes to the information are only permitted in limited circumstances.

Advertisements of timeshare rights must refer to the possibility of obtaining the document mentioned above and state where it may be obtained.

An agreement for timeshare accommodation in a building must set out certain minimum information on such matters as the nature of the property, the price and recurring costs and charges.

The purchaser is entitled to have the agreement in the language of the country of his residence or the country of which he is a national. In addition, a purchaser resident in the United Kingdom is entitled to the contract in the English language.

A purchaser is also entitled to a translation in the language of the country where the property is situated.

If the timeshare agreement relates to accommodation in a building, the notice under s. 2 of the 1992 Act will have to state that cancellation of the timeshare agreement will automatically cancel any related timeshare credit agreement. The rights to cancel a timeshare agreement for accommodation in a building are extended. The fourteen day cancellation period is extended up to three months and ten days if certain information has not been provided to the purchaser.

Advance payments are prohibited during the cancellation period. The vendor of rights to timeshare accommodation in a building will be obliged to inform any creditor forthwith on receipt of a cancellation notice which automatically cancels a timeshare credit agreement. Certain of the new obligations on vendors are statutory duties subject to civil proceedings.

ESTATE AGENCY

44. Estate Agents Act 1979

The Estate Agents Act 1979 allows the Director General of Fair Trading, if satisfied that a person is unfit to carry on estate agency work, to prohibit that person from doing any estate agency work at all, or of a specified description. This power is only exercisable if the particular person: has been convicted of an offence involving fraud, dishonesty or violence, or the provisions of the Act itself or of any offence specified by the Secretary of State for Trade and Industry: see the Estate Agents (Specified Offences) (No. 2) Order 1991, SI 1991/1091 (as amended); has committed discrimination in the course of estate agency work; has failed to comply with certain provisions of the Act; or has engaged in a practice declared undesirable by the Secretary of State: see the Estate Agents (Undesirable Practices) (No. 2) Order 1991, SI 1991/1032.

The Act outlines the procedure to be followed before an order is made and the stated procedure when an application is made for variation or revocation of an order. Appeals may be made to the Secretary of State and to the High Court on points of law.

45. Warning orders

The Director General, if satisfied that a person has infringed certain provisions of the Act dealing with interest on clients' money, information to clients as to prospective liabilities, regulation of pre-contract deposits (these particular provisions are not yet in force) and transactions in which an agent has a personal interest, and if satisfied that a repetition would make that person unfit for estate agency work, may notify that person that he is so satisfied. Failure to comply with the warning is to be treated as conclusive evidence that the person is unfit to carry on estate agency work.

46. The register

The Director General is required by the 1979 Act to maintain a register recording orders prohibiting unfit persons from doing estate agency work, warning orders, and his decisions on applications for the revocation and variation of orders. The register is open to the public and copies may be taken.

47. General duties of director

The Director General of Fair Trading is under a duty to superintend the working and enforcement of the Act and, where expedient, to take steps to

283

enforce it. As far as practicable, and having regard to the national interest and the interests of estate agents and consumers, he must also keep under review and from time to time advise the Secretary of State as to social and commercial developments relating to the carrying on of estate agency and related activities, and the working and enforcement of the Act. Furthermore the Director General is required to arrange for the dissemination of such information and advice as he thinks expedient.

The Director General, in the exercise of his functions, has the right to require any person to furnish him with such information or to produce any documents as may be specified. Non-compliance with this requirement is an offence.

48. Clients' money and accounts

Clients' money is defined as any money received in the course of estate agency work which is a contract or pre-contract deposit in respect of the acquisition of an interest in land in the United Kingdom, or in respect of a connected contract. The latter is a contract conditional on the acquisition of an interest in land or upon entering into an enforceable contract for such an acquisition. Such money is held on trust for the person who is entitled to call for it to be paid over to him, or at his direction, and to be held on trust, where the money is received as a stakeholder, for the person who may become entitled to it. Where an order prohibiting an unfit person from doing estate agency work has the effect of prohibiting him from holding client's money, the order may appoint another as trustee and may require the person to whom the order relates to make good the new trustee's expenses.

Every person who receives clients' money in the course of estate agency work is required to pay the money without delay into a client account maintained by him or his employer. Regulations specify the details of these client accounts: the Estate Agents (Accounts) Regulations 1981, SI 1981/1520. These regulations also make provision for the person holding clients' money to account for any interest earned, or which could have been earned, by putting the money into a deposit account.

49. Information to clients of prospective liabilities

An estate agent is required, before entering into a contract with a client, to advise the client as to particulars of: the circumstances in which the client will become liable for payment to the agent for carrying out estate agency work (see *Solicitors' Estate Agency (Glasgow)* v *MacIver* (1991)); the amount of the payment or how it will be calculated; payments which do not form part of the agent's remuneration for carrying out estate agency work or a contract or pre-contract deposit but which may become payable and particulars of the circumstances in which such payments will become payable; and the amount of any payment within the preceding clause, or an estimate together with particulars as to how the amount will be calculated.

Regulations require certain other information as to services and charges to be given and to offer explanation of certain technical terms (see the Estate Agents (Provision of Information) Regulations 1991, SI 1991/859). If, after the contract is made, the parties agree on a variation of the contract, the agent must give the customer details of any changes which fall to be made in the information above which was given before the contract was made. There appears to be no requirement that any of the information under this section must be in writing.

Breach of these provisions makes the contract, or the variation, unenforceable except on a court order.

50. Transactions in which estate agent has personal interest

'Personal interest' is defined as one where the agent has a beneficial interest in the land or the proceeds or where he knows or might reasonably be expected to know that any of the following has such an interest: his employer or principal; any employee or agent; or any associate of his or of any person mentioned above.

Where an agent has a personal interest in land to be acquired or disposed of, or will have an interest in land because of a disposal, he must disclose this to the other side before negotiations are entered into. These rules apply where the agent is negotiating on his own behalf as well as when he is negotiating in the course of estate agency work. Further, an agent may neither seek nor receive a contract or a pre-contract deposit in respect of the acquisition of a personal interest of his in land in the United Kingdom, or any other interest in such land in which he has a personal interest. Breach of any of the foregoing provisions gives rise to no criminal or civil penalty but can be taken into account by the Director General of Fair Trading in the exercise of his functions.

51. Bankrupts

A bankrupt person must not engage in estate agency work except as an employee. This does not include employment of him by a body corporate of which he is a director or controller. This prohibition ceases to have effect when the adjudication of bankruptcy is annulled or he is discharged from bankruptcy. Any contravention of the foregoing provisions is an offence.

52. Standards of competence

The Estate Agents Act 1979 lays down provisions for minimum standards of competence, but these have not as yet been brought into force.

53. Property misdescriptions

The Property Misdescriptions Act 1991 makes it an offence, in the course of an estate agency or property development business, to make a statement which is false to a material degree as to any prescribed matter (see the Property Misdescriptions (Specified Matters) Regulations 1992, SI 1992/2834). The defence of due diligence applies.

Case law The property in question was situated in Enfield. Mr and Mrs Leppett owned it at the relevant time and got in touch with Castles Estate Agents Ltd. They were then visited by Mr Coton, who was the firm's senior negotiator.

The house itself was a 4-bedroomed semi with a separate single storey building. This annex was fitted out as a one-bedroomed bungalow, and its general physical appearance gave the impression of a building designed for residential use.

When he looked at this particular building, Mr Coton asked if planning permission had been granted for it. He was told that it had, and he noted down this response on his instruction sheet. He made no further enquiries about the planning status of the bungalow. No attempt was made by Mr Coton or his firm to contact the local authority to determine if the response given by the Leppetts was true.

Mr Coton prepared the particulars for the property and arranged for the property to be advertised in the locality. What he then did was to send the particulars to the vendors together with a Certificate of Confirmation. The particulars made express reference to a 'one-bedroom bungalow located in the grounds'. The Leppetts were asked to sign the Certificate and to return it to Castle, thus verifying the accuracy of the information in the particulars. A letter sent with these papers stated that, without the Certificate duly signed, the firm could not go about marketing the property. The Certificate was, however, not returned: and a reminder phone call to the Leppetts provoked no satisfactory response.

Notwithstanding the absence of the Certificate of Confirmation, the estate agency went ahead with an advertisement which described it as a 'four-bedroom extended semi-detached house, plus one-bedroom bungalow'.

Castle did not have exclusive rights to the disposition of no. 267. There was another firm, Kings. When they were drafting the particulars of the property, they were advised by an 'anonymous source', that there was something suspect about that bungalow and its status. Kings contacted the Leppetts who assured them that the bungalow had been erected with all due planning consents. Kings, however, then got in touch with the local authority who said that the relevant permissions had not been obtained, and hence the property could not be sold under the description 'bungalow'.

To describe the property as a 'bungalow' was plainly an offence under the 1991 Act and this was not denied. Nor did the Castle estate agency deny knowledge of the Act. Indeed, it was said to be a 'daily topic of conversation in the office'. Mr Coton had attended a training course on its implication and it featured regularly at monthly meetings which the firm arranged.

The Property Misdescriptions Act provides for the defence of due diligence; that is to say, the person charged is entitled to be acquitted, even though the offence has been committed, if he can show that he took all reasonable precautions and exercised all due diligence to avoid commission of the particular offence. The Justices found the defence made out, and the prosecution appealed.

The court stressed that 'every case will vary in its facts', and that that would certainly be the case in the field of estate agency. Suppose, the court said, that this particular bungalow had been some 30 to 40 years old and occupied, but still without planning permission. In such a case, it would not be impossible to imagine someone in the position of Mr Coton not even bothering to ask if planning permission had been granted. An advertisement would then have been prepared much on the lines of the actual advertisement. There would then have been a breach of the Act but followed 'surely' by an acquittal because a court would have found the due diligence defence made out if only because, in such a hypothetical set of circumstances, 'there would have been no steps which would have been reasonable to take to avoid committing the offence, and due diligence would have required no further action'.

Suppose too, the court said, that if Mr Coton went to see what was 'plainly a newly completed and ugly extension tacked onto the side of a house in a conservation area', then due diligence would have required some enquiry as to planning permission. The court said that relying on the oral assurance of the vendor would, in those again hypothetical circumstances, be unlikely to suffice because the agents could have asked to see the planning consent or they could have gone to the local authority for the relevant information.

Much attention in this case had been given to the Certificate of Confirmation. In evidence, the estate agency said that it was quite common for vendors not to return the Certificate. Most needed reminding, and some never did return the form. It was the case that guidelines issued by the National Association of Estate Agents indicated that all due diligence had been taken once the Certificate of Confirmation had been sent.

The court, however, felt that little weight needed to be given to the Certificate. Sending the particulars back to the vendor for signature 'would not of itself amount to any form of verification of the information which orally the vendor had already supplied'. It was, however, recognised that in some circumstances, which the court did not specify, the use of this Certificate could be a 'modest step' towards showing due diligence.

After dismissing the relevance to the present case of the Certificate, the court considered what it reckoned was the 'vital question'. This was whether, at the time of Mr Coton's visit to the property, 'the circumstances were such as to raise in his mind (that is to say in the mind of a competent estate agent in his position) any doubts as to the planning permission'.

In cross-examination, Mr Coton had explained that he would have been alerted about planning permission if, for instance, the property had somehow looked wrong: 'but in this case it was a perfectly good bungalow situated within its own ground ... It wasn't occupied at that moment but it appeared that it had been occupied previously, so I was not suspicious'. But this led to the question, posed by the court, as to why, then, Mr Coton had asked about planning permission at all. It answered its own question by saying that, even though Mr Coton did not in fact believe there to be a problem, his experience as a sales negotiator was such as to make him think it prudent just to ask. Having being given the answer he was given by the Leppetts, 'any small doubt that he may have had was thereby completely resolved'. That meant, the court concluded, that the Justices were entitled to find due diligence because Mr Coton was really relying on his own assessment of the position supported, to a small degree, by what he was told. This all had to be assessed against the background that it was known that, in the event of a sale, the whole matter would be investigated by whoever acted for the purchaser in the eventual sale. If the circumstances had been such that Mr Coton should have been put on notice, then, the court said, it was doubtful if the defence could be said to have been made out, not least because he could have asked for the copy of the consent, or have contacted the planning authority.

The estate agency had led evidence to show that it trained its personnel and took considerable steps in that direction, but that was no evidence as to ascertaining planning permission, and that, the court now said, was 'the starting point for the investigation in the present case'. Noting that the facts of this case were 'unusual', the court ruled against the appeal and upheld the finding of the lower court that the estate agents had shown due diligence: *London Borough of Enfield* v *Castles Estate Agents Ltd* (1996)

ENERGY INFORMATION

The Energy (Refrigerators and Freezers) Regulations 1994 implement Community law. They require suppliers to provide, and be responsible for, the accuracy of labels and tables about the energy consumption of refrigerators and freezers. Dealers have to attach labels to appliances displayed or make the information available prior to sale.

It is an offence to display a mark, label, symbol or inscription which does not comply with the Regulations if the item in question would be taken to comply with the Regulations or is likely to mislead or confuse.

The Regulations contain provisions relating to enforcement, the due diligence defence, the liability of a person other than the principal offender, test purchases, obstruction of authorised officers and the disclosure of information.

Similar provisions apply in relation to washing machines and tumble dryers.

Reference should also be made to the Energy Information (Combined Washer-driers) Regulations 1997/1624.

9

Business and the environment

The law and practice relating to the environment, and to the control of environmental pollution, is complex and specialist texts should be consulted. This chapter confines itself to setting out the basic provisions of the Environmental Protection Act 1990 and the Environment Act 1995.

POLLUTION CONTROL AND WASTE MANAGEMENT

1. Integrated pollution control and air pollution control by local authorities

The provisions of Part I of the 1990 Act establish two separate systems of control: integrated pollution control, and local authority air pollution control. The two systems share a number of features, such as the prescription of processes and substances for control; authorisations, which may be subject to conditions; enforcement powers; publicity provisions; and offences. In England and Wales, however, integrated pollution control is to be in the hands of the Environment Agency while local authority air pollution control is in the hands of the local authorities. Furthermore, the former is to be exercisable 'for the purpose of preventing or minimising pollution of the environment due to the release of substances into any environmental medium'. Local authority air pollution control, on the other hand, is exercisable 'for the purpose of preventing or minimising pollution of the environment due to the release of substances into the air (but not into any other environmental medium)'.

2. Functions of the Secretary of State

Apart from prescribing the processes and substances to be controlled, the Secretary of State has considerable powers in relation to the integrated pollution control and local authority air pollution control systems; the functions of the Secretary of State include:

(1) Establishing standards, objectives or requirements (s. 3(1)).

(2) Making regulations to establish quantitative and qualitative standard limits on substances which may be released (s. 3(2)).

(3) Prescribing standard requirements for the measurement or analysis of prescribed substances, or their release.

(4) Prescribing standards or requirements as to any aspect of a prescribed process (s. 3(2)).

(5) Establishing quality objectives or standards for any environmental medium in relation to substances to be released into that medium (s. 3(4)).

(6) Making plans to establish limits for the total amount of substances to be released into the environment in the United Kingdom or any area of the United Kingdom for allocating quotas as to the release of substances to persons carrying on processes where such limits are prescribed, and using such limits so as to reduce pollution progressively and to achieve progressive improvements in quality objectives and standards (s. 3(5)).

(7) Directing that functions being exercised by local authorities should be exercised instead by the Environment Agency (s. 4(4)).

(8) Making regulations determining the allocation of functions between the Inspectorate and river purification authorities in Scotland, and consultation procedures (s. 5).

(9) Giving directions specifying conditions which are or are not to be included in authorisations (s. 7(3)).

(10) Issuing guidance as to the techniques and environmental options that are appropriate for any description of a prescribed process (s. 7(11)).

(11) Making, with the approval of the Treasury, schemes as to fees payable for applications for authorisations and variations, and charges in respect of the subsistence of authorisations (s. 8(2)).

(12) In England and Wales, making payments to the Environment Agency of such amounts as appear to be required to meet the estimated relevant expenditure of that Agency attributable to authorisations (s. 8(9)).

(13) Giving directions as to the exercise of variation powers, and what constitutes a 'substantial change' in a prescribed process for the purpose of those powers (ss. 10(6) and (7)).

(14) Giving directions as to the exercise of revocation powers (s. 12(5)).

(15) Giving directions as to the exercise of enforcement powers (s. 13(3)).

(16) Giving directions as to the exercise of powers relating to prohibition notices (s. 14(4)).

(17) Determining appeals or directing determination by an appointed person (s. 15).

(18) Making regulations as to appeals (s. 15(10)).

(19) In relation to integrated pollution control processes, appointment of inspectors and of the Chief Inspectors for England and Wales and for Scotland (s. 16).

(20) Making regulations as to procedures for sampling by inspectors (s. 17(4)).

(21) Authorisation of other persons to exercise certain powers of inspectors (s. 17(9)).

(22) Requiring information from enforcing authorities and any other persons (s. 19).

(23) Making regulations as to public registers of information to be maintained by the enforcing authorities (s. 20(1)).

(24) Giving directions as to the removal of information from registers (s. 20(6)).

(25) Determining whether the inclusion of information in a register would be contrary to national security and giving directions accordingly (s. 21).

(26) Determining appeals on whether information is commercially confidential so as not to require inclusion on the register, making regulations as to such appeals, and giving directions as to commercially confidential information which nonetheless should be included within the register on grounds of public interest (s. 22).

(27) Authorisation of inspectors to prosecute in magistrates' courts (s. 23(5)).

(28) Approval as to exercise of powers by the Environment Agency, to remedy harm caused by offences (s. 27(2)).

3. Authorisations, conditions and best available techniques not entailing excessive costs

Authorisation is required to carry on a prescribed process. The authorisation must contain such specific conditions as the enforcing authority considers appropriate for achieving certain stated objectives (s. 7(1)(a)) and may contain such other conditions as appear to the enforcing authority to be appropriate (s. 7(1)(c)). All authorisations will also be subject to a general condition as to the use of best available techniques not entailing excessive cost to minimise pollution (s. 7(4)). The importance of the phrase 'best available techniques not entailing excessive cost' should be noted. This phrase clearly requires more than simply the use of certain technology or equipment: it includes also adequate personnel and premises (s. 7(10)).

4. Relationship with other areas of control

The creation of integrated pollution control and local authority air pollution control raises issues of duplication or overlap with other areas of control. Examples are matters of health and safety at work, statutory nuisances (see **13** below), water pollution (see **11–12** below) and waste disposal (see **14–21** below).

(a) *Health and safety at work.* No condition may be imposed on an authorisation for the purpose only of securing the health of persons at work (within the meaning of Pt. I of the Health and Safety at Work Act 1974 (s. 7(J)).

(b) *Deposit of controlled waste.* No condition may be attached to an authorisation so as to regulate the final disposal by deposit in or on land of controlled waste, nor shall any condition apply to such a disposal (s. 2(1)). However, where a prescribed process does involve the final disposal of controlled waste by deposit in or on land, that fact must be notified by the enforcing authority to the relevant waste regulation authority (s. 28(1)).

By s. 33(3), the Secretary of State may make regulations excluding the deposit, treatment, keeping or disposal of controlled waste from control under Pt. II of the Act. In exercising this power, the Secretary of State is to have regard to the expediency of excluding cases for which adequate controls are provided otherwise than by s. 33: s. 33(4)(c). Thus, forms of waste disposal activity other than landfill, such as incineration, may be brought within Pt. I of the Act.

(c) *Radioactive substances.* The Radioactive Substances Act 1993 regulates the keeping and using of radioactive materials as well as regulating the disposal and accumulation of radioactive waste. For a full treatment, see **5–10** below.

5. Registration of premises using radioactive material

Any person who keeps or uses radioactive material on premises used for the purpose of an undertaking must either be registered or subject to an exemption under the provisions of the EPA 1990 (s. 6).

Applications for registration are made to the Environment Agency. Applications have to contain specified information and be accompanied by a fee (s. 7). Copies of applications are sent to the local authority unless the circulation of an application has been restricted by the Secretary of State for reasons of national security (s. 25).

The Agency may either refuse to grant a registration or grant one (which may be subject to conditions and limitations). When setting conditions or limitations the Agency must have regard only 'to the amount and character of the radioactive waste likely to arise from the keeping or use of the radioactive material on the premises in question' (s. 7(7)). Conditions and limitations may deal with the structure of premises, apparatus, equipment or appliances relating to the use of radioactive material. Additional conditions may require the production of information on the movement of radioactive material, or prohibit the sale of incorrectly labelled radioactive material.

Premises covered by available exemptions include those which are subject to a nuclear site licence (granted under the Nuclear Installations Act 1965) and premises on which clocks and watches which contain radioactive material are kept or used (although this exemption does not extend to premises on which clocks or watches are manufactured or repaired by processes involving the use of luminous material). Other exemptions are set out in statutory orders and include a wide range of low-activity radioactive materials.

6. Registration of mobile radioactive apparatus

In addition to the registration of premises, special provisions are made for mobile radioactive apparatus. Such equipment must be registered wherever it might be kept, used, lent or hired, unless such use is covered by an exemption (s. 9).

The provisions on applications and the powers of the Agency for registering mobile radioactive apparatus are very similar to those for registering of premises, although the Agency may impose any limitations and conditions that it thinks fit (s. 10). A registration of mobile radioactive apparatus is only valid in the country in which it was issued.

Exemptions from the necessity to register mobile radioactive apparatus are to be set out in statutory instruments.

7. Cancellation or variation of registrations

The Environment Agency may cancel or vary any registrations made in respect of premises or mobile radioactive apparatus at any time (s. 12). Such cancellation or variation is subject to a right of appeal (s. 26).

8. Authorisation of disposal or accumulation

It is useful to distinguish between 'disposal' and 'storage'. *Storage* of radioactive waste is where the material is placed at a facility (either engineered or natural) with the intention of action being taken at a later time for its subsequent disposal. That later action may involve the retrieval of the substances, its in-site treatment or a declaration that no further action is needed and that the storage has, in the event, become disposal. The *disposal* of radioactive waste is the dispersal of the waste into an environmental medium or placement in a facility with the intention of taking no further action apart from some possible monitoring for technical or reassurance purposes. In the United Kingdom, it is only low-level waste such as that produced by hospitals, research facilities and industry and the like, as for example contaminated packaging, gloves, rags, glass, small tools, paper, filters and effluents which may be disposed of by way of incineration, landfill or discharge to sewers. Intermediate-level waste and high-level waste are generally accumulated in long-term storage facilities at Drigg, Cumbria.

The disposal (on land, into water or by discharge into the atmosphere) of any radioactive waste, on or from any premises, is prohibited unless it is authorised by the Agency or it is exempted under the Act (s. 13). A similar prohibition applies to the disposal of any radioactive waste from mobile radioactive apparatus or the receipt of radioactive waste for the purpose of its disposal.

The exemptions cover premises with a nuclear site licence, the disposal of any radioactive waste arising from clocks and watches (on a similar basis as for registration) and others as set out in statutory instruments.

The accumulation of radioactive waste with a view to its subsequent disposal is also prohibited unless it is either authorised by the Agency or exempted (s. 14). The exemption provisions are as for the disposal of radioactive waste (s. 15).

Applications for both authorisation for disposal or accumulation are made to the Agency (s. 16). However, where the disposal of radioactive waste is on or from a nuclear site, the power to authorise resides with the Agency which must consult with such local authorities, relevant water bodies or other public or local authorities as appear to it proper to be consulted.

As for registration, authorisation may be granted or refused. Where granted, the authorisation may be subject to such limitations or conditions as the Agency, or the Agency and the appropriate Minister, may think fit. Copies of applications will be sent to the local authority except where there are overriding issues of national security (s. 25).

The Agency may vary or revoke any authorisations for disposal or accumulation of radioactive waste in which case there is a right of appeal (s. 17).

9. Central control of radioactive materials

The control of radioactive materials is a central and not a local government function. Local bodies are specifically prohibited from taking account of radioactivity when exercising their functions under public health and clean air legislation as enumerated in Sched. 3, or local enactments dealing with nuisances, pollution and waste discharges. However, the non-radioactive aspects of any substances must still be dealt with. For example, the discharge of waste effluent to a sewer must be properly authorised under the Water Industry Act 1991, regardless of whether or not it is radioactive. Where the Agency believes that the disposal of radioactive waste is likely to involve the need for any special precautions to be taken, it will consult with relevant authorities, including any local or water authorities, who would have to take special precautions before the authority to dispose of waste is granted. Only where special precautions are necessary can the authority in question make a charge (s. 18).

The Secretary of State can give directions to the Agency on the conduct of any applications or in relation to any registration or authorisation granted (ss. 23 and 24). Where the Secretary of State believes that inadequate provisions for the safe disposal or accumulation of radioactive waste are not available, he may arrange for such facilities to be provided. The Secretary of State may then make a charge for their use. The site at Drigg near Sellafield has been provided pursuant to this power. That site is owned and operated by British Nuclear Fuels Limited and is used for the disposal of solid waste which is considered unsuitable for special precaution tipping at a landfill site (s. 29).

On a similar note, the Agency has the power to dispose of radioactive waste where the premises on which it is are unoccupied or the occupier is absent or insolvent or for some other reason, and it is unlikely that the waste would be lawfully disposed of unless he intervened. The Agency may recover its reasonably incurred costs from the occupier or owner of the premises (s. 30).

Posting of certificates

A copy of any certificate of registration or authorisation must be displayed at the appropriate premises (s. 19). The Agency can require a registered or authorised person to retain and produce on request site and disposal documentation (s. 20).

Enforcement and prohibition notices

The Agency can issue enforcement or prohibition notices in relation to any registration or authorisation. It may consider issuing an enforcement notice where there is either an actual or likely failure to comply with the conditions and limitations of an authorisation or registration. Prohibition notices may be used where the continuation of an authorised or registered activity involves an imminent risk of pollution of the environment or of harm to human health.

There is no prerequisite to the service of such notice of non-compliance with any limitation or conditions.

Prohibition notices are likely to be used in the event of an unauthorised or unusual happening: ss. 21, 22.

Criminal offences

The Act creates a number of criminal offences arising out of failure to obtain authorisations and registrations as well as other provisions of the Act (ss. 32–37).

Record keeping

The Agency must keep copies of applications as well as documents issued by it or sent by it to local authorities. Additionally, it must keep a record of convictions under the Act (s. 39). The Agency must send documentation to local authorities and those documents are to be made available to the public (s. 39).

The Crown

The Crown is generally bound by the Act (s. 42). However, the Act does not apply to premises occupied for military or defence purposes, by Her Majesty in her personal capacity or by visiting forces. The Crown cannot be held criminally liable for an infringement of the Act, but the courts can make a declaration that an unlawful act or omission has been committed.

10. Other controls

Nuclear installations in the United Kingdom are regulated by the Nuclear Installations Act 1965. This Act provides for their licensing and inspection with a view to ensuring the maximum possible safety in their construction and operation. That Act also provides that where injury or damage results from the emission of ionising radiation from or in connection with a nuclear site, compensation is available.

The transportation by road of radioactive material is regulated by the Radioactive Material (Road Transport) Act 1991 and its attendant Regulations. That Act makes provision for the consignment and carriage of radioactive material in Great Britain and imposes strict requirements on the transportation of such material which are enforced by criminal sanctions.

11. Water pollution

Where the activities comprising a process prescribed for integrated pollution control include the release of any substances into controlled waters for the purposes of Chap. I of Pt. III of the Water Act 1989, control remains with the Environment Agency. Sched. 15, para. 29, amends the Water Act, s. 108, to provide that no offence is committed where a discharge is made under and in accordance with an integrated pollution control authorisation. However

(a) The Environment Agency shall not grant an authorisation if in its opinion the release will result in or contribute to a failure to achieve any water quality objective in force under Pt. III of the Water Act (s. 28(3)(a)).

(b) Any authorisation granted must include such conditions as appear to the Environment Agency to be appropriate for the purposes of Pt. I of the 1991 Act and which are notified in writing to the Environment Agency (s. 28(3)(b)) and authorisation as required by notice in writing given by the Environment Agency (s. 28(4)). This last obligation appears to apply also to processes scheduled for local control so far as they involve the release of any substances into controlled waters.

12. Trade effluent

Under the Water Act 1989, s. 74, and Sched. 9, the Secretary of State is enabled to exercise ultimate control over the discharge of certain types of trade effluent to sewers. The Trade Effluent (Prescribed Processes and Substances) Regulations 1989/1156 prescribe the relevant substances and processes. Sched. 15, para. 28 of the Environmental Protection Act 1990 amends the Water Act by providing that Sched. 9 (which confers the relevant controls on the Secretary of State) shall not apply in relation to trade effluent produced or to be produced in a process prescribed for central control under Pt. I of the Environmental Protection Act.

The definition of release into water as including releases to sewers (s. 1(11)(c)) enables the Environment Agency to control discharges to sewers from prescribed processes by means of conditions. However, the sewer and its contents are to be disregarded in determining whether there is pollution of the environment. Thus, plant subject to integrated pollution control which discharge trade effluent to a sewer will be subject to integrated pollution control conditions in relation to that discharge. They will also require consent from the sewerage undertaker under the Public Health (Drainage of Trade Premises) Act 1937, which may include conditions as to volume, composition, temperature and other matters, as well as setting the charge to be paid.

13. Statutory nuisances

In the case of statutory nuisances consisting of smoke emitted from premises, dust, steam, smell or other effluvia arising on industrial, trade or business premises, or any accumulation or deposit, a local authority may not issue summary proceedings under Pt. III of the 1990 Act without the consent of the Secretary of State, if proceedings in respect thereof might be instituted under Pt. I of the Act: s. 79(10). Given the breadth of the definitions of 'pollution of the environment' and 'harm' contained in s. 1 of the Act, control under Pt. I can clearly embrace matters of public health and, indeed, activities causing offence to people's olfactory or other senses.

Under s. 2 of the Noise and Statutory Nuisance Act 1993, noise emitted from or caused by a vehicle, machinery or equipment in a street is a statutory nuisance.

14. Planning control

There is no explicit linkage between planning control and the provisions of Pt. I of the 1990 Act.

Unlike a waste management licence under Pt. II, there is no requirement that planning permission be in force before authorisation is granted under Pt. I. Clearly there is a danger that conditions attached to planning permissions or terms contained in planning agreements could conflict with the conditions of the Pt. I authorisation. The traditional approach of the Secretary of State to planning conditions is that they will be unnecessary so far as they duplicate other, more specific, areas of control, and *ultra vires* in so far as they conflict with other such controls.

However, there have been cases where planning conditions have been upheld, notwithstanding a degree of overlap with industrial air pollution controls, on the basis that they provide better protection than the more specifically-based controls: Ferro-Alloys and Metals Smelter Ruling (1990).

15. Organisation of functions

Sections 30–32 of the 1990 Act deal with the reorganisation of waste regulation, collection and disposal functions. Three types of authority are constituted, namely: (1) waste regulation authorities; (2) waste disposal authorities; and (3) waste collection authorities. Their composition and functions are as follows:

(1) Waste regulation authorities

In England, county councils are the waste regulation authorities save for Greater London and the metropolitan areas, where the authority is either a statutorily constituted waste authority or the district council. District councils are the Waste Regulation Authorities in Wales, and islands or district councils in Scotland. The main functions of the Authorities are:

(a) Waste management licensing (s. 35)

(b) Supervision of the new duty of care as to waste (s. 34)

(c) Inspecting land before accepting surrender of licences (s. 39)

(d) Supervision of licensed activities (s. 42)

(e) Investigation of the need for arrangements for dealing with controlled waste arising within their area and preparation of waste disposal plans (s. 50)

(f) Powers to require removal of waste unlawfully deposited (s. 59)

(g) Maintenance of public registers (s. 64)

and s. 31 creates a reserve power for the Secretary of State to set up regional authorities to discharge any of the functions of the two or more authorities involved. It is open to Authorities to enter into such joint arrangements voluntarily, and the Secretary of State's power is intended for use where a regional approach would be advantageous but is not adopted voluntarily.

(2) Waste disposal authorities

Waste disposal authorities are the county councils in non-metropolitan areas; special arrangements apply in some metropolitan counties and in London, and in other metropolitan areas the district councils are the waste disposal authorities. In Wales the district councils are the authorities and in Scotland the functions fall to islands or district councils.

The functions, powers and duties of authorities under Pt. II are:

(a) Formation of waste disposal companies and transfer of relevant parts of their undertakings to such companies (s. 32)

(b) Direction of waste collection authorities as to places to which collected waste is to be delivered (s. 51(4)(a))

(c) Arranging for the disposal of controlled waste collected in the area by waste collection authorities (s. 51(4)(b))

(d) Arrangement for the provision of places at which residents of the area may deposit household waste and for the disposal of waste so deposited (s. 51(1)(b))

(e) Arrangement for the provision of places where collected waste may be treated or kept prior to removal for treatment or disposal (for example, transfer stations) (s. 51(4)(b))

(f) Making payments to waste collection authorities for savings in disposal costs in respect of waste retained for recycling (s. 52(1))

(g) Waste recycling (s. 55).

Separate provisions apply to waste disposal authorities in Scotland in relation to a number of these matters (ss. 53 and 56).

In exercising these functions, the scheme of the Act is that regulatory and disposal functions shall be kept separate (s. 30(7)). Operational disposal functions are not carried out by the disposal authorities themselves, but through 'waste disposal contractors' defined as companies formed for the purpose of collection, keeping, treating or disposing of waste in the course of a business (s. 30(5)). Such companies may be either private sector businesses or companies formed by waste disposal authorities. Section 32 and Sched. 2, Pt. I make provision for the transition of undertakings of waste disposal authorities to such local authority waste disposal companies. The intention is that these authorities and private sector waste disposal companies will compete for business on equal terms, and Sched. 2, Pt. II contains detailed provisions as to contracts and putting such contracts to tender.

(3) Waste collection authorities

Waste collection functions fall to district councils in England and Wales, London boroughs, the Common Council of the City or the Temple authorities in Greater London, and islands or district councils in Scotland. The functions of such authorities are:

(a) To arrange for the collection of household waste in their area and to arrange for the collection of commercial or industrial waste on request (s. 45)

(b) To arrange for the emptying of privies or cesspools in their areas (s. 45)

(c) To determine the nature and source of receptacles in which household waste is to be placed for collection (s. 46)

(d) To supply receptacles for commercial or industrial waste (s. 47)

(e) To deliver for disposal waste collected to such places as the waste disposal authority directs (s. 48)

(f) To carry out investigations as to appropriate arrangements for dealing with waste for the purpose of recycling and to prepare a statement of such arrangements (s. 49)

(g) To retain waste which the authority has decided to recycle and to make arrangements for recycling it (s. 48).

16. Central control

Central Government control over the activities of waste regulation, disposal and collection authorities is provided by a variety of powers conferred on the Secretary of State to give directions on a wide range of matters, including:

(1) Arrangements for transition to waste disposal companies (s. 32(2))

(2) Exercise of licensing functions, both specific directions and general guidance (s. 35(7) and (8))

(3) Disagreements as to licensing between waste regulation authorities and the National River Authority (s. 36(5))

(4) Modification and variation of licences (s. 37(3))

(5) Revocation and supervision of licences (s. 38(7))

(6) Supervision of licensed activities (s. 42(8))

(7) Content and preparation of waste recycling plans (s. 49(4) and (7))

(8) Content and preparation of waste disposal plans (s. 50(9) and (11))

(9) Acceptance of waste by holders of licences and delivery of waste by persons keeping control of it (s. 57(1) and (2))

(10) Inspection and modification of closed landfills (s. 61(1I)).

Additionally, the Secretary of State makes the various Regulations required under Pt. II (including those regulating special waste), issues the Code of Practice on the duty of care relating to waste (s. 34(7)) and exercises the appellate functions in matters of licensing (s. 43) and exclusion of information from registers (s. 66(5)).

As mentioned above, the Secretary of State also has power to establish single regional authorities for waste regulation purposes (s. 31).

17. The duty of care

Section 34 contains a new duty of care as to the keeping, control and transfer of waste. The duty covers all those responsible for the importation, production, carriage, keeping, treatment, disposal or control of controlled waste and those who have control of such waste at whatever point in the chain to final disposal.

The standard is based on reasonableness in the light of the measures applicable to the relevant person in their particular capacity. Reasonable steps are required: (a) to prevent any other person contravening the law as to unauthorised deposit, treatment or disposal of the waste; (b) to prevent escape of the waste; (c) to secure that the waste is transferred only to an authorised person; and (d) to secure that a sufficient written description of the waste accompanies it on transfer.

The duty does not, however, apply to occupiers of domestic property in respect of their own household wastes (s. 34(2)). Central to the operation of s. 34 is a Code of Practice to be prepared and issued by the Secretary of State; such a code will be admissible and relevant evidence in any proceedings as to whether the duty of care has been fulfilled (s. 34(10)).

Breach of the duty of care is an offence punishable by a fine of £5,000 in the magistrates' court and an unlimited fine on conviction on indictment.

18. Waste management licensing

A waste management licence authorises the treatment, keeping or disposal of any specified description of controlled waste in or on specified land, or the treatment or disposal of any specified description of controlled waste by means of mobile plant (s. 35(1)). 'Controlled waste' is defined in s. 75(4) to mean household, commercial and industrial waste; these categories are themselves defined in s. 75(5)-(7). The licence shall be granted on such terms and subject to such conditions as the authority thinks appropriate (s. 35(3)) and continues in force until revoked or surrendered (s. 35(11)).

Where planning permission is required for the use of land authorised by the licence, the licence may not be issued unless either: (a) such permission is in force or (b) an established use certificate is in force (s. 36(2)). Subject to this requirement and to the obligations to refer the proposal to the Environment Agency and the Health and Safety Executive, the waste regulation authority may not reject an application unless either: (a) they are not satisfied that the applicant is a 'fit and proper person' or (b) they are satisfied that rejection is necessary for the prevention of harm to the environment, harm to human health, or serious detriment to the amenities of the locality (s. 36(3)). This last ground of refusal does not apply where planning permission is in force in relation to the proposed use, presumably on the basis that in such a case, issues of amenity will have been addressed at the planning application or appeal stage.

The question whether the applicant is 'fit and proper' is completely new, and brings in considerations of technical competence, financial standing and the absence of relevant convictions (s. 74). Pt. II contains provisions as to variation of licences (s. 37), revocation and suspension of licences (s. 38) and surrender and transfer of licences (ss. 39 and 40 respectively). Under s. 39 it is no longer possible to surrender a licence at will, but only if the authority accepts the surrender – this process involves inspection of the land, consultations with the Environment Agency and the issue of a 'certificate of completion' if the authority is satisfied that the condition of the land is unlikely to cause pollution of the environment or harm to human health. The acceptance of a surrender has important implications in relation to the provisions contained later in Pt. II as to the inspection of closed sites and necessary remedial work (s. 61). Appeal to the Secretary of State lies against the various decisions of waste regulation authorities under the licensing system (s. 43).

Under s. 62 the Secretary of State may make provision by regulations for the treatment, keeping, or disposal of controlled waste that may be difficult or dangerous: such waste is known as 'special waste'. Detailed control is at present exercised over such waste by the Control of Pollution (Special Waste) Regulations 1980 No.1709. This involves a system of documentation of the waste and of pre-notification to the relevant waste authorities of disposal of the waste.

The deposit, treatment or disposal of controlled waste is an offence except under and in accordance with a waste management licence (s. 33). Other offences include: the deposit of waste other than controlled waste in certain circumstances (s. 63(2)); the making of false statements in relation to licence applications (s. 44); breach of the regulations on special waste (authority to create an offence by delegated legislation being given by s. 62(2)(g)); failure to comply with requirements to deal with pollution when a licence is suspended (s. 38(10) and (11)); obstruction of inspectors (ss. 69(9) and 70(4)); failure to comply with requirements to furnish information (s. 71(3)); and failure to comply with a requirement to remove unauthorised waste deposited on land (s. 59(5)). In addition, damage caused by waste unlawfully deposited on land may give rise to civil liability under s. 73(6).

19. Control of Pollution (Amendment) Act 1989

Pt. II of the 1990 Act has to be read in conjunction with the Control of Pollution (Amendment) Act 1989. The 1989 Act creates a scheme for the registration of carriers of controlled waste with related offences and powers. As such, the 1989 Act is an important component of the statutory framework for controlling and regulating waste, in conjunction with the 1990 Act. In particular, registration of carriers is a vital precondition to the statutory duty of care on waste producers (see above).

20. Waste recycling

Under s. 46(2) a waste collection authority may require household waste to be placed in separate receptacles or compartments according to whether the waste is to be recycled or not. Waste collection and disposal authorities may make arrangements for the recycling of waste under express powers in s. 55 (s. 56 for Scotland). In respect of waste which the collection authority decides to recycle, the usual requirement of delivery to such place as the disposal authority directs does not apply (s. 48(2)) and there is provision for the disposal authority to make payments to the collection authority in respect of net savings in disposal costs (s. 52(1)).

Waste collection authorities are under a duty to carry out investigations as to the appropriate arrangements to facilitate recycling and to prepare waste recycling plans as to such arrangements (s. 49). Finally, in determining the contents of waste disposal contracts they enter into with contractors, and in the tendering process for such contracts, waste disposal authorities must have regard to the desirability of including terms designed to maximise the recycling of waste (Sched. 2, para. 19(1)(b)).

21. Closed landfills

In relation to sites no longer in operation, new duties and powers are provided by s. 61 under which waste regulation authorities must inspect their area to detect whether deposits of controlled waste on the land have led or are leading to noxious gases or liquids being concentrated or accumulated, and emitted or discharged so as to cause possible pollution of the environment or harm to human health.

Substantial powers of entry are given, and if land is found to be in such a condition it must be kept under review until the authorities are satisfied that no such pollution or harm will be caused.

It is the duty of the authority to do works or take steps (whether on the land affected or on adjacent land) as necessary to avoid such pollution or harm. The cost of such measures may be recovered, in whole or in part, from the person for the time being the owner of the land, except where the surrender of the relevant waste management licence has already been accepted by the authority under s. 39. Since the matters on which the authority has to be satisfied before accepting the surrender are precisely those of the condition of the land and the risk of pollution or harm to health, it seems that this exception will rarely arise in practice.

22. Public information

As with Pt. I and indeed the rest of the Act, Pt. II contains comprehensive provisions for the disclosure of information on public registers (s. 64). The relevant information relates predominantly to the exercise of licensing powers, and there are provisions as to the exclusion of information on grounds of national security (s. 65) and commercial confidentiality (s. 66). In addition, each waste regulation authority must publish an annual report on the discharge of its regulatory functions (s. 67).

23. Relationship of waste licensing with other powers

Waste management licensing may to some extent be duplicated by other statutory controls. The relevant principles are as follows:

(a) Integrated pollution control

Conditions attached to integrated pollution control authorisations may not be framed so as to regulate the final disposal of controlled waste by deposit in or on any land; other forms of disposal may be so regulated: s. 29(1). Where a prescribed process involves such final disposal by deposit in or on land, the Environment Agency must notify the waste regulation authority, for the area in which the process is carried on. The Secretary of State may, by regulation, exclude the deposit, keeping, treatment or disposal of waste from licensing requirements, and from the offence of treating, keeping or disposing in a manner likely to cause pollution of the environment or harm to human health: s. 33(3).

(b) Statutory nuisances

The provisions of Pt. III of the Act on statutory nuisances could apply to accumulations of controlled waste (s. 79(1)(e)) or to smell or other effluvia from such waste (s. 79(1)(d)). The relationship of waste licensing powers and control over statutory nuisances was considered by the Court of

Appeal in *Attorney-General's Reference (No. 2 of 1988)* (1989) It was held in that case that:

(a) The primary purpose of waste disposal licensing powers under Pt. 1 of the Control of Pollution Act was to avoid water pollution, serious detriment to the amenities of the locality and harm to public health; therefore the power to impose conditions under s. 6(2) of the Control of Pollution Act was not wide enough to allow a condition prohibiting public nuisances of all kinds, whether or not they had one of those three effects.

(b) If such condition were valid, there would be no need to trace a nuisance back to a particular failure of management or operation in order to establish a breach. It is not clear how far proposition **(a)** remains correct under Pt. II of the 1990 Act, where protection of water from pollution has been broadened to protection of the environment generally, and where 'harm' to the environment receives a very broad statutory definition to include human senses.

(c) Water pollution

A waste site or installation that involves the discharge of effluent into controlled waters (for example a leachate treatment plant), or which results in polluting matter entering such waters, will require consent from the Environment Agency under the Water Act 1989, ss. 107 and 108. The Agency must be consulted before a waste management licence is issued and if the Agency requests that the licence is not issued or disagrees with the waste regulation authority as to the conditions, the licence may not be issued except in accordance with a decision of the Secretary of State, to whom either party may refer the matter (s. 36(5)). Similar provisions apply in Scotland in relation to river purification authorities (s. 36(6)). The same principles apply to proposals for modification of licences (s. 37(5)). Any proposal to accept surrender of a licence must also be referred to the Environment Agency (s. 39(7)).

(d) Radioactive substances

By s. 78, nothing in Pt. II of the Act applies to radioactive waste, but regulations may apply some or all of the provisions of Pt. II, with or without modification, for the purpose of dealing with such waste.

(e) Town and country planning

The prerequisite of either planning permission or an established use certificate before a waste management licence can be granted has already been referred to (see **18** above). Another question which can arise is the relationship between planning conditions or agreements and conditions attached to waste management licences. DOE Circular 1/85, The Use of Conditions in Planning Permission (W.O. 1/85), states (Annex, paras. 18 and 19) that a planning condition which duplicates the effect of other controls will be unnecessary and one whose requirements conflict with other controls will be seen *ultra vires* as unreasonable. However, the Circular goes on to say, conditions may be needed in the case of concurrent controls where the material considerations are different, so that it could be unwise to rely on the other systems of control to secure planning objectives. The Circular also suggests that planning conditions could be used where concurrent control is not available, for example to secure the aftercare or restoration of a waste disposal site, where the waste disposal licence could not achieve the same result upon termination. Although waste authorities are now given greater post-completion controls over matters of pollution and public health, it appears there may still be a role for planning conditions in matters of amenity, such as contours, planting and landscaping.

CLEAN AIR AND LITTER

24. Statutory nuisances and clean air

Part III of the 1990 Act deals with statutory nuisances, clean air and controls over offensive trades. The commencement of summary proceedings requires the consent of the Secretary of State: s. 79(10). A complaint may be made to a magistrates' court by any person aggrieved by the existence of a statutory nuisance. The court must make an order requiring abatement or prohibiting recurrence, if satisfied the nuisance exists, or, if abated, is likely to recur and may also impose a fine. Breach of such an order is an offence: s. 82.

Local authorities may take abatement, prohibition or restriction proceedings in the High Court if of the opinion that a prosecution for failure to comply with the authority's abatement notice would provide an inadequate remedy: s. 81(5).

Section 85 enables the Secretary of State to make regulations to control the emission of specified gases from furnaces, thus extending the controls of the Clean Air Acts 1956 and 1968 to such emissions and beyond the grit, dust and smoke controlled by those Acts.

25. Litter, etc.

Part IV of the Act contains new provisions relating to litter and to abandoned shopping and luggage trolleys. Its principal provisions are:

(1) A widened offence of leaving litter, subject to a maximum £25,000 fine on summary conviction (s. 87)

(2) Power to issue fixed penalty notices to a person believed to have committed the new littering offence (s. 88)

(3) Duties on the Crown, local authorities, highway authorities designated statutory undertakers and the occupiers of 'relevant land' to ensure land is, so far as practicable, kept clear of litter and refuse (s. 89)

(4) Power for the Secretary of State to issue a Code or Codes of Practice on the duty (s. 89(7)-(13).

(5) Power to designate 'litter control areas' (s. 90)

(6) Provision for summary proceedings by persons aggrieved by litter on highways, Crown and local authority land, other relevant land, and litter control areas designated under s. 90 (s. 91). The proceedings may lead to a 'litter abatement order' under s. 91(6), non-compliance with which is an offence.

(7) Provision for summary proceedings by litter authorities, with power to serve litter abatement notices (s. 92)

(8) Power for litter authorities to issue 'street litter control notices' on occupiers of premises adjacent to streets or fronting on to streets (s. 93)

(9) Power to apply provisions as to the seizure, removal, retention, return and disposal of abandoned shopping and luggage trolleys, with power to levy charges on the return of the trolleys (s. 99 and Sched. 4).

CONTAMINATED LAND

26. Contaminated land and abandoned mines

The scheme of the provisions

The provisions of the Environment Act 1995 follow through a sequence from the identification of contaminated land to securing its remediation. Primary responsibility for this process rests with district councils and unitary authorities, though both the Secretary of State and the Environment Agency also have very important roles to play.

(1) Identifying contaminated land

'Contaminated land' is defined at s. 78A(2) of the 1990 Act by reference to the subjective opinion of the local authority in whose area it is situated as to

309

whether it is in such a condition by reason of substances in, on or under it, that significant harm is being caused or there is a significant possibility of such harm being caused, or that pollution of controlled waters is being or is likely to be caused. The local authority is under a statutory duty to cause its area to be inspected from time to time for the purpose of identifying such land (s. 78B(1)). In making the determination as to whether the land is contaminated or not, the local authority is required to act in accordance with guidance from the Secretary of State as to the manner in which the determination is to be made (s. 78A(2)).

(2) Notification

Upon identifying contaminated land, the local authority is required to give notice of that fact to: (a) the Agency; (b) the owner of the land; (c) any person who appears to be the owner or occupier of all or part of the land; and (d) the person who appears to be the 'appropriate person', that is to say the person who caused or knowingly permitted the contamination, and as such may be served with a remediation notice.

(3) Special sites

As well as identifying contaminated land, the local authority must decide whether such land is required to be designated as a 'special site': ss. 78B(l)(b) and 78C(1). The significance of this distinction is that in the case of special sites the Agency is the enforcement authority rather than the local authority (s. 78A(9)). Before making this decision, the local authority must request the advice of the Agency and have regard to the advice received (s. 78C(3)). Land is, however, only required to be designated as a special site if it falls within a description prescribed for this purpose by the Secretary of State (s. 78C(8)). The Agency may itself consider that contaminated land falls within such a description, and may give notice of that fact to the local authority (s. 78C(4)). Disagreements between the Agency and the local authority are resolved by referral to the Secretary of Slate (s. 78D).

(4) Duty to require remediation

Where land has been identified as contaminated or has been designated as a special site, then the relevant enforcing authority falls under a duty to serve on the 'appropriate person' a remediation notice, specifying what is to be done by way of remediation and within what period (s. 78E(l)). In this context remediation can mean either works to assess the situation, or actual remedial or mitigating measures, or subsequent inspection (s. 78A(10)). This duty is, however, qualified in four respects: (a) the requirement for prior consultation under s. 78H (see below); (b) restrictions on service of a notice under s. 78H; *(c)* the requirement that remediation may only comprise those things the authority considers reasonable, having regard to the cost likely to be involved and the seriousness of the harm in question (s. 78E(4)); and *(d)* the requirement to have regard to guidance issued by the Secretary of State (s. 78E(5)).

(5) Determination of the 'appropriate person'

Section 78F deals with the vital issue of who is the appropriate person or persons to bear responsibility to comply with the remediation notice.

Responsibility rests primarily with the person or persons who caused or knowingly permitted the contaminating substances to be in, on or under the land: s. 78F(2). However, the current owner or occupier may also be liable where, after reasonable inquiry, no such person can be found: s. 78F(4),(5). Specific provision is made with regard to those acting in the context of insolvency (such as receivers): s. 78X(3). No special provision is, however, made for lenders, other than the definition of 'owner', which makes it clear that a mortgagee is not within the definition: s. 78A(9).

One very difficult issue is that of joint and several liability. The starting point is that where a number of persons have contributed the same, or different, contaminating substances, liability may be joint and several: s. 78F(2). However, this potential liability is mitigated in two respects: first, by the requirement that the remedial action required to be taken by any appropriate person be 'referable' to the substances he contributed (s. 78F(3)) and, secondly, by the obligation of the enforcing authority, in determining who is the appropriate person, to act in accordance with guidance issued by the Secretary of State: s. 78F(6) and (7). Special provision is also made for the situation where substances migrate from their original source, so as to cause other land to become contaminated: s. 78K.

(6) Consultation

The enforcing authority must use reasonable endeavours to consult with the person who appears to be the responsible person, and with the owner and the occupier of the relevant land: s. 7llH(l). The consultation must relate to what is to be done by way of remediation and no remediation notice may be served during a three-month period from the original notification (see (2) above): s. 78H(3). Certain circumstances are specified where no remediation notice may be served at all, for example where the authority is satisfied that there is nothing that could reasonably be required, having balanced cost considerations against the seriousness of the contamination, or where the authority is satisfied that appropriate steps are being or will be taken by way of remediation voluntarily, without the need for service of a remediation notice: s. 78H(5). In such cases, the outcome will be the preparation and publication of either a remediation declaration (by the authority) or a remediation statement (by the responsible person): s. 78H(6),(7).

(7) Appeals against remediation notices

Where a remediation notice is served, the recipient has a right of appeal: s. 78L. Notices served by local authorities are appealed to the magistrates' court. Appeals against notices served by the Agency are determined by the Secretary of State.

(8) Offences

Failure, without reasonable excuse, to comply with any of the requirements of a remediation notice is an offence: s. 78M(1). The offence is punishable, on summary conviction only, by a maximum fine of £5,000 and a further fine of £500 per day for which failure continues after conviction. Where the contaminated land in question is 'industrial, trade or business premises', the respective figures are £20,000 and £2,000.

(9) Default powers

As well as instigating a prosecution, an enforcement authority may itself carry out remediation works in a number of cases, for example where works are urgently required to prevent serious harm of which there is an imminent danger, or where the responsible person has entered into a written agreement with the authority to carry out the works, or where the recipient of a remediation notice fails to comply with it: s. 78N. In a number of these cases, the authority is entitled to recover its reasonable costs, subject to considerations of hardship and guidance issued by the Secretary of State: s. 78P. Additionally, the authority may serve a charging notice, the effect of which is that the sums expended carry interest and that the cost and accrued interest form a charge on the premises.

The enforcing authorities may bring their own prosecutions.

(10) Registers

The Act includes a requirement for the maintenance of public registers of remediation notices and other matters (such as appeals and convictions): s. 78R. There are also provisions dealing with the exclusion of information from the register on grounds of national security and commercial confidentiality: ss. 78S and 78T.

27. The role of statutory guidance

A number of the provisions on contaminated land require the exercise of discretion in making difficult decisions, such as whether land is contaminated; what should be required by way of remediation; or on whom should the remediation notice be served. The approach adopted has been to create a strong form of statutory guidance which the enforcing authority is required to follow, and which is itself subject to a negative resolution type of parliamentary procedure: s. 78. In other cases. the guidance is not subject to this special procedure and does not have prescriptive effect.

28. Radioactive substances

The 1990 Act amends the Radioactive Substances Act 1960. The main amendments are:

(1) Provision for the appointment of inspectors and a Chief Inspector by the Secretary of State to exercise regulatory functions (s. 100)

(2) Provision for a scheme of fees and charges payable in respect of registration and authorisation under the 1960 Act (s. 101)

(3) New powers of enforcement (s. 102)

(4) Withdrawal of the exemption in favour of the United Kingdom Atomic Energy Authority from certain requirements of the 1960 Act (s. 103)

(5) Application of the Act to the Crown (s. 104).

OTHER PROVISIONS

29. Genetically modified organisms

The main features of Pt. VI of the Act are as follows:

(1) Sections 106 and 107 contain a series of definitions of key terms and concepts.

(2) Section 108 contains a general prohibition on importation, acquisition, release and marketing of genetically modified organisms without carrying out a risk assessment of possible damage to the environment and notifying the Secretary of State of the intention to carry out the activity. Persons keeping such organisms are also under an obligation to carry out a risk assessment and to notify the Secretary of State of the keeping of the genetically modified organisms.

(3) Section 109 places a series of duties of care relating to the risk of environmental damage on persons proposing to import or acquire genetically modified organisms and persons keeping and persons proposing to release such organisms.

(4) Section 110 gives the Secretary of State power to serve prohibition notices in relation to acts or activities involving genetically modified organisms which would entail a risk of causing damage to the environment.

(5) By s. 111, in certain cases to be prescribed, the importation, acquisition, keeping, release or marketing of genetically modified organisms is prohibited, except in pursuance of a consent granted by the Secretary of State and in accordance with any limitations and conditions to which the consent is subject. In such cases the requirements of ss. 108 and 109 do not apply. Section 112 contains provisions as to express and implied conditions and limitations on such consents. Such conditions may not be imposed for the sole purpose of securing the health and safety of workers (s. 112(1)). Consents will contain a series of conditions implied by statute as to reasonable measures for risk assessment, notification and use of best available techniques not entailing excessive cost for the purpose of preventing damage to the environment.

(6) By s. 113 a scheme of fees and charges for consents may be instituted.

(7) Sections 114–117 provide for the appointment of inspectors and give various powers of entry, inspection, obtaining information, and dealing with imminent dangers.

(8) Section 118 creates various offences in relation to contravention of the requirements of Pt. VI.

(9) Sections 119–121 contain ancillary provisions on offences, including the onus of proof and powers to order matters to be remedied, or to recover the costs of remedial steps.

(10) Sections 122 and 123 make provision for public registers of information relating to matters under Pt. VI of the Act.

(11) Section 124 provides for the appointment of a committee to advise the Secretary of State on the exercise of his powers.

(12) Section 125 allows the delegation of certain enforcement functions to officers of public authorities.

Public access to information

Originally Pt. VI did not provide on its face for public access to information, save in relation to the advertising of applications for consent. However, the Government gave an assurance that it is committed to allowing access to information as for other Parts of the Act under the Secretary of State's inherent powers of disclosure. In the event, express statutory provisions to that effect were inserted as ss. 122 and 123.

30. Miscellaneous

Part VIII of the 1990 Act contains a number of miscellaneous provisions of varying importance. The most significant are:

(1) Power to restrict the importation, use, supply or storage of substances or articles for the purpose of avoiding pollution, or harm to man, animals or plants (s. 140)

(2) Power to restrict the importation or exportation of waste for the purpose of preventing pollution or harm to human health or for conserving facilities or resources for dealing with waste (s. 141)

(3) Powers to make provision for the obtaining of information about substances with potential to cause pollution or harm to human health (s. 142)

(4) Provision for public registers of potentially contaminated land (s. 143)

(5) Amendments of the legislation of control of hazardous substances (s. 44 and Sched. 13)

(6) Increase of maximum penalties in respect of water pollution offences (s. 145)

(7) Amendments on legislation as to marine deposits (s. 146) and creation of public registers as to such deposits and marine incineration (s. 147)

(8) Amendments of the provisions as to oil pollution offences from ships (s. 148)

(9) Provisions for the control of stray dogs (ss. 14–151)

(10) Provision as to banning the burning of straw, stubble and other crop residues (s. 152).

THE ENVIRONMENT AGENCY

31. Functions of the Environment Agency

Certain functions of the Environment Agency have been considered above. The 1995 Act also gives it the following new functions:

Contaminated land

Section 57 gives the Agency powers to give guidance to local authorities as enforcing authorities, and a role as enforcing authorities themselves in relation to 'special sites'. These are sites designated as such in accordance with procedures set out in the 1990 Act.

Air quality

The Agency is given a role as a statutory consultee when the Secretary of State prepares a national air quality strategy and makes regulations in relation to the implementation of the air quality strategy and international obligations regarding air quality; and generally in relation to the assessment and management of air quality: Pt. IV of the 1995 Act.

Waste strategy

Section 92 of the 1995 Act provides that, as with air quality strategy, the Agency is a statutory consultee for the Secretary of State's National Waste Strategy for England and Wales.

Producer responsibility

Sections 93 and 94 of the 1995 Act provide for regulations to be made imposing producer responsibility obligations. The Agency is charged with monitoring compliance, enforcement and guidance in relation to such obligations.

Nuclear installations

The Agency must be consulted by the Health and Safety Executive before it grants or revokes a nuclear site licence, and also before it places a condition on or varies such a licence where such condition of variation relates to or affects the creation, accumulation or disposal of radioactive waste: paras 7–9, Sch 22.

32. The Environment Agency – an overview

Legislative responsibilities

Environmental standards are set in European and United Kingdom legislation. The Environment Agency has the responsibility for enforcing some of these standards within England and Wales.

There is a great deal of legislation that has an impact on the way the Environment Agency operates or the way it carries out its enforcement duties. The main legislation includes the following Acts:

General
The Environment Act 1995

Water management, water resources
Water Resources Act 1991
Water Industries Act 1991

Flood defence
Coast Protection Act 1949
Water Act 1989
Water Resources Act 1991
Land Drainage Act 1991

Fisheries
Diseases of Fish Act 1937
Sea Fisheries Regulation Act 1966
Salmon & Freshwater Fisheries Act 1975
Wildlife & Countryside Act 1981
Diseases of Fish Act 1983
Salmon Act 1986
Water Act 1989
Water Resources Act 1991

Navigation
Water Act 1981
Water Resources Act 1991
Land Drainage Act 1976
Sea Fish Industry Act 1951
Pilotage Act 1987
Harbour Docks & Piers Clauses Act 1847
Anglian Water Act 1977
Upper Medway Navigation & Conservancy Act 11 & 14
Southern Water Authority Act 1982
Thames Conservancy Acts; 1932, 1950, 1959, 1966, 1972

Recreation
Water Resources Act 1991

Conservation
Water Resources Act 1991

Pollution regulation: discharges to water
Water Act 1989
Water Resources Act 1990
Water Industries Act 1991
Salmon & Freshwater Fisheries Act 1975

Waste regulation
Control of Pollution Act 1974
Refuse Disposal (Amenities) Act 1987
Control of Pollution (Amendment) Act 1989
Town & Country Planning Act 1990

Environmental Protection Act 1990
Planning & Compensation Act 1991

Integrated pollution control
Environmental Protection Act 1990

Air pollution
Health & Safety at Work etc. Act 1974
Alkali etc. Works Regulation Act 1906

Radioactive substances
Radioactive Substances Act 1993

Others
Deregulation and Contracting Out Act 1994
Welsh Language Act 1995

Functions of the Environment Agency

The Environment Agency's work is divided into seven main functions:

(1) *Flood defence* has the role of protecting people and the developed environment from flooding by providing effective defences and protection of floodplains. Safeguarding life is its highest priority and to meet this aim it provides a flood forecasting and warning service. Flood defence also has an aim to protect and enhance the natural environment by promoting works that are sustainable and work with nature.

(2) The *water resources* function comprises the conservation, redistribution and augmentation of surface and groundwater supplies. It includes the powers to encourage water conservation and to promote transfer schemes to balance the needs of water users and the environment by issuing licences for users to abstract water from rivers and boreholes.

(3) The *pollution control* function includes :

- Integrated pollution control regulating the most polluting, or technologically complex, industrial and other processes in air, on land or in water.
- Water quality and pollution control which prevents and controls pollution and monitors the quality of rivers, estuaries and coastal waters.
- Radioactive substances regulating the disposal of radioactive material, including from licensed nuclear sites, and regulating the accumulation, keeping and use of radioactive materials, except from licensed nuclear sites.

- Waste regulation setting consistent standards for waste management practice to regulate the treatment, storage, movement and disposal of controlled waste. The Agency also has a requirement to register and monitor those who produce waste imposing obligations to reduce, re-use, recover or recycle products and materials.
- Reporting on the extent of contaminated land and contributing to its management (primarily undertaken by local authorities).
- Abandoned mine operators are also required to give the Agency notice so that steps can be taken to prevent minewater pollution in the future.

(4) The Agency is responsible for maintaining, improving and developing *fisheries*. This is carried out by licensing, regulation and enforcement schemes which cover salmon, sea trout, non-migratory trout, coarse and eel fisheries. The Agency also carries out improvements to fisheries by improving the habitat, fish stocks and providing advice to fishery owners.

(5) The *navigation* function is responsible for monitoring and improving over 800 km of inland waterways, the Harbour of Rye and the Dee Estuary. Its aim is to make these resources widely available to the public for water or land based recreational use.

(6) The Agency must also take account of recreation and access. Over 1000 sites in their control are managed for recreational use. They also have a general duty to promote the recreational use of water and land throughout England and Wales.

(7) In fulfilling all its functions the Environment Agency is required to contribute to the *conservation of nature, landscape and archaeological heritage*, to have a regard to conserving and enhancing flora, fauna, geological or physiographical features when carrying out pollution control functions and a duty to further conservation when carrying out other functions, and also a duty generally to promote the conservation of flora and fauna dependent on the aquatic environment.

10

The United Kingdom as a member of the European Union

The United Kingdom entered what was then called the Common Market in 1973 by virtue of the enactment in the United Kingdom Parliament of the European Communities Act 1972. Including the United Kingdom, there are now 15 member states in the Union. The 'constitution' of the Union is to be found in the Treaty of Rome 1957. The Treaty on European Union, signed in Maastricht in 1992, later amended at Amsterdam, created a European Union moving towards economic and monetary union with inter-governmental co-operation in certain areas. The Maastricht Treaty was implemented in the United Kingdom by the European Communities (Amendment) Act 1993. The Amsterdam treaty has not so far been incorporated into United Kingdom law but the European Communities (Amendment) Bill, which implements the latest Treaty, is proceeding through Parliament as we go to press.

The European Union has joined with the member states of the European Free Trade Area (Iceland, Liechtenstein, Norway and Switzerland) to form the European Economic Area. There is free movement of goods, persons, services and capital within the area, as well as uniform rules on competition and state aid. The EFTA states generally adopt Union legislation.

THE INSTITUTIONS OF THE EUROPEAN UNION

1. European Commission

The European Commission is responsible for initiating and drafting legislation, implementing the decisions of the Council of Ministers of the European Union (see below), administering the various EU funds (such as the European Social Fund, the Cohesion Fund). The Commission has autonomous powers under which it may act without reference to the Council in areas such as the Common Agricultural Policy and customs union.

The Commission consists of 20 Commissioners. Austria, Belgium, Denmark, Finland, Greece, Ireland, Luxembourg, Netherlands, Portugal and Sweden each have one. France, Germany, Italy, Spain and the United Kingdom each have 2. The European Parliament (see below) is consulted before the member states appoint the President of the Commission, and Parliament must approve the full commission. Commissioners serve for 5 years. Commissioners are required to act in the best interests of the Union as a whole, and are not under the authority of their national government.

2. Council of Ministers of the European Union

Legislation is initiated by the Commission (see above) but its final adoption generally depends on the Council. Each member state has the following votes in the Council: Austria (4); Belgium (5); Denmark (3); Finland (3); France (10); Germany (10); Greece (5); Ireland (3); Italy (10); Luxembourg (2); Netherlands (5); Portugal (5); Spain (8); Sweden (4); United Kingdom (10). Some measures, notably on taxation, have to be adopted unanimously, and there are also occasions (see below) when the law-making procedure requires unanimity. Unanimity is also generally required for action in relation to a common foreign and security policy, or in relation to co-operation in home affairs. For the most part, however, the Council can adopt measures by a simple majority or by a qualified majority. This latter requires 62 votes of the possible 87 votes which may be cast.

The Council consists of representatives from each member state at ministerial level, authorised to commit the Government of that member state. Meetings are attended by different ministers. For example, agriculture ministers will discuss farm prices; employment ministers, labour and social affairs. Major Union issues will be matters for the foreign ministers.

3. European Parliament

This is directly elected by the citizens of the Union. Its role is to adopt the Union's budget, give its opinion on proposed legislation and propose amendments (see further below) and to investigate complaints of maladministration in the other institutions of the Union. Under the amendments adopted at Maastricht, the Parliament has been given the power of 'negative assent' which means that it can veto legislation in certain areas (such as education and culture) by an absolute majority. The Parliament also has the right of initiative which enables it to request the European Commission to draft legislation in areas where it feels EU action is required.

Parliament's consent is also required for the accession of new members.

4. Committee of the Regions

This was established by Maastricht. It drafts legislation on policy areas such as health, culture and certain funds, and where the Council or Commission considers it appropriate. It consists of 222 representatives from local and region authorities in the member states.

5. Economic and Social Committee

This is an advisory body also consisting of 222 representatives from the various economic and social sectors in the member states. It is divided into three groups: employers, workers, and various interests (such as agriculture, small and medium-sized businesses and transport). The Committee draws up opinions on all draft legislation referred to it by the Commission.

6. Conciliation Committee

This is made up of members or representatives of the Council and Parliament in equal numbers. It is convened when the Council and Parliament disagree on a legislative proposal (see more on the law-making process below) and it seeks to draw up and approve a text satisfying both bodies.

7. COREPER

This is an acronym for the Committee of Permanent Representatives of the member states. It is composed of civil servants and is where the initial discussion of proposals takes place between the member states.

8. Court of Auditors

The Court consists of 15 members appointed by the unanimous decision of the Council after consultation with the Parliament. Its main task is to check that all Union revenue has been collected and that all expenditure has been validly incurred, and that financial management is sound. It issues an annual report.

9. The European Court of Justice and the Court of First Instance

The Court of Justice consists of 15 judges assisted by 9 advocates-general. The members of the Court are appointed for 6 years by agreement between the Governments of the member states. Their independence is guaranteed.

The Court's role is to ensure that the European treaties are interpreted and applied in accordance with the law. The Court can find that a member state has failed to fulfil its obligations. A member state not complying with a judgement of the Court may be fined.

The Court also reviews the legality of measures taken by any of the Union's institutions and it has the power to judge when they are in breach of the Treaties by failing to act.

The Court also gives preliminary rulings, on an application by a national court, on the interpretation or validity of points of Community law. If a legal action produces a disputed point of law of such a kind, a national court may seek a ruling from the Court: it must do so if there is no higher court of appeal in the member state, in which case the judgement of the Court is binding.

> *Case law* It was decided by the Court of Appeal that the High Court and Court of Appeal have the jurisdiction to interpret Community law and that they are not obliged to grant a right of appeal to the European Court of Justice. However, if the case goes to the House of Lords on appeal, the House must refer the matter to the Court if either party so desires: *H P Bulmer Ltd* v *Bollinger SA* (1974).
>
> The obligation to refer to the Court does not arise if the question raised is not relevant to the outcome of the proceedings, if it has already been answered in a previous ruling of the Court, or if the correct interpretation is so obvious as to be beyond reasonable doubt: *CILFIT* v *Ministry of Health* (1982); *Magnavision NV SA* v *General Optical Council (No. 2)* (1987).

The Court of First Instance deals with disputes concerning the EU institutions and their staff and with EU competition rules. The CFI also has jurisdiction in all direct actions by citizens and firms against EU institutions except in anti-dumping matters. It consists of 12 judges. Appeals on points of law are only dealt with by the Court of Justice.

THE LEGISLATIVE INSTRUMENTS

10. Regulations

Under the Treaty of Rome, the Union may adopt Regulations. These apply the same law throughout the Union and apply in full in all member states. In addition, Regulations are 'directly applicable', which means that they do not have to be specifically adopted by the member states. Instead, they confer rights or impose duties in exactly the same way as domestic laws.

11. Directives

The purpose of a Directive is to ensure uniformity in the law throughout the Union but to make allowance for national traditions and structures. A Directive is binding on member states as to the objective to be achieved, but leaves the precise attainment of that purpose to whatever method is chosen by the individual member state.

Although, unlike Regulations, Directives do not have direct effect, the European Court of Justice has held that, where a member state has not implemented a Directive, nationals of that state can rely on the Directive before the national court to secure such rights as are provided by the Directive, and can even claim compensation where loss is sustained because of the failure to implement the Directive (Cases of *Frankovich* and *Boniface* (1991)).

> *Case law* A contract had been made in Italy which was within the terms of Council Directive 85/577 on contracts made by consumers away from business premises. The contract was made at a time when Italy was in breach of the time limit for the implementation of that Directive. The European Court of Justice ruled that, in the absence of measures implementing a Directive, consumers cannot make use of the right of cancellation provided for in the Directive nor enforce such rights in the national court since Directives were addressed to member states and hence could not impose obligations on individuals. However, the Court said that national courts, when applying national law, had to interpret it as close as possible to the principles contained in the Directive so as to achieve the intended result.
>
> Moreover, if the result required by the Directive could not be obtained by such interpretation, the member state would have to make good the damage caused to individuals by the failure to implement the Directive if: *(a)* the purpose of the Directive was to grant rights to individuals; *(b)* it was possible to identify the contents of those rights from the provisions of the Directive; and *(c)* there was a link between the breach of the member state's obligations and the damage suffered: *Faccini Dori* v *Recreb Srl* (1995). See too *Criminal Proceedings against Arcaro* (1997).

12. Decisions

A Decision of the Commission or Council may be addressed to member states, individuals or corporations and is binding on those addressed. An example of an individual Decision would be a Commission ruling that a firm had acted in breach of the competition rules contained in the Treaty of Rome. Such Decisions can include the imposition of a fine. An example of a

Decision addressed to a member state would be a Community instruction requiring a member state to abolish or amend measures of state aid to national undertakings.

13. Recommendations and Opinions

Recommendations and Opinions delivered by an institution of the Union have no legal effect. Recommendations will urge those addressed to adopt a particular form of behaviour; Opinions are used when the particular institution is called on to state a view on a current situation or particular event in the Union or a member state. A Recommendation was, for example, adopted in 1992 on codes of practice for the protection of consumers in respect of contracts negotiated at a distance.

14. Resolutions

Unlike the various instruments discussed above, the Treaty of Rome does not provide for Resolutions. However, the Council, the Parliament and the Commission do occasionally adopt Resolutions which do not, of course, have legal effect. In 1992, for example, the Council adopted a Resolution on future priorities for the development of consumer policy.

THE LEGISLATIVE PROCESS

15. The proposal procedure

As was seen above, it is the Council which in most cases is responsible for the adoption of a legislative proposal. However, before it actually reaches a decision, the various stages have to be completed.

The Commission will draft a measure which it can adopt by a simple majority, and this is then forwarded to the Council. The Council will then check to determine if it is required by Union law to refer the matter to other union institutions, such as the European Parliament or the Economic and Social Committee. If they are to be consulted, they communicate their opinion back to the Council.

Once these consultations have taken place, the Commission proposal is once more placed before the Council, possibly amended to take account of the opinions expressed during the consultation process. Adoption by the Council is the final stage of the legislative process.

This form of procedure operates where neither the co-operation or co-decision procedures are stated to apply (see below)

16. The co-operation procedure

The co-operation procedure involves a bigger role for the Parliament. It is applicable primarily in matters relating to the internal market, social policy, economic and social cohesion and research and development.

The procedure is essentially as follows:

(1) The Commission proposal is sent not just to the Council but also to the Parliament. This gives the proposal a first reading, and it then notifies the Council of its opinion.

(2) The Council then adopts a 'common position' which is sent to the Parliament for a second reading. Parliament then has three months to choose one of the following:

(i) It may accept the Common Position, in which case the Council can adopt the proposal.

(ii) It may do nothing, in which case it is to be taken to have accepted the Common Position and the Council can adopt it.

(iii) It may reject the Common Position, in which case the proposal can only be adopted by the Council acting unanimously.

(iv) It may propose changes to the Common Position. The question is then whether the Commission is prepared to accept these amendments. If it does, the Council may adopt the proposal by a qualified majority (see above) or, if it is departing from the Commission's proposal, unanimously. If the Commission does not accept the amendments, adoption by the Council must be unanimous.

It is always open to the Council effectively to block a measure by not taking any decisions at all on amendments proposed by Parliament or on the amended Commission proposals.

17. The co-decision procedure

The following is the essence of the co-decision procedure. It encompasses measures relating to the free movement of workers; freedom of establishment (including special rules for foreign nationals and recognition of diplomas); freedom to provide services; the harmonisation of legislation for the establishment and operation of the single market; educational and vocational training; youth, culture and health; consumer protection; research and development; and certain environmental programmes.

(1) The Commission makes a proposal which is sent to the Council and the Parliament. There is a first reading by the Parliament and its opinion goes to the Council.

(2) The Council can then accept the proposal by a qualified majority (see above) or, if it is departing from the proposal, unanimously. Either way, a Common Position is adopted, and the matter is then referred to the Parliament for a second reading. Parliament is now in the co-decision stage and it has three months in which to do one of the following:

(i) It may adopt the Common Position, or do nothing, in which case the Council may adopt the proposal.

(ii) If it wishes, it may make amendments to the Common Position. The procedure is then for the setting up of a Conciliation Committee consisting of representatives from the Council and the Parliament in equal proportion to negotiate a compromise. If a compromise is agreed on, the proposal is adopted by a joint decision of the Council and Parliament.

(iii) it may reject the Common Position outright, in which case the Council may convene the Conciliation Committee, and the procedure is then as in (ii).

(3) Where the Conciliation Committee fails to negotiate a compromise, the Council may, within six weeks, confirm its Common Position, amended as desired by Parliament, by a qualified majority. Parliament may, however, reject this position by an absolute majority of its members at third reading. In this case, the proposal is defeated, thus giving the Parliament a right of veto.

18. Infringement proceedings

The European Commission or another member states (in practice almost always the Commission) may bring a member state before the European Court of Justice if it believes that that member state has failed to fulfil an obligation imposed by EU law. If the Court finds against the particular member state, that state is required to take the measures needed to conform.

Case law It was held by the European Court of Justice that the United Kingdom, in allowing women to claim free prescriptions from the age of 60, but compelling men to wait until 65, was in breach of EU law on the equal treatment of men and women in matters relating to social security. The Department of Health then immediately issued a press release entitled 'Exemption from prescription charges to be equalised for men and women from tomorrow' which provided for men and women to receive free prescriptions from age 60: *R* v *Secretary of State for Employment* (1996).

Case law The European Court of Justice ruled that the provisions as to equal treatment were infringed by an occupational pension scheme which applied differing age qualifications between men and women.

327

Although this did not apply to state pensions, the United Kingdom took the view that it would be impossible in practical terms to maintain differing ages for men and women in this context and made provision in the Pensions Act 1995 for the state retirement age to be 65 for both sexes: *Barber* v *Guardian Royal Exchange Assurance Group* (1990).

If a member state fails to comply with a judgement it can be ordered to pay a lump-sum fine or a penalty payment.

19. Preliminary rulings

This refers to the procedure by which a national court can seek guidance on EU law from the Court. Where a national court is required to apply provisions of EU law in the case before it, it may stay the proceedings and ask the Court for questions regarding the validity of the EU legislation at issue and/or the interpretation of any legislation. The Court answers in a judgemental, not in an advisory, capacity.

> *Case law* Social security legislation applied different age qualifications between men and women in relation to certain disablement allowances. Female applicants were refused allowances by adjudication offers, but their appeal succeeded before the Social Security Commissioners, whose decision was upheld by the Court of Appeal, on the grounds that the legislation infringed EU law. The Secretary of State for Social Security appealed to the House of Lords who referred the matter to the European Court of Justice for its ruling: *Secretary of State for Social Security* v *Thomas* (1993).

PRIMACY OF COMMUNITY LAW

There is nothing in the Treaty of Rome which expressly gives EU law superiority over national law in the event of a conflict between the two. The principle of the primacy of EU law has, however, been established by the European Court of Justice. It has established that, first, the member states have transferred sovereign rights to a Community created by them. They cannot reverse the process by means of subsequent unilateral measures inconsistent with the concept of that Community. Second, it is a principle of the Treaty of Rome that no member state can call into question the status of Community law as a system uniformly and generally applicable throughout the EU: *Costa* v *ENEL* (1964).

The notion that EU law is paramount can mean that United Kingdom courts have the authority to suspend the operation of what is otherwise a valid enactment.

Case law Acting under the provisions of the Merchant Shipping Act 1988 the Secretary of State made certain regulations dealing with a register of British shipping vessels. Certain English companies did not qualify under the regulations because most of their directors and shareholders were Spanish. They challenged the legislation on the ground that it deprived them of certain rights granted by the EU. The Divisional Court requested a preliminary ruling from the European Court of Justice on the substantive provisions of EU law and granted the applicants interim relief to the effect that the relevant United Kingdom legislation was to be disapplied and the Secretary of State restrained from enforcing it. The Court of Appeal allowed an appeal and set aside the order for interim relief. The applicants appealed to the House of Lords which held that the common law did not provide the power to set aside otherwise valid legislation pending a reference to the European Court. The House of Lords, however, referred this matter to the European Court which ruled that a national court was required to set aside a rule of national law which it considered was the sole obstacle preventing it from granting interim relief in a case before that court concerning Community law, if to do otherwise would impair the full effectiveness of the subsequent judgement to be given on the substantive issue of the existence of the rights being claimed under Community law.

Following this ruling from the European Court, the House of Lords held that a court should exercise its discretion according to the balance of convenience and should, in so doing, take account in particular of the importance of upholding the law of the land in the public interest, bearing in mind the need for stability in society and the duty placed on certain authorities to enforce the law in the public interest. However, the court should not restrain an apparently authentic law unless satisfied that, having regard to all the circumstances, the challenge to its validity was *prima facie* so firmly based as to justify the taking of such an exceptional course. Applying those principles to the present case, the applicants had a strong case to present to the European Court that the evidence presented by the Secretary of State was not sufficient to outweigh the obvious and immediate damage which would continue to be caused to them if they were to be granted the interim relief, and therefore the balance of convenience favoured the granting of interim relief to the applicants whose appeal against the decision of the Court of Appeal was therefore allowed: *Factortame Ltd and Others* v *Secretary of State for Transport (No 2)* (1991).

In *R* v *Secretary of State for Transport, ex parte Factortame (No 5)* (1998), the Court of Appeal held that breaches of EU law committed in the United Kingdom when the Merchant Shipping Act imposed conditions of nationality, domicile and residence on those wishing to register to fish in UK waters were sufficiently serious to give rise to liability for any damage caused to trawler owners and managers refused registration.

Index